THINKING AND EXPERIENCE

THINKING and EXPERIENCE

by

H. H. PRICE

Wykeham Professor of Logic in the University of Oxford,
Fellow of the British Academy

HUTCHINSON'S UNIVERSITY LIBRARY

Hutchinson House, London, W.1

New York   Toronto   Melbourne   Sydney   Cape Town

First Published - 1953

Printed in Great Britain by
William Brendon and Son, Ltd.
The Mayflower Press (late of Plymouth)
at Bushey Mill Lane
Watford, Herts.

CONTENTS

CHAPTER I

UNIVERSALS AND RESEMBLANCES

WHEN we consider the world around us, we cannot help noticing that there is a great deal of recurrence or repetition in it. The same colour recurs over and over again in ever so many things. Shapes repeat themselves likewise. Over and over again we notice oblong-shaped things, hollow things, bulgy things. Hoots, thuds, bangs, rustlings occur again and again.

There is another and very important sort of recurrence which we also notice. The same pattern or mode of arrangement is found over and over again in many *sets* of things, in many different pairs of things, or triads, or quartets, as the case may be. When A is above B, and C is above D, and E is above F, the above-and-below pattern or mode of arrangement recurs in three pairs of things, and in ever so many other pairs of things as well. Likewise we repeatedly notice one thing inside another, one preceding another, one thing between two others.

These recurrent features sometimes recur singly or separately. The same colour recurs in this tomato, that sunset sky, and this blushing face; there are few other features, if any, which repeat themselves in all three. But it is a noteworthy fact about the world that there are *conjoint* recurrences as well as separate ones. A whole group of features recurs again and again as a whole in many objects. Examine twenty dandelions, and you will find that they have many features in common; likewise fifty cats have very many features in common, or two hundred lumps of lead. In such cases as these there is conjoint recurrence of many different features. Again and again they recur together in a clump or block. This is how it comes about that many of the objects in the world group themselves together into Natural Kinds. A Natural Kind is a group of objects which have *many* (perhaps indefinitely many) features in common. From observing that an object has some of these features, we can infer with a good deal of probability that it has the rest.

These constant recurrences or repetitions, whether separate or conjoint ones, are what make the world a dull or stale or boring place. The same old features keep turning up again and again. The best they can do is to present themselves occasionally in new combinations, as in the black swan or the duck-billed platypus. There is a certain *monotony* about the world. The extreme case of it is found where the same old feature repeats itself in all parts of a single object, as when something is red all over, or sticky all through, or a noise is uniformly shrill throughout its entire duration.

Nevertheless, this perpetual repetition, this dullness or staleness, is also immensely important, because it is what makes conceptual cognition possible. In a world of incessant novelty, where there was no recurrence at all and no tedious repetitions, no concepts could ever be acquired; and thinking, even of the crudest and most primitive kind, could never begin. For example, in such a world nothing would ever be recognizable. Or again, *in so far as* there is novelty in the world, non-recurrence, absence of repetition, so far the world cannot be thought about, but only experienced.

Hitherto I have been trying to use entirely untechnical language, so that we may not commit ourselves unawares to any philosophical theory. But it is at any rate not unnatural, it is not a *very* wild piece of theorizing, to introduce the words 'quality' and 'relation' for referring to those facts about the world to which I have been trying to draw the reader's attention. A *quality*, we say, is a recurrent feature of the world which presents itself in individual objects or events taken singly. Redness or bulginess or squeakiness are examples. A *relation*, on the other hand, is a recurrent feature of the world which presents itself in complexes of objects or events, such as this beside that, this preceding that, or B between A and C. It is also convenient sometimes to speak of *relational properties*. If A precedes B, we may say that A has the relational property of preceding B, and B has the converse relational property of succeeding A.

One further remark may be made on the distinction between qualities and relations. I said just now that a quality presents itself in individual objects or events taken singly, and a relation in complexes of objects or events. But it must not be forgotten that an individual object or event usually (perhaps always) has an *internal* complexity. In its history there is a plurality of temporal phases, and often it has a plurality of spatial parts as well. And there are relations between these parts, or these phases, which it has. Such relations *within* an individual object or event are sometimes said to constitute the 'structure' of the object or event. For scientific purposes, and even for purposes of ordinary common sense prediction, what we most need to know about any object or process is its structure. And from this point of view the chief importance of qualities, such as colour or hardness or stickiness, is that they often enable us to infer the presence of a structure more minute than our unaided senses would reveal. It has often been maintained that sensible qualities are 'subjective'. But subjective or not, they have a most important function. They give us a clue to what the minute structure of objects and events is. If a gas smells like rotten eggs, we can infer that it is sulphuretted hydrogen.

The terms 'quality' and 'relation' enable us to give a simple analysis of *change*. The notion of change has puzzled some philosophers greatly, ever since Heracleitus, or some disciple of his, remarked long ago that πάντα ῥεῖ, 'all things flow'. Indeed, it has sometimes led them to suppose that this world *is* a world of perpetual novelty after all, and not the tedious or boring or repetitious world which it has to be, if conceptual cognition is to be possible. They have, therefore, concluded—rightly, from their premises— that all conceptual cognition is radically erroneous or illusory, a kind of systematic distortion of Reality; so that *whatever* we think, however intelligent or however stupid we may be, we are in error. On this view, only non-conceptual cognition—immediate experience or direct intuition—can be free from error.

These conclusions are so queer that we suspect something is wrong with the premises. We can now see what it is. The notion of Change, as Plato pointed out, has itself to be analysed in terms of the notions of Quality and Relation. In qualitative change, as when an apple changes from being green to being red, an object has quality q_1 at one time and a different quality q_2 at a later time. In relational change, an object A has a relation R_1 to another object B at one time, and a different relation R_2 to B at a later time. At 12 o'clock, for example, it is six inches away from B, at 12.5 it is a mile away from B; at one time the relation it has to B is the relation 'hotter than', at another the relation 'as hot as', at another the relation 'cooler than'.

It is not necessary for our present purposes to enquire whether there are other recurrent features of the world which are neither qualities nor relations nor analysable in terms of these. Some philosophers have thought, for instance, that causality (in its various determinate forms, hitting, bending, pushing, pulling, attracting, repelling, etc.) was such an ultimate and irreducible feature of the world, recurring or repeating itself in many situations. Others have undertaken to give a purely relational analysis of causality (the 'Regularity' theory). For our present purpose, however—which is merely to explain why philosophers have thought it worth while to talk about recurrent features of the world at all—it is not necessary to decide how many irreducibly different types of recurrents there might be. It will be enough to consider just qualities and relations.

We may now sum up the results of this ontological discussion so far by introducing another technical term, again not so *very* technical, the term 'characteristic'. Characteristics, we say, are of at least two different types, qualities and relations. What has been said so far then comes to this: there are *recurrent characteristics* in the world, which repeat themselves over and over again in many different contexts. Is it not just an obvious fact about the world, something we cannot help noticing whether we like it or not, that there *are* recurrent characteristics? Now these recurrent characteristics have been called by some philosophers *universals*. And the line of thought we have been pursuing leads very naturally to the traditional Aristotelian doctrine of *universalia in rebus*, 'universals in things'. (To provide for universals of relation, 'things' must be understood to cover complexes as well as individuals. The *res* which the universal 'beside' is in is not this, nor that, but this-and-that.)

I do not propose to discuss the Platonic doctrine of *universalia ante rem*, 'universals anterior to (or independent of) things'. This is not because I think it uninteresting or unimportant, but merely because it is more remote from common sense and our ordinary everyday habits of thought than the Aristotelian theory of *universalia in rebus*. It is a sufficiently difficult task in these days to convince people that there is any sense in talking of universals at all, even in the mild and moderate Aristotelian way.

The doctrine of *universalia in rebus* may, of course, be mistaken, or gravely misleading. There certainly are objections to it, as we shall find presently. But I cannot see that it is in the least absurd or silly, as the most approved thinkers nowadays seem to suppose. Nor can I see that it arises entirely from erroneous views about language, as the same thinkers seem to suppose; for example, from the superstition that all words are names, from which it would follow that general or abstract words must be names of general or abstract entities. On the contrary, this philosophy seems to me to be the result, and the very natural result, of certain *ontological* reflections. It seems to me to arise from reflections about the world; from consideration of what things are, and not—or certainly not merely—from consideration of the way we talk about them. On the contrary, it could be argued that we talk in the way we do, using general terms and abstract terms, because of what we find the world to be; because we find or notice *recurrences* in it.

Let us now consider how the doctrine of *universalia in rebus* might mislead us, although it arises in this natural and plausible way from the ontological considerations which we have been discussing. One danger of it obviously is that universals may be regarded as a sort of *things* or entities, over and above the objects or situations in which they recur. We may indeed emphasize the word 'in'. We may insist that universals are *in* things, and not apart from them as the doctrine of *universalia ante rem* maintains. But is the danger of supposing that they are themselves things or quasi-things entirely removed? Does it not arise over again as soon as we reflect upon the implications of the word 'in' itself?

If it is our profession to be misled—as, of course, it *is* the profession of philosophers—we shall be liable to suppose that redness is in the tomato somewhat as juice is in it, or as a weevil is in it. And if so, what can be meant by saying that redness is recurrent? How can it be *in* thousands of other tomatoes as well, or hundreds of post boxes, or dozens of blushing faces? It does not make sense to say that a weevil is in many places at once. Again, when the tomato begins to decay and turns brown, where has the redness gone to, which used to be in it? (The weevil has gone somewhere else; you will find him in the potato basket.) Likewise, where has the brownness come from?

If we prefer to say that the tomato *has* redness, rather than 'redness is in it', we shall again mislead these literal-minded persons, and in the same sort of way. Does the tomato *have* redness as

Jones *has* a watch? If so, how can millions of other things have it too?

I confess that I do not think much of these difficulties. The meaning of 'in' and 'have' in this context can be quite easily exhibited by examples, just as their literal meaning can, when we say that there is a weevil in the tomato, or I have a watch. Surely we all know quite well what is being referred to when two things are said to *have* the same colour? And is it really so very difficult to recognize what is meant by saying that the same colour is *in* them both? It is true no doubt that the words 'in' and 'have' are here being used in a metaphorical sense, though not, I think, extravagantly metaphorical. But we must use metaphorical words, or else invent new and technical terms (which are themselves usually metaphorical words taken from a dead language, Greek or Latin). Our ordinary language exists for practical ends, and it has to be 'stretched' in one way or other if we are to use it for purposes of philosophical analysis. And if our metaphors can be cashed quite easily by examples, as these can, no harm whatever is done.

It could, however, be argued that the terminology of 'characteristics', which was current in the last philosophical epoch, some twenty years ago, is better than the more ancient terminology of 'universals'. A characteristic is pretty obviously a characteristic *of* something or other, and cannot easily be supposed to be an independent entity, like the weevil. Nor can we be easily misled into supposing that when something 'has' a characteristic, i.e. is characterized by it, this is at all analogous to the having of a watch. In the technical symbolism of Formal Logic, the most appropriate expression for referring to one of these recurrent features of the world is not a single letter, such as ϕ or R, which might possibly be mistaken for the name of an entity, but a propositional function, such as ϕx, or xRy, or $R(x,y,z)$. Here the x, y and z are variables, so that the propositional function is an overtly *incomplete* expression. To complete it, one must replace the variable by a constant, denoting some object which satisfies the function; or if there are several variables, as in xRy or $R(x,y,z)$, each of these must be replaced by a constant. The terminology of characteristics is an approximate equivalent in words to the non-verbal symbolism of propositional functions, and has much the same advantages; whereas if we use the more traditional terminology of universals, there is some danger (though not, I think, unavoidable) that we may be led to speak of them as though they were in themselves complete and independent entities.

Henceforth, the Aristotelian theory of *universalia in rebus* will be called 'the Philosophy of Universals' for short. If our argument so far has been correct, the Philosophy of Universals is drawing our attention to certain important facts about the world. Yet it is at the same time proposing an analysis of those facts. We cannot dispute the facts, nor can we dispute their fundamental importance. We cannot deny that something which may be called 'the recurrence of characteristics' is genuinely there. We must also admit that if it were not there, conceptual cognition could not exist. If the world were not like this, if there were no recurrence in it, it could be neither thought about nor spoken about. We could never have acquired any concepts; and even if we had them innately (without needing to acquire them) they could never have been applied to anything.

But though we cannot dispute the facts, nor their importance, we may, nevertheless, have doubts about the analysis of them which the Philosophy of Universals proposes. At any rate, another and quite different analysis of them appears to be possible. It is the analysis offered by what one may call the Philosophy of Ultimate Resemblances. (Henceforth I shall call this 'the Philosophy of Resemblances' for short.) This is the analysis which most contemporary philosophers accept, so far as they consider the *ontological* side of the Problem of Universals at all. It is also accepted by Conceptualists, like Locke. The Philosophy of Resemblances is more complicated than the Philosophy of Universals, and more difficult to formulate. It involves one in long and cumbrous circumlocutions. Yet it claims, not unplausibly, that it keeps closer to the facts which have to be analysed. The unkind way of putting this, the one its critics prefer, is to say that it is 'more naturalistic'. Let us now consider the Philosophy of Resemblances in more detail.

When we say that a characteristic, e.g. whiteness, *recurs*, that it presents itself over and over again, that it characterizes ever so many numerically different objects, what we say is admittedly in some sense true. But would it not be clearer, and closer to the facts, if we said that all these objects resemble each other in a certain way?

Is not this the rock-bottom fact to which the Philosophy of Universals is drawing our attention, when it uses this rather inflated language of 'recurrent characteristics'? The Philosophy of Universals of course agrees that all the objects characterized by whiteness do resemble one another. But according to it, resemblance is always derivative, and is just a *consequence* of the fact that the very same characteristic—whiteness, in this case—characterizes all these objects. To use more traditional language, it says that when A resembles B, this is *because* they are both instances of the same universal.

Now this is all very well where the resemblance is exact, but what are we to say when it is not? Let us consider the following series of examples: a patch of freshly fallen snow; a bit of chalk; a piece of paper which has been used for wrapping the meat in; the handkerchief with which I have been dusting a rather dirty mantelpiece; a full evening dress bow tie which has been left lying about for several years on the floor. All these, we say, are white objects. But are they exactly alike in their colour, if white may be counted as a colour for the purpose of this discussion? Clearly they are not. They are, of course, more or less alike. In fact there is a very considerable degree of colour-likeness between them. But certainly they are not exactly alike in colour. And yet if the very same characteristic, whiteness, is present in them all (as the Philosophy of Universals, apparently, says it is) ought it not to follow that they are exactly alike in colour?

To make quite clear what the point at issue is, we shall have to distinguish, rather pedantically perhaps, between *exact* resemblance in this or that respect and *total* or *complete* resemblance. To put it in another way, resemblance has two dimensions of variation. It may vary in intensity; it may also vary in extent. For example, a piece of writing paper and an envelope, before one has written on either of them, may be exactly alike in colour, and perhaps also in texture. These likenesses between them have the maximum degree of intensity. But the two objects are not completely or totally alike. For one thing, they are unlike in shape. Moreover, the envelope is stuck together with gum and has gum on its flap, while the piece of writing paper has no gum on it. It might perhaps be thought that two envelopes from the same batch *are* completely alike; and certainly they come nearer to it than the envelope and the piece of notepaper. All the same, there is unlikeness in respect of place. At any given time, envelope A is in one place and envelope B is in a different place. On the Relational Theory of Space, this is equivalent to saying that at any given time A and B are related in unlike ways to something else, e.g. the North Pole, or Greenwich Observatory.

According to Leibniz's Principle of the Identity of Indiscernibles, complete or total likeness is an ideal limit which can never quite be reached, though some pairs of objects (the two envelopes, for example) come closer to it than others. For if *per impossibile* two objects were completely alike, place and date included, there would no longer be two objects, but only one. Whether Leibniz's Principle is correct, has been much disputed. But we need not concern ourselves with this dispute. It is sufficient to point out that if there were two objects which resembled each other completely, in date and place as well as in all other ways, and this complete resemblance continued throughout the whole of the histories of both, there could not possibly be any evidence for believing there were two of them. So in this discussion we need not concern ourselves any more with complete or total resemblance, though it is of course an important fact about resemblances that they vary in extent, as well as in degree of intensity.

What does concern us is intensity of resemblance. The maximum intensity of it is what I called 'exact resemblance in this or that respect'. Now some people appear to think that even this is an ideal limit. They seem to think that no two objects are ever *exactly* alike even in one way (e.g. colour, or shape) though, of course, many objects are closely alike in one way or in several. I do not see what evidence we could have for believing such a sweeping negative generalization. It is true that sometimes, when we thought at first that there was an exact likeness in one or more respects between two objects, we may find on more careful examination that there was not. We may have thought that two twins were exactly alike in the conformation of their faces. We look more closely, and find that John's nose is a millimetre longer than William's. But still, there are many cases where there is no discoverable inexactness in a resemblance. We often find that two pennies are indistinguishable in shape, or two postage stamps indistinguishable in colour. And we should not confine ourselves to cases where two or more objects are being compared. There is such a thing as monotony or uniformity within a single object. For example, a certain patch of sky is blue, and the same shade of blue, all over. It is monotonously ultramarine. In other words, all its discernible parts are exactly like each other in colour; at any rate, we can discover no unlikeness of colour between them. Again, there is often no discoverable unlikeness of pitch between two successive phases of the same sound. Will it be said that such monotony is only apparent, not real? But what ground could we have for thinking that no entity is ever really 'monotonous' in this sense, not even in the smallest part of its extent, or throughout the smallest phase of its duration? Thus there is no good ground for maintaining that resemblance of maximum intensity never occurs at all, still less for maintaining that it never *could* occur. Nevertheless, it is not so very common for two objects to be exactly alike even in one way, though monotony within a single object or event is more frequent. What we most usually find in two or more objects which are said to be 'alike' is *close* resemblance in one respect or in several.

We can now return to the controversy between the Philosophy of Resemblances and the Philosophy of Universals. It is argued that if the Philosophy of Universals were right, exact resemblance in one or several respects (resemblance of maximum intensity) ought to be much more common than it is; indeed, that *in*exact resemblance in a given respect, say colour or shape, ought not to exist at all. Of course, there could still be incomplete or partial resemblance, resemblance between two objects in one respect or in several, and lack of resemblance in others. But whenever two objects do resemble each other in a certain respect, it would appear that the resemblance ought to be exact (of maximum intensity), if the Philosophy of Universals were right; either it should be exact, or else it should not exist at all. The Philosophy of Universals tells us that resemblance is derivative, not ultimate; that when two objects resemble each other in a given respect, it is because the very same universal is present in them both. This seem to leave no room for inexact resemblance.

Now if we consider the various white objects I mentioned before[1]—the whole series of them, from the freshly fallen snow to the unwashed bow-tie—how can anyone maintain that the very same characteristic, whiteness, recurs in all of them? Clearly it does

[1]See p. 14 above.

not. If it did, they must be exactly alike in their colour; and quite certainly they are not. If we are to use the language of universals or characteristics, shall we not have to say that each of the objects in this series, from the snow to the unwashed tie, is characterized by a *different* characteristic, or is an instance of a *different* universal? In this case, then, the resemblance seems to be ultimate and underivative, *not* dependent on the presence of a single universal in all these objects, although they certainly do resemble each other.

Let us consider another example. Two pennies may be exactly alike in their shape. If so, one may plausibly say that the very same characteristic, roundness, is present in both of them, and that their resemblance is dependent on this. But what about a penny and a sixpence? They certainly *are* alike in shape; but not exactly, because the sixpence has a milled edge and the penny a smooth one. So here again, it would seem, there is no *single* characteristic present in them both, upon which the resemblance could be dependent. This resemblance again seems to be ultimate and underivative.

Thus the Philosophy of Universals, when it makes all resemblance derivative, appears to forget that resemblances have degrees of intensity. Resemblance is treated as if it were degreeless, either present in its maximum degree or else not present at all. In practice, the Philosopher of Universals concentrates his attention on *close* resemblances, and averts his attention from the awkward circumstance that few of them are exact; and resemblances of a lower degree than this (small or moderate ones, not intense enough to be called 'close') are just neglected altogether. But is it not a glaringly obvious fact that resemblances do differ in degree or intensity?

That being so, shall we not be inclined to *reverse* this alleged dependence-relation between 'being alike' and 'being characterized by'? Surely we shall be inclined to say that it is resemblance which is more fundamental than characterization, rather than the other way round. We shall, of course, be willing to go on using terms like 'characteristic' and 'characterized by'; they are part of ordinary language, and everyone has a sufficient understanding of them. But we shall define 'characteristic' in terms of resemblance, and not conversely. Where a number of objects do happen to resemble each other exactly in one respect or three or fifteen, there, and in consequence, we shall be quite willing to say that they have one, or

B

three, or fifteen 'characteristics in common'. But in other cases, where the resemblance is less than exact, we shall not be willing to say this. We shall just say that they resemble each other in such and such a degree, and stop there. In a given set of objects there is whatever degree or resemblance there is. Let us be content to take the facts as we find them.

Turning for a moment to the epistemological side of the matter, surely it is obvious that the applicability of concepts does *not* require an exact resemblance in the objects which a concept applies to? Of course there does have to be a considerable degree of resemblance between all the objects which 'satisfy' a given concept. As we say, there has to be a sufficient likeness between them, e.g. between all the objects to which the concept White applies. What degree of likeness is sufficient, and where the borderline comes between something which falls just within the concept's sphere of application and something else which just falls outside it, is often difficult to decide. For instance, one may wonder whether the *very* dirty bow-tie is white at all. Indeed, it is difficult to see how such a question can be definitely answered, at least in the case of whiteness and many other familiar concepts. The right way to tackle it, perhaps, is to refuse to answer it as it stands. Perhaps we should rather say that a concept may be 'satisfied' in many different degrees; or, in more commonsensical language, that there are good instances and bad instances, better and worse ones, and some so bad that it is arbitrary whether one counts them as instances or not. Thus the piece of chalk is a *better* instance of whiteness than the rather dirty handkerchief is. The patch of freshly fallen snow is a better instance still, perhaps a perfect one. We may give it the mark α $(+)$. Then $\alpha\beta$ is about the right mark for the piece of chalk, and we will give the unwashed bow-tie $\gamma=$, to denote that it is just on the borderline between 'pass' and 'failure'.

It is not easy to see how the doctrine of *universalia in rebus* can make any room for this important and familiar notion of degrees of instantiation. But there is plenty of room for it in Conceptualism, which is the epistemological counterpart of the ontological philosophy of Resemblances. We must add, in fairness, that there is also plenty of room for it in the Platonic doctrine of *universalia ante rem*. Indeed Plato, or perhaps Socrates, was the first philosopher who noticed that there are degrees of instantiation. This is one of the points, and a good point, which Conceptualism and Platonic Realism have in common.[1]

In the last few pages, I have been discussing the difficulties which the Resemblance Philosophers find in the Philosophy of Universals. But the Philosophy of Resemblances has its difficulties too. The most important ones are concerned with resemblance itself. I shall discuss two of them, and the solutions proposed for them. The first arises from the phrase 'resemblance in respect of. . . .'

It is obvious that we must distinguish between *different* resemblances. Objects resemble each other in different respects, as well as in different degrees. Red objects resemble each other in one respect, round objects in another respect. The members of a natural kind, for instance cats or oak trees, resemble each other in many respects at once. Thus it would be much too vague if we said that red objects, for example, are just a set of objects which resemble one another, or sufficiently resemble each other. That would not distinguish them from blue objects, or round objects, or any other class of objects one cares to name. We must specify what resemblance it is. Red objects are those which resemble each other 'in a certain respect'. But in *what* respect? And now it looks as if we should have to introduce universals again. Our first answer would probably be that they resemble each other in respect of colour; and this looks very like saying that they are all instances of the universal Colouredness. That is bad enough; but we shall be driven to go farther, because we have not yet said enough to distinguish red objects from blue ones or green ones. Can we stop short of saying that red objects are just those objects which resemble each other in respect of *redness*? And here we seem to be admitting the very point which the Philosophy of Universals is so anxious to maintain; namely that the resemblance between these objects is after all derivative, dependent upon the presence of a single universal, Redness, in them all. To generalize the argument: whenever we say that A, B and C resemble each other in a certain respect, we shall be asked 'In *what* respect?' And how can we answer, except by saying 'in respect of being instances of the universal ϕ' or 'in respect of being character-

[1] In Christian Platonism, where Plato's transcendent 'forms' become concepts in the mind of God, the differences between Platonic Realism and Conceptualism are still further diminished, though they do not disappear altogether.

ized by the characteristic ϕ'? We may try to get round the difficulty by saying that they resemble each other in a certain *way* (avoiding the word 'respect'), or that there is a certain *sort* of resemblance between them. But when we are asked to specify in *what* way they resemble each other, or what sort of resemblance there is between them, surely we shall still have to answer by mentioning such and such a universal or characteristic? 'The way in which red objects resemble each other is that all of them are instances of the universal Redness, or all of them are characterized by the characteristic Redness.'

This is one of the classical objections to the Philosophy of Resemblances. The argument purports to show that resemblance is not after all ultimate or underivative, but is dependent on the presence of a universal or characteristic which is common to the things which resemble each other. There is something about this objection which arouses our suspicions. It comes perilously near to the tautology 'red things are the things which are red'. The Resemblance philosophers were not undertaking to deny this tautology. They do not deny that *x is red* entails *x is red*. They are only concerned to offer an analysis of *x is red* itself.

Let us now consider the answer they might make to this celebrated objection. Roughly, it consists in substituting 'resemblance *towards* . . .' for 'resemblance in respect of . . .' Resemblance towards what? Towards certain standard objects, or *exemplars* as I shall call them—certain standard red objects, or standard round objects, or whatever it may be.

It is agreed by both parties that there is a *class* of red objects. The question is, what sort of a structure does a class have? That is where the two philosophies differ. According to the Philosophy of Universals, a class is so to speak a promiscuous or equalitarian assemblage. All its members have, as it were, the same status in it. All of them are instances of the same universal, and no more can be said. But in the Philosophy of Resemblances a class has a more complex structure than this; not equalitarian, but aristocratic. Every class has, as it were, a nucleus, an inner ring of key-members, consisting of a small group of standard objects or exemplars. The exemplars for the class of red things might be a certain tomato, a certain brick and a certain British post-box. Let us call them A, B and C for short. Then a red object is any object which resembles

A, B and C as closely as they resemble one another. The resemblance between the exemplars need not itself be a very close one, though it is of course pretty close in the example just given. What is required is only that every other member of the class should resemble the class-exemplars *as* closely as they resemble one another. Thus the exemplars for a class might be a summer sky, a lemon, a post-box, and a lawn. These do resemble one another, though not very closely. Accordingly there is a class consisting of everything which resembles these four entities *as* closely as they resemble each other. It is the class of coloured things, whereas the previous one was the class of red things.

It may be thought that there is still a difficulty about the resemblance between the exemplar objects themselves. In *what respect* do the tomato, the brick and the post-box resemble each other? Surely this question still arises, even though it does not arise about the other members of the class? And how can one answer it, except by saying that these three objects resemble each other in respect of being red, or of being characterized by redness?

But this assumes that we know beforehand what 'being red' is, or what 'being characterized by redness' amounts to. And this begs the question against the Resemblance Philosophy. The Resemblance Philosophers maintain that our knowledge of what it is for something to be red just consists in a capacity to compare any particular object X with certain standard objects, and thereby to discover whether X does or does not resemble these standard objects as closely as they resemble each other. It does not make sense to speak of comparing the standard objects *with themselves*, or to ask whether *they* resemble one another as closely as they do resemble one another. Yet that is just what we should be trying to do, if we tried to say 'in what respect' they are alike. To say that *they* are red, or are characterized by redness, would not be an informative statement, but a tautology.

This objection does however draw our attention to an important point. According to the Philosophy of Resemblances, there cannot be a class unless there are exemplar objects to hold the class together. Nevertheless, the same class may have *alternative* sets of exemplars. The class of red things, we said, consists of everything which resembles the post-box, the tomato and the brick as closely as they resemble each other. It could equally be said to consist of everything which resembles a certain bit of sealing wax, a certain blushing face and a certain sunset sky as closely as *they* resemble each other. In that case, it does make sense to ask whether the post-box, the tomato and the brick are red, or are characterized by redness. And the answer 'Yes, they are' is now no longer tautologous. We are no longer trying, absurdly, to compare them with themselves. We are comparing them with three other things, and discovering that they do all have a sufficient degree of resemblance to these other things. But because there are (within limits) alternative sets of standard objects for the same class, we are led to suppose, erroneously, that a class can exist without any standard objects at all. This or that set of standard objects can be deposed from its privileged position without destroying the unity of the class; and we then suppose, by a process of illegitimate generalization, that the class would still remain what it is if privilege were abolished altogether. There must be *a* set of standard objects for each class, though within limits it does not matter which set of objects have this status.

Thus in the Philosophy of Resemblances, as well as the Philosophy of Universals, there does after all have to be something which holds a class together, if one may put it so. Where the two philosophies differ is, in their view of what that something is. In the Philosophy of Universals, what holds a class together is a universal, something of a different ontological type from the members. In the Philosophy of Resemblances there is no question of different ontological types. There are just particular objects, and there is nothing non-particular which is 'in' them, in the way that a universal is supposed to be 'in' the particulars which are its instances. What holds the class together is a set of nuclear or standard members. Anything which has a sufficient degree of resemblance to these is thereby a member of the class; and 'resembling them sufficiently' means 'resembling them as closely as they resemble each other'.

Again, to turn for a moment to epistemological considerations, it is their relationship to the standard objects or exemplars which enables all these objects to satisfy the same concept, e.g. the concept Red, and likewise enables the same word or other symbol, e.g. the word 'red', to apply to them all. But this is to anticipate. The Philosophy of Resemblances is an *ontological* doctrine, though it may be used as the starting point for certain epistemological theories (Conceptualism, Imagism and Nominalism), just as the

Philosophy of Universals may be used as the starting-point of a Realist epistemology. If the Philosophy of Resemblances is true at all, it might still have been true even if there had been no thinkers and no speakers. As it happens, there are thinkers and speakers too. But there may be many classes in the world, which do exist (because the requisite resemblances do happen to be there) although no mind happens to have formed the corresponding class-concepts, and no speaker has acquired the habit of using the corresponding class-symbols. Thus there is nothing subjectivist or anthropocentric about the Philosophy of Resemblances. It denies that there are universals *in rebus*, but it asserts that there are resemblances *inter res*. Certain objects really are as like the objects A, B and C as these are to one another, whether anyone notices the fact or not. Known or not, spoken of or not, the relationship is there; just as in the Philosophy of Universals objects are instances of universals whether they are known to be so or not. In this respect, both these philosophies are equally 'realistic'.

We must now turn to the second of the classical objections against the Philosophy of Resemblances, an objection so familiar that one might almost call it notorious. It is concerned with resemblance itself. Surely resemblance is itself a universal, present in many pairs or groups of resemblant objects? It is of course, a universal of relation. The instances of it are not individual objects taken singly, but complexes, and each of these complexes is composed of two objects or more. In their attempt to 'get rid of universals', the Philosophers of Resemblance seem to concentrate their attention on universals of *quality* (e.g. redness, colour, shape) and say little or nothing about universals of relation. Hence they have failed to notice that resemblance itself is one of them. But if we are obliged to admit that resemblance at any rate is a genuine universal, a relation which does literally recur in many different situations or complexes, what ground have we for denying that there are other *universalia in rebus* as well?

It may seem audacious to question this formidable argument, which has convinced many illustrious men. But is it as strong as it looks? The Resemblance philosophers might very well reply that it begs the question at issue, that it just assumes what it purports to prove. For after all, what reason is given for the crucial assertion that resemblance is a universal? Apparently none. It is not enough just to say 'surely resemblance at any rate is a universal'. Could any reason be given? We might perhaps try to find one by starting from the linguistic side of the matter. The word 'resemblance', we might say, is an *abstract* word, like the words 'redness' and 'proximity'; therefore it must stand for a universal or characteristic (a relational one, of course). But if this is the argument, it seems to beg the question. For if one does start from a linguistic point of view, the very question at issue is whether abstract words and general words do stand for universals. And if the argument is to be cogent, it ought to be an argument about the noun 'resemblance' in particular, or about the verb 'to resemble' in particular. We ought to be shown that it is somehow peculiarly obvious that *this* word at any rate (or this pair of words) stands for a universal, even though it may be less obvious that other general words do.

Perhaps it will be said, the peculiar obviousness consists in this, that even the people who try to get rid of universals have to use *this* general word at least, or equivalent general words such as 'similar', 'like'. True enough, one cannot speak in a language consisting entirely of proper names and demonstratives. One cannot say anything at all without using some general words. As an observation about the nature of language, this is perfectly indisputable. But the question is, what are its implications? Does it follow that because we must use general words, there are, therefore, general somethings *in rerum natura* which they stand for? That is just the point at issue. One cannot just assume that the answer is 'Yes'. Of course the Philosophy of Resemblances admits that we do use general words, and cannot avoid using them if we are to speak at all. It does not at all deny the fact. But it does deny the conclusion which the Philosophy of Universals draws from it—namely that because we use general words, there must be *general somethings* (universals) which they mean. Has anything been done to show that this denial is mistaken? Nothing. The Philosophy of Universals has just repeated over again the principle which has to be proved, the principle that every general word stands for a universal; adding—what is obvious—that *if* this principle is true, the word 'resemblance' is an illustration of it. Of course. But *is* the principle true?

If the Philosopher of Resemblances is asked to explain how the general word 'resemblance' is used, or what kind of meaning it has, he will presumably point out that there are resemblances of *different orders*. Two cats, A and B, resemble each other, and two sounds, C and D, also resemble each other. These are first-order resemblances. But it is also true that the two-cat situation resembles the two-sound situation, and resembles many other situations too. This is a second-order resemblance. The A–B situation and the C–D situation really are alike, though the constituents of the one are unlike the constituents of the other. In virtue of this second-order likeness (a likeness *between* likeness-situations) we may apply the same general word to both of them; and the word we happen to use for this purpose is the word 'resemblance', in a second-order sense. There is nothing wrong or unintelligible in the notion of second-order resemblance. Or if it be said that there is, we can reply with the *tu quoque* argument that universality must itself be a universal. When it is said that 'cathood is a universal' the word 'universal' is itself a general word, just as 'cat' is when we say 'Pussy is a cat'. So according to the Philosophy of Universals, there must be a universal called 'universality'. And if it is a universal, universality must accordingly be an instance of itself. But this is a contradiction. For according to this Philosophy, anything which is an *instance* of a universal is *ipso facto* a particular, and not a universal. To get out of this difficulty, the Philosophy of Universals must introduce the notion of 'different orders' too. The word 'universal', it has to say, stands for a second-order universal, whereas 'green' or 'cat' or 'in' stand for first-order ones. This is equivalent to saying that the expression 'a universal', or the propositional function 'ϕ is a universal', can occur only in a metalanguage.

This suggests another way in which the Philosophy of Resemblances might reply to the objection that 'resemblance is itself a universal'. The objection assumes that resemblance is just one relation among others: a relation of the same type as 'on top of', or 'near to', or 'side by side with'. But according to the Philosophy of Resemblances, resemblance is not just one relation among others. Indeed, according to this philosophy, it would be misleading to call it 'a relation' at all. It is too fundamental to be called so. For what we *ordinarily* call 'relations' (as well as what we call 'qualities') are themselves founded upon or analysable into resemblances. For example, the relation 'being inside of' is founded upon the resemblance between the Jonah-whale complex, the room-house complex, the match-matchbox complex, etc. Moreover, the Philosophy of Universals itself does not really hold that resemblance is just one relation among others, and in pretending that it does, it is abandoning one of its own fundamental principles; indeed it is abandoning the very one which this argument ('resemblance is itself a universal') is ultimately intended to establish, the principle, namely, that all resemblance is derivative. In the Philosophy of Universals itself, resemblance has a status quite different from relations like 'side by side with' or 'on top of'. Resembling is connected with *being an instance of* . . . in a way that ordinary relations are not. When A resembles B and C, this is supposed to be a direct consequence of the fact that A, B and C are all instances of the same universal; and not only when A, B and C are individual objects (in which case the universal is a universal of quality) but also when they are complexes, so that the universal they are instances of is a relational one, such as 'being inside of'. If resemblance, in the Philosophy of Universals, is to be called a relation at all, it is a relation of a very special sort, quite different from anything to which the word 'relation' is *ordinarily* applied. We should have to say that it is a 'formal' or 'metaphysical' relation (as opposed to a 'natural' or empirical one) just as the relation of instantiation is, if that can be called a relation at all.

So much for the reply the Philosophy of Resemblances might make to this celebrated argument that 'resemblance is itself a universal'. First, it might be objected that the argument begs the question, by just assuming (what it ought to prove) that because 'resemblance' is admittedly a general word, it must stand for a universal. Secondly, the argument overlooks the fact that there are resemblances of different orders. Thirdly, it treats resemblance as one relation among others, parallel in principle to 'side by side with' or 'on top of', whereas the Philosophy of Resemblances maintains that it is too fundamental to be called a relation at all, in the ordinary sense of the word 'relation'. Fourthly, the Philosophy of Universals itself admits, in its own way, that resemblance does *not* have the same status as other relations, in spite of maintaining in this argument that it has.

Thus the Philosophy of Resemblances has an answer to these two classical objections, the one about 'resemblance in respect of' and the one we have just discussed 'that resemblance is itself a universal'. But the Philosophy of Universals also has an answer to the objection about inexact resemblances, and to the complaint that it ignores the different degrees of intensity which resemblances may have.[1] We must consider this answer if we are to do justice to both parties.

The first step is to distinguish between *determinable* and *determinate* characteristics. Universals or characteristics, it is said, have different degrees of determinateness. The adjectives 'determinable' and 'determinate' are too fundamental to be defined. But their meaning can be illustrated. Thus the characteristic of being coloured is a determinable, and the characteristic of being red is a determinate of it. Being red is again a sub-determinable, and has under it the determinates being scarlet, being brick-red, being cherry-red, etc. Likewise, being a mammal is a determinable characteristic, a highly complex one this time. There are many different ways of being a mammal. Being a dog, being a whale, being a man are some of the determinates of this determinable.

Now whenever two objects resemble each other with less than the maximum intensity (i.e. whenever they have what was called an 'inexact' resemblance) we can always say that the same *determinable* characteristic characterizes them both, though not the same determinate one. Two objects may each have a different shade of red. A is scarlet, and B is brick-red. They resemble each other fairly closely, but by no means exactly. That is because redness itself is a determinable characteristic, a sub-determinable falling under the higher determinable colouredness. The two objects do have this determinable characteristic in common, though each of them has a different determinate form of it. So we can still maintain that this resemblance, though inexact, is derivative, dependent on the presence of the same determinable universal in both objects.

Let us apply these considerations to the two examples given on pp. 14 and 17. (1) the various white objects; (2) the penny and the sixpence. It may now be maintained that all my different white objects—from the freshly fallen snow at one end of the series to the unwashed bow-tie at the other—do have a *determinable* characteristic in common; though 'whitish', rather than 'white', would be the appropriate word for it. 'White' might be taken to mean

[1]See pp. 14-17, above.

pure white. And pure white is only one determinate of the determinable *whitish*. We certainly should not say that all the objects in this series are pure white. At the most, only the freshly fallen snow is pure white, but not the piece of chalk, or the rather messy bit of paper, or the rather dirty handkerchief, or the very dirty unwashed bow-tie. But we should admit that all of them are 'whitish'.

Let us now consider my other example, the penny and the sixpence, which resemble each other in shape, but inexactly. The penny with its smooth edge and the sixpence with its milled (slightly serrated) edge have different determinate shapes. How is it, then, that they do still resemble each other in shape, though inexactly, and both would be called 'round coins' in ordinary speech? Because the same *determinable* shape—we might more appropriately call it 'roundish'—characterizes both of them; and it characterizes many other things as well, e.g. slightly buckled bicycle wheels, cogwheels with not too large teeth, which resemble each other a good deal less closely than the penny and the sixpence do.

By this expedient the Philosophy of Universals is able to maintain its thesis that all resemblances, inexact ones too, are derivative, and not ultimate, as the Philosophy of Resemblances would have them. Inexact resemblance, we are invited to say, depends upon or is derived from the presence of the same *determinable* characteristic in a number of objects; exact resemblance (resemblance of maximum intensity) depends upon their being characterized by the same *determinate* characteristic.

Perhaps this will also enable us to dispense with the notion of 'degrees of instantiation' which was mentioned on p. 18 above. It was not easy to see what could be meant in the Philosophy of *universalia in rebus* by saying that one object is a *better* instance of so-and-so than another, though this notion fits well enough into the Platonic theory of *universalia ante rem,* and into Conceptualism too. Perhaps it could now be suggested that the determinates of some determinables, e.g. 'whitish', 'roundish', are serially ordered. Thus the various determinates of whitishness which characterize the patch of snow, the piece of chalk, the paper, etc., may be arranged in a series beginning with 'pure white'. After this comes 'nearly pure white' (the colour the piece of chalk has), then 'farther from pure white' and then 'farther still from pure white', until we come to a characteristic which is as far from pure whiteness as it can be without ceasing to be a determinate of whitishness at all. The system of marking ($a+$, a, $a-$, $\beta+$, etc.) which we suggested for indicating the 'goodness' or 'badness' of instances can still be used: only it is now applied not to the objects themselves, but to the determinate characteristics by which they are respectively characterized.

Thus this objection to the Philosophy of Universals, that it can make no room for inexact resemblances (resemblances of less than the maximum intensity), turns out after all to be indecisive, although it looked so convincing at first sight. The facts to which this argument draws our attention are of course perfectly genuine, and important too. It is, for example, an important fact about language that most of our general words apply to sets of objects which inexactly resemble one another; and it is an important fact about thinking that the various objects which 'satisfy' a given concept, e.g. the concept of Crow, do not have to be exactly alike. Nevertheless, this argument does not at all refute the Philosophy of Universals, as it is often supposed to do. All it does is to point out what was lacking in our first rough-and-ready formulation of that philosophy. Certainly the Philosophy of Universals would be quite unworkable *without* the distinction between determinable and determinable universals. The doctrine that universals or characteristics have different degrees of determinacy is an indispensable part of it. But the distinction between determinables and determinates is perfectly consistent with the contention that there are recurrent characteristics in the world, and with the accompanying doctrine that resemblances are derivative, not ultimate. Indeed, it could be argued, the fact that recurrent characteristics do differ in their degree of determinateness is just as obvious as the fact of recurrence itself.

Finally, it is worth repeating that the phrases 'inexact resemblance' 'not exactly alike' are sometimes used in another way, to mean *incomplete* or *partial* resemblance. If A and B are closely alike in a large number of respects, but unlike or not closely alike in one or two, we sometimes say that they are very like each other but not exactly like each other. For example, within the same species of bird we often find that there are slight differences of size or colouring between two individual specimens, although they also resemble each other closely in very many ways. It is obvious that if the phrase 'inexact resemblance' is used in *this* sense, the Philosophy of Universals has no difficulty at all about inexact resemblances. We merely have to say that many universals are common to the two birds, or recur in both of them; and consequently the two individuals resemble each other in a great many respects. We then add that bird A is also an instance of a certain universal ϕ, while bird B is not an instance of this, but of a certain other universal ψ; and consequently there is a respect in which they are *not* alike. (It may be found, of course, and in this example it almost certainly will be, that though ϕ and ψ are different determinate universals, they are determinates of the same determinable universal, say 'mottled'). It must not be forgotten that every individual object is an instance of several universals at once, and often of very many at once. When we compare it with another object, we may easily find that some universals are common to both of them, and other universals are not. It would be a strange misunderstanding of the Philosophy of Universals to suppose that in this philosophy every particular is held to be an instance of only *one* universal. When we say that something is a cat, we are saying that it is an instance of many universals conjointly, and not just of one.

Our discussion has been long and complicated. What conclusion shall we draw from it? It would seem that there is nothing to choose between these two philosophies, the Philosophy of Universals or characteristics (*universalia in rebus*)[1] on the one hand, and the Philosophy of Ultimate Resemblances on the other. At any rate, it would seem that there is nothing to choose between them so long as they are considered as purely ontological doctrines, which is the way we have been considering them in this chapter. Both seem to cover the facts, though only when both are stated with sufficient care. Moreover, they both cover the *same* facts. This strongly suggests that they are two different (systematically different) terminologies, two systematically different ways of saying the same thing. It does not follow that both alike are just pieces of solemn and elaborate trifling. On the contrary, the thing which they both say is of the first importance, and we do need a way of saying it. The efforts

---

[1] It may be worth while to remind the reader that the phrase 'the Philosophy of Universals', as it has been used in this chapter, is *not* intended to cover the Platonic doctrine of *universalia ante rem*.

which each party has made to provide us with a systematic terminology for saying it have not been a waste of time. For if there were
no recurrent characteristics, *or* no resemblances between different
objects—whichever way you choose to put it—there could be no
conceptual cognition, and no use of general symbols either.

Now if there is only a (systematic) difference of terminology
between these two philosophies, it is well to be familiar with both.
Each of them may have its misleading features; and when we are
in danger of being misled by the one, we may save ourselves by
changing over to the other.

The danger of the terminology of Universals has been pointed
out already. If we can only do our philosophizing in this terminology,
we may be led to regard universals as *things* or *entities*. We reduce
this danger by using the word 'characteristic' instead; or by using
phrases like 'being red' 'being a cat' 'being side by side with . . .'
instead of noun-substantives like 'redness', 'cathood', 'side-by-side-
ness', which do look like *names* for entities; or by using the propositional function notation ϕx, xRy, $R(x,y,z)$, etc., where 'x', 'y'
and 'z' are variables. But perhaps we do not avoid the danger
altogether, especially when we make very general statements, as
we have to in philosophy; for example 'characteristics are divided
into two sorts, qualities and relations' or even 'the characteristic of
being red entails the characteristic of being coloured'. Such statements may mislead us into supposing that 'there are' characteristics
in the sense in which 'there are' dogs, or planets.

We can avoid these dangers by changing over to the terminology
of Resemblances, and by recalling that everything which can be
said in the language of Universals or Characteristics can also be
said (though usually less elegantly) in the language of Resemblances.

Perhaps there is another danger as well. The Philosophy of
Universals may tend to make us think that the world is a more
neat and tidy place than it is. If one may say so, there is sometimes
a certain air of infallibility or omnicompetence about its exponents,
as if the basic structure of the universe were perfectly clear to them,
and only a few rather unimportant details remained to be settled.
The Philosophy of Resemblances delivers us from this danger, by
reminding us that most of the resemblances we think and talk of
are by no means exact ones. It restores to human thought and
language that fuzziness or haziness, that absence of hard and fast

boundaries, which do belong to them, and even in a way to the world itself.

On the other hand, the terminology of Resemblances has its defects too. It is clumsy, complicated, and difficult to handle. Moreover, it tends to make us too much preoccupied with the inexactitude of resemblances; and so we may come to forget the vastly important fact that after all they *are* resemblances, and some of them pretty close ones too. There is such a thing as too much attention to 'marginal cases'. Attention to them is a philosophical virtue, but exclusive preoccupation with them is a philosophical vice. If that is our temptation, we may escape it by changing over to the terminology of Universals. In this terminology, we remind ourselves, there are determinable characteristics and not only determinate ones; so that even where objects resemble each other inexactly, there is still *recurrence*.

CHAPTER II

RECOGNITION

IN this chapter we turn from ontological to epistemological questions, from questions about the nature of the world to questions about the nature of intelligence and the relation of intelligence to the world. Intelligence displays itself most conspicuously in thinking or conceptual cognition, which is the main subject of this book. But thinking is not the only way in which intelligence is manifested; and if we supposed it was, we should misconceive the nature of thinking itself, especially in the earliest phases of its development. There is also such a thing as intelligent behaviour. The skill of a musician or a fighter-pilot, and even the cunning of a fox or a cat, in so far as it is an acquired cunning learned from experience, are forms of intelligence. And they manifest themselves in what these agents do, not in the way they think. Indeed, it is a difficult and controversial question whether, or in what sense, the fox and the cat are capable of conceptual cognition at all. There is a traditional belief that behaviour is never intelligent in its own right, but only in a derivative manner,[1] in so far as it is the putting into execution of a plan thought out beforehand. This Rationalistic belief, recommended by schoolmasters and other high-minded persons, is a superstition, and it does less than justice to the subtlety of Nature or the wisdom of Nature's Author. Intelligent behaviour is not necessarily, but only occasionally, preceded by a process of conceptual planning. Indeed, its intelligent character is most conspicuous in sudden emergencies, where there is no time to make plans. And some agents—children, primitive adults, and animals—who are quite capable of intelligent action, are either quite incapable of thinking out their actions beforehand, or can only do so in the vaguest and most general way. Most of us can tie a bow-tie with fair skill. But even the most sophisticated and civilized conceivers are lost if they try to think out each twist and tug before they execute it.

[1]For a criticism of this belief, cf. Professor G. Ryle *The Concept of Mind*, chap. 2.

C

Yet in these skilful or cunning actions there is the application of past experience to new situations, obstacles are circumvented, mistakes are retrieved; and these, surely, are marks of intelligence. In adapting his means to a not yet actualized end, and varying them with varying circumstances as the end requires, the agent is behaving with reference to something not at the moment present to sense. Thinking is characteristically cognition of the absent. And if cognition of the absent is a manifestation of intelligence, behaviour with reference to the absent is a manifestation of intelligence too. 'Transcendence of the given', to use a traditional phrase, can occur in action no less than in thinking. Not only so. In intelligent behaviour, although unplanned and unthought-out, provision is made not merely for the not-yet-actual but for possibilities which may never be actualized at all. The skilful pilot, as he brings his aircraft in to land, is alert to correct bumps and gusts if and when there are any. And his actions still have this alert or vigilant quality, directed to this possibility, even though in fact the air is as smooth and calm as a mill-pond. Yet the pilot does not *think* to himself, in words or images, 'there may be a bump, and I must at once move the control-stick or the rudder-pedal if there is'. Such conceptualizing is not a sign of having all one's wits about one, as Rationalistic theorists would apparently suppose; at the best, it is a prophylactic—and a not too effective one—against losing them.

Of course, one may say if one pleases that the skilful or cunning performer is thinking after all. But then we must explain that he is thinking *in his actions,* and not in words or images; it is his hands or feet that he thinks with. Again, we may say if we please that intelligent action is guided by an 'idea' of the end to be achieved; perhaps it will even be said that this must be so, because otherwise the action, by definition, could not be called intelligent. But then we must add that an idea may manifest itself, or make itself effective, in more ways than one. It may manifest itself through our actions and in the manner one action follows upon another, and not merely by what goes on in our consciousness; indeed, it may manifest itself in our actions (and perhaps all the more effectively) at times when it is not manifesting itself in our consciousness, and even though it never manifests itself in our consciousness at all.

The fundamental intellectual process seems to be the experience of *recognition*. On this, both thinking and intelligent action depend. According to the traditional account of conceptual cognition, we have to distinguish between the basic concepts which are abstracted directly from observed instances, and derivative concepts (traditionally called 'complex ideas') which we acquire by intellectual operations performed upon these basic ones. The concept of Dragon is one which we possess without ever having observed any dragons. But this concept is derivative, not primary. In conceiving of a dragon we are conceiving of a winged fire-breathing reptile, and we *have* observed winged creatures, reptiles, breathing, and fire. Or if we have not, or having done so have since forgotten what reptiles, or winged creatures, or breathing, or fire are like, then for us the word 'dragon' is a word without meaning.

There are basic concepts, then; basic in the sense that they have been acquired, not by any operation upon other concepts already possessed, but by direct abstraction from instances. And unless there were some concepts acquired in this way by direct abstraction, there would be no conceptual cognition at all. Now abstraction, whatever account we give of it, is preceded by an earlier stage, in which we learn to *recognize* instances. Before I can conceive of the colour violet *in abstracto* (that is, in the absence of observed instances) I must first learn to recognize instances of this colour when I see them. To think of it in absence, I must first learn to recognize it in presence. Recognition, then, is the first stage towards the acquisition of a primary or basic concept. It is, therefore, the most fundamental of all intellectual processes. Without it, we should acquire no basic concepts; and without basic concepts, we should not be capable of thinking at all. Nor is its importance merely genetic. Recognition is not like the ladder which we can kick away once we have used it to climb with. It is essential not merely to the acquisition of concepts, but to their possession when acquired. For whatever else a concept may be, to possess a concept is at least to have the capacity of recognizing instances when and if they are observed. And this is true of the most elaborate and advanced concepts, as much as the humble and basic ones which are acquired by direct abstraction. The concept of Dragon is not acquired by direct inspection of instances. But if I really do possess it, I must be capable of recognizing an instance if by any chance I should ever meet with one. The economic concept of Inflation, the political concept of Revolution, are very advanced and elaborate concepts, only to be acquired by complicated intellectual operations. Yet anyone who really does possess them must *ipso facto* be capable of recognizing an inflationary or a revolutionary situation if and when he encounters one. Unless he can do this, he does not possess these complex concepts, however much he may talk and write as though he did. To say it another way, it is part of the nature of a concept to be 'cashable' by instances, whether or not it is actually cashed. And the basic concepts from which all others are directly or indirectly derived, must actually at some time or other have been cashed. The acquisition of basic concepts requires the actual recognizing of instances; the possession of any concept requires the capacity for recognizing them.

It is hardly necessary to point out that the recognition of instances is not less fundamental to intelligent behaviour. A man would hardly know how to play a violin, if he did not recognize a violin or a violin-bow or a musical score when he saw them. The cat, having learned to mew outside a closed door when he wants to come in, can only exercise this piece of acquired cunning if he can *recognize* that this object is a door and is closed. And in this way, knowledge in the *practical* sense, 'knowing how to' (skill, cunning, sagacity) depends on knowledge in the cognitive sense, 'knowledge of'. Both to acquire my 'knowledge how to', and to exercise it when acquired, I must be capable of recognizing the objects or situations to which it applies. The Philosophy of Universals would describe this situation by saying that intelligent behaviour, no less than thinking, depends on the awareness of *universalia in re*. It should follow (though this conclusion was not generally drawn, and was sometimes even denied) that even animals must have some awareness of universals, since they are certainly capable of intelligent behaviour; at any rate, they must be capable of recognizing universals 'in their instances', even if they cannot conceive of universals *in abstracto*.

We can safely conclude, I think, that the analysis of recognition is the first task which any epistemology of conception must undertake. It may appear at first sight that recognition is a process so simple that there is nothing to be said about it. But we shall find that it is a good deal more complicated than it looks.

It is sometimes supposed that no intellectual activity of any kind can occur without the use of words. This is not true of recognition. Of course, in talking animals, like ourselves, recognition *is* quite often expressed in words. Recognizing something to be a cat, I may say 'cat' or 'this is a cat'; and when I do not say it publicly, I may say it privately by means of sub-vocal speech or verbal imagery. But it is not necessary that I should say anything at all, even privately. Recognition is a *pre-verbal* process in the sense that it is not dependent on the use of words. To all appearance, even the quite elaborate and complex form of recognition which I shall later call 'recognition by means of signs' can occur in animals, who never learn to use words at all, and in young children who have not yet learned to use them. And even when we have acquired the use of words, we may still have no word for just that type of object which we are now recognizing. A person ignorant of botany can recognize quite a number of different sorts of trees when he sees them, though he does not know what any of them are called.

Again, even when we have acquired a very large vocabulary, and are complete masters of our language, there is still no one-to-one correspondence between our recognizings and our recognition-statements. Entering a familiar room, I recognize many individual objects, and many different sorts of objects, all at the same time. But I cannot make many recognition-statements simultaneously. It has been remarked that we 'say less than we see'. We also say less than we recognize. Any recognition-*statement* I do make will apply only to a small selection of the objects simultaneously recognized; and very likely I make none at all. Suppose I do utter a long catalogue, 'table here, chair there, fire-place over there, cat on hearth, etc.', as we must imagine that some very intelligent philosophers habitually do whenever they enter a familiar room. Even so, the verbal catalogue will take a long time to utter, and I was recognizing the later-mentioned items long before I mentioned them; and in point of fact, I can recognize all these objects without mentioning any of them.[1] And if I *must* always be talking (which, according to some philosophers, is the essential mark of an intelligent being) my talk, private or public, may be about some quite different subject, such as politics, or theology, or tomorrow's weather, and have no appli-

---

[1] There is not very much difference between the philosophers of a generation ago who maintained that an intelligent being must always be 'judging', and those of today who say he must always be talking to himself or to others.

cation at all to the multitude of things around me which nevertheless I recognize perfectly well.

Finally, words themselves have to be recognized. If I am to speak or listen understandingly, to write or to read, I have to *recognize* the sounds or black marks as being the words they are. I have to recognize this visible mark or noise as a sensible 'token' of a certain 'type'-word. Otherwise it will not function for me as a word at all; it will be just a curious sound or mark and nothing more. Now I do not recognize the word 'cat' by saying to myself 'this is the word "cat"'. And if I did, the words in this sentence would themselves have to be recognized as being the words they are (i.e. as sensible tokens of certain type-words). At some stage or other, we just have to recognize words 'straight off' without again using words to do the recognizing with. Thus the recognition of words is itself pre-verbal. Nor is this a paradox. What is recognized is in this case verbal, but the recognizing is not. And unless we did recognize words pre-verbally, verbalized recognition would not be possible, and no other kind of verbalized intellectual operation would be possible either; because words must be recognized as being the words they are, if they are to be used understandingly.

Recognition of individuals and recognition of characteristics.

Recognition might be described as an experience of 'the same again'. But there are two sorts of sameness, the sameness of an *individual* and the sameness of a *characteristic*. Correspondingly, there are two sorts of recognition, the recognition of an individual object or person or place, and the recognition of a characteristic. I recognize my friend Jones when I see him again, I recognize the front quad-rangle of my college when I enter it. I recognize my hat or my mackintosh, at least usually, when I see them hanging on the peg outside the room where I have had lunch. But equally, when I see a cat, I recognize that it is *a* cat; though I have never to my know-ledge seen that particular cat before, I recognize the complex characteristic of being a cat (felinity) in a new instance. And when I see a blue flower, I recognize that it is blue and is a flower. The same characteristics, *blue* and *flower*, which I have often noticed before, present themselves to me in a new instance, and I recognize them.

In a discussion of concepts, it is the second sort of recognition,

recognition of characteristics, which mainly concerns us. But we may notice in passing that recognition of individuals itself depends on recognition of characteristics. Contrary to what we might suppose, it is a more complicated process, and correspondingly a more fallible one, than the recognition of characteristics. It belongs to a higher, and a more precarious, stage of intellectual development. It involves abstraction, the conceiving of characteristics in absence, as well as the recognition of them in presence. To recognize an individual person or object, I must first recognize a characteristic, characterizing a present particular. But I must do more than this. I also *remember* an earlier particular—Jones-as-he-was-last-Wednesday—which was an instance of that same characteristic. And then, further, I *believe*, or unquestioningly take for granted, that there has been a spatio-temporally continuous series of particulars intervening between these two, in such a way that the whole series of particulars constitutes the history of one persisting individual. This belief of mine need not be true. It may not be Jones at all, but merely someone very like him, his twin brother perhaps. If so, there has probably been *a* series of particulars continuously exemplifying the characteristic now noticed. But it is not the series I took it to be, because the particular I observed last Wednesday, and now remember, was not a member of it. The particular now perceived does not form part of the same continuum as the remembered one.

It would seem, then, that recognition of individual objects, persons or places is a more complicated process than recognition of characteristics. Recognition of characteristics is indeed a part of it. But something more is needed: what may be called the postulation of continuance through time, or the disregarding of intervals of non-perception. This postulation is no doubt a function which is as primitive, or nearly as primitive, as the recognition of characteristics itself. For it already occurs at a level of mental development where cognition and action are not yet clearly differentiable. When the mouse disappears into a mouse-hole, the cat remains on the watch outside. We may say that *in his actions* he postulates the continuous existence of the mouse through an interval of non-perception. In the same way he regularly returns to his own home after an outing. He assumes *in his actions* that the drawing-room has continued to exist during his absence, and recognizes it, in his actions, as the same individual place when he comes back.

But probably animals are only capable of this kind of recognition when the individual identity of the object is of practical importance to them. In other cases, we may imagine, they are in a state where no clear distinction is drawn between sameness of individual and sameness of character. We may imagine this, because such a condition is not uncommon in ourselves. The visitor to Oxford when he sees a Gothic gateway, notices that it is in *some* way the same as a gateway he saw two hours before, when his breathless tour of the university began. But whether it is the same individual gateway as he saw after lunch, or merely has the same architectural characteristics, he does not know; and, what is more relevant, he is in such a state of bewilderment and fatigue that he does not even ask himself the question. Yet he is certainly aware of sameness in the sense that what he sees has a familiar feel, and reminds him of something seen earlier in the day. Indeed, such a state of mind is not at all uncommon when we are first accustoming ourselves to a new environment, physical or social. Is this the same heavy-jowled man I saw at breakfast, or only another like him? Is it the same room that we had lunch in yesterday, before that tedious committee meeting, or another one furnished in the same Edwardian style? We do not know; and hurried from one impression to another, we do not even ask. It is enough for us that in the bewildering chaos there are samenesses of *some* kind to hold on to.

A sane, sober, rational man may wonder how such a muddled state of mind is possible, even to an animal, and still more to our rational selves. How could anyone be so idiotic that he confused numerical and qualitative identity? It would be insufficient, though it might be true, to reply that excessive sanity may be a disqualification for philosophic enquiries, especially when one is trying to explore the more primitive levels of mental activity. But this confused state of mind is not really so puzzling as all that. It may best be described, perhaps, as an *unanalysed sense of familiarity*. And 'confused' is too unkind a name for it. It is rather that certain questions are not asked than that their answers are mixed up with each other. First, we do not ask just what character it is, in respect of which the situation feels familiar. We are aware of 'same again', without clearly discriminating what it is that is the same. And secondly, we do not ask whether it is sameness of character only, or whether, in addition, there has been a series of intervening particulars (all having that same character), and joining up this present particular with another experienced in the past. The difference between sameness of character *per se*, and sameness of character combined with temporal continuity, does not at the moment interest us. It is enough that the situation has *something* familiar about it. Identity of character at least is there, relating this present particular to a previously experienced one. And we do not even ask whether there is or is not a relation of indirect temporal continuity as well. If we were rats or hedgehogs or bullfinches, we should probably never ask the question at all, not even in our actions, unless it were of pretty urgent practical importance. Human beings do normally ask it (of course they may give the wrong answer) but in times of stress or bewilderment they fall back into the unanalysed feeling of familiarity which I have been trying to describe.

Our conclusion so far is that recognition of individuals is derivative. It is recognition of characteristics which is fundamental. There can be no recognition of individuals (not even mis-recognition of them) unless there is already recognition of characteristics. And there are probably forms of consciousness in which recognition of characteristics occurs but recognition of individuals does not. On the other hand, without the capacity of recognizing some characteristics at least, however dimly, mental life of any kind could hardly exist at all. This has sometimes been denied. It has been thought that there are conscious beings whose experience consists of nothing but pure sensation. But what could a consciousness be like to which nothing ever felt in the least degree familiar, a consciousness wholly incapable of the experience of the 'same again'? (We may observe that if nothing is familiar nothing can be strange or novel or disconcerting either). At any rate, if such a consciousness could exist, it would be absolutely useless to its possessor. From a biological point of view it would be a sheer luxury. Teleologically, the point of being conscious, of having experiences, is that it enables one to *recognize* one's food or one's enemies when they are within the range of one's sense organs, or to recognize other things which are biologically helpful or harmful (for example, a suitable place for concealment, a safe place for building a nest). The owl who cannot recognize a mouse when he sees one or hears one will soon starve, however acute his senses of sight and hearing may be.

It is possible that in some creatures the capacity of recognizing their food or their enemies is unlearned, 'instinctive' as we say; and that the function of sense-experience is merely to actualize these already existing recognitional powers. But in most animals, perhaps in all, sensation has another function as well. It enables one to learn from experience, and thereby to respond more effectively to one's environment. To put it rather extravagantly, sense-experience exists for the sake of *induction*. We cannot, of course, suppose that inductive generalizations are consciously formulated in the animal mind, as they sometimes are in ours. The cat does not say to himself 'when there is tea there is usually milk'. Yet in some sense he has acquired the information which these words formulate; and he has learned it inductively, by experiencing a conjunction which has repeated itself in varying circumstances. It exists in him, we may suppose, in the form of a disposition to expect milk when a cup of tea is poured out in his presence. This expectation may or may not manifest itself in his consciousness in the form of a vivid milk-like image. If it does, an inductive generalization for him is much what Hume says it is for us. But the disposition is also a disposition to act in a milk-expectant manner when tea is seen or smelt: for example, to prowl round the chair of the lady of the house or to jump on her knee. The difference between such unformulated animal inductions, and the very similar inductions made by ourselves are only these: first, we can sometimes formulate our inductive generalizations, if the resources of our vocabulary permit. But we made them and relied upon them long before we tried to formulate them. And sometimes we cannot formulate them even when we do try. The weather-wise countryman or sailor can tell by the look of the clouds that the rain-storm is passing. But he cannot describe that look in words. The phrase 'cold-front cumulus' is not part of his vocabulary. Secondly, it would appear that animal inductions are a good deal less *disinterested* than ours. We notice more regularities than animals do, because a knowledge of 'how Nature works' gives us a certain satisfaction in itself, though in some men the satisfaction is small. The animal achieves the ideal which the Practical Man only approaches; he only notices the constant conjunctions which are directly relevant to his biological needs. His inductions, such as they are, are based upon these regularities. He does not bother his head with generalizing about others, and so his generalizations are few, and very closely bound up with action. When A recurs, its occurrence is not so much a premiss from which B can be inferred, as an opportunity for B-seeking action; or in other cases (as when a loud bark announces the approach of a dog) an urgent signal for B-avoiding action. The animal mind is the Pragmatist's paradise.

The point for us to notice, however, is not that these animal inductions have limitations, but the fact that they do exist. If learning from experience, however limited, occurs even at the animal level, this throws some light on the nature of consciousness. Locke was surely mistaken when he said that 'brutes abstract not' and that 'we observe no foot-steps in them of the use of general ideas'; though, as we shall see, abstraction and the use of general ideas are matters of degree and it is not always easy to decide whether they are present or absent. At any rate, it is a mistake to suppose that there is a level of consciousness in which one is aware only of particulars and not in any sense at all aware of universals. A being whose consciousness was in such a state could never learn anything; and if *per impossibile* it could, its learning when acquired could never be applied. For both learning and the subsequent use of it depend upon the capacity of recognition—the sort of recognition called recognition of characteristics just now. This follows from the nature of induction itself. Induction, at any rate the crude and primitive induction we are here considering, can only occur through experience of *repeated* conjunctions. Nor is it enough that the conjunctions should in fact be repeated. One must notice their repetition, or, to put it more cautiously, their repetition must 'make an impression' upon one. And I must be able to *recognize* that this is tea and that is milk when I see them or smell them again, before I can be 'impressed' by the fact that these characteristics have again been conjoined, as they have been before. Moreover, having made my generalization, having learned to expect milk (in my actions at least) whenever tea is observed, I cannot apply what I have learned or use it as a guide to my future behaviour, unless I can also recognize later instances of tea when I meet them; even though I may be as incapable of conceiving of tea *in abstracto*, as the cat is in Locke's opinion.

I am tempted to add that the philosophical myth of a purely sensitive consciousness, aware only of particulars, is one of the most important reasons for the rise of Behaviourism. The Behaviourist maintains that the conception of consciousness is useless for purposes of psychological explanation. And the hypothesis of such a purely sensitive consciousness *is* indeed useless for the explanation and prediction of the observable behaviour of animals. If you say that this is the only kind of consciousness they have, you might as well say they have no consciousness at all; or that, if they have, it is not of the remotest biological importance and may quite safely be ignored by the student of Animal Psychology. We can only save the animal consciousness if we consent to allow it some degree of intelligence as well as sensation. Whether animal intelligence deserves the honorific title of 'reason' is a question the reader must decide for himself.

Primary and Secondary Recognition.

We have distinguished between recognition of individuals and recognition of characteristics. We have now to draw another distinction which is equally important, but much less obvious. Its nature may be roughly indicated by saying that recognition of characteristics may be either direct or indirect, either intuitive or inferential, either immediate or mediate. When one sees a red object in a good light, one recognizes the redness of it directly or not at all. Familiar colours, shapes, sounds, tastes, smells and tactual qualities are recognized immediately or intuitively, when one observes instances of them. But when I see a grey lump and recognize it as a piece of lead, this recognition is indirect or mediate. In taking the object to be a piece of lead, I am recognizing it as something metallic, heavy in proportion to its bulk, soft and easily bent or cut, bright when at first cut but liable to oxidize quickly when exposed to air, liable to make dirty marks on the fingers or on paper, etc. These characteristics are not directly observed to be present in the object, in the way the grey colour is. We cannot claim that we just *notice* them, as we do notice the grey colour when we see the object lying at our feet. As a first rough approximation (we shall have to modify it later) let us say that they are *inferred*, by an inductive inference; for it is a fairly reliable inductive generalization that when that particular sort of dull-grey colour is present, those other characteristics are present as well. The same sort of thing happens when I recognize a bird as a raven. I *notice* its blackness and its shape as it flies overhead. I also notice a certain familiar *gestalt*-quality about the way it flaps its wings, though I could not possibly describe this quality in words. But in recognizing it as a raven, I attribute to it many other characteristics which I do not at the moment notice at all: a harsh croaking voice, good soaring capacities, a tendency to indulge in dives, side-slips and other aerobatic manœuvres, a disposition to feed on carrion, and to inhabit hilly and rocky places.

Indeed, it would seem that most of the recognitions which interest us—unless we happen to be psychologists or painters or phenomenologically minded philosophers—have something of this character which we are tempted to call indirect, or mediate, or inferential. Even when we recognize something as a man, or a chair, or a flower-pot, we go beyond the characteristics which we actually notice the perceived object to have. In addition, we attribute other characteristics to it which we are not at the moment noticing at all; though we believe, or rather take for granted without question, that further examination of the object would enable us to notice them if we wished. For instance, when I recognize the thing over there to be a chair, I am assuming without question that it is a moderately rigid body capable of supporting a man or a pile of books, and unlikely to change its shape or its chemical constitution within the next five minutes; but the only characteristics I actually notice it to have at the moment are a certain set of colours distributed over the front part of its surface, and a certain visible shape.

Nevertheless, the words 'indirect', 'mediate', 'inferential' are not quite the right ones, though they will do well enough as a first approximation. And consequently their contraries—'direct', 'mediate', 'intuitive'—would also be misleading without further explanation. It will be better to use the deliberately colourless phrases *primary recognition* and *secondary recognition*. Primary recognition is the sort I have hitherto called direct, intuitive, or immediate; I have also called it 'noticing'. Secondary recognition is the sort I have been calling indirect, mediate, or inferential.

But what is wrong with those words 'indirect', 'inferential', 'mediate'? Surely when you recognize something as a piece of lead or as a raven, you *are* making an inductive inference? Perhaps I should make one later, if I were challenged or if some other cause for doubt occurred. Perhaps I used to make one on similar occasions long ago, when I was less familiar with lead or with ravens. Perhaps

I *ought* to be making one now—if I were a perfectly rational being on the Cartesian model. But as a matter of fact I am not inferring at all, however much philosophers may tell me that I ought to be. To say that I am inferring is to misdescribe the experience which I have. What makes us want to misdescribe it in this way is, of course, the fact that secondary recognition is fallible, and fallible in the same kind of way as inductive inference is. (The thing may not be lead at all but only a bit of painted wood, and the bird may be a carrion crow, not a raven.) And to add to the temptation, there is the further fact that we did make inductive inferences at an earlier stage, when we were still *learning* to recognize ravens or pieces of lead. But be that as it may, our present experience is not an experience of inferring. To put it crudely, it does not *feel* like inferring at all. It feels like recognition, however discreditable this may be to human nature. There is no transition of the mind from a premiss to a conclusion. There is not even an associative transition of the mind, as when I see a man and a second later the sight of his face reminds me of his name. If one may put it so, secondary recognition has a totalistic character. The thing is recognized as a piece of lead or a raven 'straight off', as soon as I look at it. Sometimes it is not even necessary to look (if we distinguish looking from mere seeing). I may have the merest glimpse of the bird flying by, while my attention is occupied in painting a picture of a rock-strewn stream, or in trying to follow my companion's obscure exposition of Existentialism; and yet I recognize the object as a raven without difficulty and straight off. Indeed, this 'all at once' character of secondary recognition is so striking that one is strongly tempted to describe it by the very adjectives which were applied to primary recognition just now—'direct', 'immediate', 'intuitive'.

Perhaps the best way to put it is this: secondary recognition is recognition by means of *signs*. The noticed characteristics are taken as signs of others which are not at the moment noticed. The dull-grey colour is a sign to use of the heaviness, softness, etc., which go to constitute the complex characteristic of 'being lead'. But if we put it this way, we must be careful to insist that the sign-significate relation has nothing temporal about it. As I have pointed out, there is no transition of the mind from the sign to the signified; neither an inferential transition, nor even an associative one. Sign and significate present themselves together to the mind (perhaps they ought not to, but they do). Moreover, we react to them in a practical way as one indivisible whole. I react to the approaching bomb as if I saw it, by prostrating myself on the ground, though all I see—at the most—is the approaching aircraft. There are not two stages in the action, any more than there are in the cognition.

Perhaps this all-at-once character of secondary recognition was what some psychologists had in mind when they introduced the conception of 'complication' and distinguished it from ordinary association, in which there is a transition from the 'cue' to the 'associate'. They pointed out, for example, that ice *looks* cold and water looks wet; and these are also excellent illustrations of secondary recognition. When I see the ice, I certainly do not infer the coldness from the glimmery look; nor would it be true that the glimmery look reminds me of the coldness, by causing a transition of the mind from the one characteristic to the other. In the same way, the distant mountain *looks* bulgy, though physically and physiologically it is far beyond the range of stereoscopic vision. The sharp contrast of light and shade on its visible surface is one of many sorts of 'depth-sign'. The sign-characteristic and the signified bulginess present themselves to my mind together, as soon as I look at that part of the landscape. Indeed, the two characteristics are so little separated that the difficulty is, on the contrary, to get them apart. It is only by the utmost effort that I can get myself to see the object as just a mass of variegated light and shade.

With these precautionary remarks, it will perhaps be safe to indicate the nature of secondary recognition by calling it recognition by means of signs. Primary recognition, on the other hand, is not recognition by means of signs. It is by primary recognition that we recognize the sign-characteristics themselves—the dull grey colour which is a sign to us of lead, the blackness and the visual *gestalt*-quality which are signs to us of a raven. In earlier days, primary recognition would have been called 'intuitive awareness' or 'immediate apprehension', and it would have been said that a primarily recognized characteristic is something 'given'. It would also have been said that primary recognition is 'logically' as well as psychologically immediate, whereas secondary recognition has only psychological immediacy.

Perhaps the reader may suspect that, by accepting the distinction between primary and secondary recognition, he is committing himself to the Sense-datum Analysis of perception. Before going further, it will be well to show that this suspicion is groundless.

By secondary recognition I recognize the black flapping object in the sky as a raven. But in so doing I am recognizing, by primary recognition, the blackness and the 'flappy' *gestalt*-quality of something. Now philosophers differ about the nature of that something. According to one school, it is a visual sense-datum which I take (fallibly) to belong to a moving material object, or to be in some way a constituent of a moving material object. On this view, it would seem that all recognition of material-object characteristics must be secondary recognition. Even recognizing something as a black object would be secondary recognition, if 'object' here means 'material object'. According to these philosophers, it is only sensory or sense-given characteristics which can be recognized by primary recognition; and *sensible* blackness, which can be primarily recognized (indeed must be, if recognized at all) has to be distinguished from *physical* blackness, which cannot. Physical blackness, blackness considered as a public characteristic independent of a particular point of view and a particular observer, could only be recognized by secondary recognition.

Other philosophers have rejected this Sense-datum Analysis of perception. The alternative analysis which they prefer is not easy to state satisfactorily. Perhaps we may best describe it as an 'Appearing' Analysis. One way of formulating it is 'There are no sense-data, there are only percepts'. And it is claimed that if we try to describe the basic or minimal percept, what one would reach if one abstained from all inference and all secondary recognition, it would still have to be described in material-object terminology; though words like 'appear' or 'look' would still have to be used, as they would not be if one were trying to describe objects in themselves, without any reference to perception. Thus in my example of the raven, one would say 'there appears to me now to be a black flapping object in the sky' (where 'object' means 'material object'). Of course, I may be having an hallucination; and then there is in fact no such object in the sky. I may be having an illusion, and then though some material object does exist and is being perceived by me, it is not really black, or it is not really flapping, or it is not really in the sky. But still it is an ultimate and unshakeable fact that there does now *appear* to me to be a black, flapping object in the sky, whether there really is one or not. On this view, then, the primary-recognizables are always characteristics of percepts, and never characteristics of mere sense-data. Sense-data are either abolished altogether; or if it is conceded that there are certain rare and queer experiences which are most appropriately described in the sense-datum terminology, these experiences only occur (so it is said) when painters or phenomenologically minded philosophers apply a peculiar psychological or psycho-physical technique to their percepts and replace them by something quite different. Of course, we cannot just say, on this view, that the characteristics of percepts are characteristics of material objects; if we did, we should be making no allowance for the awkward facts of illusion and hallucination. But at any rate we can say that they are characteristics such as material objects do have. There may appear to be a black, flapping object when really there is not. But still, some material objects really *are* black in precisely this sense of the word 'black', and some material objects do flap.

At first sight these two philosophies do seem to draw the line between primary and secondary recognition in different places; and that in turn seems to throw doubt on the distinction itself. But I believe this is a misconception of the point which is at issue in the sense-datum controversy. On the question *what* characteristics are primary-recognizables, both parties agree. If asked to indicate them, they would indicate the very same ones. They differ concerning the entities to which these characteristics are to be ascribed, the entities, or the situations, *characterized* by them. One party says they characterize a special sort of particulars called sense-data; the other, to put it roughly, says they characterize apparent material objects. But the two parties do not differ at all as to what characteristics they are. We can see this if we consider our example of the piece of lead. One can recognize a piece of lead 'straight off', 'at a glance', by its peculiar dull-grey colour. Neither party would deny that this is secondary recognition, by means of signs. Again, neither party would deny that the dull-grey colour itself is recognized in a different and more fundamental way, directly or intuitively, in a manner which is independent of past inductions.

Controversy only arises when we ask what it is that *has* this dull-grey colour. One party says it is a visual sense-datum which has it,

D

a colour expanse situated at a certain depth in my present visual field, with a slightly bulgy visible shape.[1] The other party prefers to say that there appears to be a slightly bulgy material object having this colour, and spatially related to various other material objects (e.g. a road, a hedge) which there also appear to be.

We may conclude then that the controversy between the Sense-datum Philosophers and their critics is irrelevant to our present inquiry. All that matters to us is the distinction between primary and secondary recognition; and the distinction remains just what was, whether we accept sense-data or reject them. This conclusion is not very surprising. Anyone who denied it would in effect be denying the possibility of empirical verification.

But suppose the Anti-sense-datum Philosophers had maintained that there is no primary recognition at all? In that case, their contention would certainly have been relevant to the questions which concern us. On the other hand, it would have been obviously absurd. It does not make sense to suggest that *all* recognition is recognition by means of signs. The signs themselves must be recognized, if they are to perform their signifying function; and that recognition itself is not recognition by means of signs. Whatever our philosophy of perception may be, in one way or another we must make room for the distinction between primary and secondary recognition.

Wherever there is secondary recognition, we have said, there must also be primary recognition, even though there is no transition of the mind, either inferential or associative, from the primary recognized characteristic (the sign) to the secondarily recognized characteristic (the signified). It must now be pointed out that secondary recognition presupposes primary in another and not less important way. When I recognize an object as a raven, a complex set of characteristics is before my mind (in what sense 'before' it will be discussed later).[2] One or two of them are signs, and these are primarily-recognized; all the rest are merely signified. But such

[1] It is an absurd misunderstanding, though not at all an uncommon one, to suppose that according to the Sense-datum Philosophy all visual sense-data are 'flat' (i.e. two-dimensional). Why should a Sense-datum philosopher, of all people, deny perfectly obvious phenomenological facts? His peculiar terminology, misleading as it may be, was invented precisely in order to enable him to describe them.

[2] See ch. XI, below.

secondary recognition cannot occur, unless I am *able* to recognize each of the signified characteristics in the primary way, when and if an instance of it is presented to me; presented, that is, in the direct, perceptual manner in which the black colour and the 'flappy' visual *gestalt*-quality are presented to me now. In my secondary recognition, one of the characteristics I attached to this black and flappy entity is a tendency to croak in a peculiar way, and another is a tendency to perform aerobatic manœuvres such as sideslips, dives, and half-rolls. To recognize these characteristics now, by secondary recognition, I must be *capable* of recognizing them in another and more fundamental way when and if I actually hear the croak or actually see the aerobatic manœuvres. And this would be primary recognition, as the recognition of the black colour and the visible *gestalt*-quality of the flapping bird are now. To say the same thing in another way, secondary recognition is always subject to *verification* (that is how its fallibility is discovered) and in this respect it really does resemble inductive inference. Primary recognition is not thus subject to verification; on the contrary, it is that by which the verification is done. If I want to make sure that this really is a piece of lead, I have to look at it and handle it. I have to subject it to physical tests; either crude and everyday ones—such as cutting it and bending it, estimating its weight in my hands, putting it in the fire-shovel over the hot coals to see if it melts quickly—or the more refined ones which would be carried out in a scientific laboratory. And the whole point of these procedures is that they are perceptual procedures, designed to provide opportunities for *primary* recognition.

Moreover, secondary recognition has to be *learned* by means of primary recognition, and in that way also it is derivative. As I have tried to explain, it is not inductive inference, nor inference at all. But as I have also mentioned, inductive inferences (no doubt of a crude and unsystematic kind) are part of its pre-history. I can recognize a piece of lead 'at sight' now, simply by noticing its peculiar dull-grey colour. But there was a time long ago when I did have to infer the other lead-characteristics from the colour, by an inductive inference. And that inference in turn was made possible by the sheer, simple noticing of perceptible conjunctions; the conjunctions, and the characteristics conjoined, had to be recognized by primary recognition. This was what enabled me first to infer from one of these characteristics to others by an inductive inference; and then, much later, when such inferences had been repeatedly performed, that in turn made one of them a sign to me of the others, and so at last I acquired the capacity of recognizing a piece of lead from its colour 'straight off', by secondary recognition.

Thus however important secondary recognition may be, both biologically and epistemologically—and certainly it is one of Nature's most ingenious and successful devices—primary recognition must be analysed first. If we can get some grasp of what primary recognition is, we shall be well on the way to a satisfactory theory of conceptual cognition in general; otherwise not. Primary recognition is either the basic operation of intelligence, or at any rate it is the indispensable preliminary without which the operations of intelligence could never begin.

Analysis of Primary Recognition.

First, we must make it quite clear, if it is not clear already, that recognition can occur without abstraction. We may call this *pre-abstractive* recognition. Or, if it be said that abstraction is a matter of degree, then the degree of it which is required to make this sort of recognition possible is the minimal degree, and can exist long before full and perfect abstraction is attained, and even if it is never attained at all.

Of course recognition can and does occur *after* abstraction as well; there would be very little point or use in abstraction if it did not. When one possesses an abstract idea—an explicit concept—one is *ipso facto* capable of recognizing instances when and if they are presented. Anyone who possesses the concept ϕ is thereby capable of verifying the existential proposition $\exists x \phi x$; and such verification of an existential proposition is obviously post-abstractive. In order to entertain this proposition at all, one must be able to conceive of the concept ϕ in the absence of instances.

Perhaps a word should be said here on a more advanced and sophisticated form of recognition, which may be called *recognition by means of a definition*. The concept ϕ, whose possession enables me to verify the existential proposition $\exists x \phi x$, need not itself have been directly abstracted from observed instances (as the concept Red is). It may have been acquired by means of a definition, formal or in-formal. Of course this definition, in turn, referred to two or more concepts, ψ and χ say, which *were* directly abstracted from instances. But we need not have met with any instances of ϕ itself. To acquire it we only need to 'compound' or 'think together' the concepts ψ and χ which we already possess. An example would be the concept of Dragon. Nevertheless, if I really do possess this concept, I must be *capable* of recognizing an instance supposing I ever should observe one, though in fact I never have. Another example would be the concept of Helicopter. Before 1935 or thereabouts a student of aeronautics in this country was not at all likely to have seen a helicopter. He had not abstracted the concept from observed instances, because there were none available. He had acquired it by means of a definition ('an aircraft supported by a rotating lifting surface which is driven by engine power'). Nevertheless, every student of aeronautics was able to *recognize* the first helicopter he saw; and this capacity for recognizing an instance was inherent in his possession of the concept itself. Of course he could only do this because he had observed instances of the simpler concepts in terms of which 'helicopter' is defined. But he had to possess these concepts explicitly and *in abstracto* before he could form the complex concept at all. And the subsequent recognizing of instances of it is the clearest possible example of post-abstractive recognition.

Let us now return to pre-abstractive recognition. We can often recognize a characteristic in a new instance, long before we are capable of thinking of that characteristic in absence. And this applies not only to simple characteristics, but also to some which are highly complex; not only to determinate characteristics, but also to determinable ones. There is a traditional view, derived from Locke, that the basic concepts—those which are directly abstracted from observed instances—are 'simple ideas', such as Red, and the most determinate forms of them at that, such as Brick-red. It was supposed that complex concepts, and determinable concepts likewise, are only acquired by a subsequent intellectual operation, directed upon those simple and completely determinate ideas, an operation of synthesis or analysis as the case may be. This traditional view seems to be erroneous.

Let us consider something with a very complicated shape, for example a blackberry bush. Most of us can recognize a blackberry bush quite easily when we see one. We can recognize it even in rather unfavourable conditions, when it is seen in a poor light or at a considerable distance. To judge from behaviour, blackberry-eating animals, such as pheasants, can do the same. This, of course, is secondary recognition, since it contains predictions or extrapolations concerning characteristics which are not at the moment noticed. I take the thing seen in the distance to be a very thorny object, hard to push one's way through, and loaded with blackish and juicy fruit which I cannot at this distance discern. But the primary recognition, which is the core or nucleus of this secondary one, is the recognition of a very complicated visible shape. I may be quite unable to conceive such a complex geometrical concept in absence; and if I cannot do it, it is almost certain that the pheasant cannot. Very likely I cannot even form a visual image of this shape in absence—perhaps the simplest and most elementary way in which the possession of an abstract concept can manifest itself. But these incapacities (however shocking to rationalistically minded persons) do not in the least prevent me from recognizing new instances of this complicated shape-quality when I meet with them.

We may notice further that this shape-quality is a *determinable* characteristic, as well as a complex one. Blackberry bushes vary a good deal in their shape. Some spread themselves flat along the ground. Others rise up into vast and variegated lumps. Sometimes they grow in continuous hedges, sometimes in splendid isolation. But this variability does not prevent me from recognizing the blackberry-bush shape. I still recognize the determinable in all the many determinate forms it assumes. And the pheasant, to all appearance, can do the same.

Another example of pre-abstractive recognition of determinables occurs when we recognize an individual object, especially one which changes fairly rapidly. As we have seen, the recognition of an individual always contains the recognition of a characteristic or characteristics. I recognize the individual, Jones, by recognizing the 'Jonesy' gait and voice and features which I have observed before; and then I believe, truly or falsely, that the present exemplification of these characteristics is indirectly continuous in space and time with previous exemplifications observed before. Now these 'identifying' characteristics are highly variable. Jones is pale today, though he was ruddy three years ago when I saw him last. His face has an expression of patient resignation instead of the air of cheerful enterprise which it then wore. There are touches of grey in his hair, though last time it was copper coloured all over. He was plump then; now he is thin. Yet there is still a Jonesy something about his face and gait and voice. It has assumed a new determinate form since I last saw him. But it is still perfectly obvious, and I recognize it at once, in spite of all. This illustration is a good one for our purpose. For even in the most inveterate and sophisticated conceivers (unless they happen to be professional physiognomists) this recognition of the 'individualizing' characteristics of an individual human being is nearly always pre-abstractive and pre-analytical. What enables us to recognize Jones at sight is something we cannot describe, even to ourselves. Very likely we cannot even form a visual image which would serve as a rough and ready illustration of it,[1] when no actual observable exemplification is present. Or if we can, it is excessively vague; and as psychologists have acutely pointed out, the more familiar we are with Jones, the vaguer it is likely to be. Here then is a characteristic at once determinable and complex, which is perfectly recognizable; but it can be conceived *in abstracto* either very imperfectly, or more likely, not at all.

I must now remind the reader of the two theories which were distinguished in the previous chapter: the Philosophy of Universals (*universalia in re*), and the Philosophy of Resemblances. Both these theories, as we described them there, were ontological ones: theories about the nature of the world, or if it be preferred terminologies for describing it. Either of them could be held even if no one had ever reflected on intellectual operations at all, or indeed on any other cognitive processes. But as soon as anyone does start reflecting on intellectual operations, his ontological theory—whichever of the two it is—will partly determine the *epistemological* theory to which his reflections will lead him. His ontological philosophy will acquire an epistemological offshoot or appendix. And the first problem he will have to tackle, if he begins at the beginning, will be the analysis of primary recognition. Let us now consider how the Philosophy of Universals would analyse it. Later, we shall turn to the very different analysis which the Philosophy of Resemblances would give.

In the Philosophy of Universals, intelligence is conceived in a very simple and straightforward manner. (This manner of conceiv-

[1]On this illustrative or 'quasi-instantiative' function of mental images, see ch. VIII.

ing it is the epistemological theory traditionally called Realism.)
The distinctive feature of intellectual processes—what differentiates
them from other forms of cognition—is held to be just this, that
they are concerned with universals. Intelligence is that special kind
of cognition whose objects are universals. And primary recognition,
it would be said, is the most elementary way of being aware of a
universal. It is the most elementary, because we are only aware
of the universal in the act of observing an instance. We are not
being aware of it *in abstracto* or in absence. Sometimes, of course,
we could be. Looking at the surface of this box, I recognize in it
the universal Red; but I can also conceive of that universal *in
abstracto*, and frequently do. And even though at present I can only
be aware of a certain universal 'in' its instances, and cannot yet
conceive it *in abstracto*, I may learn to do so later. It would probably
be said, however, that the lower animals can *only* be aware of
universals in this elementary, pre-abstractive way, by recognizing
them 'in' perceived instances.

What more can the Philosophy of Universals say about primary
recognition? Nothing much, it may seem. There *are* universals,
existing and subsisting *in rebus*. We are sometimes aware of them
'in' their instances, either pre-abstractively or post-abstractively; and
that is what primary recognition is. What more can be said?

But this would not be a fair way of putting it. The Philosophy
of Universals does not offer us quite such a jejune account of primary
recognition. In the first place, it is part of the analysis of something
to distinguish it from what it is not, and especially from other things
which are liable to be confused with it. One must distinguish primary
recognition from other sorts of recognition, and a large part of
this chapter has been concerned with that task. The reader will
have noticed that everything said in it has been said in the terminology of Characteristics and nothing (or almost nothing) in the
terminology of Resemblances. There is a good reason for this. The
terminology of Characteristics is far simpler and easier to handle.
It accords with our ordinary habits of speech in a way the terminology of Resemblances does not. Now the terminology of Characteristics is the terminology of Aristotelian Realism, which is the
epistemological counterpart of the philosophy of *Universalia in re*.
The Philosopher of Universals, then, may fairly claim the credit
(for what it is worth) of everything we have said so far to dis-

tinguish the different sorts of recognition. All this, he may say, is part of *his* analysis of primary recognition; although, to be sure, when we ask what primary recognition itself is, and have finished distinguishing it from what it is not, there is little more he can add except this—that primary recognition is the awareness of universals or characteristics 'in' their instances.

Even so, there is still something more to be said; though historically, exponents of the Philosophy of Universals have not often troubled to say it. If we hold that there are recurrent features in the world, characteristics or *universalia in rebus*, of course we shall naturally hold also that primary recognition is the awareness of such recurrent features. When I recognize, we shall say, I am just noticing a recurrent characteristic. But there is an ambiguity here. Am I merely noticing a characteristic which is in fact recurrent—a universal which has in fact been 'in' some earlier particular than this one 'in' which it is now recognized? In that case, the man who first discovered a duck-billed platypus must have recognized the creature at once; for there had in fact been earlier duck-billed platypuses, and though unseen by human eyes, that individual one had in fact existed for some time. Clearly it is not sufficient that the characteristic recognized should be in fact recurring—should as a matter of fact have had earlier instances. At least one of these earlier instances must have been observed by myself, if I am to recognize the characteristic now. (For it is primary recognition we are speaking of; not recognition from definitions,[1] which does not require experience of previous instances, but that more fundamental kind which might be expressed by the words 'the same again'.) Yet it would be too much to claim that the characteristic is explicitly *known to be the same as* one noticed before in other instances. That would require that I must be consciously recollecting a previously recognized instance, and consciously comparing it with the one recognized now. This does happen occasionally. Unaccustomed to Baroque architecture, I gaze with astonishment at the portal of one of the more bizarre churches in Rome. Where have I ever seen pillars like that before, twisted as if they were bits of sugar-candy? Ah! now I remember. It was in the porch of the University Church in Oxford. But when this kind of thing happens, it is because I have not *fully* learned to recognize the architectural characteristics in

[1]On recognition by means of definitions, see pp. 52-3, above.

question. I am still in process of learning. Normally, however, the recognition occurs 'straight off', without any process of recollection at all (indeed, that is what happens even in the more complex process of secondary recognition).

Perhaps the best way of describing the situation is this: In primary recognition a characteristic is not only noticed; it is also *familiar* in some degree. And this does not entail that it reminds us of some particular past occasion when we noticed the characteristic before; that may happen or may not, and commonly does not. No doubt, if the characteristic feels familiar to us, we have as a matter of fact experienced at least one previous instance of it; but we need not recall when or how. Moreover, our previous awareness may have been relatively inattentive. Mere use and wont, without discrimination or study, will suffice to render a characteristic familiar to us. It is in that way, for the most part, that we come to recognize the 'identificatory' characteristics—the distinctive 'look' of a room or of a face—which in turn enable us to recognize individual persons and places.

Recognition of a characteristic, then, does not require the conscious recollection of past instances; it only requires that the characteristic recognized has become familiar. Nevertheless, recognition is only possible to a being which has the capacity of *retentiveness*, whatever the right analysis of that capacity may be. A conscious being without any power of retaining his past experiences (if such a being can be conceived of) might notice many things as they happened, but could not recognize anything—neither characteristics, nor *a fortiori*, individual objects. Thus memory in a large sense of the word is essential to recognition, even though conscious recollection of the past is not. Of course this is perfectly obvious. But its importance has been overlooked. Examiners and other academic persons are accustomed to contrast intelligence with memory. Williams has a very good memory, but his intelligence is third class. The antithesis serves well enough in certain limited contexts. Some specialized forms of memory are independent of some specialized forms of intelligence. A man may have a great capacity for remembering historical facts, and a very small capacity for mathematical reasoning. But if we generalized this antithesis, if we concluded that intelligence as such is independent of memory as such, we should be making a fundamental mistake. On the contrary, conceptual cognition in all its phases, from recognition to the most abstract forms of reasoning, is itself a function of memory, whatever else it may be besides. Without memory in a large sense of the word, there would never be any concepts at all. Without memory, there would be no primary recognition; without primary recognition, no abstraction, and therefore no basic concepts; and without basic concepts there would be no derivative concepts, which are acquired by intellectual operations directed upon these basic ones. It is equally clear that intelligent action depends upon the power of recognizing the situations to which one's skill or knack or *expertise* is applicable. As Mr. C. J. Holloway has put it, an intelligent being is one who 'does not waste his past'.

If all this has sometimes escaped notice, it is because memory has been equated—mistakenly—with the capacity of conscious recall, the recollecting of particular past experiences. But this is only one manifestation of memory, and one of the least important, both biologically and epistemologically; certainly far less important than the sense of familiarity, which makes recognition possible.

To put my point in a more grandiloquent manner: intellectual operations, from primary recognition upwards, are only possible for a being who has the power of 'transcending time'. But lest this should seem too exciting, I hasten to add that even the humblest slug (unless it is a mere automaton) must have this capacity of time-transcendence as well as we. For unless we admit that it can learn to recognize characteristics, however few and however slowly, we might as well say it is not a conscious creature at all.

We can now see that even though the reality of *universalia in rebus* is admitted, yet when it comes to conceptual cognition a simple and straightforward Realistic epistemology leaves something out. In the sort of Realism which was current in the first quarter of this century, it was apparently supposed that nothing more was needed on the mind's side but a bare capacity of being aware. Sometimes one was aware of particulars, sometimes of universals; sometimes (as in the more advanced forms of conceptual cognition) one was aware of several universals, with the relations between them. The objects of awareness differed, but the awareness was the same. All one could say about it was that it entailed, or perhaps consisted in, a direct relation between the mind and whatever sort of object it happened to be. But it is by no means enough to talk of 'being aware of' universals, as if the thinking mind had nothing to do but just open its intellectual eyes and look at them. In other words, universals may be as objective as you please, but conceptual cognition (intelligence) in all of its forms, from recognition upwards, is something more than merely noticing them. Memory enters into it as well—not memory in the form of explicit recollection, but memory in the form of retentiveness. Knowledge of universals (if we like that terminology) requires a process of *familiarization*, long or short. And this familiarization is something which happens in ourselves, not in the external world; however true it may be that the external world contains recurrent features, each of which is the same in many instances. Thus even though we accept the ontological theory which I have called the Philosophy of Universals, we shall still have a use for words like *concept* or *idea*, to mean a certain sort of mental disposition in ourselves. It will by no means be enough to say, as these Realists often did say, that the words *concept* or *idea* can be dispensed with, since they seem to mean something 'in the mind', and nothing (it was said) is in the mind, when we are aware of a universal, except the bare awareness of it. There is something else 'in the mind', namely the memory of past instances; and this, not in the form of conscious recollection—which might have been written off as just another act of pure awareness, directed this time on the past—but in the form of a retentive disposition, which is undoubtedly a state of ourselves.

It must be added that these criticisms would by no means apply to the Realism of Aristotle, the founder of the Realist Epistemology; nor would they apply, I believe, to the medieval Aristotelians. Aristotle is careful to emphasize the part which φαντασία plays in our awareness of universals. And φαντασία, usually translated 'imagination', seems in fact to mean the power of forming memory-images. Aristotle seems to hold that it is from these memory-images, and not directly from perceived particulars, that universals are abstracted. And in a famous passage he takes care to point out that our knowledge of universals is a gradual growth. He does not say much about the pre-abstractive recognition which now concerns us. But he certainly does maintain that awareness of universals would be impossible without memory; even though we may think that he sometimes over-emphasizes the importance of memory-images, and under-emphasizes the other ways in which a memory-disposition may manifest itself. There is a celebrated passage in the *Posterior Analytics* in which he says quite clearly that memory is essential to the awareness of universals. "So out of sense-perception comes to be (γίνεται) what we call memory, and out of frequently repeated memories of the same thing develops experience (ἐμπειρία); for a number of memories constitute a single experience. From experience again—i.e. from the universal now stabilized in its entirety within the soul, the one beside the many which is a single identity within them all—originate the skill of the craftsman and the knowledge of the man of science. . . . It is like a rout in battle, stopped by first one man making a stand and then another, until the original formation has been restored."[1] The gradual growth of conceptual cognition—first, familiarization, then recognition, and finally explicit abstraction—could not be better described; though Aristotle was more interested in what follows abstraction—in explicit conceptual thinking, and especially deductive reasoning— than in the dimmer and only imperfectly intellectual stages of consciousness which precede it.

So much for the present about Primary Recognition in the Philosophy of Universals. According to that philosophy, primary recognition is the awareness of a universal *in re*, 'in an instance'. And in the pre-abstractive phases of consciousness, that is the *only* way in which we are aware of a universal. (Of course, primary recognition occurs after abstraction as well as before. The capacity for recognizing universals 'in' their instances is an essential feature of intelligence in all its phases, from the most elementary to the most developed. But for the moment, it is the pre-abstractive stage of consciousness which interests us.) This awareness of a universal, however, is not merely the noticing of something now present; it is also a function of memory. A universal, according to this philosophy, is a *recurrent* feature of the world. And in being aware of it, I am aware of it *as* recurrent, as something which is common to this present object and some past object or objects experienced before. To be aware of it, I have to 'retain' those past experiences of mine, though I do not have to recollect them, and may even be incapable of doing so. This retention shows itself by making some feature of

---

[1] *Posterior Analytis*, Book II, ch. 19, 100A lines 3-13 (Clarendon Press Translation). Aristotle's word 'experience', corresponds roughly with what I have called 'being familiar with'.

the present object *feel familiar*. The recurrent characteristic which feels thus familiar need not be a determinate one, nor yet a simple one. It is often determinable, rather than determinate; and it is often complex, as in our earlier example of recognizing the shape of a blackberry bush.

Let us now consider how primary recognition would have to be analysed if we rejected the Philosophy of Universals, and accepted the Philosophy of Resemblances instead. Can we give any account of recognition at all, if universals are dispensed with? Certainly we shall have to say it is awareness of a resemblance, not of a universal. Primary recognition is a pre-verbal experience; but if we do try to express it in words, the words the Philosophy of Universals would use are 'The *same* again', whereas the words the Philosophy of Resemblances would use are 'There has been something *very like* this before'. We might say that in the Philosophy of Universals recognizing is *identifying*, but in the Philosophy of Resemblances it is *assimilating* (so long as 'identifying' means not making, but finding an identity, and 'assimilating' means not making, but finding a resemblance; and despite etymology, that is the way these two words are commonly used).

Let us suppose that I have previously observed three objects, A, B and C, and have noticed that they resemble each other closely; for instance, the blushing face, the tomato and the sunset which were mentioned on an earlier page. This close likeness has 'impressed us'; it has set up a memory-trace in us. Now, some time afterwards, we observe a fourth object D, and we become aware that it resembles those three objects as closely as they resemble each other. A, B and C, thanks to the impression their resemblance made on us, have become for us *exemplars*, the nucleus of a possible class composed of anything which resembles them as closely as they resemble each other. The new object D, which has a 'sufficient' degree of resemblance to these exemplars, is accordingly classified along with them. And this, it can be said, is what we mean, or ought to mean, by saying that D has a 'characteristic in common with' A, B and C (for instance, has 'the same colour as' they had). The terminology of characteristics—of qualities and relations—is the one we normally use when we come to the use of language. But according to the Resemblance Philosophers it is a mere shorthand, not to be taken literally (as the Philosophy of Universals takes it). And this is the experiential cash-value of it. I emphasize this point, because I have hitherto been using the language of characteristics throughout this chapter. For example, I have called the sort of recognition we are now discussing 'recognition of characteristics' as distinguished from a more complex sort, 'recognition of individuals'. It must not be thought that in adopting this distinction we commit ourselves irrevocably to the Philosophy of Universals, on the ground that in the Philosophy of Resemblances the distinction between characteristics and individuals disappears. It does not. Neither does the distinction between the two types of recognition disappear; it merely has to be described in a more complicated way.

Let us consider what recognition of an individual would amount to, according to the Philosophy of Resemblances. By 'an individual' we mean what has been called a *continuant*, something which endures through a long period of time and retains an identity through change. In order to give *any* analysis of individual-recognition at all (whether in terms of resemblances or anyhow else) we shall have to divide this continuant into a series of temporally brief phases. These I shall call *particulars*, as before. If we accept the Philosophy of Resemblances, we shall then proceed as follows. I have in the past experienced certain particulars A B C which resemble each other very closely, and were moreover spatio-temporally continuous with each other. Now, after an interval, perhaps a long one, I observe a new particular M, and notice that it resembles A, B and C as closely as they resembled each other. So far we have only recognition of a characteristic. For this is what recognition of a characteristic amounts to, according to the Philosophy of Resemblances. It is noticing that a present particular resembles certain past particulars as closely as they resembled each other. This recognition might be pre-verbal, and frequently is. If we did use words, it might be expressed by saying that the new particular has 'the Jonesy look'; but that would only be a short way of saying that it resembles these past particulars as closely as they resemble each other. The past particulars A B C are the *exemplars* for the class of Jonesy-looking particulars. Any other particular which has sufficient resemblance to them is classified along with them, any other particular which does not have it is excluded.

But if recognition of an individual is to occur, a further step must be taken. In addition to noticing that M resembles A B C as closely as they resemble each other, we must also believe or take for granted that there has been a spatio-temporally continuous series of particulars, joining up the present M to the past A B and C, in such a way that the whole series forms one continuing individual persisting through time. Thus the distinction we drew between recognition of characteristics and recognition of individuals still survives in the Philosophy of Resemblances; so does the connection which we indicated between them—that recognition of individuals consists in recognition of a characteristic together with a postulation of temporal continuity. It is only that the phrase 'recognition of a characteristic' is replaced by something which comes nearer (so the Resemblance Philosophy claims) to giving its experiential cash-value: namely by a terminology of resemblances between particulars.

The Philosophy of Resemblances has the advantage of emphasizing from the start that recognition is a function of memory; whereas exponents of the Philosophy of Universals, at least some of them, only admit it as an afterthought, and start by declaring that recognition is just the awareness of a universal in an instance, as if memory did not enter into the situation at all. In the Philosophy of Resemblances, this reference to the past is made perfectly explicit from the first. The exemplar-particulars, which the present one resembles, are particulars I have experienced in the past. But this very virtue of the Philosophy of Resemblance appears to involve it in an insoluble difficulty. As we have seen, recognition may occur, and commonly does, without any *recollection* of past particulars at all. My retention of these past experiences shows itself not by the explicit recalling of them, but by the 'tone' or 'colouring' which the present experience has as a result of them, by the fact that a feel of familiarity attaches to some element within it. Yet the Philosophy of Resemblances, it may seem, is bound to maintain (in spite of the facts) that recognition does involve the conscious recollecting of exemplars. How am I to notice that M resembles the past particulars A B and C as closely as they resemble each other, unless by recalling these very particulars, and comparing it with them? How can I be aware that M stands in this many-term relation without having the other terms of the relation before my mind?

Shall we be content to say that the present particular M just feels familiar as a result of these past experiences, though they are not recalled? Certainly there is a feel of familiarity when we recognize (for example) the colour of M, and certainly it does result from past experiences of similar particulars. That is a fact independent of any theory. But *to what* does this feel of familiarity attach? In the Philosophy of Universals, we can say it attaches to a *universal of quality* (redness, for example) which is actually 'in' the object M. Shall we now say, instead, that it attaches to a *relational property* which is 'in' the object M—the property of sufficiently resembling the past, but unrecalled, exemplar objects A B and C? There are two objections to this. First, we have fallen back into the terminology of characteristics, which we were trying to get rid of. A relational property, as much as a quality, is a characteristic. And secondly, if that objection can somehow be got round by conducting our analysis in successive stages, how can we be aware of a relational property of something without being aware of the other term or terms to which that something is related?

Perhaps it will be helpful to point out that this difficulty arises about other relational properties as well, and not merely about the relational property of having a resemblance to so-and-so. I can see 'straight off' that this man is short and that one is tall, this one is fat and that one is thin, without any process of recollection and comparison. Now these are plainly relational properties. To be fat is to be *more* voluminous *than* the majority of men, to be thin is to be less so. To be tall is to have the crown of one's head *farther* from the soles of one's feet than the majority of men have, to be short is to have it nearer. These properties—tall, short, fat, thin—are, as we say, relative, relative to a standard. And the standard, for each of us, is his memory of the size and bodily proportion of the majority of men he has met with. When we notice that Jones is fat, one might accordingly expect that we should *recall* the look of the majority of the men we have met with: recall (and notice) their height and their voluminousness in proportion to their height; and having paraded them and inspected them, *compare* this present man with them, and discern that he is more voluminous in proportion to his height than they are. But in actual fact there is no recollection, no inspection-parade, and no comparison. Here then is another case where we are aware of a relational property (and here the relation is a many-

E

term relation too) and yet we are aware of only *one* term of the relation.

The same kind of thing happens in many everyday estimates of quantity. How long is this sheet of paper? I answer without hesitation 'about a foot long'; that is, its length is about equal to the length of a standard foot-rule. I do not recollect the foot-rules I have seen and handled, nor compare the piece of paper with them. How heavy is this parcel? I want it to go by letter post, and must decide whether it weighs less than five ounces. I weigh it in my hand, moving my wrists up and down, and decide that it is a good deal under five ounces. Here I do not answer the question straight off. I hesitate for a considerable time. It cannot be argued in this case (as it might have been in the last one) that there is no time for recollecting standard weights and comparing the object with them. But how is the time occupied? Not in recollection and comparison at all, but just in attending carefully to the feel of the package itself. As I do so, various estimates suggest themselves, until at last one of them seems 'about right'. As a matter of fact, my own power of tactuo-muscular recollection is very defective. I could not *recall* the feel of a standard ounce weight if I tried.

The same thing happens too with estimates of degrees of quality —as when I estimate that the bang I heard just now is a loud one, that the moon is shining very brightly tonight, that this candidate's paper is a third-class one. Here again, we might expect that we should recollect previously observed standard objects and compare the present one with them. But we do nothing of the kind. And very likely we could not recollect a standard object of the relevant sort even if we tried.

Of course all the different sorts of estimates I have mentioned are liable to be mistaken. If we want to check them, we do have recourse to a standard object—a present one, however, not just a recollected one—and we do compare the estimated object with it. Conceivably we might even parade the majority of our acquaintances, not in memory but actually before our eyes; we might measure their height and volume with foot-rules, do the same with Jones, and so confirm or refute our original comparative judgement that he is fat. The point, however, is not that such estimates are sometimes mistaken, but that they are often right, and much more frequently right than they would be by chance alone. It is plain that there *is* a mental power of estimating relational properties at a time when only one term of the relation, and not both of them or all of them, is present to consciousness.

Now if so, it cannot be an objection to the Philosophy of Resemblances that in its account of recognition it is obliged to postulate such a power. The postulate has to be made in any case, whether we accept universals or reject them. Or rather, this mental power does not have to be postulated at all. We just have to admit that we have it. From a merely polemical point of view, then, the Philosophy of Resemblances is in a strong position.

But this will not satisfy the reader if he is as indifferent to mere polemics as a philosopher should be. After all, he will say, this power of detecting a resemblance without recollection and comparison is exceedingly puzzling. It may be true that the power is manifested in other cases, in the detection of other relational properties where only one of the related terms is present to the mind, but does that make it any less puzzling? Not exactly. But it does make it less shocking. We shall be less inclined than we were to suppose that the human mind has no business to do any such thing, and that if it has the appearance of doing it (as in recognition it certainly has) the appearance must somehow be explained away. We now see that there cannot be anything disreputable about this non-recollective and non-comparative primary recognition, to which the Philosophy of Resemblance is committed. We begin to suspect, on the contrary, that like secondary recognition ('straight off' recognition by means of signs) it is just another of those subtle and ingenious devices of Nature, which a Rationalistic philosopher, if he had been constructing a human or animal mind *de novo*, would never have been clever enough to invent.

But even though shocked surprise may have given place to admiration, of course we are puzzled still. And the way to remove the puzzle is not to solve it directly, but to ask what the source of it is. Its source, I believe, is a much too narrow conception of what *memory* is, or ought to be. Though we may officially deny it, we are still in our secret hearts inclined to believe that the conscious recollecting of individual past experiences is what remembering 'really' is, and that having a memory of something (in the sense of a persistent memory-disposition) is 'really' just the capacity for recalling it. We have this inclination, because this is the only sort of remembering in which philosophers, up to very recent times, have been interested. Memory has been far less discussed by epistemologists than other forms of cognition, such as sense-perception, or self-consciousness, or mathematical inference. And what discussion there has been, has been almost entirely concerned with the recalling or recollecting of individual past events. Philosophers have been troubled by the errors to which memory is liable, and have asked how, if at all, they can be corrected. This has led some of them to ask whether there is such a thing as memory-*knowledge* at all; or is all memory just fallible belief? They have enquired into the part which images play in memory and the relation they have to what is remembered. All these are problems about the recalling or recollecting of the past. And so, later students of the Theory of Knowledge have come to assume, tacitly, that this is the only sort of remembering there is. I do not at all deny the importance of these traditional discussions of memory, nor the difficulty of solving these traditional problems about it. But I do deny the tacit assumption that remembering *is* nothing but the recollecting or recalling of past experiences. That is one way in which a memory disposition may manifest itself in consciousness, but by no means the only one. Recognition is another, and a feeling of surprise or strangeness or disconcertment is still another. And memory-dispositions sometimes manifest themselves not in cognition, but in action. That happens in any kind of acquired skill. I remember 'how to' tie up my shoe-laces, and this memory of mine manifests itself regularly once a day by the movements of my wrists and fingers, without any recollection of the experiences by which I learned to perform this operation.

More important for our purpose: the recollective sort of remembering enjoys no priority, causal or temporal, over the other sorts. I come into Smith's room and experience a feeling of strangeness on seeing the table in the middle of the floor. This feeling is felt, and strongly felt, *before* I recollect that the last time I was there the table was right up against the wall. Indeed, the feeling of strangeness is itself the stimulus which makes me try to recollect. And when I do try, I may easily fail. Quite probably I do not at all recollect where the table was at the time of my last visit. All I can feel sure of is that it must have been somewhere else. But as the word 'must' shows, this is not recollection, but an inference from the present feeling of strangeness itself. We may notice further that in the experience of strangeness there is no trace of an act of *comparing* the present state of the room with its past state (unless of course we choose to say that the experience of strangeness is itself a queer kind of comparing). That comes later, if it comes at all, when I have succeeded in recalling what the past state of the room was.

Someone will say perhaps 'You have *no* memory of the previous position of the table; you have just admitted that you do not remember where it was'. In saying this, of course, he is equating memory with recollecting. Be it so. We may use the verb 'to remember' in that narrow way if we like. But then it will not follow that because I fail to remember A (even after an effort), in this sense of the word 'remember', I therefore have no memory of it; and it will not follow that this memory is not being actualized at this very moment. If I had altogether lost the memory of how the room looked last time, if I had wholly forgotten it, there could be nothing strange in the look it has at present. The previous experience, though unrecalled, and even unrecallable, is still somehow active in me. It has a very marked effect on my experience at present: a mediate effect, as we generally suppose, mediated by a 'memory trace' of some kind in my brain or mind or both,[1] but at any rate the effect is certainly produced. That being so, it seems better to widen, rather than narrow, the use of the verb 'to remember'; to say not that I fail to remember the past experience of the room, but that I do remember it, and the experience of surprise is itself the *way* in which the remembering happens, the form which it takes on this particular occasion. If this sounds too paradoxical, and if remembering (in the active, not the dispositional sense of the word) is to be reserved for acts of recollecting, at any rate we must say that my feeling of strangeness is an actualization of a memory-disposition; quite a different sort of actualization from an act of recollecting, and independent of it. Moreover, it can still occur when the corresponding capacity to recollect has been lost.

Nearly everything I have said about the experience of strangeness would also apply to (primary) recognition. In one way, of course, they are opposites, but in a more important way they are

---

[1]In *The Analysis of Mind* Lord Russell suggests that such 'mnemic causation' may conceivably be direct, and that the hypothesis of memory-traces may be unnecessary.

parallel. We might call them complementary opposites. And they are not independent of each other, in the way that both of them *are* independent of recollection and comparison. If I have the experience of strangeness on finding the room unlike what it used to be, it must also be true that I should have had the experience of recognition had I found it *like* what it used to be. Indeed, I do have the experience of recognition now, *in so far as* the room is like what it used to be.

It comes to this: the awareness of a resemblance (or equally a disresemblance) between something experienced now and something experienced previously is one of the fundamental manifestations of memory; fundamental, in the sense that it is not analysable in terms of any of the other ways in which a memory-disposition may manifest itself. And so far from being reducible to recollection —the explicit and conscious recall of past experiences—it is, if anything, *more* fundamental than recollection is. And this in two ways: First, it is more primitive. The capacity of being aware of a resemblance between present and past can exist *before* we are capable of recollecting the relevant past experiences, and can continue to exist *after* we have become incapable of recollecting them. Secondly, in so far as recollection occurs by means of memory-images, the image itself has to *feel familiar*. And that is just another way of describing this primitive awareness of a resemblance between present and past. To speak more sophisticatedly, I have to be aware that the image resembles something-or-other in my past, before I can recollect what in particular that something-or-other was.

Let us now return to recognition as the Philosophy of Resemblances describes it. I have a memory of certain exemplar-objects experienced in the past. This memory-disposition is now actualized by a certain present object which is like them, though I do not recall or recollect those past objects, and am even perhaps incapable of it. Shall we say, then, that recognition (according to the Philosophy of Resemblances) is just the name for the peculiar and not further analysable experience we have when a memory-disposition is actualized in this way? We cannot quite say this. It is not enough that the present object recognized should be like the exemplar-objects. It must be like them to a 'sufficient' degree—*as* like them as they were like one another. But, as a matter of fact, in this primitive awareness of present-to-past resemblance, we can and do distinguish greater and lesser degrees of resemblance. This thing here is extremely like something I have experienced before: or again, rather like it; or again, a little like it. I can detect these distinctions, even though I cannot at all recollect what that past something was.

But, of course, what we ordinarily call recognition of a characteristic (say, redness) cannot merely consist in being aware of some degree of likeness, great or small, between the present object and some past object or other. The likeness we are aware of is likeness to a *set* of past objects which were like one another. And this is not all. It was a special sort of set, whose members were *un*like each other as well as like. If our Red Exemplars had been an apple, a tomato, and a cherry, they would not have served their purpose. They might as well have been Round Exemplars, or Fruit Exemplars, or Juicy Exemplars, as Red ones. To go back for a moment to the language of characteristics which the Resemblance Philosophy is trying to analyse, these three objects have other characteristics in common besides redness. What we need, then, for a set of exemplar objects, is not just that they should be all alike, but that they should be alike in the midst of unlikeness, if one may put it so. There should be one likeness between them, along with as many unlikenesses as possible.

We shall have to suppose, I believe, that the human mind has an innate (unacquired, unlearned) tendency to notice and remember —to be 'struck by' and 'impressed by'—this special sort of likeness-situation, where there is one likeness in the midst of many unlikenesses. This supposition is not so alarming as it looks. It only amounts to saying that intelligence itself is an innate or unlearned capacity. For the noticing and remembering of likeness-situations of this special sort is the indispensable first step in the growth of conceptual cognition. And this is true whichever of the two philosophies we hold, *either* the Philosophy of Universals *or* the Philosophy of Resemblances. In the Philosophy of Universals too we shall need to notice and remember likenesses of this sort—likeness in the midst of unlikeness—if we are ever to acquire any *clear* or discriminating awareness of universals, in which one universal (redness say) is distinguishable from others (roundness, say, or juiciness).

We shall further have to suppose that when we have observed

such a set of objects, alike in the midst of unlikenesses, we thereafter have a memory of the set *as a whole*, a 'totalistic' memory, if one may put it so. If we like to state the point in the terminology of 'traces', it comes to this: there is *one* memory-trace for the set of objects as a whole (say for the Red Exemplars), 'one' in the sense that in the effect it has upon subsequent experience and action it operates as a psychological unit. Moreover, this totalistic memory-disposition may exist, whether or not there are also individual memories of the individual exemplar-objects severally; and certainly it may continue to operate, to make a difference to subsequent experience and action, after the memories of the individual exemplar-objects have been lost—all the more effectively, perhaps, because they have been lost.

Now in the experience of primary recognition, as the Philosophy of Resemblances explains it, it is the totalistic memory of such a set of objects (alike in the midst of unlikenesses) which is manifesting itself. 'Recognition' is the name we give to the special kind of experience we have when a present object resembles such a remembered group as a whole, and thereby activates one of these totalistic memory-dispositions. To put it otherwise: recognition is just the *way* we (actively) remember an exemplar group when we perceive a new object which resembles that group as a whole; a way or mode of remembering which is quite different from the recalling of individual past objects, and quite irreducible to it. But of course there are not *two* processes, perceiving the new object *and* remembering the exemplar group. We remember the exemplar group *in* perceiving the new object. To use a familiar metaphor (not such a bad one) we perceive it 'in the light of them'. And we could equally well say that we remember them 'in the light of' *it*. Similarly in the parallel cases discussed above, we have a totalistic memory of the lengths of many foot-rules, and the heights of many men; and we estimate the height of this man here, or the length of that piece of metal there, 'in the light of' this totalistic memory which gives us our standard of reference. Recollection of individual past objects—individual men or foot-rules—is quite unnecessary.

This, or something like this, is the way primary recognition has to be analysed in the Philosophy of Resemblances. It may be complained that the analysis does not take us very far. Surely the analysis we began with (and rejected) in which we were supposed to recall

individual objects severally, compare them with each other, and
then compare the new objects with them, was much more detailed
and therefore more satisfying—if only it had fitted the experience
which had to be analysed! True enough, but it is not to be complained of. For our new analysis, jejune as it may seem, has brought
something to light which ought to have been obvious, but is in
fact frequently overlooked. It shows us that recognition is one of
the primary and irreducible functions of memory; it delivers us
from the epistemological superstition that the recalling of individual
past objects is all that memory 'really' is, or ought to be. And it
makes us see how very close the connection is between memory
and intelligence. Indeed, the connection turns out to be even closer
than I have said. For in the totalistic memory of a set of exemplar-
objects as a whole, we have the first faint beginnings of an abstract
idea. Only its beginnings, of course; because so far this memory-
disposition manifests itself only in the presence of some perceived
object which arouses it. At this primitive stage, it does not yet manifest itself *also* in the absence of such a reminding object, as it will
when the capacity of conceiving *in abstracto* is fully developed. But
even at this stage, when we are capable of recognizing-in-presence,
but not yet capable of conceiving-in-absence, we can see that there
is something *abstractive* about memory itself. It is not only that
intelligence depends upon memory, and would remain wholly
latent—an unactualized capacity—unless past experiences were somehow retained. It is that memory itself is a form of intelligence, or at
least has something intellectual about it. If this seems paradoxical,
it is partly because of our inveterate tendency to suppose that the
recalling of individual past experiences is the only function of
memory; and partly it is because we are misled by the language of
faculties—'this is an operation of intelligence on the one hand, and
that is an operation of memory on the other'. The language of
faculties is not to be rejected altogether. It is right and proper to
use it as a rough and ready 'first aid' in a preliminary classification
of mental processes. But if it is a useful servant, it is also a bad master,
and we must not allow it to tyrannize over us.

Before leaving this difficult part of our subject, I will add one
further remark. Whichever of the two philosophies we accept, either
the Philosophy of Universals or the Philosophy of Resemblances,
we shall have to admit that the experience of recognition may have

different degrees of *vagueness* or *clearness*, and is not the all-or-nothing occurrence we at first took it to be. We shall even have to admit, I think, that the mere awareness of some resemblance or other between the present object and some past object or other is *already* an experience of recognition in its vaguest and most primitive form. In the Philosophy of Universals it would perhaps be described as the undifferentiated awareness of several universals 'in' a single instance. At any rate, any creature which can be aware of a present-to-past resemblance at all has taken the first step towards conceptual cognition also, though it has still a very long way to go and may never be able to complete the journey.

CHAPTER III

ERRORS OF RECOGNITION

CAN recognition be erroneous, and if so, in what ways? I have throughout been using the word 'recognition' in such a way that the question makes sense. (If the reader dislikes this usage, he may put the question thus: can one seem to recognize when one does not really recognize, and if so, how?) It is clear at once that *secondary* recognition is often mistaken. It is recognition by means of signs; and few signs, if any, are 100 per cent reliable. We have already given examples. What I recognize as a raven may in fact be a carrion crow. The dull grey object which I recognize as a piece of lead may turn out to be only a bit of painted wood. Again, recognition of *individuals* is frequently mistaken. The *déjà vu* illusion is a notorious example; and everyone has had the painful experience of misrecognizing individual persons, buildings and localities.

The mistakes which occur in these two sorts of recognition are best described as illusions. Nothing like an act of 'judgement' need occur. It is not quite clear what philosophers have intended to refer to when they have used the word 'judgement'. But it seems to be a mental act or occurrence which involves the use of symbols, whether words or others, and it seems to involve the use of concepts *in abstracto*. Now secondary recognition, whether mistaken or correct, may be pre-abstractive and pre-verbal. To all appearance, it occurs in young children and in animals; as we might expect when we consider its enormous biological utility. Or if it be said that abstraction is a matter of degree, and that the first faint beginnings of it are already present as soon as anything has begun to feel familiar to us, at any rate secondary recognition can occur long before the process of abstraction has been completed. But if we are to 'judge'—rightly or not—that this object has the character ϕ, it would seem that so far as ϕ is concerned the process of abstraction must already be complete. Much the same argument applies to recognition of individuals, whether correct or incorrect. This too may be pre-abstractive and pre-verbal.

Of course, secondary recognition may occur after abstraction, as well as before. The skilled ornithologist, who recognizes the black object in the sky as a raven, is perfectly capable of conceiving the complex concept of Raven *in abstracto*. But in the act of secondary recognition he is not so conceiving it. What is occurring is more like what psychologists call 'complication', as when ice looks cold or water wet. The black flappy object in the sky *looks* raven-ish to him. And if it is only a carrion crow after all, his mistake is rather an illusion than an erroneous judgement. Likewise, if you and I hear a pitter-patter 'rainy sounding' noise on the roof, which is in fact caused by a shower of little pebbles thrown by a mischievous small boy, our mistake is rather an illusion than an erroneous judgement. The character of rainishness was blended with the auditory sensation; the mistake was a perceptual one, not a mistaken opinion. And the *déjà vu* experience, again, is rightly called an illusion. The room or the village green *looks* familiar, as the faces of my friends do when I meet them. I do not just judge or opine that I have been there before; or if I do, the look of familiarity comes first, and is the evidence on which my erroneous judgement is based. That is why mistakes of recognition are so peculiarly disconcerting. We feel as if the world itself—not our own minds or intellectual processes—had somehow let us down. Something has actually *presented* itself as being what in fact it is not.

Are there illusions of primary recognition too? Many philosophers suppose that there are. It is true that they have discussed the question in a rather limited context. They have asked whether certain sorts of empirical *statements* are ever incorrigible, and have concluded that they are not. The statements in question are those called basic statements or protocol statements, e.g. 'this is scarlet', 'that is a loud noise', 'here and now a headachy feeling is occurring'. In the terminology I am using, these would be primary-recognition statements. But this way of putting the problem is too narrow. As I have argued earlier, primary recognition may be pre-verbal or non-verbal (indeed secondary recognition may be pre-verbal too). It occurs before we have learned to use words. It occurs in animals, who never learn to use them. Even when we have learned to use words, we may still have no word for just that characteristic which we are at the moment recognizing; and even if we have, we need not use it, not even privately and sub-vocally. At any given time we recognize far more characteristics than we name; and if we always have to be talking, privately or publicly, so long as we are conscious (as some philosophers suppose) we may be talking about something quite different, not present to sense at all. Finally, words themselves have to be recognized if they are to be understood, and they are recognized 'straight off', without using other words to recognize them with.

Thus if we only ask whether primary recognition statements are incorrigible, we shall narrow the question too much, by ignoring pre-verbal or non-verbal recognition. Moreover, in another way we shall complicate it irrelevantly. It might be that primary recognition *statements* were always corrigible, though primary recognition itself was not. Mistakes in formulation are always possible. I may use the wrong word, though there was no mistake in the recognition itself. 'I said "left", but of course, I meant "right".' I may do this through sheer inadvertence or fatigue, or from some more disreputable reason—some piece of 'active forgetting'—such as Freud has indicated in his discussion of slips of the tongue.[1] Again, my usage of words may differ from other people's. I may use the word 'round' to cover egg-shapes and not too eccentric ellipses, as well as circles; whereas you restrict it to shapes which are circular or very nearly so. In that case, my recognition-statement 'this is round' may be perfectly correct according to my own usage of the adjective; and yet it may cause you to make a mistake, either about the shape I am seeing or about the one you will see if you move into my present point of view. But these misformulations and failures of communication, vexatious as they may be, are irrelevant to the question which concerns us. The question, at least for an epistemologist, is whether primary recognition itself can be mistaken, whether formulated in words or not; though a logician, no doubt, will only be interested in recognition statements.

It must be remembered also that primary recognition may be pre-abstractive. When I cannot yet think of a certain shape *in abstracto*, I may still be able to recognize instances of it. (Cf. the example of the 'look' of a blackberry bush, above, pp. 53-4.) Indeed, with basic concepts at any rate, the pre-abstractive recognition of instances is a necessary condition of abstraction itself. Of

[1] Cf. S. Freud, *The Psychopathology of Everyday Life*, ch. 5.

course, primary recognition occurs after abstraction as well as before; and I shall suggest later that a concept or abstract idea is fundamentally a recognitional capacity. But it is important to mention pre-abstractive recognition at this point, because it is so obviously pre-verbal, whereas post-abstractive recognition is frequently (though not invariably) expressed in words; and if we confined our discussion to the corrigibility or incorrigibility of recognition-*statements*, we should be ignoring pre-abstractive recognition altogether.

But even though we set aside all questions about verbal formulation or misformulation, it may still appear that primary recognition can be erroneous. We analysed primary recognition into two component factors: a memory-component, and another which we called 'noticing'. According to the Philosophy of Universals, primary recognition is an experience of 'the same again', an awareness of recurrence. According to the Philosophy of Resemblances, I am aware of a resemblance between something now present and a set of mutually resemblant entities experienced before, though I do not and perhaps cannot recall them individually. But on either view, primary recognition is a compound of two factors, the noticing of what is present and the memory of what is past.

Let us first consider the memory-component. Surely this can be a source of error or illusion? Is it not generally agreed that all the operations of memory are fallible? But there are some difficulties in this contention, and we must pause to consider them.

For we have to admit, I believe, that no one memory can be validated or invalidated without relying on other memories. This awkward fact is sometimes overlooked. It is often supposed that we can validate or invalidate a memory-judgement by means of a present perception, for example by consulting documents or records. Again, it is supposed that we can do it by appealing to the established laws of nature: your memory of being in London at 11 a.m. last Tuesday cannot be right, because you were seen in Oxford at 11.3 that morning, and no human being can travel from the one place to the other in three minutes. But in both cases we are using memory over again, because we are relying on inductive generalizations. It is not a self-evident truth that ink-marks retain a constant shape over long periods of time. For all we can tell *a priori* they might change their shape every other minute, writhing and twisting like worms in a flower-bed. Our grounds for believing that they do not are purely inductive. Our grounds for believing that a human being cannot travel fifty-four miles in three minutes are likewise inductive. And however great the probability of an inductive generalization may be, its probability is derived from *past* observations. We have only memory to assure us that those past observations existed, or what sort of observations they were. In the second example, moreover, it is only memory which assures us that you *were* seen in Oxford at 11.3 a.m. last Tuesday. And finally, once a memory judgement has been made it itself is something past. In order to question it or doubt it, we must *remember* that it occurred.

But though we can only cast doubt on one memory by relying on others, it will not follow from this that any act of memory is infallible. Our principle rather is to treat each memory as having a finite degree of 'weight' or a finite claim to acceptance, and this claim is never absolute, though for some memories, e.g. memories of the very recent past, it is greater than for others. We then try to form a system in which as many of these claims as possible are accepted, having due regard to those which are greater. As Plato said in another connection, our aim is 'to save the appearances'.[1]

It will be objected, perhaps, that it is self-contradictory to speak of erroneous memories. If we hold a false belief about the past we cannot be remembering; we only seem to remember. This 'short way with fallibility' does not take us very far. How am I to tell whether this mental event which now occurs in me is a case of really remembering, or only of seeming to remember? Presumably I shall have to check it by reference to the objective facts about the past. But how am I to do this except by another mental act of the same sort—what ordinary people would call another act of remembering? And then the same question arises again about this second act, which purports to tell me what the objective facts about the past were. Is it a case of really remembering, or only of seeming to remember? Thus by this rigid way of defining memory, which makes it infallible by definition, fallibility is not got rid of. It is merely transferred to another place. What is now fallible is the decision that this or that mental event is a case of 'really' remembering as opposed to seeming to remember. No doubt ordinary lan-

[1] Plato said this with regard to the apparent movements of the heavenly bodies.

guage gives some countenance to this narrow definition of memory, which makes incorrect memory logically impossible. But it also gives countenance to the wider one which allows memory to be fallible ('Jones has a very unreliable memory', 'I cannot trust my memory for a thing like that'). In this matter, as in others, ordinary language is confused and inconsistent; and even if it were not, we should be entitled to depart from it, so long as we say clearly what we are doing. At any rate, I propose to use the word 'memory' and its derivatives in such a way that it makes sense to say there are mistaken memories. The facts which make it convenient to speak so are not seriously disputed. If anyone chooses to refer to them otherwise, for example by substituting 'ostensible memory' whenever I say 'memory', of course he may.

Let it be agreed, then, that no operation of memory is infallible. What are the consequences? It would seem that primary recognition might easily be illusory. Conceivably, this feature which I now discern in the present particular has *not* been observed by me before. And then, to use the terminology of the Philosophy of Universals, my consciousness of recurrence—of 'the same again'—will be mistaken. Likewise, to speak with the Philosophy of Resemblances, it will *not* be true that I have in the past observed a set of mutually resembling particulars which this present particular resembles; or if I have, I may be mistaken about the degree of resemblance they had to each other, or the degree of resemblance this present particular has to them.

We have all heard of the *déjà vu* illusion, and most of us have experienced it at some time or other. In its commonest form it is the illusory recognition of an individual object, such as a room or a landscape. I enter a house or see a village green from a bus, and for a second or two I have an overpowering feeling of having been there before. Yet on further consideration, I find the strongest reasons for believing that I never was there before in my life.

Perhaps this form of the *déjà vu* illusion is irrelevant to our present discussion. As we have seen, recognition of individuals is a complex process. There is first the recognition of a characteristic, a complex visual pattern-quality in this case; I recognize it as having characterized some particular or other which I have experienced in the past, without recalling the precise occasion on which I did so. Then, in addition, there is the belief or taking for granted that there has been a continuous series of particulars joining up that past particular to this present one, in such a way that the whole series constitutes the history of one persisting object. It would not be at all surprising if this second stage of the process, the postulation of intermediate particulars, were mistaken; nor would it be relevant to the present discussion. It is the first stage, the recognition of a characteristic, which concerns us at present. Now in this form of the *déjà vu* illusion, it would be very difficult to prove that there was anything illusory about the first stage. Two rooms often look very much alike; so do two village greens. And even if I have never seen a room or a village green which looked just like this one, it is perfectly possible that I may have dreamed of it. Perhaps I cannot recall such a dream. Nevertheless, it may perfectly well have occurred, and it may have left behind it a memory-trace which is quite sufficient to cause this present experience of recognition, though insufficient to cause an act of explicit recalling. If the likeness between a past dream-image and a present visible scene is so close and detailed that it cannot reasonably be attributed to chance, we say that the dream was a precognitive one; and such dreams do occasionally occur. There is no reason at all why precognitive dreams, like others, should not be forgotten in the sense of being unrecallable, and yet unforgotten in the sense of being able to affect subsequent experiences. (They might, of course, become recallable if the subject were hypnotized or if psycho-analytical methods were applied to him.)

There is, however, another form of the *déjà vu* illusion which concerns not a persistent object, such as a room or a village green or a landscape, but an event. Listening to a conversation or seeing a street accident, one may have the feeling 'all this has happened before'. It is as if one had seen or heard it all already. Now, of course, numerically the same event cannot happen twice, nor does one feel as if it had. The sameness referred to in 'all this has happened before' is sameness of quality, not numerical sameness. What one feels is that one has experienced an event exactly like this before; and yet on reflection one is convinced that one cannot have done so.

It is to be noticed that the event may be quite complex. The man with red hair leans down and lifts up a half-empty tea-cup from the hearthrug, disturbing a large black and white cat as he does so. Straightening himself and ruffling his hair with his other

F

hand, he says in an ironical tone of voice, 'Of course, you expect me to believe that'. The whole of this complex event seems somehow familiar as a whole, including the order in which its episodes occur. It is not just that it is a combination of simpler events each of which is familiar separately; if that were all, there would be no problem. As each of the successive episodes occurs, the spectator has the feeling 'of course that *had* to happen next', as if somehow he could have predicted it beforehand. The illusory feeling of recurrence, the feeling 'all this has happened before' attaches to the complex event as a whole. It is as if one had previously experienced an event having just this pattern-quality.

Does not this example make it clear that there can be illusory recognition of characteristics, as well as of individuals? Not quite clear, I think. For here again we cannot quite exclude the possibility of an unrecalled precognitive dream. I may have at some time experienced a sequence of dream-images, visual and auditory, which really did possess as a whole the same complex characteristic which this present series of perceived events has. In the language of the Resemblance Philosophy, I may have experienced a sequence of dream-images which exactly resembled these present perceived events. In that case, I shall only be in error if I claim to have had a previous *perceptual* experience exactly like this present one. And no such claim seems to be contained in the *déjà vu* experience itself. We may observe also that at least one of the current physiological explanations of the *déjà vu* illusion amounts in effect to abolishing its illusory character. It is suggested that the two hemispheres of the brain are as it were out of step in time; one is affected by the sensory stimuli a little earlier than the other. Thus there are two successive perceptions of the same event; the earlier one is subconscious, but causes the later, and conscious, one to be invested with a feel of familiarity. In that case, however, it is true, and not false, that 'I have heard (or seen) all this before', though only a very short time ago. (I leave it to more subtle-minded persons to decide whether, if this physiological explanation were right, we should perceive numerically the same event twice, or two exactly similar ones, or two numerically different appearances of the same one.)

Still, even though it is difficult to establish that illusions of primary recognition occur, surely it must be possible in principle that they should? How can we deny this if we admit that no operation of memory is infallible? I shall now try to show, however, that if or so far as primary recognition is illusory, its illusoriness is irrelevant to our present discussion, which is concerned with conceptual cognition.

Recognition of every sort, whether primary or secondary, recognition of individuals or of characteristics, pre-abstractive or post-abstractive, can be considered from two quite different points of view. First, we may consider it as a source of information about the past, like other operations of memory. But secondly, we may consider it as an experience which is intimately connected with conceptual cognition; in that pre-abstractive recognition is a necessary stage in the process by which basic concepts are acquired, while post-abstractive recognition is one of the most important ways in which our possession of a concept manifests itself, once we have acquired it. Now it is this second aspect of recognition which concerns us at present, recognition as an intellectual function, whether pre-abstractive or post-abstractive. And it might be that so far as it is an intellectual function, primary recognition, at any rate, is incapable of being erroneous, though it may easily be a source of erroneous information about the past.

Lord Russell somewhere invites us to entertain the hypothesis that we came into existence only a second ago, with all the memories we have now. Suppose that this were true (though doubtless we have the best of reasons for thinking it *causally* impossible). Then any experience of primary recognition I now have will be erroneous, so far as its reference to the past is concerned; unless by any chance I happen to have observed an earlier instance of the now-recognized characteristic within the last second. And this time my *déjà vu* experience will certainly be an illusion. It will not be true that I have met with this characteristic before, not even in an unrecallable dream; for *ex hypothesi* I have had no dreams at all. And if it be said that one second is long enough for the out-of-step operation of the two hemispheres of the brain, we can easily imagine that the time-interval which has elapsed since I came into existence is shorter still, or even infinitesimal.

Thus if this extravagant hypothesis were true, primary recognition would be wholly delusive in so far as it is a source of information about one's past. But in so far as it is an intellectual function, it would not be impaired at all. What matters then is not what my past actually was, or even whether I had one; it is only the *memories* I have now which matter, be they false or true. I recognize something here and now as being red. In actual fact, we are supposing I have never seen anything red before. But what of it? I still have all my memories, erroneous as they are. Among them are memories of many red things, and that is enough to enable me to recognize this one.

The point may be brought out in another way by making a supposition which is much less extravagant than Lord Russell's. Suppose I *did* long ago experience a number of instances of a characteristic C, but have wholly forgotten them. Not only am I unable to recall them, even when hypnotized or psycho-analysed; the memory-disposition which resulted from these experiences has altogether ceased to exist.[1] I now observe a new instance of C, and notice it too. Shall I recognize this characteristic? Clearly I shall not, however true it is that I have in the past experienced other instances. The mere *de facto* existence of past experiences, without any memory of them, is not a sufficient condition for recognizing what I experience and notice now; the memory of them *is* a sufficient condition for it, without their *de facto* existence.

Finally, let us try to reformulate this contention in the terminology of Resemblances. I see a red apple and recognize its colour. According to the Philosophy of Resemblances, we have said, I am being aware that this object sufficiently resembles a set of mutually resembling objects (the Red Exemplars) perceived by me in the past. We can now see that this analysis will have to be modified a little. What makes a set of past particulars A, B, C into exemplars, usable thereafter for the recognizing of later ones, is not just the fact that I did actually perceive A, B and C and did actually notice their mutual resemblance. It is the fact that I still retain a memory of them, though very likely I cannot recall them individually. It is not past objects as such, not even perceived past objects, which are exemplars, but *remembered* objects. And it makes no difference if

[1]According to some authorities, this supposition too is causally impossible. They hold that no experience one ever has is totally forgotten. It is true that some, which *seemed* to have been totally forgotten, turn out to be recoverable later by means of hypnosis or psychoanalytical methods. But at any rate some come so near to being totally forgotten, at least for the time being, that we are quite unable to recognize new instances when perceived.

the memory of them is inaccurate. I said earlier that for a set of objects to function as exemplars they must have 'resemblance in the midst of differences' (see p. 71, above). Now in my memory of them either the resemblances, or the differences, or both, may be exaggerated. It is even abstractly conceivable that I never experienced such a set of mutually resemblant objects at all, though we have very good reasons for thinking this causally impossible. But however inaccurate my memory is, even if it is totally delusive, it will not matter. Provided I do have a memory of them, and a memory of them as mutually resemblant in the midst of differences, they will serve as perfectly good exemplars for later recognitions. And whatever resemblances or differences there actually were between them, they will *not* serve as exemplars unless I do have a memory of them.

So much for the memory-factor in primary recognition. However fallible memory may be, it will not follow that primary recognition itself is fallible in so far as it is an *intellectual* function, a manifestation of, or a stage in the growth of, conceptual cognition. It is only fallible *per accidens*, in so far as it is source of information about the past.

What of the other component factor in primary recognition, the one I called 'noticing'? Noticing is a cognitive function which is too elementary to be erroneous. The only possibility is that it may fail to occur when its occurrence might have been expected. A man with good eyesight, in a good light, may fail to notice what is under his nose; or even what is on it, his spectacles for instance. But this is absence of noticing, not erroneous noticing. Again, there may be a partial absence of noticing even when it is not totally absent. One may notice the determinable character of something and fail to notice its determinate character. I notice the reddish colour and the roundish shape, but not what shade of reddish colour it is, nor whether the shape is circular or ovoid or elliptical. And another sort of partial non-noticing is possible, indeed very frequent. If something complex is presented to me, I may notice some elements in the complex and fail to notice the rest. I notice the colour of the flower, but not the shape of the petals or the leaves or the hairs on the stem.

Absence of noticing, total or partial, may easily give rise to erroneous *statements* which have the verbal form of primary recognition-statements. But it does not follow that there is anything erroneous in primary recognition itself. It merely fails to occur, totally or partially, owing to the total or partial non-occurrence of the requisite noticing. Ignorance, total or partial, may always lead to false statements, especially if it occurs in circumstances where the speaker would not normally be expected to be ignorant. But ignorance is not error for all that. It is merely absence of cognition.

I conclude that so far as the noticing factor in it is concerned, primary recognition cannot be erroneous; while so far as the memory factor in it is concerned, it can only be erroneous *per accidens* in respect of the information it gives about the past experience of the recognizer.

Shall we say then that primary recognition is infallible, or as near to infallibility as we can get? This might be misleading, because it might suggest that mistaken primary recognitions are theoretically possible, though by a fortunate dispensation of Providence they never in fact occur. It will be better, perhaps, to say that primary recognition is *non*-fallible, because the notion of fallibility does not apply to it.[1]

This is not a very surprising conclusion. Anyone who denied it would in effect be denying the possibility of empirical verification and falsification. Incidentally, he would also be precluded from indulging in the favourite occupation of doubting other people's protocol statements, or his own. For what ground does one have for thinking that these statements occurred at all? What makes you so sure that I *did* say 'this is scarlet' (when I ought to have said 'brick-red') or that these words are to be found in my protocol-book? If the statement was not uttered, or if the words are not there on the page, *cadit quaestio*; there is nothing for you to doubt of, and what is all the fuss about? But if you are sure that the statement was actually made, how are you sure of it? Because you *noticed* certain sounds or black marks, and in noticing you *recognized* them, by primary recognition, to be a token of a certain type-sentence.

But if primary recognition is incapable of being erroneous, this is only because it is a mental occurrence so primitive and elementary that the antithesis of correct and incorrect does not apply to it. There is nothing particularly grand about such inerrancy, and there

[1] I owe this point to my colleague Mr. W. F. R. Hardie, the President of Corpus Christi College, Oxford.

is no occasion for taking off one's hat to it. On the contrary: it is the fallible forms of recognition, secondary recognition and recognition of individuals, on which we should congratulate ourselves (and the lower animals too) if we are in the mood for congratulations. Let us rather take off our hats to any creature which is clever enough to be caught in a trap. It is the capacity of making mistakes, not the incapacity of it, which is the mark of the higher stages of intelligence. The whole importance of primary recognition, both biologically and epistemologically, consists in this, that it is the indispensable basis for the higher, and fallible, levels of intellection.

CHAPTER IV

SIGNIFICATION

IN this chapter we shall discuss Sign-Cognition: the type of cognition in which something not immediately experienced is brought before the mind by means of a sign. (What 'before the mind' means in this context is one of the questions we shall have to consider.) In the previous chapters we have already examined an elementary form of signification, namely Secondary Recognition, as when one recognizes an object 'straight off' as a raven or a piece of lead. But secondary recognition is not the only form of signification. In secondary recognition the sign and the significate are tied together in a peculiarly close union. In traditional terminology, they are characteristics of the same substance. In the example of recognizing the piece of lead, the softness, ductility and heaviness which are signified are taken to be *coinherent* with the grey colour which is the sign. Again, the complex of characteristics which constitute 'being a raven' are attributed to that very same flappy object which I now see moving across the sky. But there may be signification without coinherence. When I hear the bell ring, it is a sign that there is some human being standing outside the front door. But I do not take the sound itself to be a rational animal, nor to be standing outside the door. The signified characteristics and the signifying one are attributed to different entities. If I see a halo round the moon, it is a sign of rain to come. But I do not anticipate that the characteristics of being wet and descending from the sky will characterize the moon itself.

It comes to this: sign-cognition, as we have seen already, is an inductive mode of thinking. It is made possible by observation of constant or more-or-less constant conjunctions. The typical form of an inductive generalization is 'when there is an instance of characteristic C_1 there is also an instance of characteristic C_2'. In some inductions C_1 and C_2 are characteristics of the same thing. In others they are not. In some there is a time-interval between the *conjuncta*, in others there is not. In secondary recognition the *conjuncta* are characteristics of the same object, and they all characterize it at the same time.

It might be thought that if we substituted a terminology of Particulars for the terminology of Substances, the difference to which I am drawing attention, between secondary recognition and other forms of sign-cognition, would disappear. When I take this object to be a raven, am I not after all taking for granted the existence of *other* particulars in addition to the one I now experience? (The raven, or any other material object, is a complex of many numerically different particulars, according to this way of thinking.) And when I take the watery moon to be a sign of rain, am I not likewise taking for granted the existence of *other* particulars, future ones in this case? This does bring out an important point, which the terminology of Substances and Coinherence may conceal: namely that in all sign-cognition we are believing, or taking for granted, an existential proposition. What is signified is not just a characteristic, as we have too loosely said hitherto, but the proposition that this characteristic has an instance, the proposition that *there is*—or was or will be—something characterized by it. Nevertheless, the distinction I have been trying to draw still remains, though in this terminology of Particulars it is less clear cut and shades off into a distinction of degree. Suppose we do say that a single thing or object is a system of very many numerically diverse particulars. Still, the various particulars into which the piece of lead is to be analysed are much more closely related to each other than (say) a particular which is a constituent of the moon and another particular which is a constituent of a rain storm. The complex of particulars which is a piece of lead is bound together by relations of spatio-temporal continuity within a common boundary, and by laws or regularities of the immanent-causal type. The relationship between a lunar particular and a pluvial particular is much more remote than this, though both situations alike are covered by the formula 'When ϕx, then usually ψy'. When the sign-cognition is concerned with a *complex* substance, such as a machine or an organism, we have an intermediate case. The observed movement of the clock-hand is a sign that the pendulum is moving and the spring is in a state of tension. Here we can say that the signified state of affairs is 'in the same thing as' the signifying one, namely in the

clock; or we can say that it is 'in a different thing' on the ground
that the clock-hand is one object and the spring or the pendulum
is another.

Secondary recognition, then, is not the only sort of sign-cognition. And perhaps no one except a philosopher would even consider
the possibility that it might be. On the contrary, most people are
surprised to find that signification enters into recognition at all. In
our ordinary everyday consciousness, for very good biological
reasons, we easily overlook the difference between primary recognition, which does not depend on the interpretation of signs, and
secondary recognition which does. It is easily supposed that we
recognize a piece of lead or a bomb-explosion in the same direct
and 'knock down' manner in which we recognize the greyness of
this colour or the loudness of that noise. To put it otherwise, we
easily overlook the *inductive* element which there is in very many
of our everyday recognitions.

But though secondary recognition is not the only type of signification, there are advantages in beginning with it. For the paradoxical
character of sign-cognition appears here with special clearness. All
sign-cognition has two features which at first sight appear difficult
to reconcile. It is at once thought and perception. It is a form of
cognition in which ideas or concepts are somehow blended with
immediate experience.

It has other curious features too. It is a pre-verbal form of
cognition, though, of course, it is sometimes formulated in words
when once the use of words has been acquired. It is also independent
of the use of images. Sometimes the signified event may incidentally
be imaged. When I see the smoke, I may have a visual image of a
fire. But usually I take the smoke as a sign of fire without having
any images at all. Perhaps this is specially clear in what is called
'immediate expectation', where the sign refers to the very near
future, as when a vivid flash of lightning signifies an imminent clap
of thunder. The sign certainly operates upon me. Indeed, it operates
very effectively. I am put into a state of tense anticipation. But I
am very unlikely to have an auditory image of a thunderclap. Such
an image will only arise if the anticipated event fails to happen, or
is deferred. At first sight it may appear strange that one should
'have an idea' of a thunderclap not only without words, but even

without images. And yet one evidently does 'have an idea' of it, in some good sense of that puzzling phrase.

We notice too that signification is very closely connected with practical behaviour, so closely that it is almost as much a form of action as of cognition. Sign-cognition is the characteristic mode of mental operation at a level of mental development where cognition and action are not yet sharply differentiated. The sign *of* some future state of affairs (or present unobserved one) is also a sign *for* doing something about it—what students of Animal Psychology call 'a releaser'. To the cat, the loud sound of a bark is a sign of the presence of a dog. It is also a sign *for* running up a tree or taking other evasive action. When I am driving a motor-car, and a cyclist wobbles into the middle of the road ten yards ahead, this spectacle is a sign *of* an imminent collision with him, and equally a sign *for* pressing the brake-pedal—a 'releaser' for a piece of appropriate action. (Incidentally, it is quite clear in this example that the sign operates without words or images; there is no time to indulge in the luxury of verbalizing or mental picturing.) And even when the sign does not 'release' a full-scale or complete action, it may still be a sign for an incipient or a preparatory action. If the wobbling cyclist is twenty-five yards ahead instead of ten, I do not actually press the brake pedal. But I am in a state of readiness to press it, and this readiness manifests itself by an incipient tension in my left ankle.

Here we may notice another curious feature of signification. There is often a kind of conflict between its cognitive aspect and its practical aspect. When A is a sign *of* B, it is often a sign *for* an action which will prevent B from happening. The sign 'releases' an action which falsifies the signified proposition. Pressing the brake pedal falsifies the proposition 'I am about to run into the cyclist'. Still more often, the sign releases an action which prevents the signified proposition from being verified by the sign cognisant. This happens whenever the sign is a sign for a movement of escape or of concealment. A mewing sound signifies the presence of a cat. By running away into its hole or under the dresser, the mouse prevents itself from having experiences which would verify the signified proposition.

But, of course, this conflict between the two aspects of signification, the cognitive and the practical, does not always occur. If the thing signified is something I desire, I act in a way which is likely to make the signified proposition true, and likely also to give me experiences which will verify it. When I hear the sound 'Hullo!' behind me uttered in a familiar voice, this is both a sign *of* the presence of Jones and a sign *for* the action of turning round which enables me to verify the signified proposition. And when I see the sun setting, which is a sign of approaching darkness, nothing that I can do will prevent the signified proposition from being true.

Finally, A is not a sign of B *per se*, but only to someone—to some conscious being. 'Being a sign of' is a three-term relation. There is something paradoxical about this too, because our ordinary ways of speaking tend to conceal it. In a mindless world (or a mindless part of this world) there would be no signification, though there would still be constant conjunctions. Signification only occurs when someone notices, and retains, such conjunctions; or at least believes, on the evidence of testimony for instance, that they are there. In other words, the sign-relation only exists as a result of *learning*. Moreover, a given sort of sign-relation only exists for someone who has undergone the particular sort of learning which is needed. For a countrified person, a peculiar rank smell at the garden gate is a sign of the recent presence of a fox. For the townsman it is not a sign at all, but just a disagreeable smell. There is a certain sound which to the expert signifies the presence of a jet-propelled aircraft. To the layman it does not. It merely signifies the presence of some sort of aircraft or other.

In secondary recognition, these paradoxical features of sign-cognition are specially evident. It is so closely connected with perception that it is commonly taken to *be* perception. It is pre-verbal, and images play no part in it. It passes so easily into appropriate action that its cognitive character is hardly noticed. By secondary recognition, I recognize this gleaming something in the road as a puddle, but this recognizing is not easily distinguished from the action of stepping out of the way. It may appear that the conflict between the practical and the cognitive aspects of signification is absent; my action, it may be said, has no tendency to falsify the signified proposition as the motorist's action had when he put on the brake. No; but still, in recognizing the thing as a puddle, I was taking it to have certain disagreeable causal properties—a capacity for making my feet cold and wet, and my shoes dirty. And my evasive action does prevent these causal properties from being actualized, though it does not prevent them from existing. It also prevents me from having experiences which would verify their existence.

We may now consider these characteristics of sign-cognition in more detail. First, it is a combination of perception and thought, in which 'ideas' (whatever exactly they are) are somehow blended with immediate experience. As to its perceptual character, not much needs to be said. It is only necessary to mention a point of terminology. The phrase 'is a sign of' is most commonly used in a *dispositional*, not an occurrent sense. When we say that a high temperature is a sign of influenza, we do not usually mean that any patient's high temperature is actually being perceived at the moment either by himself or anyone else. For this reason, and for the further reason that the relation is commonly spoken of as it were a two-term one, the perceptual character of sign-cognition is liable to be overlooked. But when A is actually functioning as a sign of B for a person X, it is obvious that X must be perceiving A, or at any rate is in some way directly aware of it. As a matter of fact, the perceptual character of sign-cognition is referred to in dispositional sign-statements too, and only a little analysis is needed to reveal it. The dispositional statement contains a latent if-clause. 'Stratus cloud is a sign of rain' says that the speaker, or all persons of a certain class to which he belongs, *would* expect rain *if.* . . . If what? If stratus cloud were to cover the sky? Clearly this is not enough. They would have this expectation not just if the stratus cloud were there, but if they saw it. Indeed, the actual existence of the cloud is not even a necessary condition of this expectation. If they had a visual hallucination of stratus cloud, they would still expect rain. In short, a sign, when it is actually operating as a sign, has to be perceived, or at any rate experienced in some way, by the conscious being for whom it is a sign.

The complementary feature of sign-cognition, the fact that it involves thought as well as perception, is perhaps less obvious. Some people might hold that when someone takes A as a sign of B, he is not thinking at all. How can he be thinking, when there are neither words nor images in his mind? This is partly a matter of definition. One may decide that no process is to be called thinking

unless words or images enter into it. But there are two objections
to this decision. First, there is the danger that the mental processes
excluded by this definition may be overlooked altogether. Traditionally, the epistemologist is supposed to study perception, thought,
memory and self-consciousness. If sign-cognition is none of these,
as by this definition it will not be, it will just be ignored; as in fact
it has been, by almost all philosophers except Hume. The student
of perception will ignore it; for sign-cognition is obviously something more than mere perception, although there is a perceptual
factor in it. The student of thought will not study it either, on the
ground that it is pre-verbal and independent of images. Secondly,
and more important, even if we do define thinking in this narrow
way, we still cannot deny that there are very striking resemblances
between sign cognition and the word-using and image-using processes which are admittedly processes of thinking. Indeed, sign-
cognition has so much in common with what is universally admitted
to be thinking that the presence or non-presence of words or
images seems trivial in comparison. It is, therefore, expedient to
accept a more liberal definition of the term 'thought' and to allow
that sign-cognition *is* a form of thinking, or rather a blend of
thought and perception, as was suggested before. We may still
admit, of course, that there are different grades or levels of thinking,
and that the thinking which occurs in sign-cognition is of a relatively
primitive and low-grade sort; though, even so, the subtlety and
delicacy of which it is capable must not be underrated, as we shall
see.

The reasons for saying that sign-cognition is a form of thinking
are these. First, it is capable of being *erroneous*. It makes no sense to
say that immediate experience can be erroneous. If we have such
and such an experience, then we do have it, and there is no more
to be said. In the traditional phrase, immediate experience is below
the level of truth and falsity. The same can be said of primary recognition. But with secondary recognition, recognition by means of
signs, the possibility of error begins. What I take to be a raven may
be a carrion crow. What I 'see as' a sheep on the distant hillside
may turn out to be a bit of grey rock. What I 'hear as' rain falling
pitter-patter on the roof may be only a shower of dried peas or
pebbles thrown by some naughty little boy. With the possibility
of error and deception, an enormous step forward has been taken

in our mental development. We have crossed the boundary-line between immediate experience and intelligence. 'Transcendence of the given' has begun. We have passed beyond mere sensation, and abstract ideas (or something approximating to them) have begun to operate.

All sign-cognition is tied to perception. But often the tie with perception is a good deal less close than it is in secondary recognition. And when this is so, it is obvious without argument that error is always possible. When I see a cumulo-nimbus cloud, it is a sign of a thunderstorm, and if I have no mackintosh or umbrella it will be prudent to go home. But the thunderstorm may not occur after all. Signification is an inductive process, and shares in the fallibility of induction. Few signs, if any, are 100 per cent reliable. And even if there are some which are, if the conjunction of B with A is absolutely invariable (not just more or less constant) it still makes sense to say that this B might not have been conjoined with this A. In principle, any sign-relation is capable of being deceptive, even if in fact there are some which may be wholly relied on. I would emphasize again that this is not a defect of sign-cognition, but a virtue. The fallibility of sign-cognition shows that it is a form of thought or intelligence, though perhaps a humble one. A purely sensitive being cannot err. Only *thinkers* are capable of so distinguished an achievement as making a mistake.

Secondly, sign-cognition is cognition of the absent, and this is another feature which it has in common with thinking. To make the point clear, let us use the terminology of Universals to begin with. In thinking, it may be said, we are aware of a universal by experiencing a particular which is *not* an instance of it. The word 'red', for example, is not an instance of redness, and a cat-like visual image is not itself a mouse-eating animal. In this sense, thinking may be described as cognition of the absent. That is what distinguishes thinking from primary recognition. In primary recognition we are aware of a universal by experiencing a particular which *is* an instance of it; and this, unlike thinking, is cognition in presence, not in absence. Now by this criterion, sign-cognition must clearly be counted as a form of thinking. The cumulo-nimbus cloud is not itself an instance of the universal 'Thunderstorm'. True, we might sometimes call it 'thundery' or 'thundery-looking'; and this is a way of emphasizing the tied-to-perception character which sign-cognition has. But the tie, however close and important, is not that of instance to universal. The cloud *is* not a thunderstorm.

The terminology of Universals may, of course, be objected to. And even if we consent to use it, we may still think it inadvisable to say that in thinking one is *aware of* a universal by experiencing a particular which is not an instance of it. For this suggests that thinking is a kind of inspection.[1] It would be safer, perhaps, to say that in thinking we 'refer to' universals by experiencing particulars which are not instances of them; or that our (dispositional) knowledge of universals is actualized or made operative by the experiencing of such non-instantiative particulars.

In any case, the point I am making still holds good if we prefer not to use the terminology of Universals at all. Let us use the terminology of Resemblances instead. Then thinking, as opposed to primary recognition, is cognition of a class of objects by means of a particular which is *not* a member of the class; that is, by means of a particular which does not resemble the class-exemplars as closely as they resemble one another. Indeed, it need not resemble them at all. The word 'red', for example, does not resemble the Red exemplars at all. And a visual image of a cat, though it does resemble the Cat exemplars in some degree, certainly does not resemble them as closely as they resemble one another. It is certainly not itself a member of the class of cats, which is thought of by means of it. By this criterion, again, sign-cognition has to be counted as a form of thinking. The cumulo-nimbus cloud is not a member of the class of thunderstorms. A knock at the front door is not a member of the class of postmen, and has not even the most distant resemblance to the entities which are.

But will this apply to secondary recognition? Surely the grey thing I see (the signifying particular) *is* an instance of lead, the characteristic signified? Or, if we prefer the language of Resemblances, surely the particular which I see *is* itself a member of the class of leaden objects, and does sufficiently resemble the Lead exemplars? It would follow that secondary recognition, by this criterion at least, would not after all be thinking; it would not be cognition in absence, even though other forms of signification are.

This objection would only hold good, at the most, for *correct*

[1] This 'inspective' conception of thinking will be examined in ch. xi, below.

or veridical secondary recognition. When the thing which I 'see as' a bit of lead is not lead at all, but only a piece of painted wood, the signifying particular is certainly not an instance of the characteristic signified. It does resemble the Lead exemplars in some degree, but certainly not in a sufficient degree. Erroneous cognition must always be 'in absence' just because it is erroneous. Indeed, that is what makes error the exciting and important thing that it is, the most obvious of all the manifestations of intelligence.

Even in correct secondary recognition, however, there is still cognition in absence. It will be remembered that in secondary recognition the sign and the significate both belong to the same Thing or Substance. (That is how we distinguish secondary recognition from other forms of signification.) Now traditionally a Thing or Substance is assumed to be a *single* particular. The objection we are discussing depends on that assumption. But as we have seen, one may reject the traditional doctrine and maintain instead that a Thing or Substance is a very complicated system of many numerically diverse particulars, bound together by spatio-temporal continuity and immanent causal laws.[1] It then becomes clear that the signifying particular is not itself an instance of the characteristics signified. The grey particular which I sense is not itself an instance of ductility, or heaviness, or low melting-point. What is characterized by these characteristics (which, be it noted, are not qualities but causal properties) is the whole complex system of particulars of which the immediately experienced one is taken to be a member; and the other members of the system are not at the moment experienced at all.

Even if one is unwilling to be as Russellian and untraditional as this, one must still admit that a Thing or Substance is at any rate a highly complex particular, however much its singleness is insisted on. The grey something which is immediately experienced and functions as a sign is still only one element or factor in the complex entity which is, as a whole, an instance of Lead. And so far as all the *other* factors in its being are concerned, this complex entity is still being cognized in absence, however much you insist that it is unitary as well as complex.

We may conclude, then, that if cognition in absence is one of the distinguishing features of thinking, signification does have that

[1] Cf. pp. 89-90, above.

G

feature; and this is true of secondary recognition as well as other forms of signification.

So far we have found that sign-cognition has two of the distinctive features of thinking: it is liable to error, and it is cognition in absence. We have now to notice another and very important characteristic of sign-cognition. There is a certain abstractness or generality about it. If we think of sign-cognition in a rather old-fashioned way as a blend or union of immediate experience and 'ideas', then we have to say that those ideas are *abstract* ideas. From one point of view this is not surprising, since the 'ideas' here are obviously not images; sign-cognition can occur, and usually does, without any images at all. But from another point of view my contention may well appear surprising, because we are so accustomed to suppose that abstraction is impossible without words; and sign-cognition is pre-verbal as well as pre-imaginal. One may admit perhaps that there are degrees of abstractness, and that verbalized thinking is more abstract, or more explicitly abstract, than sign-cognition is. But we must still insist that some degree of abstraction, and even a very considerable degree of it, is present in sign-cognition, pre-verbal as it is.

If this is right, it follows that Locke was wrong when he said that 'brutes abstract not'. For sign-cognition is the typical achievement of the animal mind, or of mind at the animal level. Cats are not mathematicians, and rats are not poets. But sign-cognition plays a very large part in their lives (indeed, even amoebas seem to be capable of it); and if it were not so, they might as well have no sense-organs at all. Of course, signification in them is very closely bound up with action, as it frequently is in us. Their intelligence is practical and not theoretical. But though it may sound odd to say so, intelligent behaviour has something abstract about it no less than intelligent cognition; and indeed at the animal level it is unrealistic to separate the two.

Let us first consider an example in which sign-cognition is tied very closely to sensation. To most of my readers, ice looks cold. Of course it would not look so to a tropical African who was seeing ice for the first time in his life. But to Northern Europeans and others who live in cold climates it does look cold. Similarly, water looks wet and walls look hard. I emphasize the word 'look'. It is not just that when I see the gleamy semi-transparent object I am reminded of coldness, by association. There is no transition of the mind from the gleaminess to the coldness. That might happen with a visitor from tropical Africa who had seen ice a few times before and handled it once or twice. But to us, who are familiar with northern winters, the ice actually *looks* cold. Some philosophers, it is true, have denied on *a priori* grounds that this can happen. An object, they say, can only look to have visible qualities, and coldness is not a visible quality. But phenomenological facts cannot be got rid of by *a priori* arguments. The sentence 'ice looks cold' is a very natural and perfectly intelligible way of describing something which really does happen. If we need a technical name for it, psychologists have suggested one. It has been called 'complication', to distinguish it from ordinary associative reminding. The idea of coldness, it is said, is 'complicated' (or 'blended') with the visual sensation, and does not just follow it or accompany it.[1] In the terminology I have been using, complication is a specially striking form of secondary recognition.

But though the idea is so closely tied to sensation, and even has a quasi-sensational vividness, there is still something abstract about it. This lump of ice looks cold. But *how* cold does it look? Very cold, perhaps, or rather cold. But usually there is not even this degree of determinateness about it. The object just looks cold; and if we are pressed to say how cold it looks, we cannot answer, because there *is* no answer. What is complicated or blended with the visual sensation is just the idea of cold in general. Similarly, the wall I see looks hard. It may perhaps look harder than a mattress, and less hard, possibly, than a diamond. But within these very wide limits it does not look to have one degree of hardness rather than another. And ordinarily it just looks hard *et voilà tout*. Of course if the percipient had been Demetrius Poliorcetes,[2] or some other general accustomed to storming walls, it might have looked to have a more determinate degree of hardness. It might have looked to him as hard as a wall feels when it will resist a catapult-missile, but less hard than it feels when it will resist a battering-ram. But even then,

---

[1]Most of the examples given by Berkeley in his *Theory of Vision* are instances of complication, rather than ordinary associative reminding. It is a pity that he did not make the distinction explicitly.

[2]Demetrius 'the Besieger', a Hellenistic king of the third century B.C.

the hardness which it looked to have would not be completely determinate. It would still have been a determinable (in the language of W. E. Johnson) even though nearer to complete determinateness than it is in my experience now.

It may be useful to give two other examples, non-visual ones this time. As I sit writing this in my rooms, I hear the familiar and distracting sound of the College choir doing its daily choir practice. The notes are 'heard as' a sound of many voices. They *sound* multi-vocal, as the wall *looks* hard. But how many voices? More than three, perhaps, and less than twenty. But beyond that point, the multi-vocal character cannot be further specified. Again, I hear a knock at the door. The knock *sounds* human and visitatorial. There is someone outside the door. But is he tall or short, fat or thin, old or young, pink-faced or grey-faced? The knock just sounds 'human' without providing any answer to these questions. If we must answer, we shall have to say that he is like Locke's triangle 'all and none of these at once'—just someone, just *a* man. The idea which is blended with the auditory sensation, so intimately blended that it has a quasi-sensational vividness, is nothing more nor less than the abstract idea of man-in-general.

If this is true of complication, where the *significatum* is so closely tied to sensation, it is still more obviously true of other forms of signification. As one drives along an unfamiliar road, the sight of a hill in front signifies *some* piece of country lying beyond it. But what sort of country? Arable, pasture, town, marsh? Often one has 'only the most general idea' of what sort of country it is. Again, the sky is covered with stratus cloud. It will rain soon. But how soon? Within the next three hours, perhaps. But in the sign-cognition itself the precise minute when the rain will fall is left unspecified. So is the degree of heaviness which it will have. If one were a very skilled professional meteorologist, the look of the sky might signify a rainstorm of medium heaviness. But even so, the degree of it would be far from determinate. And if one is just an ordinary empirical sky-watcher, what is signified is only rain in general.

If the significate has this determinable and not determinate character, it is obvious that what are traditionally called 'abstract ideas' must be at work in sign-cognition. Signification, in fact, is one manifestation of the presence of concepts, though if a given concept could *only* manifest itself in sign-cognition and primary recognition, we should probably say that it was not fully explicit. Again, we might say that what is called 'possessing a concept' is a matter of degree, and that it is not completely possessed unless it can be used in image thinking and verbal thinking, as well as in sign-cognition.

I have been emphasizing the determinable rather than determinate character of some *significata*, in order to show in what way sign-cognition is abstract. But important as this is, it must not be exaggerated. Otherwise we might underrate the subtlety and delicacy of which this pre-verbal form of cognition is capable. To a skilled ornithologist a little bit of broken egg shell is a sign of the recent presence of a quite determinate species of bird, e.g. a hedge sparrow, though to the layman it only signifies the recent presence of some bird or other, or some rather small bird or other.

Moreover, when sign-cognition manifests itself by practical behaviour, as it frequently does, the practical response may be most delicately adjusted. Consider a skilled marksman shooting at a snipe. In spite of, or even because of, the creature's zigzag flight, he can estimate very accurately where it will be a fraction of a second after he has pressed the trigger. This estimating is a form of sign-cognition. The visible course of the bird's flight during a certain half second is an inductive sign of what its course will be in the next half second. And the signified movement is highly specified as to direction and velocity. The marksman shows his excellent 'judgement', as we say, in directing his gun in just this direction and pressing the trigger at just this moment. But his good judgement does not manifest itself by what philosophers call an 'act of judging', that is by asserting a proposition in words, not even in private and imaged words. His 'act of judging', if we must call it by that name, is wholly pre-verbal. It is manifested to other people by what he does, and to himself by muscular sensations. If he stopped to put his 'judgement' into words, even sub-vocal words or verbal images, he would certainly miss his aim. He cannot afford the luxury of such a verbal exercise. Indeed, the chances are that he could not put his sign-cognitional estimate into words, even if he tried. He would have to use the technical mathematical vocabulary which is needed for accurate description of lines, angles, distances, and velocities; and he may be quite uneducated or even illiterate. Gamekeepers and poachers are not usually very expert in handling mathematical symbols, but they may be excellent marksmen for all that. Indeed, in some people at any rate, and perhaps in all, such pre-verbal estimation shows an accuracy and a delicacy, and a rapidity too, which are much greater than verbalized thinking can achieve. It is commonly supposed that pre-verbal thinking—if it is allowed to count as thinking at all—must always be vague and clumsy in comparison with the thinking which is conducted in words. I am not sure that this is wholly true even of image-think-ing,[1] the only sort of pre-verbal thinking which philosophers have usually considered. But it certainly is not true of all sign-cognition. Indeed, in examples like the one we have been considering the truth is the other way round. In such significational estimations, pre-verbal thinking shows itself superior and not inferior to verbalized thinking. Its only defect is that it is incommunicable. It can be demonstrated but it cannot be told. Like tact, which is an exercise of sign-cognition in social relations, it cannot be taught by means of verbal instructions.

We observe also that birds and beasts of prey, which have to make their living by their wits (that is, by their powers of sign-cognition) can make these significational estimates as well as we can, and sometimes better. The peregrine falcon, when he dives at a swiftly moving pigeon a hundred feet below, has to estimate very accurately where his victim will be a second hence. The present movement of the target-object is a sign to him of what its future movement will be, and the *significatum* is highly specific. Of course the falcon may be wrong; so may the marksman, and the verbal thinker may be wrong too. Such significational estimates are fallible, like any other form of sign-cognition. The point, however, is that this form of pre-verbal thinking is capable of being right, and frequently right, in cases where there is a very minute difference between a correct estimate and a mistaken one.

I argued previously that there are sign-cognitions in which the *significatum* has a high degree of generality, and just now I have been trying to show that in some sign-cognitions it has a high degree of specificity. There is no inconsistency between these two conten-

[1] Cf. ch. VIII, pp. 235-7, below.

tions. But does it not follow, at any rate, that there are two sorts of sign-cognition, one in which the significate is abstract and another in which it is concrete: one into which abstract ideas enter, as when ice looks cold but with no determinate degree of coldness, and another in which there is no abstractness at all, as when the marksman or the hawk makes an exact estimate of the future position of his target-object? No, this does not follow. It still remains true that all sign-cognition involves the operation of abstract ideas. To suppose otherwise would be to confuse the concrete with the specific. I began by emphasizing the determinable—as opposed to determinate—character of some significates, because determinables are so obviously *abstracta*. Where the significate is just coldness in general, or *a* man unspecified outside the door, it must be an abstract idea which is operating in our minds. Or if there is any doubt about it, the doubt can only concern the use of the word 'idea' and not the abstractness. There is clearly *something* abstract about this mode of cognition even if the 'idea' terminology is thought objectionable. But a highly determinate significate is abstract too. Moving exactly north-north-west with a velocity of just sixty-five feet per second is a shareable characteristic, which many different particulars may have, though it is both complex and determinate. In old-fashioned terminology, it is still 'a universal'. And in any case, not all the characteristics of the significate are determinably specified, even though some of them are. For instance, the precise angle of incidence of the snipe's tail one second hence is not determinately specified, nor the distribution of light and shade over its surface; whereas the concrete is determinate in respect of *all* the characteristics which it has. And finally, it is self-contradictory that something should be at once concrete and non-existent. But any significate, however determinate, may always be non-existent. The marksman's estimate may be very precise, but for all that it may be falsified. Indeed, the more precise it is, the more ways there are in which it can be false. That is why the combination of determinateness and correctness, which some sign-cognition displays, is a proper subject for surprise and admiration. It is this combination which we have in mind when we congratulate the marksman, or the falcon, on the 'accuracy' of his sign-cognitive estimations.

We have seen that sign-cognition has three features in common with what is admittedly thinking. It is capable of being erroneous. Moreover, the significate is cognized 'in absence', by means of an experienced particular which is not an instance of it, or not a member of the class to which the significate itself belongs. And finally, the significate is something abstract or general, though in some cases it is more determinate than in others. We shall also see later that there is something which may be called a 'logic' of sign-cognition. The logical notions of *if*, *or* and *not* have a place in sign-cognition, pre-verbal though it is.[1] Since there are these very important resemblances between sign-cognition and processes which everyone admits to be examples of thinking, it is expedient to adopt a wide, rather than a narrow, definition of the term 'thinking', and to allow that sign-cognition *is* a form of thinking. At any rate, it is certainly a form of intelligence.

Nevertheless, we are still inclined to say that sign-cognition is a primitive or not fully developed form of thinking. Why is this? Some psychologists have distinguished between 'tied' ideas and 'free' ideas. If we are willing to use the Idea terminology at all, we have to admit that ideas are operative in sign-cognition, and abstract ideas too. But we also have to admit that these ideas are 'tied' and not 'free'. Verbal thinking and image thinking have a certain autonomy. To a very considerable degree they are independent of the perceived environment. The course they take is largely controlled by the thinker himself, either by his own voluntary decision, or at any rate by his own desires, emotions, interests and associative habits—in either case by factors within himself. In the midst of the Sahara, he can think of green fields, cool breezes and babbling brooks; he can image them vividly, and can discourse about them in words either public or private. In a German prison, he can think about Chinese politics, or Roman history, or pure mathematics. He can think of the sun by night, and of the stars by day. And even when it is not controlled wholly by processes within himself, his verbal thinking (and his image thinking too) is still controlled by what *other thinkers* say to him, or by their writings which he reads. The course of an animated discussion or debate is very little affected by what is going on in the physical environment of the speakers.

Sign-thinking is not thus autonomous. It is capable of great delicacy and precision (as I have tried to illustrate) but it is *tied* to

[1]See ch. v, below.

sensation. Not necessarily to peripheral sensation, it is true. Organic sensations may be signs too. A familiar sort of headache is a sign that something is wrong with one's digestive apparatus. Shivery feelings and aches in one's back are a sign that one has influenza. Thus it might be wrong to suggest that all signs are environmental. And yet perhaps it would not be wholly wrong either. For to the verbal thinker and the image thinker, even his own body, with all its aches and pains, is something extraneous and 'given'. From the point of view of the thinker himself, when he is thinking in these autonomous ways, his own organic sensations come to him *ab extra*. If I may dare to say so, to the autonomously thinking self even his own body may be environmental, though to the practical self it is a part of 'me'. Even if he is in a daydream, when there is little or no *conscious* control of the course of his thoughts, his body is still something environmental—something which 'breaks in' upon his thoughts with its itches or aches or pains. And this is still more obviously so, if his thought is consciously purposive and voluntarily controlled, for example when he is composing a sonnet or trying to solve a mathematical problem.

The doctrine that mind is 'inward' and body 'outward' has no doubt been a source of muddles and paradoxes, as Professor Ryle has so brilliantly shown.[1] Mind, and especially intelligence, shows itself in public and outwardly observable performances as well as in private processes detectable only by their owner. But it does not follow that the whole antithesis of 'inward' and 'outward' is a mistake. (If it were, why has it been so familiar in all ages and nations?) There really is a sense in which autonomous thinking is more inward than actions ever are, however justly 'mental' predicates may be applied to these. 'Environmental' and 'outward' are relative terms, after all. It all depends where your 'centre' is. To the rock-climber, when he is actually engaged in climbing rocks, his boots are almost as much parts of himself as his toes. The motorist says, '*I* ran over a dog' and not 'a vehicle which I was driving ran over a dog'. In autonomous thinking, on the other hand, especially when it is conducted in images (either verbal images or pictorial ones) the thinker's own feet and stomach are as environmental as the dog was to the motorist.

Nevertheless, the autonomy of verbal thinking and image think-

[1] G. Ryle, *The Concept of Mind, passim.*

ing, their independence of the environmental and the outward, is an advantage which has to be paid for; and sometimes the price is rather a stiff one. Just because these forms of thinking are 'free' and not 'tied', they avert our attention from the world around us. This autonomy may be biologically disastrous. The thinking of Archimedes was so autonomous that he was killed by the Roman soldier while working out a geometrical problem. Even from a purely cognitive point of view, such 'free' thinking has its dangers, as well as its virtues. It may turn our attention away from empirical matters of fact, so that we 'lose contact with reality'. This happens not only with poets and day-dreamers, but with theorists too, and not least with philosophers; and not only with speculative meta-physicians, but with Empiricist philosophers too, for theorizing about experience is not the same as having it. 'Much learning hath made thee mad' is sometimes true, however false it may have been when it was first said. Sign-cognition, on the other hand, keeps us in touch with reality, just because it is not free but tied to sensation. Being an inductive form of thinking, however crude and primitive, it is perforce concerned with empirical matter of fact; and with just those matters of empirical fact which are most likely to be biologically relevant at the moment, because signs only operate when the sign-event is actually experienced. So long as we remain at the level of sign-cognition, we may make mistakes; but at least we can never be clever but silly, as 'free' thinkers too easily can.

I have been emphasizing the difference between tied thinking and free thinking. Nevertheless, the distinction is not an absolutely hard and fast one. Though sign-cognition is always tied to sensation, the tie may be more tight or less. And there are certain factors in sign-cognition itself which tend to loosen the tie, though they never abolish it altogether. To see this, we must consider certain differences which there are between one sign-situation and another; certain dimensions of variation, if the phrase be permitted, to which sign-cognition is subject.

First, there are *short-range* signs and *long-range* signs. (Of course this too is a difference of degree.) A very loud thunderclap signifies an almost immediate flash of lightning. When you feel the doctor's hypodermic syringe applied to your skin, this tactual experience is a sign to you of an almost immediate stab of pain. But when the distant hillside across the valley looks very clear, this signifies that rain is coming in a few hours' time, not at once. To some people, a plentiful crop of hedgerow berries in autumn signifies a hard winter. (It does not matter whether this sign-cognition of theirs is right or wrong; the point is that it is a long-range one.) When I see workmen digging drains in a green field, that is a sign to me that some day there will be houses there; but certainly not at once—in two or three months, perhaps, or more.

There are similar degrees of remoteness when the sign points backwards in time, signifying something past instead of future. The sound of a door opening and closing is a sign that someone has *just* passed through. A faded footprint in the mud signifies that a deer has been here a day or two ago; and to a botanist, the vegetation he sees on a hillside is a sign that trees were cut down there several years before. We may add that both forward-pointing and backward-pointing signs are often indefinite in their temporal range. If I see a full-grown apple tree in your garden, this signifies to me that someone planted it some years ago, more than two and less than fifty; but to me the date of the signified event is not more specific than that, and even to an expert it would not be absolutely specific.

Secondly, there are *strong* signs and *weak* signs (of course this again is a difference of degree). We have seen already that no sign-cognition is infallible. The point now is that one sign may be more reliable than another. The very loud thunderclap is an all-but-certain sign of an immediate flash of lightning. The drain-laying is a far from certain sign that the houses will be built. The Chancellor of the Exchequer or the Minister of Town Planning may change his mind (there is plenty of inductive evidence that this can happen). There may be a war, or a strike of building-workers or brick-makers. The significate is merely rather more probable than not. The perceived event, in this case, is only a weak sign; whereas the loud thunderclap is a very strong sign of a lightning flash, and the sight or feel of a hypodermic syringe applied to one's skin is a pretty strong sign of pain to come.

It must be made clear that the distinction between strong signs and weak ones exists not only for the outside observer, but also for the sign-cognisant himself. He himself learns, by experience, to rely more confidently on some signs and less confidently on others.

Even animals can learn to distinguish strong signs from weak ones in matters which are biologically important for them. It may seem odd to suggest that cats or rats can distinguish different degrees of inductive probability. But to judge from their behaviour they undoubtedly do. They can distinguish dangerous situations from safe ones. And 'danger' is a conception which has to be analysed in terms of inductive probability. A dangerous situation is one in which there is a probability of death or injury or some other biological evil. Animals appear to recognize quite small probabilities of this kind. Nothing is more characteristic of the animal mind than the state of vigilance, or wariness, or being on one's guard. The cat is wary even when he is eating. Interesting as that occupation is, he keeps half an eye on his surroundings—'just in case'. He takes account, in his actions, of the bare chance (that is, the small but finite inductive probability) that something will go wrong. Again, an animal which is in a dangerous situation can recognize, from signs, that there is a chance of escape. It likewise recognizes that there is an opportunity of getting food, or of slipping into its hole unobserved. 'Chance of' and 'opportunity of' are probability notions of the inductive kind. Indeed, if animals could not learn to distinguish between strong signs and weak ones, they might as well be incapable of learning from experience altogether. If any sign, to be a sign at all, had to be relied upon with 100 per cent confidence, the capacity of sign-cognition would be biologically disastrous instead of advantageous. It would be better not to learn from experience at all than to learn from it in this indiscriminating and undoubting manner. In the very earliest stage of one's sign-cognitive career one may be in a state of undoubting 'primitive credulity'. But one must quickly learn to get out of it, if one is to escape disaster. If a sign lets me down—if one of my sign-cognitive expectations is falsified—I shall do well to treat it as a weak sign in future, though I may do ill to treat it as no sign at all. 'Once bitten, twice shy' is a very salutary maxim, both for animals and men.

Short-range signs are often also strong ones (as in the examples I have given); and long-range signs are often also weak ones. But the two distinctions do not wholly coincide. When I see the swallows gathering in flocks on the telephone wires, I can expect with great confidence that they will begin their southward migration in a day or two. It is a relatively long-range sign, but a strong one. When

I get into the ocean liner at Southampton, I can expect with great confidence to arrive in New Zealand a month or so from now. On the other hand, some short-range signs are relatively weak. I am watching a polite game of tennis. The lady makes a feeble shot. It looks as if the ball *must* hit the net. But no, it scrapes over, with half an inch to spare. I see you pull the trigger, and I expect an immediate bang. There is no bang. You forgot to load the gun. These are very short-range signs, and yet they are certainly not cast-iron ones.

Nevertheless, the situation is more complicated here than it is in long-range signification. The sign-cognisant may be aware that these short-range signs have some degree, at least, of weakness, because he has experienced their fallibility in the past. But if their weakness is not too great, his state of 'immediate expectation', at the moment when he actually perceives the sign, tends as a matter of psychological fact to be undoubting. The expected event, though still future, is presented to the mind with a quasi-sensible vividness. The idea of it blends with the present sensation, as in the examples of 'complication' discussed earlier (e.g. where ice looks cold or a wall looks hard).[1] One 'sees the tennis shot as' a net-hitting shot; one sees the trigger movement as bang-producing. Even though I noticed the small boy outside preparing to throw his handful of dried peas, I still cannot help hearing the pitter-patter sound on the roof as 'rainy' or 'rainish'.

But this does not happen even with short-range signs if their weakness is very considerable. There is a certain gentle soughing sound which is a sign that a glider is passing close overhead. It is a short-range sign, but a pretty weak one, because sounds almost indistinguishable from it can be produced in other ways, for example by a broad-leaved bush waving gently in the wind. In this case the significate is not accepted undoubtingly, and the idea of it does not acquire the quasi-sensible vividness which occurs in cases of 'complication'. In cases of complication, one experiences a most disconcerting shock of surprise if the sign-cognition is falsified; for example, if the wall when touched feels quite soft. I experience no such shock of surprise when I look up and see no glider overhead, but only a bush waving in the wind.

Finally, there may be *mutually conflicting* signs, and one and the

[1]See pp. 76, 99, above.

same sign may be *ambiguous* or ambivalent. The barometer is high, signifying continued fine weather; but at the same time the clouds look threatening. The sound of church bells is a sign that Divine Service is about to begin, but equally it is a sign that the Campanological Society is indulging in its anti-social exercises. Where there is a conflict of signs, it is obvious that both are weakened. The same thing happens when a single sign is ambiguous. Neither of the two (or more) alternative significates is accepted with whole-hearted confidence. It must be noticed, however, that the same sign may be ambiguous and therefore weak for one person, whereas it is unambiguous and strong for another. When I hear a cooing sound, it is a sign to me that there is either a wood-pigeon or a stock-dove in the tree overhead; and for me, each of these alternatives is weakly signified. To a skilled ornithologist the same sound is an unambiguous sign and a strong one. In his mind there is no doubt which of the two sorts of birds it is.

If some signs are weaker than others, this obviously has an important bearing on the relation between sign-cognition and *belief*. In the classical account of sign-cognition in Hume's *Treatise*, in the Sections on Belief and on Necessary Connection,[1] we are told that when A is signifying B, the significate B is always believed. Indeed Hume in effect *defines* belief in terms of sign-cognition, as that state of mind which we have towards the significate of some experienced sign. That is what 'a lively idea associated with a present impression' comes to. Again, he explicitly says that he is discussing inference (that is, inductive inference). And according to most logicians, the distinctive feature of inference—what distinguishes it from mere awareness of an implication—is that an inference both premise and conclusion are 'asserted', in other words, believed or assented to. But if there are weak signs, and if the sign-cognisant himself is sensitive to their weakness, as we have seen he often is, this account of the matter is over-simplified. We must at any rate say that in sign-cognition there are *degrees* of belief; and when the sign is weak, the significate is accepted with something much less than whole-hearted and undoubting conviction. Indeed, we must go further.

[1]*Treatise*, Book I, Part 3, Section 7 'Of the nature of the Idea or Belief' and Section 14 'Of the Idea of Necessary Connection'. It may be noticed that the last section of Part 3 is called 'Of the Reason of Animals' (Part 3, Section 16), though Hume's readers do not seem to have paid much attention to it.

When the sign is *very* weak, we do not believe at all. Jones has promised to come to my rooms at 12 o'clock. At 11.57 I hear a knock at the door. This is a sign that he has arrived. But it is a very weak sign, because he is nearly always late rather than early, and many other people knock at my door from time to time. In such a case, I certainly do not *believe* that Jones has arrived. The thought that he has is suggested to my mind by the sound, and I do not reject it, but neither do I accept it. There is only an inclination to believe, an inclination which is inhibited by the weakness of the sign. If I were to express my state of mind in words, I should say 'Good heavens! Can that be Jones already?' (or, if I were a logician, 'there is a finite but very small probability that Jones has come').

The absence of belief is most obvious when there are conflicting signs. The sky is blue and well-formed cumulus clouds are floating across it. On the other hand, the wind has gone round a point or two towards the south, and the distant landscape looks clearer than it did. Will it rain before we have got down from the mountain, or will it continue fine? I believe neither, because the signs point opposite ways. It is true that each set of signs arouses an *inclination* to believe, but the two inclinations inhibit each other, and I am left in a state of suspended judgement. In short, once we grasp the distinction between strong and weak signs and the fact that their various degrees of strength and weakness are often appreciated by the sign-cognisant himself, we see that sign-cognition is a more rational, or at least more intelligent, operation than Hume thought it was. Something like a rational estimation of inductive probabilities enters into it, in that the intensity of our inclination to believe is regulated to some extent by the 'weight of experience' behind this sign-cognition or that. In the section on the Idea of Necessary Connection, and also in the section on Belief, Hume tacitly assumes that all signs are maximally strong and that signification has, so to speak, an 'all or nothing' character—either you believe undoubtingly in the significate, or else no signification occurs at all. It is true that he modifies this extreme view in a later section on 'The Probability of Causes',[1] but he did not revise the earlier sections accordingly.

These characteristics of signification, that signs differ from each other in range and in strength and may be conflicting or ambiguous,

[1] *Treatise*, Book I, Part 3, Section 12.

have an important bearing on the logic of sign-cognition, as we shall see later.[1] For the moment, however, we are more concerned with the effect they have in loosening the tie between idea and sensation. Although all sign-cognition is 'tied' thinking, some sign-cognitions are less closely tied to sensation (or more nearly 'free') than others. In this connection, there is another difference of degree which we should consider, though this time it is a difference in the significates, and not in the way in which sign and significate are connected. The significate may be more interesting or less. It may appeal much or little to the 'needs' (innate or acquired) of the sign-cognisant subject. What is signified may be very exciting to him, or rather exciting, or almost indifferent. To be sure, if the significate had never had any interest for him at all, that particular sign-relation would never have been established; the relevant constant conjunctions, or more or less constant conjunctions, would never have been noticed. The mouse which lives in the front hall is probably not interested enough in letters or parcels to associate a particular sort of knock at the front door with the arrival of the morning's post, though this conjunction has been constant or almost constant throughout the mouse's lifetime. Again, although the significate must have been interesting at some time or other, it need not be interesting at this particular moment when the sign-event happens to be perceived again. In a recently fed animal or human being food-signs arouse no response, though they are very exciting at other times. The domestic cat, with an open back door in front of him and a comfortable chair waiting for him beside the drawing-room fire, is more or less indifferent to the attractions of a thick bush which would provide him with a good place of refuge to sleep in. The lair inside the bush, signified by the thickly interlacing twigs, interests him very little, because the seat in front of the fire, signified by the open back door, appeals to him much more. If the house were shut up, the bush would interest him a good deal.

The most favourable conditions for loosening the tie between idea and sensation seem to be these: the sign must be a relatively long-range one, and the significate must be highly interesting or exciting to the sign-cognisant subject. If the sign is also weak, rather than strong, this will help, but it is not sufficient by itself. In these conditions the signified idea, though brought to mind by a sensation

[1] Cf. ch. v.

and so far 'tied', will tend to remain in mind after the sensation has ceased—perhaps for a long time after. During the waiting period which elapses between the sign-cognition and the later event which is to verify it or falsify it, the significate will be thought of independently, apart from, or not wholly in union with, the sign by which it was originally brought to mind. (What kind of thinking this is, or what sense of the word 'think', we shall consider presently.) In very short-range sign-cognition this cannot happen, simply because there is no time for it to happen.[1] The anticipation of the bang cannot occupy my mind for its own sake, because the actual bang succeeds the flash so very quickly. But the anticipation of rain, signified by a falling barometer, may occupy one's mind for the whole morning, provided that the difference between wet weather and fine is sufficiently interesting; and this despite the fact that the barometer itself was only quickly glanced at, and is out of sight and almost (though perhaps never quite) out of mind thereafter. Here the thought of the coming rain is partly, though not entirely, 'freed' from the sense-given sign which originally suggested it.

But in what sense is the rain 'thought of' during this waiting period? If one is an adult human being, or even a non-infantile human being, words and images will certainly play some part in this thinking, and very likely a preponderant part. But then one has reached a level of mental development which does not yet concern us. At the level which does concern us, an idea can only be brought to mind in two ways: by an actual perceived instance (primary recognition), or else by means of a sign. How then can it remain before the mind when no instance is being perceived, and when the sign which brought it there has lapsed from consciousness?

'Before the mind' is a stop-gap phrase, not to be taken too literally. If we do take it literally, it suggests what may be called an Inspection Theory of thinking. I shall discuss this theory later, in chapters X and XI, and shall try to show that it is much more false than true. Even in verbal thinking, the 'freest' sort of thinking that there is, it is most misleading to suggest that anything is being

[1]One should not perhaps ignore the possibility that the span of the 'specious present' may vary considerably in different creatures. The event which is a short-range sign for human percipients may be a relatively long-range one for birds or insects. Conversely, we can at least imagine that there might be intelligent beings whose specious present is very much longer than ours. For them our long-range signs might be short-range ones.

inspected by the thinker. And the tied or half-tied thinking which concerns us now is about as unlike inspection as anything can be. If the phrase 'before the mind' has these implications for the reader, we had better say 'in the mind' instead, or just 'in mind'. Let us ask then in what way the signified idea remains 'in mind' when the sign itself has lapsed from consciousness.

Perhaps it remains in mind in this sense, that I continue to be ready or prepared for an instance of it—for a perceived situation which 'satisfies' it. And I am ready or prepared for this, not just in the sense that when and if an instance is perceived, I shall recognize it to be one. For that is true of me at all times, once I have acquired the relevant abstract idea or concept (the idea of Rain in this case) and have not lost it. To have a concept or abstract idea *is* to have the capacity of recognizing instances and of distinguishing them from non-instances, or at any rate that is part of what it is. Yet, it may seem, this capacity of mine is not being actualized either; recognition of an instance is not actually occurring now, though it will occur later, when and if the sign-cognition is verified. Thus there is something more than the mere capacity of recognition, and something less than an actualization of it. To clear the matter up, we have to introduce the notion of *degrees* of actualization. As Leibniz pointed out in his criticism of Locke's chapter on 'Powers', it is an important fact about powers or capacities that they can be actualized in different degrees; at any rate this seems to be true of mental powers, whether or not it is also true of purely physical ones. There are intermediate stages between complete latency on the one hand—where a mental capacity, though I do still possess it, is not at the moment being actualized at all by any occurrence, mental or psycho-physical—and complete actualization on the other. The capacity to add 2 and 2 is completely latent when I am in dreamless sleep or completely absorbed in eating an egg. It is not wholly actualized until I do actually add 2 and 2. But it passes some way beyond complete latency whenever I see and recognize a column of figures, even though the numeral 2 is not among them; and it emerges still further towards complete actualization when I am adding 5 to 5.

The same point is sometimes formulated quite differently by means of the Herbartian notion of the threshold of consciousness. An idea, it is said, may be far below the threshold ('unconscious') or just below the threshold ('subconscious') or just on it, or well above it. This way of speaking is very useful in some contexts, and it is a pity that contemporary philosophers have almost ceased to make use of it. But for our present purposes it is misleading. It is liable to suggest the Inspective Theory of thinking, as if ideas— abstract ideas too—were quasi-preceptible entities which can 'come into view' or pass out of it as visible objects can. The same may be said of another visual analogy (which also has its uses) where ideas are spoken of as 'focal' or 'marginal'. A more useful term for our present purpose is *sub-activation* or *sub-excitation*, where the prefix 'sub-' has the force of 'partially', 'faintly,' 'on the edge of'. A mental or psycho-physical capacity can be sub-activated by certain cues or stimuli which are not sufficient to actualize it completely. We may say that the capacity to add 2 and 2 is sub-activated by seeing the column of figures or by the activity of adding 5 to 5. Similarly, the capacity for recognizing rain is sub-activated when one sees a man carrying a folded up umbrella or hears a pitter-patter sound on the roof, though neither of these is an instance of rain, and only an actual perceived instance would actualize the capacity completely.

It is, of course, natural to suppose, with Locke, that a mental capacity is either completely actualized or else completely latent, and that there is no half-way house between the two. The notion of degrees of actualization is paradoxical and unfamiliar, and so is the connected notion of sub-activation. But before the reader rejects them as absurd, he ought to wait and see what can be done with them, what clarificatory power they have. If there are puzzling facts which can be understood by means of a somewhat queer-seeming notion, and cannot be understood otherwise, he will be unwise to maintain that the notion itself is unintelligible.

Let us now see whether this one does help us to understand sign-cognition better. In all sign-cognition, we say, an abstract idea or concept, is sub-activated by a sensational sign. Let us suppose, as a first approximation at least, that possessing an idea of X consists in having the capacity to recognize instances of X, when and if they are presented. This capacity is only fully actualized when an X-ish particular is actually presented. But it can be partially actualized, sub-activated, when *other* particulars are presented. Suppose that we have experienced a sufficiently constant conjunction of Y-ish and X-ish particulars in the past (it need not be an absolutely constant

one). Then the X-recognizing capacity will be sub-activated, partially though not completely actualized, when a Y-ish particular is
presented. This is what happens in sign-cognition. Y is then a sign
for us of X, though it will not be for others who have not observed
that more-or-less constant conjunction. (When we have learned to
understand words, Y can become a sign of X though the testimony
of other people who have observed the constant conjunction, even
though we ourselves have not. But at present we are only concerned
with pre-verbal thinking.) For example, smoke is for me a sign of
fire; that is, my fire-recognizing capacity is sub-activated or sub-
excited, partially but not completely actualized, by seeing the smoke.
In some degree I approach, though I do not reach, the state in which
I should be if a fire were actually being seen or felt.

We may pause for a moment to compare this account of the
matter with Hume's. In Hume's analysis of sign-cognition, the idea
of the significate is 'enlivened' by the impression which is the sign.
There would be little to object to in this formula, if Hume's theory
of ideas themselves were more satisfactory than it is. But unfortunately he has a tendency to identify ideas with mental images;
and this in turn distorts his account of the 'liveliness' which the
significate-idea acquires from the presentation of the sign-impression. When he says that my idea of X is made lively by a present
impression of Y, he appears to mean, usually, that I just have a
vivid X-like image when the Y impression occurs. And even when
he is writing more carefully, as in the section 'Of Abstract Ideas',[1]
he seems to equate an idea with an image-producing *capacity*. We
shall have to discuss this Imagist theory of thinking later.[2] For the
moment it suffices to point out once again that sign-cognition can
occur without images, and commonly does. Even if one does have
an image of the significate, it certainly need not be vivid; and in
short-range sign-cognition, as when a very loud thunderclap is a
sign of an almost immediate flash of lightning, there is no time for
an image to present itself.

But if we alter Hume's theory of ideas, and substitute recognitional capacities for image-producing capacities, what he says about
sign-cognition is substantially true. In sign-cognition a recognitional capacity *is* enlivened by a present impression. My capacity

[1] *Treatise*, Book I, Part I, Section 7.
[2] See Chapters VIII and IX, below.

for recognizing fire is enlivened by my present impression of smoke; and this happens, as Hume says it does, because there has been a constant conjunction of fire with smoke in my past experience. On the other hand, as Hume also says, the idea is not enlivened completely. That only happens when and if we experience an actual fire-impression. We have only to add, what Hume admits but insufficiently emphasizes, that there are not just two degrees of 'enlivening', complete and incomplete. The less-than-complete enlivenment, which occurs in sign-cognition, itself admits of degrees. In the phenomenon of complication, as when ice looks cold or water wet, the idea is so closely blended with the sensational sign, and so powerfully enlivened, that it is almost as if we were actually experiencing and recognizing an instance. It is almost as if the coldness or wetness were actually felt—almost, though still not quite. But when I see a red sky in the evening and take it as a sign of a fine day tomorrow, my capacity for recognizing fine weather is enlivened to a much smaller degree than this.

We may now return to our question concerning the 'tied' (as opposed to 'free') character of significational thinking. Though this form of thinking is always tied to sensation, we noticed that the tie is weaker in some cases than in others. With long-range signification particularly, the significate can remain in mind long after the sign itself has lapsed from consciousness. The significate-idea is partially emancipated from the sensational sign. The sign was needed to bring the significate idea to mind; but once brought to mind, this idea remains in mind on its own account. This does not mean that we as it were continue looking at it. The Inspection Theory of thinking, whatever merits it may have, does not fit this level of cognition at all. What happens is rather that we continue to be prepared or ready for the perception of an instance. And the being prepared for an instance is one of the ways in which an idea, a recognitional capacity, is partially actualized. In some measure we approach, though we by no means reach, the state in which we should be if we were actually recognizing an instance. When we have seen the stratus cloud spreading over the sky, our rain-recognizing capacity, sub-excited by this sensational sign, remains sub-excited for some time after.

This preparedness for an instance manifests itself in various ways.

If we are word-using creatures it may manifest itself by the production of words (rain-mentioning sentences or phrases), but it need not. It may manifest itself by the production of rain-like images. But again it need not, though images are more likely to occur in long-range than in short-range signification. It may manifest itself, and probably will, by the noticing of further and later weather-signs which either support or weaken the original one. I shall be more 'sensitive' than usual to changes in the look of the sky and to increases or decreases in the felt dampness of the air. Most important of all, my preparedness for rain manifests itself in actions and incipient actions, such as fingering my umbrella from time to time or half-opening it, getting the mackintosh out of my haversack, or walking in the valley among trees rather than on a bare and shelter-less mountainside. It would be quite wrong to regard these per-formances as mere physical movements, though, of course, they *are* physical movements. They are manifestations of the possession and partial actualization of an abstract idea or concept, ways in which it reveals its continuing sub-activation. In a minded creature, bodily movements are one of the ways in which ideas operate; they operate not only psychically but also psycho-physically. (A speculative metaphysician might even suggest that this is why minds have bodies.) We could almost say that the action of finger-ing the umbrella is one of the ways in which one *thinks* of rain; though this thinking is not at all like the inspecting or envisaging of some kind of 'intelligible object' (e.g. a subsistent universal or a subsistent proposition) and need not even involve the sort of envisaging which occurs when one has images. At any rate, the fingering of the umbrella 'has a reference to' rain, and is not fully described unless this reference—and what it is a reference *to*—is mentioned. Moreover, this action refers to rain in absence, as some-thing which is not at the moment actual.

The more interesting the significate idea is, the more likely it is to remain in mind when the sign-sensation has gone. And this is still more likely to happen if the sign is weak, rather than strong, or if there is some conflict of signs. The state of being prepared for an instance then takes the intensified form which may be called *vigilance*. Here we are not only prepared for an instance of the significate-idea but also for a counter-instance, if one may put it so; that is, for an experience which will 'dissatisfy' the idea, as well as for an experience which will 'satisfy' it. In other words, one is prepared not only for the verification of the signified proposition but also for its falsification. (At this pre-verbal level of consciousness, no sharp distinction can be drawn between having an idea or concept in mind, and entertaining a proposition.) Moreover, if the significate-idea is a determinable one with several alternative determinates, as it commonly is, the sign-cognisant is prepared for any one of these determinates, at any rate if the differences between them are sufficiently interesting. And then the different alternatives are 'taken account of' in the actions of incipient actions which fill the period of waiting. Or if there is immobility, it is the immobility not of quiescence but of muscular tension, ready to explode as it were in this direction or that, according to the determinate form the verifying situation takes when it comes. Here is a sleeping dog. The cat sitting on the doorstep across the street has seen this formidable creature, and is on his guard. This visual sensation is for him a sign of a dangerous situation, though it is a relatively weak and long-range sign. The dog may continue to sleep for another half-hour. When he wakes, he may go straight home for his dinner. The dangerous situation may never occur at all. But the cat is on his guard 'just in case'. And he is prepared for alternative moves on the dog's part, and for alternative forms of evasive action to suit them. He will dash across the street and over the wall if the dog moves slowly. If there is no time, or if that escape-route is cut off, he will run up the tree which is close beside him on his own side of the street. Or at the worst, he is prepared to stand and fight. I am not, of course, suggesting that the cat 'thinks out' these alternative possibilities, as we might think them out by means of words or images if we were situated as he is. But he takes account of them in what he does, and a state of alert immobility is part of what he does. To use the same language as before, his behaviour 'has reference to' them, and it has reference to them *as alternatives*.

Vigilance is often emotionally toned, with a flavour of anxiety; and animals in a state of vigilance often display bodily symptoms of anxiety, as we do ourselves. The cat's tail, for example, may be observed to twitch slightly. This anxiety, or 'nervousness' as it is vulgarly called, is interesting to the epistemologist and even in a way to the logician. It is not just a self-contained psychical state, any more than the bodily actions spoken of before are just physical movements. It too has a referential character. And what it refers to is a set of alternative possibilities. Anxiety, in fact, is a primitive and non-disinterested form of the cognitive activity of questioning or wondering, and involves something like the entertaining of a disjunctive proposition.

On its cognitive side, vigilance is still a form of sign-cognition. The idea which remains in mind during the period of vigilance, and manifests its presence in the ways I have described, was brought to mind in the first place by a sensational sign. The thinking or practically-enacted thought which occurs in vigilance is tied thinking, not free; it is still tied to sensation. But the tie has been very considerably weakened. The signified idea, once brought to mind by the sensational sign, is dwelt upon for its own sake. Yet it would be too much to say that it is 'before the mind', in the sense in which this *can* be said quite plausibly of the ideas which we think of when we think 'freely', by means of words or images. Shall we say, then, that the significate-idea is not present *to* us but rather operates *in* us, by maintaining a state of preparedness for an instance and controlling a series of preparatory actions and incipient actions, with a concomitant emotional tone of anxiety? These actions and incipient actions, including the bodily state of tense and alert immobility, and the concomitant feeling-tone of anxiety as well, are ways of *taking account of* the significate and of the various alternative determinates which it includes, though they are not ways of contemplating it or inspecting it. If this sounds queer, it is because philosophers are not accustomed to considering a level of mental development at which cognition and action are not yet sharply differentiated, and a level, moreover, at which words are not used and even images can be dispensed with; and so when we try to describe it, we have no ready-made terminology for the purpose. At best we have to proceed by clumsy approximations and at worst by paradoxes.

In this discussion of the ways in which a significate may remain in mind after the sign has ceased, I have been concerned entirely with predictive signs, those which point forward in time. But there are, of course, also signs which point backwards in time, 'retrodictive' ones. Thus a heap of ashes on the ground is a sign that there *has* been fire and a footprint is a sign that a man *has* been here. There are 'juxtadictive' signs as well, where the sign points to something contemporary with itself but at the moment unobserved. The sight of a closed door signifies the *present* existence of a room behind it. In these cases too, we can say that the significate-idea is sub-activated or sub-excited by the perceived sign. The capacity which I have to recognize fire, if I perceive it, is partially but not completely actualized by the sight of the ashes; and similarly with my room-recognizing capacity when I see the closed door.

Retrodictive signs, like predictive ones, may be long-range or short-range. A very loud thunderclap is a sign that there was a lightning flash a second or two ago. Ruinous walls signify that there was an inhabited house here many years ago. But naturally there is no question of a waiting-period, long or short, as there is with predictive signs. The signified event or state of affairs is past and gone, and I can never hope to observe it. At the most, I can only hope to recall that I did formerly observe it, though perhaps I had forgotten all about it until the retrodictive sign reminded me. But often, of course, it is not something which I formerly observed and can now remember; I did not see the lightning flash, and I never saw the house in its previous inhabited state. Thus if the significate-idea is to remain in mind after the sign has lapsed from consciousness, it can only be because it is specially interesting to the sign-cognizant subject. In what sense, then, does it 'remain in mind'? From the nature of the case I cannot be prepared or ready for the signified event to happen.

No, but I can be prepared or ready for *other* signs which will strengthen or weaken the original one, as I was in the meteorological example already mentioned, when I was on the look-out for other signs that rain was coming. Thus I am prepared for other signs that a fire has been burning here, burnt out matches, for example, or an abandoned match box, or scattered tea leaves. Again, if the signified past event is one which concerns us very closely, we may be prepared for a *repetition* of it. A bang signifies that someone has just fired a gun in our direction. This puts us into a state of vigilance in case the man fires again. In that way the significate-idea, 'gun fired towards us' remains in mind when the original bang is no longer heard. The significate idea may also remain in mind in other ways, provided it is sufficiently interesting. Its continuing sub-activation may be shown by emotional states, such as distress, regret, horror, with their accompanying bodily symptoms (tears, sighs, trembling).

It may also be shown by the occurrence of images depicting the signified past event, or possibly by dumb show imitating it, and, of course, by the occurrence of words, overt or private, if the sign-cognizant is a word-using creature. As we have seen before, in predictive signification words or images are more likely to occur when the sign is a long range one, and there is a waiting period during which 'nothing can be done about' the signified event. In retrodictive signification, nothing can be done about the signified event in any case, because it is already past and gone. In this state of non-urgency, there is ample opportunity for imaging or verbalizing.

In juxtadictive signification, however, where the sign signifies something contemporary with itself, the significate is usually a *continuant*, which may be expected to remain in existence long after the sign-percept has ceased. Thus the sight of the door signifies not only that the room is there now, but also that it is likely to be there for a long time to come. Thus juxtadictive signs usually have a predictive character as well. To the extent that they have, we anticipate a future verification of them; and when the significate remains in mind after the sign-percept has ceased, the account which we have given already, in terms of preparedness or readiness, will still apply. We can also 'do something about' the significate, just because it is taken to be a continuing object. Actions or incipient actions can occur which have reference to it. For instance, we can walk round the house and look in at the room through a window, or knock on the door or unlock it, or be on the point of performing such actions, even though we do not actually perform them.

CHAPTER V

THE LOGIC OF SIGN COGNITION

It is usually supposed that the logical notions of *not, or, if,* etc., play no part whatever in pre-verbal thinking, and this is one of the grounds for the opinion that such thinking cannot 'really' be thinking at all. Logic, it is supposed, is the study of talk, or even of print; or rather, it is one way of studying them, concerned with the formal factors which are detectable in spoken or written sentences, or perhaps only in written ones. I believe that these opinions are mistaken. These formal factors, though they are more obvious and explicit in verbalized thought, are already present in pre-verbal thought, and even in that 'enacted thought' or 'thinking in actions' which is mistakenly supposed to be nothing but bodily movement. They certainly play a part in sign-cognition, and also, as I shall try to show, in desire. Desire too has its cognitive aspect, and the epistemologist cannot afford to neglect it. The reader must be warned, however, that the terminological difficulties, referred to at the end of the last chapter, will now be even greater than before. When something is present in the mind, but present only obscurely or inexplicitly, there is no easy and straightforward way of describing the situation.

As soon as we possess any concept, to the extent of being capable of recognizing instances, there is some dim appreciation of negation. If I can recognize this thing as being red, I can also recognize other things as *not* being red. As soon as I possess a concept, I can distinguish between instances and non-instances, between particulars which 'satisfy' the concept and particulars which 'dissatisfy' it. At any rate, I can do this in easy cases (with a poppy and a crow for example) even though there are borderline cases where I hesitate. It is true that this capacity for 'disrecognition', if it may be called so, is not exercised *in vacuo*. One does not go about the world noticing non-instances of the concept. The concept must already have been sub-activated, if one is to be aware that this or that particular *dis*satisfies it. But once we have reached the level of sign-cognition, this sub-activation readily occurs. If ϕ has become for us a sign of ψ and a ϕ-instance is experienced, the concept of ϕ will be sub-activated, as we have seen. We are then prepared for an instance of ψ. This readiness for an instance is one of the ways in which the sub-activation of a concept shows itself both in consciousness and in behaviour. And if no instance of ψ in fact occurs, the particulars which do occur will clash with this ψ-referring preparedness, and we shall have an experience of Negation. Disappointed expectation is what brings NOT into our lives.

This very elementary and primitive experience might also be called an experience of *falsification*. It is said, of course, that where there are only concepts and not propositions there is as yet no distinction between truth and falsity. But as we have seen, at the level of mental development which concerns us now there is no difference between conceiving a concept and entertaining a proposition. To conceive a concept or abstract idea A, in the only way we can conceive it at this level—namely, by being prepared for an instance— is to entertain (and usually also to believe) the proposition 'there is to be something A-ish'. It will be noted that the proposition is an existential one. It is also what logicians call 'general', because the notion of *something* enters into it. In the symbolism of Russell and Whitehead it would be written $\exists x \, Ax$. It may seem strange to suggest that logical notions so advanced as those of existence and generality should enter into such a primitive form of thinking. But I see no way of denying that they do. Of course the thinker himself does not reflect on them. Yet what he thinks, if analysed, is found to contain them. As soon as we are in any degree able to conceive of a concept in the absence of an instance, we are entertaining an existential proposition (though we may or may not be believing it as well); and in some degree, however primitively, we *are* conceiving of a concept in the absence of an instance when we are prepared or ready for an instance which is not yet actually experienced. *In ordine cognoscendi*, then, the most primitive form of proposition is $\exists x \, \phi x$. Anyone who possesses a concept at all is *ipso facto* capable of entertaining a proposition of this form, and actually does entertain it as soon as the concept is sub-activated in the absence of an instance. He is also capable of the experience of falsification, which is only another way of saying that he can distinguish particulars which *dis*satisfy the concept from those which satisfy it. It might be too much to say that from henceforth he 'has' the logical concept of *not* or *it is false that*, because this might suggest that he is capable of reflecting on it; but at any rate negativity or falsification has begun to play a part in his life, both cognitive and practical. It would indeed be a strange way of possessing a concept, if one could not distinguish at all between particulars which satisfy the concept and particulars which dissatisfy it. If I cannot distinguish at all between red things and green ones, there is something rather defective in my concept of Red.

We can now see what a fortunate thing it is that some signs are weak. If every sign had been a 'cast-iron' one, 100 per cent reliable, the distinction between p and not–p would have been much more difficult to learn. It is true that in any world in which there are qualitative unlikenesses, there will be not–ϕ things as well as ϕ things. But our attention will not be called to the difference unless two conditions are fulfilled. The concept ϕ must be already in mind in the absence of a perceived instance. This condition is fulfilled when ϕ is brought to mind (sub-activated) by some sign, so that we are prepared or ready for an instance of ϕ when no instance is as yet being experienced. But secondly, it is also necessary that the sign-cognition should sometimes be falsified. The sign must 'let us down', so that the particulars which come may manifestly clash with or dissatisfy the concept ϕ. This salutary shock not only makes us aware of negation. It is also what makes us aware that there *are* weak signs; and this discovery is the beginning of wisdom. It is not, of course, that we make the generalization 'some signs are less than 100 per cent reliable'. At this level of mental development we are quite incapable of such a feat of philosophical reflection. It is rather that we learn to rely upon them in future with some degree of caution or reserve. Once bitten, twice shy.

At first, it may be supposed, we are in a state of 'primitive credulity', and when anything is a sign for us at all we treat it as if it were 100 per cent reliable, undoubtingly. The experience of falsification does something to chasten our primitive credulity (though perhaps it is never entirely eradicated even in the most rational men). We pass from the state in which a proposition, if entertained at all, is accepted with unquestioning conviction, into some dim appreciation of degrees of inductive probability. As I have mentioned before, even animals seem able to acquire this.

Within limits, and in matters which are of biological importance to them, they learn to distinguish strong signs from weak ones. At any rate, they take account of this difference in their actions and incipient actions, as the state of animal vigilance illustrates.[1] The notion of inductive probability, and of different degrees of it, is another of the *logical* notions which play a part in sign-cognition.

It is possible, however, that even in a world where all signs were maximally strong we might still have acquired some appreciation of negation, provided that there were long-range signs as well as short-range ones. With a long-range sign (by definition) there is a waiting period between sign and fulfilment. Even if the fulfilment always came in the end, there would still be an experience of NOT YET during the waiting period. The dinner-bell might be for the cat an absolutely infallible sign of milk at the end of the meal. In all his experience this sign-cognition might never once be falsified. But until the family has finished eating, the sight of the empty saucer will still clash with the concept of milk which has been sub-activated by the audible sign he experienced some time ago. There is falsification for the present, though there is verification to come.

The falsification of sign-cognitions also leads to the discovery of *negative* signs; that is, of sign-situations with negative significates. (These signs, like others, may be strong or weak, long-range or short-range.) When A signifies B and B fails to occur, I may recollect that in this case A was accompanied by something else X; and I may notice later that when A is thus accompanied, B regularly or fairly regularly fails to occur. If this happens frequently, X becomes for me a negative sign, a sign (strong or weak) of the *non*-occurrence of B.

Negative signification cannot, however, occur *in vacuo*. Thunder-claps, in my experience at least, are constantly conjoined with the absence of hyenas. But I have no tendency to take a thunderclap as a sign that there is not a hyena in the neighbourhood. If X is to become for me a sign of not-B there must be something about the X situation which suggests the thought of B, or brings the concept B to mind. X must be accompanied by something (A for example) which is a *positive* though weak sign of B. In mountain country we notice sometimes that the clouds are high, which is a weak sign of continuing fine weather. But at the same time the distant hillside

[1]Cf. p. 108, above.

looks unusually clear; and when this is so, it is usually found that the expectation of continuing fine weather is falsified. In other words, negative signification only occurs when there is some *conflict* of signs; p can only signify not–q when there is something else p' which weakly signifies q. Or, if it be preferred, there is only *dis*signification when there is also signification. (Instead of saying that p signifies not–q, we may say if we like that it *dis*signifies q.)

As we have seen already,[1] signification may also be *disjunctive*. In many sign-situations, the significate is a determinable; and the state of preparedness, into which the sign puts us, is a preparedness for *either* this determinate *or* that *or* the other. The cat as he crouches ready to spring is prepared for any one of many movements of the mouse. The mouse's present visible position is a sign that he is about to make a dash for safety, either to the left or to the right or somewhere in between. The velocity of his dash and the geometrical character of his future path (rectilinear, curvilinear, zigzag) are likewise only determinably signified. He may move in any one of several alternative ways. The vigilant cat is ready for an instance of any one of these alternative determinates which fall under the determinable significate. It would be too much to say that he entertains and believes a disjunctive proposition. But he 'takes account' of a disjunction in his tense and vigilant state of psycho-physical preparedness. It is clear that ambiguous signs likewise involve an 'either or'. To the not very expert ornithologist a faint churring sound heard in the twilight signifies *either* a nightjar[2] *or* a very distant motor-bicycle. So too when signs conflict, like the high clouds and the unusually clear atmosphere. But here the disjunction takes the simple form 'either p or not–p'.

The most formidable and difficult of all logical concepts is the notion of *if*. It is the word IF which the logician inscribes over the door of his study to keep unwanted callers away. Can we show that *if* enters into sign-cognition, pre-verbal as it is? In that case there could be no doubt at all that sign-cognition deserves the name of thinking. But can there really be such a thing as hypothetical or conditional signification?

[1] Cf. pp. 99-101, above.
[2] A crepuscular insectivorous bird (*caprimulgus Europaeus*) akin to the American whip-poor-will.

Of course the proposition 'A is a sign of B', taken in its dispositional sense, is itself hypothetical. Indeed, it is a general or variable
hypothetical, equivalent to 'If anything A-ish occurs, something
B-ish is likely to occur'. But this proposition, however true it is,
does not occur to the mind of the sign-cognizant himself until he
reaches a degree of reflectiveness far more advanced than the one
we are now concerned with. Each particular A, as it comes, is
treated by him as a sign of B, without any consciousness of the
general rule 'If A, then probably B'. There is also, no doubt, a
general hypothetical which is true *about* the sign-cognizant: namely
that if anything A-ish is presented to him, he is prepared for an
instance of B. But again, he himself is not aware that this general
rule is true about him, even though his cognitive and practical
procedures do repeatedly exemplify it.

What we have to show is not merely that there is always an
if-then relation between sign and significate—an obvious but irrelevant truth—but that there is sometimes an if-then relation within
the significate itself, where A signifies not just B, but B *if* X, or *if*
X *then* B. That is what I meant just now by 'conditional or hypothetical signification'. Can there be such a thing?

For adult human beings, of course, there can. The sound of the
clock striking eleven is a sign for me that I shall shortly get a cup
of coffee, *if* the milkman has come. But this, it may be said, is no
longer pure sign-cognition, but sign-cognition aided, and modified,
by verbalized thinking. Can there be hypothetical or conditional
signification when the sign-cognition is pre-verbal? I shall try to
show that there can.

Here again, the crucial and most fortunate fact is that some signs
are weak. If a world in which all signs were cast-iron ones, infallibly
reliable, sign-cognition could never rise to the level of *if*. But where
signs are weak, or mutually conflicting, there is more hope. It may
be noticed that where the significate is a determinable, as it often is,
each of the alternative determinates is less strongly signified than
the determinable itself. The determinates divide between them the
probability which the sign-event confers on the determinable, and
there may be nothing in the sign-situation which favours any one
of them more than any other. If so, the probability of any one
determinate may be quite small, even when the probability of the
determinable is 1. In the terminology I have been using, a

determinate, taken singly, may be quite weakly signified, even when the determinable is signified with maximal or 'cast-iron' strength. The noise I hear may signify infallibly that a motor-car of some sort is entering the street, but it signifies very weakly that a Rolls-Royce is there and equally weakly that a Morris Minor is there.

The importance of this point may be seen if we consider the example of the cat and the mouse once more. Let us suppose that the present position of the mouse signifies infallibly that he will be in rapid motion in a short time. Even so, that he will be moving in just *this* direction, with just *this* velocity, and just $\frac{1}{10}$ of a second hence, is signified very weakly. Now the cat is prepared for any one of many possible mouse-movements. We have seen that this preparedness for alternatives is one of the characteristic features of animal (and human) vigilance. But this is not all. The cat is prepared to jump in the appropriate direction, whichever of these alternatives is realized. He is ready to spring to the left *if* the mouse goes to the left, and ready to spring to the right *if* the mouse goes to the right. By this I do not merely mean that if A_1 were to occur, the cat would be ready to do B_1, and if A_2 were to occur he would be ready to do B_2 instead. I want to suggest that the 'if' is so to speak *within* what he is prepared for. He *is* ready, now, to do B_1 if A_1 occurs, and also ready to do B_2 instead, if A_2 occurs. Of course this 'conditional signification' is more practical than theoretical. Formulated in words, the significate would be more like a conditional imperative than a conditional proposition. What is signified by the sign is 'if A_1 occurs, then B_1 is to be done, if A_2 occurs, then B_2 is to be done . . . etc.' rather than 'if A_1 occurs, then B_1 will occur, if A_2 occurs, then B_2 will occur . . . etc.'. Nevertheless, an *if* does enter into the situation, even though it is a practical *if* rather than a purely cognitive one. Practical reason, rather than theoretical, is Pussy's strong point.

Sign-cognition is so closely connected with action that it is not easy to find an example of conditional signification which is purely cognitive. Perhaps we may find something approximating to it when several signs are in mind together, but only one of them is actually being experienced, or at any rate not all of them. This may happen in various ways. Let us suppose for simplicity that there are just two signs in mind, one actually experienced, the other not. First, they may be *co-significant* signs. Both are signs of the same significate, and they strengthen each other, though each by itself is weak. The water in the mountain stream is high this evening and is running fast. There will very likely be a flood in the valley tomorrow, *if* it rains heavily tonight. High water this evening is a sign of a flood tomorrow; a weak one, because sometimes the water-level subsides in the course of the subsequent twelve hours, and then no flood follows. Heavy rain tonight is also a sign of a flood to-morrow; again a weak one by itself, because a flood follows some-times but not always. It all depends how high the water-level is already. But when *both* the two signs occur together, or within a shortish interval, they strengthen each other. The two together, heavy rain in the night *and* a water-level already high, are a pretty strong sign of a flood tomorrow. Long experience of the English Lake District has made me familiar with such significations as these. So when I look at the stream this evening, it naturally occurs to me that there will be a flood tomorrow, *if* it rains heavily in the night. Conversely, I may notice that it is raining heavily in the night, though I did not look at the stream this evening. Then again it occurs to me that there will be a flood tomorrow, *if* the water-level is already high.

Secondly, there may be what I will call *chain-signification*, where A is a sign for me of B, and B in turn is a sign for me of C. We must suppose again that one of these signs has actually been observed and the other not. A has been observed, but B has not, or at least not yet. (We will assume that the A–B signification is a relatively long-range one.) So far, B has only been signified, not actually observed. But, being in mind, it suggests its own significate C. At the pre-verbal level, such chains of signification cannot be carried far. But they do seem to occur. And when the initial sign is a weak one, so that there is room for doubt whether its significate will, in fact, occur, a feeling of *if* arises. The occurrence of A brings to mind not just B, but *if* B, then C. It has rained continuously from 10 a.m. till lunch-time. This is a sign, though a somewhat weak one, that it will go on raining all day. And a whole day of rain is a sign, in turn, that the lane will be very muddy for some time after. Suppos-ing I have some interest in the lane (say, because it is my favourite route for an evening walk) it may occur to me, when I look out of the window at lunch-time and see the rain pouring down, that *if* the rain goes on all the afternoon the lane will be exceedingly muddy in the evening.

But there is a difficulty here. It may appear at first sight that the relation of signification is *transitive*. Surely when A is a sign for me of B, and B is a sign for me of C, then A is a sign for me of C? In that case the observation of A will arouse a categorical belief in C, with no 'if' about it. This is the situation which Lord Russell calls 'telescoping'.

Signification *is* transitive when both the component sign-relations are maximally strong. If A makes the occurrence of B certain, and B makes the occurrence of C certain, then A does make the occurrence of B certain. Again, if I *take* both the component sign-relations to be maximally strong (whether they are so or not) then for me the signification is transitive. When A is presented, I shall believe categorically that C is going to occur. But where there is any weakness in either of the component signs, and this weakness is appreciated by the sign-cognizant himself, the situation is different. The chain as a whole is no stronger than its weakest link; and it is no longer true that because A signifies B, and B signifies C, A therefore signifies C. What specially concerns us now is the case where the *initial* link A–B is weak. Let us consider an example in which it is very weak indeed.

We are in an aircraft, and we find that we have very little petrol left. This gives us just a chance of reaching the aerodrome ten miles away, where we can be sure of making a safe landing. Here the initial sign A is a very weak one. It confers a very small though finite probability on its significate B. The second sign relation, B–C, may be as strong as you please. Getting to the aerodrome may absolutely ensure a safe landing. But however strong its second link is, the chain-signification as a whole, A–B–C, is still a very weak one. It must be at least as weak as its initial link A–B. Now in such a situation few of us would categorically believe that we shall make a safe landing. Obviously we should not be rationally justified in believing this. But the important point is that we are not in fact likely to believe it. The state of mind we are likely to be in might be represented thus: 'A, so just possibly B; and *if* B, then C'. And in any chain signification where the initial sign-relation is weak enough to arouse some doubt in us, the significate brought to mind by the initial sign is likely to be '*if* B then C' or 'C *on the condition that* B'.

Unfortunately, both the logic and the psychology of weak chain-signification are made more difficult to understand by our custom of formulating sign-relations in indicative sentences: A *is* a sign of B, and B *is* a sign of C. We easily confuse this timeless *is* with the temporal *is* of 'is actually signifying'. But though A (in the case supposed) is actually observed and is actually signifying B, it is not true that B is actually signifying C. B has not happened yet, and it may very well not happen at all. The truth is only that *if* B were to happen, it *would* signify C. And the sign-cognizant himself is aware of this when the occurrence of B is doubtful enough, i.e. when the initial sign-relation A–B is weak enough. This prevents him from 'telescoping' the two sign-relations into one, in the way described by Lord Russell. If the initial sign is weak enough, he does not treat A as though it were a direct sign of C. Instead, he has the feeling of 'if' or conditionality. He does not expect C, but only C *if* B.

It is true that with very short-range signs such telescoping may occur, even when the initial sign-relation is less than maximally strong. A logician, of course, would say that it ought not to occur, but as a matter of psychological fact it does. When I see a grim-looking individual on the other side of the street pointing a revolver at me, with his finger on the trigger, this is a sign that he is about to fire. And his firing the revolver, *if* he does fire it, would in turn signify the almost immediate arrival of a high-velocity bullet in the place where I am standing. The initial sign-relation is not, of course, maximally strong. People do sometimes point revolvers at other people without firing them. The man may be bluffing. Even if he is not, he may have forgotten to load the revolver, or the trigger-mechanism may have gone wrong. All I am rationally justified in expecting is that he is very likely to fire, and *if* he does, the bullet will arrive here. And even this conditional sign-cognition would not be an absolutely cast-iron one. The second sign-relation, like the first, is less than maximally strong. Even people with faces like that sometimes miss their aim when they do fire. He is very likely to fire, and *if* he does, the bullet will arrive *if* he has taken good aim. But I do not consider these *ifs*. They do not even occur to me. As soon as I see him pointing the revolver at me, I conclude categorically that the bullet is coming, and prostrate myself immediately on the pavement. Where the signs are such very short-range ones, a certain amount of weakness in them makes no difference. Something much less than cast-iron strength is strong enough for me.

Moreover, such telescoping of short-range signs is not confined to cases where one's own safety is concerned. You are watching some men cutting down a tree. You are a good hundred yards away, and in no danger at all. The men have all but cut through the tree trunk. They are already grasping the rope. This is a sign that the tree is about to fall. And the falling of a tree is in turn a sign of a loud scrunching crash. The crash, of course, will only occur *if* the tree falls. And the tree may not fall after all. The cut the men have made in the trunk may not be quite big enough. They may not pull hard enough, or the rope may break. But here again, this *if* will not occur to your mind. You categorically expect to hear the crash. To use the same symbolism as before: A, which is already occurring, is a sign of B; and B, *if* it occurs will be a sign of C. But on perceiving A, you treat it as a *direct* sign of B, as though the sign-relation were transitive.

Such telescoping of short-range signs has an obvious biological utility, at any rate where both the two component sign-relations are pretty strong ones. When A is a short range and pretty strong sign of B, and B, if it occurs, will be a short-range and pretty strong sign of C, it is biologically useful to treat the sign relation as transitive, and to be prepared for C as soon as B is observed; much as one would be, if B itself were already being observed, instead of merely signified. Treating A as *equivalent* to B (for that is what it comes to) may lead to error sometimes. But provided that our expectation of C is correct more often than not, there are great advantages in its unhesitating and non-conditional character. It is better to be ready sometimes for an imminent event which does not happen, than to be unready for one which does. In such circumstances a nice weighing of chances and a consideration of *ifs* are luxuries we cannot afford.

But though telescoping of signs does sometimes occur, the important point is that sometimes it does not. When the initial sign is long-range and weak, chain signification does give rise to hypothetical thinking, or at least to a feeling of *if*, though, of course, at the level of mental development we are considering there is no explicit conception of 'conditionality'. And the same thing happens in what I called co-signification, where two weak and long-range signs strengthen each other, but only one of them has so far occurred.

In both cases, the feeling of *if* arises through the experience of questioning or doubting. It never could arise at all if we had not learned to distinguish weak signs from strong ones; but as we have seen, even animals can learn to do this in matters which are of bio-logical interest to them. Given that A is for us a weak sign of B and a sufficiently long-range one, our thought of B, which the occurrence of A arouses, will be tinged with a feeling of doubt or unsureness. The B-recognizing capacity is sub-activated by the perceptual sign A. We are prepared or ready for an instance of B in the way described before. That is the form which the 'thought of' B takes at this level of mental development. But the preparedness has a flavour of 'just in case' about it. It would be a mistake to say that we actually recall past examples in which A has not been followed by B. Our appreciation of the weakness of a weak sign is nothing so conscious and explicit as that. Yet we do have a memory of such past examples, in the sense that they have left a permanent effect upon us. We do not recall them, but we are not as we would be if we had never observed them at all. Our preparedness for an instance of B (e.g. for a flood tomorrow) has something less than the full weight of our past experience behind it. And this fact manifests itself in consciousness by a feeling of doubt, and in behaviour by hesitation. We *are* prepared for an instance of B, but it is a question-ing or doubting preparedness. If B is something we greatly want, or greatly fear, the feeling of doubt is intensified, and has the affective tone of acute anxiety.

Nevertheless, a feeling of 'Is it going to happen after all?', even though raised to painful intensity, is not yet an *if*. For *if* to arise, something more is needed. In old-fashioned terminology, the idea of B which is already in mind must bring to mind other associated ideas.

But to say this, though it is true (if the 'Idea' terminology may still be allowed to pass for the present) is still not enough.[1] The association might be merely association by resemblance, or by contrast, and then no *if* would emerge. Thus the thought of a flood tomorrow, suggested by the present perceptual sign, high-water level and strong current, may merely bring to mind other floods one has seen elsewhere. It may even bring to mind, by contrast, a memory of seeing this very stream-bed completely dry a few years ago, and of walking dry-shod among the stones at the bottom. Here there is no *if*, but only at most an *and* or a *but*.

Indeed, the association might even be association by contiguity, and still no *if* would arise. The thought of a flood might recall the mewing cry of a buzzard which I heard when I last saw a flood in this valley, or the difficulties I had in trying to paint a picture of the swirling waters. It is only one special sort of association by contiguity which will do, the sort which arises from experience of constant or nearly constant conjunctions; in short the special sort of associative linkage which there is between a sign and its significate. The idea of B, already in mind because of the perceptual sign A, must bring to mind *other sign-relations* into which B enters either as sign or as significate. What is brought to mind must be either another sign which would also signify B (co-signification) or another significate which B, if it occurs, would signify (chain-signification). It is this special sort of associative linkage, where the significate-idea recalls other sign-relations into which it itself enters, which gives rise to an *if*.

We may notice that it is association controlled by a sense of *relevance*. It is precisely the absence of such control which we are pointing to, when we say that many associations are 'random' or 'casual' (for example the association which recalls the buzzard's cry to mind when I think of a flood), though from a causal point of view they, of course, are not random at all, since they certainly exemplify psychological laws. The relevance which here concerns us is inductive relevance. The thought of C is relevant, in this sense, to the thought of B if there is a relation of inductive probabilification between B and C, in either direction. It is obvious that sign-cognition, even in its most elementary forms, is controlled by a feeling for or sensitivity to inductive relevance, or at least by a

[1] Cf. Hume's *Treatise*, Book I, Part 3, Section 9, 'Of the effects of other relations and other habits' (i.e. of relations other than constant conjunction).

tendency to notice and retain inductively relevant relations between observed events.

Let us now try to describe the situation without using the idea terminology. In the language I have suggested, 'ideas' are equivalent to recognitional capacities, and association of ideas is association of two or more recognitional capacities. The essential point is that when one recognitional capacity is activated (whether completely or partially) this in turn tends to sub-activate others.[1] So far, then, what we have is this. A perceptual sign sub-activates the recognitional capacity B, and this in turn, by association, sub-activates the recognitional capacity C; the association being of the special sort which is produced by experience of constant, or more or less constant, conjunctions. But, it may be objected, this only shows how we come to think of B *and* C, for example of continued rain *and* the muddiness of the lane; and we are still as far as ever from *if* B, then C, or C *on condition that* B.

Perhaps we may come closer to them if we consider Hume's account of inductive inference, i.e. of sign-cognition. Such inference, he says, consists in a mental transition which has a special sort of 'feel' about it, a feeling of necessity. And he holds that this feeling is the source of the idea of necessary connection.

It may be doubted whether this feeling of necessity is an invariable feature of such inferences. When I see the sun setting, I expect that darkness will come; and usually I expect it without any feeling at all. But Hume's feeling does occur when the significate is for any reason disliked. It is a feeling of 'whether one likes it or not'; no matter what my wishes are, the thing is going to happen. Perhaps I have a strong wish for daylight to continue, because my head-lamps have gone wrong and I am still twenty miles from home. Then the transition of mind from the perceptual sign, sunset, to the significate, darkness, does have a feel of necessity about it. Whether I like it or not, darkness is coming soon. And given the strong opposing wish, the feeling still occurs even when the sign is relatively weak. (In this part of his discussion, Hume takes no account of the difference between strong and weak signs.) I suddenly notice a cyclist come wobbling out of a side turning thirty yards

[1]Bradley was not far wrong when he remarked that 'association marries only universals'. But, of course, it is not just universals subsisting *in re* which are thus married, and still less universals subsisting *ante rem*. By 'universals' Bradley here meant just concepts.

ahead. This is a sign, though a weak one, of an accident. And the thought of a slightly probable and by no means certain accident comes to me with a feel of 'whether you like it or not', because collisions with cyclists are things I very much dislike. If I had been as indifferent to them as I am to colliding with a leaf which drifts across the road, the 'feeling of necessity' would not have occurred.

But, of course, the Humian transition of the mind, with the feeling of necessity which sometimes accompanies it, is not quite the one which now concerns us. It is a transition of mind from a sign-percept ('impression') to a signified idea. And this, put into words, corresponds to 'because . . . therefore' rather than 'if . . . then'. As Hume himself insists, he is discussing *inference* (inductive or significational inference). What we have to discuss at present is not inference, but the awareness of an implication or significational connection. In Hume's own impression-idea terminology, we are concerned not with the transition of mind from impression to idea, but with the transition from one idea to another. It is plain that any creature which is capable of sign-cognition at all can get as far as 'because . . . therefore' or '*p*, so of course *q*'. The question is, how it can get as far as 'if *p* then *q*', or '*q* on condition that *p*'. Our examples have suggested that some sign-cognizants can do it, once they have learned to distinguish weak signs from strong ones. But how?

Let us consider chain-signification again. A is a sign for me of B, and B is a sign for me of C. A is actually perceived. The idea of B, therefore, is already in mind, brought there by this perceptual sign. I have a standing tendency to infer C from B, because of their constant or fairly constant conjunction in my past experience. (That is only another way of saying that B is a *sign* for me of C.) This tendency is aroused in some degree by the fact that B is in mind already. I have an inclination to make this inference here and now. But my inclination is held in check, or inhibited, by my sense of the *weakness* of the sign-relation A–B. I am prepared for or ready for an instance of B, but only with some doubt or hesitation. The inference from B to C is suggested, but not made. Out of this conflict-situation, where an inclination to draw a sign-inference is inhibited, and yet not abolished, by the doubtfulness of its premise, *if* emerges. An idea is still felt as 'pointing towards' its significate, though an actual inference from the one to the other is inhibited.

To put it otherwise, we become aware that B is still *a sign of* C, though it is not now *signifying* C, because no actual instance of B is yet there, and perhaps is not going to be. And as we have seen already 'ϕ is a sign of ψ' is a hypothetical proposition. It is equivalent to 'An instance of ϕ *would* (not does) signify an instance of ψ'. And this 'would' involves an 'if'. *If* an instance of ϕ were to occur, then an instance of ψ would probably occur. The perceived rain signifies, but only doubtfully, that rain will continue for the rest of the day. Continued rain *would* signify mud in the lane this evening. An inclination to expect mud is aroused, and yet inhibited.

Something like this happens in co-signification too. But here the inclination which is inhibited is an inclination to infer from something else to B, rather than from B to something else. The idea of a flood tomorrow is signified, but only doubtfully, by the sight of the high-water level tonight. This idea brings to mind the thought of heavy rain tonight, which *would* likewise signify a flood tomorrow. Here I have an *inclination* to make the inference 'heavy rain tonight, so flood tomorrow', and here again it is inhibited. But this time it is inhibited just by the fact that no heavy rain is as yet perceived, and for all I know it is not going to be.

This brings us to another way in which a feeling of *if* can arise. There is something which may be called the *if* of yearning. Let us begin with a rather fantastic example. If only I had the wings of a dove, I should fly away and be happy. The point of this, of course, is that I have *not* the wings of a dove, and know very well that I have not. The idea of having dove-like wings is very manifestly *dis*satisfied by all that I see and feel when I examine my bodily frame. Yet I do as it were toy with the sign-inference 'I have the wings of a dove, so I can fly away whenever I like'. I have some inclination to make this inference (in a dream I might actually make it). The inclination is strongly inhibited by the manifest falsity of its premise; yet the inclination is still there, and remains there, because the significate is so strongly wished for, and continues to suggest to my mind the sign which *would* make it true or probable. To take a less fantastic illustration: It is Thursday afternoon, and all the shops are shut. You are very hungry, and through the window of a baker's shop you see a large pile of appetizing currant-buns. It will then occur to you that 'if only' the shop were open, you would be able to eat a bun. This 'if only' is again the *if* of yearning. The openness of the shop *would* be a sign of almost immediate eating. Your desire to eat, intensified by the sight of the buns, has made you inclined to draw the sign-inference 'I am going in, so I shall shortly be eating'. The inclination is inhibited by the only too evident fact that you cannot go in. But it does not disappear altogether, because your interest in the significate is so strong. To judge from behaviour, this 'yearning if', or some approximation to it, is found sometimes even in animals; as when the cat, on a chilly night, stands mewing outside the window, attracted by the sight of a cosy fire which he sees inside but cannot reach.

It can now be seen that there is after all a certain parallel between Hume's feeling of necessity and the feeling of 'if' which we have been trying to describe. Hume's feeling of necessity corresponds to 'because' and not to 'if'. But the two feelings are alike in this, that both of them arise from a conflict-situation. In Hume's case, the sign-inference actually occurs; but it does have to *conflict* with desire (though he did not see this himself) if the feeling of necessity is to be felt. Otherwise the transition of mind from sign-impression to significate-idea occurs without any feeling at all. In our case, the sign-inference does not actually occur. But the inclination to make it does occur, and this inclination conflicts with something that inhibits it. In chain signification, it conflicts with the weakness of the initial and already actualized sign-situation, whose significate is accepted only with doubt and hesitation. In co-signification, and also in 'yearning', it conflicts with the present falsification of the premise from which we have the inclination to infer. Hume's case might be symbolized thus: 'q is too bad to be true? All the same, p, therefore q'. Our case might be symbolized thus: 'p, therefore q? No! not-p, or quite probably not-p'.

It may also be noticed that both these feelings, the feeling of *if* as well as Hume's feeling of necessity, require a certain 'sense of reality' on the subject's part. We can conceive of a conscious being who is just incapable of believing what is too bad to be true. A motorist twenty miles from home, with no headlights, might be quite unable to believe that darkness was coming when he saw the sun set. The sign-inference might be totally inhibited by his strong desire for the falsity of the significate. Again, there might be a creature which did actually draw the sign-inference 'p ..., so q'

whenever q was suggested to its mind, even when p was empirically falsified. The mere thought of black clouds might cause it to believe that rain was imminent, even though the sky was in fact cloudless.

It is plain from these examples that the 'sense of reality' is by no means perfect in ourselves. (Perhaps it is more nearly perfect in animals.) We do sometimes avoid making even the most obvious sign-inferences, because the significate is too bad to be true. And we do sometimes make sign-inferences, even not very obvious ones, from the mere thought of the sign, even though the sign-idea is manifestly falsified by all the available empirical facts. We will not believe that rain is coming, though the barometer is falling, the wind is backing to south-west, and the air feels damp. On the other hand, the mere thought of a signpost saying 'to Oxford' suffices to persuade us that we are on the right road, though all the signposts we have seen for the past twenty minutes have borne the name of Wolverhampton. Such instances of non-empirical thinking are not so very common in waking life. But they suggest that the human mind is not perhaps entirely at home in this world, and that its native element, so to speak, would be a world in which everything desired was *ipso facto* fulfilled, and all propositions verified by the mere fact of being thought of. In dreams we do live in a world of somewhat this kind; thought and desire are uncontrolled by sensation, and the 'sense of reality' ceases or almost ceases to operate. Perhaps dreaming is more natural to the human mind than waking life is.

Another point may be noticed. In the Humian feeling of necessity there is an element of self-consciousness. When we put it in words, we can hardly help using the word 'I'. This is going to happen, whether *I* like it or not. Our own wishes come into view as something different from and contrasted with 'hard facts'. If facts were always soft (as in the hypothetical world mentioned just now), if they always accommodated themselves to our desires, we should have no feeling of contrast between what *we* want and a world 'over against us'. The objective, it has been said, is the objectionable.[1]

---

[1] This was a saying of an Oxford Idealist philosopher, the late Professor J. A. Smith.

In the feeling of 'if', which I have tried to describe, there is likewise something of self-consciousness. Here again the hard facts clash with something in me, this time an inclination to infer; and just by this clash, my thought-operations reveal themselves as something other than the processes which go on in the perceptible world. Indeed, there is already something of self-consciousness in the primitive 'not', the experience of falsification. Just because some idea is dissatisfied by or clashes with perceptible fact, it becomes clear that ideas are something other than perceptible facts, and that the world revealed by sense-perception is not the whole of what there is. This discovery, again, would not be made if every idea was verified as soon as it was entertained. Here again the objective is the objectionable. It is what breaks in upon our thought processes and refutes our beliefs.

Thus the 'sense of reality' seems to be a necessary condition of even the dimmest kind of self-consciousness. A certain humility is needed, a readiness to accept the control of empirical fact; though this humility is also what we call 'hard headedness'. If the sense of reality did not operate (or to the extent that it does not) subjectivity would, of course, still be there. But the subject himself would have no means of recognizing it for what it is. It would present itself to him only in a 'projected' form, as the way in which this or that *appeared* to him. Such 'projected' subjectivity of course occurs now. My hatred or liking for Jones presents itself as a kind of quality of Jones himself, and not as an emotional attitude of my own towards him. I just 'see him as' horrid or nice. There is something similar when ice looks cold. An idea or belief of mine presents itself as a quasi-sensible quality of the object. This projected subjectivity presumably occurs at all levels of mental life, even in those creatures, if there are any, which are incapable of the experience of falsification. But the subject himself is incapable of discovering that there *is* anything subjective about these 'projected' qualities until he has had the experience of falsification. Until then, he has no means of distinguishing the way things appear to him from the way they in fact are; the difference is there, but it cannot be brought home to him. If thought begins as soon as there is the possibility of falsity, self-consciousness begins when falsity is detected. By finding that facts are other than they were thought to be, by the experience of NOT, one becomes aware that there is a difference between thought and the world. The distinction between subjective and objective was there all along, but now at last it is realized—felt at least, if not yet known—and self-consciousness has begun to dawn.

In this chapter I have tried to show that the logical notions of *not, or* and *if* play a part in sign-cognition; and likewise the logical notion of degrees of inductive probability, in so far as sign-cognizants distinguish between stronger signs and weaker ones. I am not, of course, suggesting that sign-cognizants have anything like an explicit concept of Negation or Disjunction or Conditionality or Inductive Probability. That is quite out of the question at the pre-verbal level of cognition which we have been considering. Even word-users, unless they are unusually reflective and sophisticated, can hardly be said to have explicit concepts of *not* and *if*. To be a verbal thinker, one does not have to be a logician. We can even conceive of a language, and quite a complicated one, in which there were no logical *words* corresponding to our words 'not', 'or' and 'if'. Their functions might be performed by inflections, by pauses between utterances, by gestures, or even by special tones of voice. 'He comes, I go' might be equivalent to 'if he comes, I go'. Instead of saying 'not *p*' one might just say '*p*' in a special tone of voice, or with a shrug of the shoulders. To negate a written sentence, one might write it in red ink, or one might write it upside down, as Ramsey has pointed out.[1]

I do, however, suggest that in sign-cognition, even when it is wholly pre-verbal, the sign-cognizant is sensitive to the *differences* which are indicated (in a sufficiently developed language) by such pairs of words as 'negative, affirmative', 'categorical, disjunctive', 'categorical, hypothetical', 'more probable, less probable'. He is able to *distinguish* between the sort of situation which word-users describe in an affirmative sentence, e.g. when an expectation is verified, and the sort of situation they describe in a negative sentence, e.g. when an expectation is falsified. Likewise, he is able to distinguish between the situations which word-users would describe by using categorical sentences, and those they would describe by using disjunctive or again conditional sentences; and between those in which they would say 'it is (inductively) very likely that . . .' and those in which they would say 'it is (inductively) quite likely that . . .' or

[1] F. P. Ramsey, *Foundations of Mathematics,* p. 146.

'there is (inductively) just a chance that . . .'. Even animals take account of these differences in their actions, and in the state of preparedness-to-act which I have called vigilance. Thus there is a *logic* of sign-cognition; as we should expect if sign-cognition is a form of thinking, however humble.

CHAPTER VI

SIGNS AND SYMBOLS

IT is often said that we must distinguish two senses of the word 'meaning': meaning in the *sign* sense (e.g. black clouds mean rain) and meaning in the *symbol* sense (e.g. the word 'rain' means rain). Meaning in the symbol sense is not confined to words; other entities and occurrences, for instance gestures, diagrams, pictures, mental images, are also supposed to have meaning in this sense.

In this chapter we shall discuss the relation between signs and symbols, or between meaning in the sign sense and meaning in the symbol sense. It is, of course, pretty clear that not all signs are symbols. The black clouds can hardly be said to symbolize the rain of which they are a sign. But still it might be true that all symbols are signs; a symbol might be a special sort of sign—what sort, we shall have to consider. On the other hand, it might be that symbolization and signification are irreducibly different; or if there are some resemblances between them, the resemblances might be less important than the differences.

What is the relation between these two senses of the word 'meaning'? That is what the question comes to. Why should a student of the Theory of Knowledge concern himself with a question so trifling and pedantic as this? Whichever way we answer it, will our answer throw any light on the epistemology of thinking? We may hope that it will. It has already been argued that sign-cognition, the taking of one event or state of affairs as a sign of another, is a form of thinking. There can be no doubt that meaning in the sign sense is an epistemologically important notion. Now symbolic cognition is also a form of thinking. Notoriously we very often think 'in' words or images. And these, it is said, are symbols. How is this sort of thinking related to the sort which we have already discussed under the name of sign-cognition? In what ways do the two sorts of thinking resemble or differ from each other? Until we have discussed this question we cannot be clear about the nature of either.

Indeed, the question about the relation between meaning in the sign sense and meaning in the symbol sense is even more important than this. For some philosophers hold that thinking *is* nothing but cognition by means of symbols. If our conclusions in the last chapter are right, this extreme view must be rejected; there must be some thinking which is non-symbolic or pre-symbolic (as when black clouds are taken as a sign of rain). But it might still be said that such thinking is primitive or undeveloped or low-grade thinking. And it might still be said that mature or fully developed or high-grade thinking is nothing but cognition by means of symbols. This point may be put in another way. Thinking may plausibly be equated with *conceptual* cognition. I tried to show in the last chapter that concepts or abstract ideas do enter into sign-cognition. But it may be argued that the characteristic of 'being conceptual' admits of degrees, and even that the possessing of a concept admits of degrees (the lowest degree of it would consist in the bare capacity of recognizing instances). Thus one form of cognition might be more conceptual, or more fully conceptual, than another. Now perhaps we do not fully possess any concept until we have acquired the capacity to use symbols; and perhaps conceptual cognition, in its complete and fully developed form, consists just in the exercising of this capacity—in the actual using of symbols.

The doctrine that thinking is symbolic cognition has been accepted in one form or another by many philosophers. Some of these philosophers have not paid much attention to sign cognition, and therefore have stated the doctrine in an unrestricted form. But they would not be seriously troubled if it were pointed out that sign-cognition too is a form of thinking, provided we admit (as we can) that it is thinking of a low-grade or undeveloped sort. The thesis that all fully developed thinking is symbolic cognition is too plausible to be ignored. And if we are to do justice to this 'symbolistic' conception of thinking, we must clearly consider the relation between symbols and signs. For example, could it be said that symbols are a species of signs, and that meaning in the symbol sense is just a special case of meaning in the sign sense?

Before we discuss this question, we must point out that the Symbolistic Theory is using the word *symbol* in a very wide sense. The term covers not only words and complexes of words, e.g.

K

sentences, descriptive phrases. It also covers what could be called pictorial symbols, whether public or private: for example, pictures, diagrams, mental images. In addition, it covers gestures, both imitative gestures ('dumb show') and deictic gestures, e.g. pointing at something with one's finger or one's walking stick; and quite elaborate pieces of non-verbal behaviour, for example ceremonial or ritual actions, would likewise be counted as symbols.

Again, in ordinary English we sometimes distinguish between symbols and words. In a treatise on Algebra, for example, or Mathematical Logic, there are many symbols but very few words. A symbolic logician is one who eschews the use of words: for example he writes '⊃' instead of 'implies' and '∼' instead of 'not'. But in the Symbolistic Theory of thinking, no such distinction is drawn between symbols and words. Words themselves are regarded as symbols; indeed, they are regarded as the most important of all symbols. It will accordingly be pointless to say that an algebraical or logical book is written in symbols, because that would be true of all books whatever. We must say instead that they are written in *non-verbal* symbols.

Moreover, in this theory no antithesis is drawn between the symbolic and the literal. We sometimes say of a myth, for example the myth of Prometheus, that it is to be taken symbolically and not literally. If taken literally it is false, if taken symbolically it may be true. We might say the same of the story of the Fall in the Book of *Genesis*; it is not to be understood literally, but it symbolizes certain important truths about human nature. We might say the same of the Social Contract theory of the state. The language of mystics, we say, is symbolic and not literal. The things they wish to tell us cannot be said literally at all; therefore they have to be said symbolically. In a rather similar way, psychotherapists tell us that dreams, hysterical actions, slips of the tongue or the pen, are symbols of unconscious wishes or unconscious mental conflicts. In the Symbolistic Theory of thinking, such statements as these would not be denied, but they would be formulated differently. A distinction would be drawn between words used literally, and words used metaphorically or analogically; but both alike would be called symbols. In some of the examples I have mentioned, it would be said perhaps that there are two layers of symbols. The words used by the author or authors of *Genesis*, or by Hobbes in the *Leviathan*, directly symbolize certain actions which did not in fact take place. The actions described, if they did occur, would in turn symbolize certain propositions about human nature: the inherent wickedness of all human beings, or the dependence of government upon a tacit agreement between the persons who are governed. For instance, the story of the Fall, or Hobbes' account of the Social Contract might be acted on the stage as a Miracle play; and then the actions of the players would directly (though non-verbally) symbolize the propositions about human nature which those authors had in mind.

Thus the Symbolistic theory of thinking does use the word 'symbol' in a 'stretched' or extended sense, to cover some events or entities, or types of events or entities, which would not ordinarily be called symbols. But this is no reason for rejecting the theory out of hand. It could quite well maintain that the resemblances between all these entities (or rather between the functions which they have in conceptual cognition) are much more important than the differences. In so far as words, images, gestures, etc., are 'things we think with' or 'think in', we need a common term to cover them all. 'Symbol' is the most natural term to use for this purpose, and it is not easy to find a substitute. Likewise, we think in or with such written marks as '$\supset$' or '$\sim$' or '$\sqrt{}$' just as we think in or with such words as 'implies' 'not' 'square root of'. And we think in or with myths and parables, as well as literal descriptions. We have to, when our vocabulary does not provide the literal descriptions we need. On this ground, 'not' has as good a right to be called a symbol as '$\sim$' has; and a literal description symbolizes something as much as a myth or parable. Moreover, this stretched sense of the word 'symbol' is not so stretched as to be unintelligible to the ordinary speaker. We cannot say that an old word is being used in a completely new way, as perhaps the words 'heat' and 'light' are in physics. On the contrary, when someone is told for the first time that thinking is symbolic cognition, he knows at once what kind of theory he is being asked to accept, though he may or may not accept it. In any case, what is called 'ordinary usage' cannot be reduced to a set of cast-iron rules. Such rules as there are in ordinary language are constantly being stretched and modified. If such stretchings occur in the barrack-room and the bar, why may they not occur in the writings of philosophers?

*   *   *   *   *

So much for the sense in which the term 'symbol' is used, when it is said that thinking is cognition by means of symbols. It remains to mention certain distinctions which must be drawn if this theory of thinking is to be understood. The first and most celebrated of them is the distinction between type-symbols and token-symbols. There is a sense in which the same symbol can occur on many different occasions. The same word 'cat' can be uttered by you on Monday and by me on Tuesday, and by millions of other people on other occasions; and it is the same word whether it is spoken, or written, or imaged either in a visual or an auditory form. Likewise the same gesture, for instance a salute, can be made by many different people in many different times or places. Here the word 'cat' or the salute is a *type* symbol. On the other hand, there is also a sense in which no symbol can recur. In this sense, when you and I both salute the Commanding Officer, there are two salutes; you make yours and I make mine, and no one can make the same salute twice. Similarly when you say 'cat' and I say 'cat' there are two different words, and no one can utter the same word twice. Here we are speaking of *token* symbols. The same type-word 'and' occurs fifty times on a certain page of print. But the printer, in making out his bill, will count these fifty printed marks as fifty different words, not as one. The shorthand writer will count in a similar way, when he claims that he can write fifty words a minute. To test his claims, you say 'cat, cat, cat . . .' to him for a minute and he writes down what you say. Then you tell him that he has only written one word in all that time. He certainly will not agree with you. The printer and the shorthand writer are concerned with *token* words.

Secondly, two different ways of using symbols are commonly distinguished. They are used descriptively or referentially, to refer to objects (in a very wide sense of the term 'object'). It is only symbols used in this way which are *true* or *false*. In a well-developed system of symbolism, it is only complex symbols which are true or false, and these complex symbols have to be constructed on a specifiable syntactical plan. Thus in a well-developed verbal symbolism only sentences can be true or false. But single words (other than purely syntactical words like 'and', 'or', 'if') can still have a referential function. Thus the word 'red' refers to a certain sort of quality, and the word 'above' to a certain sort of relation, though neither word in isolation is true or false. In a non-verbal symbolism, e.g. a symbolism of pictures or gestures, the distinction between the two sorts of symbolic reference—the sort which is true or false, and the sort which is neither—cannot be so easily drawn, if it can be drawn at all. An upward gesture of the hand could be taken to stand just for the relation 'above', but it could equally be taken as an assertion (true or false) that something is above something else. And in a primitive verbal symbolism, such as baby language or Lord Russell's Object Language,[1] a single word in isolation can likewise be true or false. Thus the word 'cat' might be equivalent to the assertion 'here is a cat'. Even adults sometimes use single words in this true-or-false way, when they are speaking a foreign language which is unfamiliar to them, or when they are suffering from aphasia.

But symbols, it is commonly said, have other functions besides this one of describing or referring. They may be used *emotively*: either to express the mental attitude of the man who uses them (this is sometimes called the expressive use), or to arouse mental attitudes such as fear, surprise, desire, in other people and even in domestic animals (this is sometimes called the evocative use).

There are some symbols which have a *purely* emotive function; for example, words like 'faugh!' or 'pshaw!' or 'Boo!', or gestures like putting one's thumb to one's nose and spreading out one's fingers, or rapidly waving one's forearm up and down to make someone go away. Adjectives like 'damnable' or 'horrid', nouns like 'cad' and 'villain' are almost purely emotive; their descriptive function, if they have any, is excessively vague. In a well-developed verbal symbolism special syntactical devices may exist whereby a complex symbol as a whole may be emotive, although some or all its constituents taken separately are not: e.g. 'What a cold day for the time of year!' or 'get out!' In practice, most emotive utterances are both expressive and evocative at the same time. In uttering them, we not only give vent to our own mental attitude, but also seek to evoke a mental attitude (e.g. an emotion or wish) in the hearer. Thus 'get out!' gives vent to my own annoyance, and tends at least to arouse in the hearer a feeling of fear and a wish to be gone. And 'What a cold day!' both expresses my own discomfort and

[1] Cf. *An Inquiry into Meaning and Truth*, ch. 4.

incites my hearer to sympathize with it, or to have a similar attitude himself.

It is important to distinguish the emotive use of symbols from their autobiographical use. When I say 'get out!' I am not *stating* that I am displeased with you and wish you to go. Otherwise my utterance would be true or false, and plainly it is neither. And when I say 'Boo!' or 'Faugh!' I am not *stating* that I am displeased by something, or feel disapproval of it. It would not be appropriate for my hearer to dispute my utterance, or question it, as he might if I had autobiographically imparted to him the results of a process of introspection. When I say 'Boo!' it will be inappropriate for him to reply 'I am surprised to hear it' or 'so am I', as he might if I had said that I was disgusted. Of course he may draw inferences from my utterance of these (token) symbols; many pieces of behaviour provide evidence from which one may infer the state of mind of the person behaving. Nevertheless I did not *tell* you anything about myself when I said 'Boo!': or if I did, it was only in that meta-phorical sense of the word 'tell' in which a cumulo-nimbus cloud may be said to 'tell us' that a thunderstorm is coming. When a schoolmaster sighs while beating a small boy, the small boy may infer, falsely, 'It hurts him more than it hurts me'. But the sigh itself is not false. The vice which the schoolmaster may be accused of is not mendacity (as if he had made a false introspective report in a psychological experiment); it is only hypocrisy, or perhaps just inadvertence. And very likely there is no vice at all. He may have sighed to express the sinking feeling he experienced at the thought of all the examination papers he has to correct between now and midnight.

Unfortunately, however, many symbols which are used refer-entially are used emotively at the same time. The statement I make (or the equivalent gesture) is true or false; but in producing these noises or gestures I am usually, and perhaps invariably, expressing my own mental attitude, and unless the remark is a piece of soliloquy it also evokes mental attitudes in others. At the very least, I express some degree of interest, however faint, in the proposition asserted, and provided you understand me (if you do not, the symbols I produce are not symbols for you) some faint degree of interest is likewise evoked in you. When I say 'it is still raining' my utterance is true or false. But it also expresses my disappointment; or perhaps my relief, if I have promised to play cricket this afternoon or to do some other distasteful thing from which rain will save me. And it has at least some effect on the mental attitude of my hearer: for example, it directs his attention to the state of the weather, and distracts it from the crossword puzzle which he was trying to solve. All statements *are* true or false, but quite often their truth or falsity is not the most important thing about them. When I say to the porter at the railway station, 'This compartment is locked' my statement is undoubtedly true or false, and we may assume that it is true. But this is not the most important thing about my utterance, as we can see by the way the porter takes it. He takes it as expressing my distress, and as a request that he should get a key and unlock the door. Even scientific and historical statements, as we know too well, may be used as propaganda. When so used, they still have a descriptive function. They are true, or at least false; but it is their evocative function which is important—the tendency they have to alter the emotional and conative states of the persons who hear them or read them.

Nevertheless, in the philosophy of thinking, it is the referential or descriptive function of symbols which concerns us, and not their emotive function, however important this may be in other fields of inquiry, such as ethics, political theory, aesthetics, sociology or anthropology.

Perhaps it may be complained that in thus concentrating on the descriptive or referential function of symbols we are guilty of a 'vicious abstraction'. It might be allowable for the student of thinking to ignore symbols which have no referential or descriptive function at all, such as 'Bah!' or 'Faugh!', or to ignore syntactical devices which have a purely emotive use, such as the imperative or optative moods of the verb. But if any symbol which does have a descriptive function, or at any rate any token symbol which has it, turns out to have an emotive function at the same time, can it be justifiable to fix our attention on the descriptive function and ignore the emotive function altogether? It might be that the emotive function was primary, and the descriptive function derivative. And thus our philosophical theory of the descriptive function of symbols would be distorted, if their emotive function were ignored.

But there is something topsy-turvy about this suggestion. The truth is just the other way round. If charges of 'vicious abstraction' are to be made, they must be made against those aestheticists and sociologists who concentrate on the emotive function of symbols, and ignore the descriptive one. It is the descriptive function which is primary, and the emotive function which is derivative. Apart from a few exclamations like 'Faugh!' or 'Bah!', symbols are only able to express and evoke emotions or conations because they refer to or describe something. To suppose otherwise is to misconceive the nature of emotion and conation. Emotions and conations are directed towards something, whether real or fictitious. They have objects, as some philosophers put it, or 'accusatives' as others have said. One cannot be just afraid or surprised. One is afraid *of* something. (The psychologically minded reader will notice that this is true of 'unconscious' fears and wishes, as well as 'conscious' ones; here too one wishes *for* something, and is afraid *of* something, though one does not know what that something is.) It follows that cognition is not just an accompaniment of emotion and conation, but an essential constituent of them. With some emotions, for example animal rage or animal terror, the cognition is perceptual. One is enraged with, or terrified at, what one actually sees or touches or hears. And these perhaps are the only emotions which *purely* emotive symbols (such as 'faugh!' or 'bah!') can express and evoke, because the object of them does not need to be described; the context of the utterance (or of the equivalent gestures) shews sufficiently what that object is. But with all other emotions the object of them is something which is wholly or partially 'absent' at the time when the emotion occurs. And the same is true of conations. What I am afraid of or wish for is something which has not yet happened, and even something merely possible, which may not in fact happen at all. I am afraid that the dog will bite me, though it has not bitten me yet and perhaps is never going to. I want to get out of the room when I am in it, not when I am out of it. Such reference to the future and the possible, as opposed to the present and actual, is conceptual and not perceptual cognition. It is thinking. According to the theory we are to examine, it is cognition by means of symbols. And symbols, when they are instruments of cognition, are being used descriptively. Unless they were so used, they could not also be used emotively, to express or evoke emotions and conations towards the objects thus described. Their emotive function is, so to speak, parasitic upon their descriptive function, however useful, or noxious, this parasitic growth may be.

Finally, there are two other distinctions to be considered. Symbols may be used either publicly or privately; and they may be used either as instruments of communication or as instruments of thought. Neither distinction is quite so simple as it looks, and the two distinctions are not equivalent with each other, though often treated as if they were.

Let us begin with the distinction between public and private. I speak aloud, or write words on paper; I draw pictures or diagrams with a pencil, or 'draw things in the air' by movements of my hand; I make gestures with my arm, or enact a piece of dumb show. All these are public symbols. On the other hand, I may also talk sub-vocally by means of incipient movements of the speech organs without making any sound. Again, instead of speaking or writing, I may use verbal imagery (visual, auditory or kinaesthetic), and visual or kinaesthetic images may be substituted for the gesture or the dumb show. Again, I may think of a thunder-clap or the bark of a dog by means of an auditory image, or of velvet by means of a tactual image of the 'feel' of it; and some people, though not all, can think of petrol or castor oil by means of an olfactory image, or of kippers and onions by means of gustatory ones. All these would be called private symbols.

But the distinction between 'private' and 'public' is not altogether clear. It is not even certain that images are wholly private; at any rate some supernormal occurrences studied by psychical researchers suggest that an image may sometimes be public to two or more minds, and that the privacy which images normally have is merely a *de facto* privacy, not privacy in principle. Again, sub-vocal speech is a difficult borderline case; and there is a similar difficulty about the incipient gesticulations which might be substituted for complete and full-blooded gestures. These incipient movements might be publicly observed, if the observer had sufficiently delicate instruments. Will it be said that the symbols here are not the incipient bodily movements, but the accompanying kinaesthetic sensations, which are private? But then it is not absolutely certain that kinaesthetic sensations and other 'bodily feelings' *are* in principle private, though they are so *de facto* and in normal conditions.

Moreover, there are two senses of the word 'private', and even though images and kinaesthetic sensations are private in the one sense, they are not private in the other. 'Private' may mean 'not publicly observable'; it may also mean 'not publicly describable'. Let us admit that images and kinaesthetic sensations are not publicly observable. In that sense, they are private, at least in normal conditions. It by no means follows that they are not publicly describable. One man can describe his visual images to another. He may describe them in great detail, and he may be understood. You cannot be acquainted with my visual images; but you may know them by description if you have visual images yourself. Some people have none; but then some people are blind too, and cannot understand descriptions of the public visible world. Again, I can describe my visual images to you by painting pictures of them, as Blake did, and as some of Galton's correspondents did. Kinaesthetic sensations are not so easily described; our verbal vocabulary for describing bodily feelings is exceedingly defective. But still I can convey to you what sort of kinaesthetic sensations occur in sub-vocal speech by getting you to speak sub-vocally yourself. Thus if 'private' means 'cognitively inaccessible', images and kinaesthetic sensations are not private. Other people may 'know what they are like', or may have well-grounded beliefs about them.

This is not the end of our difficulties. For unfortunately the antithesis between 'private' and 'public' is sometimes used in quite another way. Some children are said to have a private language, and some philosophers are accused of having one. By this we mean that these people use queer words which no-one else understands, or use ordinary words in a way which no-one else understands. But this is a different antithesis from the one we are discussing. The trouble with these words is not that other people cannot observe them. The child utters his private words aloud; the philosopher uses his in public lectures and in printed books. They are private only in the sense that they are not publicly intelligible.

But this antithesis between public and private is not a hard and fast one either. With sufficient time and patience, other people could learn what meaning the child or the philosopher attaches to his 'private' words, by noticing on what occasions or in what contexts they are uttered; their users might even be able to explain to us what meaning these words had, by defining them in terms of other words whose meaning is already publicly known. In this sense of the word 'private' no symbol is irremediably and in principle private, any more than the language spoken by the sole survivor of an otherwise extinct Red Indian tribe is. The privacy exists only *de facto* and *rebus sic stantibus*; it exists only so long as the hearers (or the speakers) have not taken the trouble to remove it.

Despite all these ambiguities, the words 'public' and 'private' are too useful to be abandoned, and I shall continue to use them myself in discussing the Symbolistic Theory of thinking. I shall say, for example, that images and kinaesthetic sensations are private symbols, and that words written on paper or uttered aloud, gestures, dumb show, pictures and diagrams drawn on paper, are public ones. But the ambiguities I have pointed out must be borne in mind. Moreover, it would appear that in all its uses the distinction between 'private' and 'public' is a distinction of degree, and not a hard and fast one. It is the notion of utter and irremediable privacy which we must guard against.

We now turn to the distinction between the use of symbols in thinking and their use in communication. First, we must be clear that symbols may be used publicly and yet *not* used for communication. A man may do his thinking by talking aloud ('to himself' as we say) or by writing words on paper. It is not that he first thinks, and then talks aloud, or first thinks and then writes. He thinks *in* the uttered words or in the written ones. Similarly, he might do his thinking by performing some piece of ritual or ceremonial behaviour. If he does any of these things he is producing symbols. And they are public symbols, capable of being observed, and understood too, by other people. But for all that, the man who produces them is not making any communication in doing so. If other people overhear his talk, or see his note-book or the diagrams he drew on the blotting-paper, if they discern through field-glasses the gestures he is making in solitude on a mountain-top, then they may be able to discover what he was thinking. But he has not communicated anything to them. His symbols, though they happened to be public, were not addressed to the people who observe them. They were not addressed at all; for they were not uttered with the intention that other people should perceive them and understand them. In respect of their cognitive function, they might as well have been mental images (verbal or other) though in respect of their intrinsic nature they happened to be publicly observable events.

What is meant here by 'addressing'? The obvious analysis, taking the case of spoken words, is this: he *intends* that the noises he produces shall be heard and understood. In the example given before, where he was 'overheard' talking to himself or thinking aloud, the man did not intend that his words should be heard and understood, though in actual fact they were; nor did he necessarily intend that they should not be—perhaps he just did not care.

But this analysis is not altogether satisfactory. The difficulty arises partly over the implied belief that there are other conscious beings capable of hearing and understanding the noises one utters (this will be considered later[1]); but partly from the notion of 'intending'. It *is* intending which is relevant, not just wishing. I might shout words at the top of my voice in the desert, wishing very much that someone else would hear and understand them. But this would not be communicating. I can wish for what I do not believe is in my power; but I can only intend what I do believe to be in my power.

What then is this 'intending'? It is only exceptionally a separate mental process which precedes the actual production of the sounds. I may conclude, after a period of doubt, that the other man is awake, not asleep; that he knows English, though he looks like a foreigner, for I suddenly recollect hearing him speak it the day before yesterday; that he is not deaf. Again, I may wonder whether it is prudent or kind to give him such and such a piece of information (e.g. that his dog has bitten me) and conclude after some hesitation that it is. In such cases it may be that there is a previous act of intending which precedes my utterance and is a cause-factor in producing it. Such an act, it may be noticed, would itself require the use of symbols. In intending him to hear and understand, I have to think of him as hearing and understanding, and this absent and not yet actual state of affairs has to be conceived of by the use of symbols.

There would be no logical difficulty in this, as there would be if we said that *all* using of symbols (communicatively or not) required a previous act of intending to use them. Nevertheless, it does not usually happen. Usually there is no separate and preceding mental occurrence which could with any plausibility be called an

[1]See ch. VIII, pp. 241-2.

act of intending. It would be better to describe the facts by means of adverbs or adverbial phrases; he utters the words 'intentionally', 'with the intention of' being heard or understood, but not as a result of a previous act of intending. But if so, how shall we distinguish utterances made 'with' this intention from utterances made without it, such as the soliloquies described above? By the differences there are in the speaker's reactions (both overt and introspectible) when he finds that he *has* been heard and understood. If he spoke with the intention of being heard and understood, he will be satisfied when he finds, or has reason to think, that he has in fact been heard and understood; for example, if the other person runs to the nearest gate and jumps over it when the speaker says, 'There is a bull coming'. If on the other hand he had spoken with no such intention, he will be either annoyed or indifferent when he finds that in actual fact someone else has heard and understood him; and any further words he produces will probably be produced inaudibly in a sub-vocal or an imaged form.

To return from this digression: we have seen that symbols usually regarded as 'public' (words spoken aloud or written on paper, visible gestures, etc.) need not necessarily be used for communication. Conversely, symbols usually regarded as 'private', such as mental images, *are* sometimes used for communication; for example, in a telepathy experiment, though this form of communication is only in its beginnings as yet, and little is known about its *modus operandi*. Thus the two antitheses, (1) between using symbols for thinking and using them for communication, (2) between using symbols privately and using them publicly, must not be equated.

Moreover, the first antithesis is not really an antithesis at all, but only a distinction. It is often supposed that we first think something and then subsequently set about communicating it, as if the thinking and the communicating were entirely separate processes. This does occasionally happen. A man may think out beforehand what he is going to say to his neighbour, and then subsequently say it. In thinking it out beforehand he does, of course, use symbols, and they may happen to be public ones too, as we have just seen. He may think aloud in planning his utterance, or write a draft on the back of an envelope. But as yet he has not communicated anything; and then later, by a separate act, he does so. But such 'rehearsed' or 'planned' communication is not very common. The celebrated injunction of the governess 'Think before you speak' is not very often obeyed (did she obey it herself when she said this?) and social life would be almost impossible if it were. The notion that *all* symbol-production must be planned or rehearsed beforehand is, of course, logically absurd, if the Symbolistic conception of thinking is correct; the planning or thinking out of what symbols you are going to produce would itself require the use of symbols. The notion that all *communication* must be planned beforehand is not logically absurd, but none the less erroneous. For very often (though not quite always) we think *in* the token words, or other symbols, by which the communication is made. The words or other symbols which we produce have both functions at the same time; we are using them *both* to think with, *and* to communicate with. This contention is indeed platitudinous. It only amounts to this, that when I speak to someone, I usually understand what I am saying; and likewise when I use any other sorts of symbols for communicating (written words, gestures, diagrams or visual images in a telepathy experiment) I understand the symbols I am using. It is true that there are a few exceptions to this, where the process of communicating is for some reason particularly difficult. In speaking to a very large audience, or shouting to somebody who is a long way away, or writing with one's toes because one's fingers are frozen, one's whole attention is absorbed by the physical movements of producing the noises or marks, etc., which are required. The same thing may happen when I have to speak very quietly to my neighbour, to avoid being overheard, or when I have to make a gesture to him which no one else will notice. (It may happen in a telepathy experiment too; one's whole attention may be absorbed in producing and holding before one's mind the images which are needed.) In such cases, I am not myself at the moment thinking in or with the symbols by which I communicate. At the time when I am producing them, these noises or marks, etc., are not functioning as symbols for me, though they are for my reader or my audience. For me, at the moment, they are just noises or marks, or bodily movements which I have to produce as carefully as I can. (Similarly in a telepathy experiment, the image or drawing or written mark which I have to 'transmit' may be for me just a shape; its sensible or imageable characteristics may absorb my whole mind.) And then it *is* necessary that I should have planned the operation beforehand, though there need not be any temporal interval between the end of the rehearsal and the beginning of the performance.

Much the same may be said if we consider communication from the side of the recipient. Ordinarily, he thinks *in* the symbols he hears or sees, just as his informant thinks *in* the symbols he utters or otherwise produces. It is true that the governess may enjoin us to think *after* we hear, or after we see, as she enjoins us to think *before* we speak. But ordinarily, this injunction is no more acceptable than the previous one. For example, 'first see, and then read' would be a very odd rule. Ordinarily we read in the act of seeing. And reading is just another name for thinking in or by means of the written words we see. Here again, however, there are occasional exceptions. The sounds we hear may be so faint and indistinct (or again so deafening), the gestures or written marks may be so difficult to recognize, that our whole attention has to be concentrated on listening or looking; and it is only when the sounds or gestures are recollected afterwards, or the writing looked at again, that we begin to think in them or with them. But then, until we do think in them or with them, the process of communication is not complete. The communication has not yet been received when we are still wholly occupied in looking or listening, nor even when we subsequently recollect what we looked at or listened to. It is only received when we ourselves proceed to think in or with these perceived or recollected particulars.

Our conclusion then is this:—It is true that symbols are used in two ways, for thinking on the one hand, for communicating on the other. But these two ways do not exclude each other. We may use symbols for thinking without at the same time using them for communication. But ordinarily the converse is not true. Ordinarily we think in the act of communicating; and the very same symbols (words, gestures, diagrams, ritual actions, and in telepathy mental images) are used in both ways at the same time. We may think aloud without communicating, as has been shown. But ordinarily when we communicate by word of mouth we are also thinking aloud; and the same applies, *mutatis mutandis,* to other forms of communication. We may think publicly without communicating; but ordinarily, when we communicate we are also thinking publicly.

It remains to add that the theory we are to consider is concerned mainly with the use of symbols for thinking, and only incidentally with their use for communication: just as it is concerned mainly with their descriptive or referential use, and hardly at all with their emotive use. The social sciences are interested only in public symbols, and in them only in so far as they are used for communication. The epistemologist is interested in private symbols as much as public ones, or even more; and public symbols interest him because they are used for thinking with, just as private ones are, and not because they are used (often, though not always) for communication as well. Here again it may be complained that he is guilty of 'vicious abstraction', on the ground that the communicational use of symbols is primary and their use for thinking is derivative, just as it was objected before that the emotive use was primary and the descriptive use derivative. But here again the answer is that the truth is just the other way round. It is only because symbols are already used for thinking with that they can also be used for communication, for giving and receiving information. Thus it is the use of symbols in thinking which is primary, and their use in communication which is derivative. This point will be discussed more fully below.

The Sign-Theory of Symbolization

So much by way of explaining what is meant by the word 'symbol' when it is maintained that thinking is symbolic cognition or cognition by means of symbols.

We have now to consider the relation between symbols and signs. On this point we find almost inextricable confusion. Sometimes the words 'sign' and 'symbol' are used as if they were synonymous. Some writers who accept what I have called the Symbolistic conception of thinking do not use the word 'symbol' in their exposition of it. Instead, they say that all thinking is cognition by means of signs; and they use the word 'sign' to cover all the different entities—spoken words, written words, gestures, pictures, diagrams, mental images both verbal and non-verbal—which were called 'symbols' just now.

Whatever objections there may be to the wide use of the word 'symbol' discussed above, this wide use of the word 'sign' is still more objectionable. Black clouds mean rain, and the word 'rain' means rain. It is as plain as anything can be that there is some important difference between the two situations. Of course there may also be some important connection between them. But to obliterate the distinction altogether, by calling the word as well as the black clouds a *sign* of rain, and leaving it at that, can only lead to confusion. It is, if possible, even more odd to say that a visual image of falling raindrops is a sign of rain in the way that black clouds are a sign of it.

Other writers who accept what I have called the Symbolistic conception of thinking do not go as far as this. They do not just equate signs with symbols. Instead, they hold that symbols are a special *sort* of signs. This doctrine is plausible and deserves careful examination. I shall call it the Sign Theory of Symbolization. In effect, it maintains that meaning in the symbol sense is a special case of meaning in the sign sense. It would allow us to say that sign-cognition, as discussed in the previous chapter, is a form of thinking; and at the same time it would explain why that form of thinking is inferior, or undeveloped, or primitive. Fully developed or mature thinking, it would be said, *is* also sign-cognition; but it is sign-cognition of a special sort, because the signs are of a special sort, and differ in an important way from those we discussed in the last chapter.

This is the theory held by Messrs. Ogden and Richards. 'When we consider the various kinds of sign-situations . . . we find that those signs which men use to communicate one with another and as instruments of thought occupy a peculiar place. It is convenient to group these under a distinctive name; and for words, arrangements of words, images, gestures, and such representations as drawings or mimetic sounds, we use the term *symbols*.'[1] According to this definition, a symbol is a sign which is used as an instrument of thought or communication. This would not prevent us from holding that thought also occurs in the non-symbolic sort of sign-situation, e.g. when black clouds are taken as a sign of rain. Of course the black clouds are not instruments of thought, in the way that the word 'rain' is, and it could not be said that we *use* them for thinking with, as we do use words and images. But it could still be said that in taking them as a sign of rain we are thinking or displaying intelligence.

Miss L. S. Stebbing takes a similar view. 'It is impossible to think without using signs, for to think is to go beyond what is sensibly

---

[1] C. K. Ogden and I. A. Richards, *The Meaning of Meaning*, 8th edition; p. 23. Authors' italics.

L

presented. This is not to say that it is impossible to think without words, for words are only one sort of signs. In the widest sense of the word "language" we use language whenever we deliberately use something as the sign of something else. A sign *consciously* designed to stand for something will be called a *symbol*.'[1]

She then distinguishes two kinds of language (in this wide sense of the word 'language'). In the one, the occurrences which we deliberately use as signs are *natural* signs, as for example in gesture-language. Here the signs are either demonstrative gestures, where we indicate something by pointing at it, or else they are imitative gestures, which resemble the thing or action signified. Similarly, there might be a 'natural' picture-language, as in some very primitive forms of writing. Sounds can also be used as imitative signs, signifying by resemblance; thus the sound 'cuckoo' is used to signify a certain bird because it resembles the sound made by this bird, and the sound 'ping-pong' is used to signify a certain game.

In the other type of language, she goes on, the signs used are not natural, but conventional or artificial. All words, except onomatopoeic ones like 'ping-pong' and 'cuckoo', are conventional signs. Miss Stebbing also points out that even gesture-language may be partly conventional; while picture-writing may gradually develop into an almost wholly conventional system of ideographs.

It is not clear whether Miss Stebbing would or would not regard 'natural signs' as symbols. In so far as they are consciously designed to stand for something, it would appear that she should, as Messrs. Ogden and Richards clearly do in the passage quoted above. 'Gesture-language,' she says 'is the simplest system of *consciously devised* signs.'[2] It would follow from this that there are natural *symbols*: symbols, that is, which are non-conventional, because their meaning is known 'straight off', without having to be learned. If so, what is consciously devised or designed in their case would merely be the *token*-symbol, the occurrence of a particular gesture or imitative sound on a particular occasion. But the *type*-symbol, e.g. 'cuckoo', would not stand for a certain bird as a result of any-one's conscious devising, but would stand for it 'by nature', because it resembles the noise which that sort of bird habitually makes at certain seasons of the year. Later, however, she seems to suggest

[1] *Modern Introduction to Logic*, ch. 2, p. 11; her italics.
[2] *Op. cit.*, p. 11; my italics.

that a symbol is always an artificial or conventional sign, and even that words—i.e. non-onomatopoeic ones—are the only symbols ('A word is the special kind of sign called a "symbol" '[1]).

There is no need to pursue these expository difficulties further. Enough has been said to show that it is not easy to discover just what the Sign Theory of symbolization is maintaining. It certainly does maintain that symbols are a special sort of signs, but just what is supposed to differentiate them from other signs is by no means clear; and the distinction between 'natural' and 'conventional' signs bristles with difficulties, as we shall see.

What has suggested such a theory, and why has it been so widely accepted? I suppose it is because we all speak of *making* signs, for example when one person communicates with another by means of gestures or dumb-show. The familiar phenomenon of sign-making suggests that the signs which are made have something in common with the signs which 'just happen', as when a clear sky at evening is a sign of a frosty night. The signs which are made by human beings are clearly symbols of some sort. Some signs, then, are also symbols. And perhaps the difference between the signs which are symbols and the signs which are not consists merely in this, that symbols are humanly made signs ('consciously devised', 'used as instruments') whereas non-symbolic signs 'just happen' without being made by anyone.

It is true, of course, that we do usually distinguish between making signs and speaking. I cannot talk to an Eskimo, but we can communicate with each other by means of signs. Nevertheless, we should be prepared to admit that there is a fairly close analogy between these two forms of communications; we speak of a sign-*language* and gesture-language, and even of a language of smiles, shrugs and grimaces. One would hesitate to say that written words are signs in the way black clouds are. But writing is something like *making* signs, though the signs here are relatively permanent; and drawing pictures or diagrams is something like it too. Again, a sign which someone makes is usually made *to* someone else. But it is not inconceivable that one might make signs, or at any rate produce them, without addressing them to anyone. In that case, to borrow a phrase from Messrs. Ogden and Richards, one would be using signs 'as instruments of thought' and not 'as instruments of

[1]*Op. cit.*, p. 13, *fin.*

communication': but they would still be made by oneself and would not just happen, like the black clouds or the clear sky at evening. The signs which one made in this uncommunicative way might even be private; and so the notion of making signs could be extended to cover the producing of mental images, as it is in the passage from *The Meaning of Meaning*, already quoted.[1]

The theory discussed and dismissed a few pages back, which just equates signs with symbols, may also have arisen from reflection on such examples as these. But if it did, the reflection was incomplete. For in all these examples the crucial point is that the signs are made or produced by someone. They do not 'just happen' like the black clouds which are a sign of rain, or the flushed face and shivery feelings which are signs of a fever. The only signs which can at all plausibly be identified with symbols are the signs which are made by human beings (or perhaps, occasionally, by non-human animals). The important fact is that there is *sign-making*, as well as signs which occur apart from human agency.

But though the Sign Theory of symbolization must distinguish between the signs which are made and the signs which merely occur, of course it must also maintain that these two sorts of sign-situation have something in common. Clearly we must ask what kind of signification-relation there is when someone makes a sign. Is it at all the same kind of relation as the one which holds between black clouds and rain, or between squeaky brakes and defective lubrication? If it is, the relation between a 'made' sign and its significate should be an inductive one. Let us consider an example given by Miss Stebbing.[2] A man makes the motions of raising a cup to his lips, and this signifies that he is thirsty. Now if he did really have a cup in his hands and raised it to his lips, this *would* be inductive evidence that he is thirsty. But, of course, the whole point of the phrase 'making the motions of' is to make clear that in actual fact there is no cup in his hands. To the spectators, his gesture does bring to mind the proposition that he is thirsty. But it does so indirectly, not by *being* an inductive sign of thirst, but by *resembling* one. He does not produce an occurrence which is itself an inductive sign of thirst, as the phrase '*making* a sign' would suggest. He only produces an imitation of it, as indeed Miss Stebbing herself points out.

[1]See p. 161, above.   [2]*Op. cit.*, p. 11.

Consider the following parallel example. If there is a thick pall of smoke filling a mountain pass, because someone has set the heather on fire, this smoke resembles a thick black cloud filling the pass, which would be a sign that heavy rain is falling there. No one would say that the smoke is a sign of rain falling there, but only that it resembles something else which *is* a sign of this. It might very well bring to mind the proposition that heavy rain is falling, but not in the way that an actual black cloud would. There is no signification, but only a reminding or suggesting. What we observe when someone makes the motions of raising a cup to his lips affects us rather in the way this pall of smoke does. It does not signify thirst—at any rate not in the inductive way—but reminds us, by resemblance, of something else which does. Now this reminding by resemblance is something for which the Sign Theory of symbolization has not provided. And this non-inductive element is essential to the effectiveness of many so-called 'natural signs', not only imitative gestures (dumb show) and imitative sounds, but also pictures and diagrams, and mental images, if we can bring ourselves to regard mental images as signs at all. And some of them, it would seem, do not even have to remind us of inductive signs, as the gesture of the thirsty man did; they seem to perform their office directly and immediately, just by resembling the object symbolized. This is true of many pictures and diagrams, and of many mental images. If we call them signs, we shall have to say that they signify just by resemblance, and not at all in the way that black clouds signify rain.

Let us leave the matter at that for a moment,[1] and turn to the other main variety of 'natural signs', namely demonstrative gestures such as pointing. The word 'demonstrative', however, is unfortunate because of its associations with demonstrative argument or deductive proof, as when we speak of 'demonstrating' a mathematical truth. Instead, I shall use the word *deictic*.[2] The topic we are now to consider, then, is deixis and deictic gestures.

Deixis and Deictic Gestures

Deictic gestures are usually regarded as 'natural signs'. In what way do they signify? Is it wholly or partly by resemblance, as with

[1] See below, pp. 179-80.
[2] From the Greek δεῖξις, literally 'pointing out'. The Greek word for 'demonstration', in the deductive proof sense, is ἀπόδειξις (hence 'apodictic proposition').

other 'natural signs'? It is not easy to see how pointing at something could resemble the thing pointed at. Perhaps they signify in a unique and unanalysable manner, and all we can say of them, over and above this, is that their mode of signification is 'natural', i.e. extra-conventional and unlearned? Some people have thought so. But we must not agree with them too easily. It is a good methodological principle to distrust such claims to unanalysability and uniqueness. And in this case, the claim is weakened when we observe that pointing with a finger or a walking-stick is not the only sort of deictic situation; at any rate there are others which have a fairly close analogy with it. An arrow-like mark (→) drawn on the ground or on the wall has a deictic function; so has a sign-post. Suppose I leave a book on a friend's table in his absence and am afraid he will overlook it. I may find it useful to arrange one or two elongated objects on the table, say a pencil, a ruler and a straight piece of string, all pointing towards the book from different directions. In this way, I may hope that his attention will be directed to the place where the book is. This set of elongated objects is at least a quasi-deictic sign.

Again, in days when few people could read, heraldic signs were in common use, and signs were put up outside shops; a shop which sold brushes might have a picture of a brush hung above the door, or a brass shape resembling a brush. Inn signs, even now, are often purely pictorial and contain no words. It might appear that such signs are not deictic at all and have a purely representative function, like dumb-show or drawing pictures in the air; it might be thought that in a verbal symbolism the equivalent of a brush-like picture or piece of brass was just the abstract noun 'brush' or 'brushes'. But this is not the whole story. We have to consider not merely the resemblance-relations which the picture or piece of brass has, but also the place where it is situated. Translated into verbal symbolism, what the picture or brass sign says is not just 'brushes' but 'brushes *here*'. Again, when we see a man in armour with a leopard painted on his shield, what is brought to our mind is not just the concept of 'leopard', but the proposition '*This* is the Knight of the Leopard'. Here again the spatial location of the sign gives it a deictic function.

Indeed, the same is true of the example discussed above, making the motion of raising a cup to one's lips. What is conveyed is not just 'thirst' but '*This man* is thirsty'. In itself the gesture is just a general symbol. But because of its spatial location, it has a deictic function as well. The man who makes the gesture is calling attention to himself, exactly as he would if he pointed at himself with a finger. In this case he gives information as well, whereas if he had merely pointed a finger at himself his gesture would have been purely deictic. Pointing a finger at oneself may be called a purely auto-deictic gesture. But here again there is nothing unique about it. There are other auto-deictic actions which are almost or quite as effective: for example, waving a handkerchief or a shirt, uttering an inarticulate (non-verbal) shout, firing off a pistol, lighting a fire whose smoke can be seen, flashing an electric torch in the dark. The purpose of such actions is simply to direct our attention to the person who does them. We may notice that, in order to be effective, they have to be sharply contrasted with their spatio-temporal context. For example, it would be useless to flash an electric torch in broad daylight or to fire off a pistol in the midst of an artillery barrage; and if one were sitting in a field of green corn, it would be better to wave a white or red shirt, rather than a green one.

We see from these examples that deictic gestures, such as pointing, are by no means the only 'made' signs which have a deictic function. It is, therefore, very unlikely that pointing signifies in a unique and unanalysable manner. There is nothing *sui generis* about it. On the contrary, it is one of a very large class of different entities and procedures which may be used for drawing attention to something, whether to oneself or to something else. Is there anything which all these entities and procedures have in common, over and above the fact that all of them are deictic in one way or another?

There is at least this, that all of them perform their deictic function in virtue of the spatio-temporal location in which they occur, or exist. Even a sound, such as an auto-deictic shout or pistol shot, is at least vaguely located; for instance it is from my right, a good way off. Moreover, what those signs draw our attention *to* is a spatio-temporal region. Perhaps this may be disputed: when a man points to a fox, surely my attention is drawn to the fox? Surely the shop-sign draws my attention to the shop, and an auto-deictic shout draws my attention to the person who makes it? But this happens only indirectly, and sometimes does not happen at all. The immediate effect of the sign is to draw our attention to a *place*. What is in the place, I must find out for myself, if I can. A man points to a fox which he sees. I see him pointing, but it does not follow that I see the fox too. From where I stand, there may be a bush in the way. Nevertheless, the man's gesture is for me a deictic sign. And this not merely in the sense that I know or believe that it is one, without knowing what it indicates; it does then and there have an indicative function for me. It indicates a place, a region of space. Similarly an auto-deictic shout may be uttered by a man who is out of sight, lying in a gully on a mountain side. No doubt there is a sense in which this sound 'indicates' the man who makes it. But this indicating is conceptual, not purely deictic. It involves the inductive sort of sign-cognition discussed in Chapter IV. I have discovered inductively that noises of that sort are usually made by human beings (I certainly do not know this *a priori*; it has to be learned from experience). All that the sound directly does is to draw my attention to the place from which it comes; and with this, its purely deictic function is exhausted. It does not cause me to *perceive* the man, which is what the word 'indicate' would naturally suggest.

Sometimes the place or region is indicated rather vaguely, as being pretty near the place where the sign itself is. The brushes are in the shop which is more or less under the brushlike sign. The Leopard Knight may be directly behind the shield which bears the leopard-like device. But perhaps this man in armour is only a herald or a subordinate, and the Leopard Knight himself is lurking in the background somewhere. Or again, he is somewhere or other in the castle over which the leopard flag is flying, but where exactly he is, one does not know.

But with some deictic signs, the region to which our attention is to be drawn is indicated more specifically, because the sign itself is not merely located but also directed. The finger or the walking-stick is pointed *towards* the place which I am to look at. A picture of a hand with outstretched finger similarly indicates direction, and so does an arrow-sign drawn on the road or on a wall. The place to which we are to attend is indicated still more specifically when there are several directed signs which are convergent. When I arrange the pencil, the ruler and the straight piece of string on the table of my absent friend, I place these elongated objects in such a way that they all point from different directions to the same part of the table. A number of people scattered about a field may all point from different directions at the place where the fox is. Signs

which are informative as well as deictic may likewise have a
'directed' character. A finger post with a place-name written on
it is an obvious example, but an irrelevant one for our present purpose, because we are discussing non-verbal signs. There could,
however, be a sign-post with a picture of a teapot on it, or a schematic drawing of a railway engine, to tell us that a tea-
shop or a railway station lies in such and such a direction from here.

So far we have concluded that the function of a deictic sign—
or of an informative sign which is also deictic—is to draw our
attention to a place, a region of space. We now see that there are
two ways in which it may do this. One may be called 'contextual',
the other 'directional'. An example of the first is the shop sign or
the shield or flag bearing an heraldic device. Here the region indicated is somewhere in the (fairly near) neighbourhood of the sign
itself. The most obvious example of the second or directional sort
of deixis is pointing. But it is not the only one. An arrow-like sign,
or a finger-post, or even a set of elongated objects arranged on a
table, may have the same 'directional' deictic function.

Can anything further be said, or must we be content to admit
that these two sorts of place-indications, the contextual and the
directional, are incapable of further analysis? Let us first consider
how the sign itself catches our attention. I have already suggested
that it does so by contrasting with its spatio-temporal surroundings,
though the degree of contrast needed is smaller if the spectator is
in a state of vigilance, expecting the sign to occur. The shout or
the pistol shot 'stands out from' the (relative) silence which precedes
and follows it. The arrow sign, drawn in white chalk, stands out
from the blue-black surface of the road which is its background.
As to this, we can only say that human beings have an unlearned
tendency to notice any thing or occurrence which is 'sensibly
abrupt'.

But having caught our attention, the sign must not retain it.
If it does, it will have failed in its signifying function, and will not
be, for us, a sign at all. An anatomist might be so interested in the
queer conformation of my forefinger that he quite failed to notice
that I was pointing. When I utter an auto-deictic cry, I may fail to
draw attention to the place where I am, if my hearer is a musician.
His whole attention may be absorbed by the harmonious, or inhar-

monious, quality of the ululation itself. For this reason deictic signs should be as simple and schematic as possible. An arrow sign is more effective if drawn without feathers, and we do not put a sleeve or cuff-links on a finger-post.

How then is our attention transferred from the sign itself to the place or region which it indicates? Where the deixis is of the contextual sort, we can only appeal again to an innate (unlearned) tendency. When some object or event A catches our attention, we have an unlearned tendency to be curious about A's spatial context; and this tendency is actualized unless there is something to inhibit it, for instance the internal details of A itself.

But where the deixis is directional, perhaps something more can be said. It is true that the directional sort of deixis may at first appear to be simpler than the contextual sort, and even to be 'ultimate and unanalysable'. But on further examination it turns out to be more complicated, and more puzzling too. I would suggest that it contains an element of imitation or dumb-show, though of a very schematic kind. Pointing at something resembles moving towards it. The movement which it resembles, and therefore suggests to the mind of the spectator, may be a movement of the man's whole body, e.g. running or walking to the place where the fox is. Or it may be a movement of some part of one's body. If I point with my finger to a letter on the table, this is rather like reaching out with my hand to grasp the letter. Indeed, to make quite sure that you understand me I may actually tap the letter with my forefinger, instead of just pointing at it. (Likewise when the pointer dog points towards the place where a shot bird has fallen: the dog is perfectly immobile, but the directedness of its posture suggests a movement towards the place where the bird is.) And the arrow sign, though it does not move at all, resembles something which does. Here again we come in the end to an unlearned tendency, a biologically useful tendency to be interested in moving objects as such and to follow their movement with our gaze. But the tendency is aroused indirectly, by an object which reminds us, by resemblance, of a moving object, without actually moving itself.

This explanation, however (supposing there is any truth in it), is still incomplete. Where an arrow sign or a finger points to the left, why is our attention directed to the left rather than to the right? If it suggests a movement, why a leftward movement rather than a rightward one? The line along which the object is disposed goes in both directions, after all. It would seem that in the directional sort of deixis the sign-object must have a certain *visual asymmetry*. One end of it must be visually prominent in a way the other end is not. Arrow signs used as weathercocks are sometimes difficult to read because their tail ends are too elaborately ornamented, and deceive us into thinking that the wind is north-west when it is really south-east.

Let us see whether this explanation will apply to human pointing. (The pointing of sign-posts and finger-posts is fairly obviously derivative. The sign-post performs its deictic function by resembling a pointing human being.) Suppose we see someone with his arm outstretched and an outstretched finger at the end of it. The outstretched arm is an elongated object, and its long axis gives the line, north and south let us suppose, along which we are to look. This elongated object has two ends, which we will call outer and inner; we will suppose that the outer end, where the finger is, is to the northward and the inner end, where the shoulder is, to the southward. Why is it that the outer end, and not the inner end, determines the direction in which we are to look?

This question, once we ask it, is very difficult to answer. Does the outer end have a visual prominence which the inner end lacks, and if so, how does it acquire this? Not because of colour contrast. Sometimes, of course, there is a fairly abrupt colour contrast between the hand and the arm, because the hand is unclothed and the arm is clothed with a sleeve. But the deixis would be just as effective if the man were wholly naked, or if he were wearing a dark blue glove exactly matching his dark blue suit. Perhaps the explanation is that the finger is thinner than the rest of the deictic object, and this is what gives visual prominence to the end where the finger is. It may be noticed that if we wish to make our pointing more emphatic and arresting, we prolong our arm by holding out a thin object like a walking-stick or a pole. A thick or fat object held in the hand, such as a plum pudding or a football, would have just the opposite result, and might even destroy the deictic effect altogether. But this explanation is not complete. Suppose the man was pointing in the dark with a phosphorescent finger, so that all the rest of him, except the finger, was invisible. However thin his finger was, we should not know whether he was pointing northwards or southwards. What is important is that one end of the outstretched limb should be visually thinner than the rest of it; and for this the rest of the limb must be seen. The thinner portion of the object contrasts more abruptly with its sensible background than the thicker portion does; and that is why it has visual prominence.

If this is right, we were also right in saying that a sign-post indicates direction derivatively, by resemblance or imitation (p. 171, above). It is true that the arm of a sign-post does not have to be thinner at its outward end. But the sign-post as a whole, post and arm, is a rough and schematic representation of a pointing human being. And in a pointing human being the direction is unambiguously indicated by the fact that one end of the outstretched limb is thinner than the other.

This explanation is confirmed by considering the curious example of the pointer dog. This creature makes itself useful by pointing at the place where a shot bird has fallen. Its nose is towards the place, while its tail is held out stiffly in a straight line behind. In such circumstances, the thin end of the dog is its tail; and this points in just the wrong direction, away from the place where the bird is and not towards it. Accordingly, the innocent spectator, unfamiliar with the animal's habits, is greatly puzzled. Some sort of deictic performance is clearly going on. But which is the important end of the deictic object, the nose or the tail? So far as visual prominence goes, the tail would appear to be the significant end. On the other hand, pointing suggests movement; and he knows inductively (not of course *a priori*) that dogs commonly move head foremost. There is a conflict between visual prominence and induction. Only further inductive researches, directed upon the peculiar habits of this particular species of dog, will enable him to settle the question. He will then discover that in this case visual prominence must be disregarded. Thus the pointing of the pointer dog is not (in the terminology we are at present using) a 'natural' sign, but an inductive one.

Perhaps human pointing *is*, in this terminology, a 'natural' sign? Even here, I think, induction cannot be completely excluded. There is something else, besides the visual prominence due to relative thinness, which helps us to decide that the finger, rather than the shoulder-joint, is the significant end of the diectic object. I have already remarked that pointing resembles movement. And signification by resemblance, in the present terminology, is 'natural'. But as we have also seen, this resemblance which pointing has to movement only suggests the line along which the movement might occur, say a north-and-south line, and does not decide whether the movement is to be thought of as northward or southward. That was why the notion of visual prominence had to be introduced. But it would seem that induction plays some part as well. It is not only that pointing *resembles* movement. It is frequently also *followed* by movement. When the man's finger is at the northward end of his outstretched arm, we frequently find that a northward movement follows shortly afterwards. He walks or runs to the northward, or stretches out to grasp or touch something which lies in that direction. We should usually describe this situation by saying 'he moves in the direction in which his finger points'. But perhaps we should rather say that he points in the direction in which he is going to move.

There is no need to pursue these curious questions further. Enough has been said to shew that the directional sort of deictic signs, so far from indicating 'in an ultimate and unanalysable manner', perform their deictic function in an exceedingly complex way, which is not at all easy to unravel.

'Natural Signs' and Signification by Resemblance.

Perhaps something should now be said about the conception of a natural sign itself, which we have hitherto accepted without question. As we have seen, Miss Stebbing holds that imitative gestures and deictic gestures are natural signs, but that almost all words, and some gestures too, are conventional or arbitrary signs.[1] Now if 'natural' is thus opposed to 'conventional' or 'arbitrary', inductive signs could quite well be called natural too. There is nothing conventional or arbitrary about the fact that cumulo-nimbus clouds are a sign of a thunderstorm. Perhaps we shall be told that the antithesis between natural and conventional applies only to humanly made signs, and not to those which 'just happen' without human agency, like the cumulo-nimbus cloud. Even so, we still have to ask whether humanly made non-conventional signs signify inductively or non-inductively or in both ways at once. And this is the most important question which can be asked about them, because the truth or

[1] p. 162, above.

falsity of the Sign Theory of Symbolization depends on it. The use
of the word 'natural' diverts our attention from this question. It
is one of those words which put a stop to further inquiry. When
something is called natural, this is much like calling it 'ultimate
and unanalysable'; it does not occur to us to ask whether there
might not be different sorts of naturalness.

But perhaps Miss Stebbing, in using the phrase 'natural sign',
has a double antithesis in mind. Perhaps 'natural' means not only
'extra-conventional', but also 'non-inductive'. A natural sign may be
one whose meaning does not have to be learned *either* in the way we
learn conventions *or* in the way we learn inductive correlations; it
may be a sign whose meaning we know 'straight off', without any
learning at all. Indeed, in discussing imitative gestures she seems to
go further, and to say that natural signs not merely do not signify
because of any kind of learning, but also that they do signify by
resemblance. (*Op. cit.*, p. 11. Whether this is intended to apply to
deictic signs as well is not clear.)

Now if by a 'natural' sign we are to mean one which signifies
by resemblance, two comments must be made. First, it would seem
that if there are signs which signify by resemblance, the Sign Theory
of Symbolization, which Miss Stebbing herself accepts, cannot be
wholly true. For according to that theory, all signs signify inductively and symbols are just one species of inductive signs. Surely
there is all the difference in the world between inductive signification and signification by resemblance, even though the two often
go together? The first is learned by experience of more or less
constant conjunctions. The second has nothing to do with constant
conjunctions at all, and the only experience it requires is experience
of other things (one at least) to which the now-presented object
has a likeness.

Secondly, if 'natural' is to mean 'signifying by resemblance', we
have to ask whether there *are* any natural signs in the sense of the
phrase. Certainly, imitative gestures, onomatopoeic sounds, pictures,
diagrams, and even some deictic gestures, do resemble the things
or situations they stand for. And mental images, if they are to be
called signs at all, do resemble what they stand for. But we should
still have to ask whether there are any *purely* natural signs in this
Resemblance Sense of the word 'natural'. Let us ignore mental
images for the present. It is very odd to call them signs at all, and

in any case the part which they play in conceptual cognition will have to be discussed later, when we examine the Imagist theory of thinking.[1] With this reservation, I believe we shall have to conclude that there are no signs whatever which signify purely and simply by resemblance. It may be true that many humanly made signs could not perform these functions unless they reminded us, by resemblance, of the thing or situation signified. But neither could they perform it, if this was all they did. Resemblance, though it may sometimes be indispensable, is never sufficient by itself (except, perhaps, with mental images) but needs to be reinforced by something else.

We have already seen that there are other unlearned factors, beside resemblance, which play a part in deictic signification at least: visual prominence, an unlearned interest in moving objects, and (with the contextual sort of deictic signs) an unlearned tendency to be curious about the spatial context of anything which catches our perceptual attention. If 'natural' is equivalent to 'signifying by resemblance', these factors will have to be called non-natural; most paradoxically, for we have an almost irresistible inclination to say that they are natural, if anything is.

What may be called 'reminder by resemblance' is a very familiar sort of mental process. It is one of the many ways in which our memory, or retention, of past experience is manifested, and it is closely connected with recognition. Indeed, according to the Philosophy of Resemblances (which dispenses with subsistent universals) recognition itself is just a specially important case of reminder by resemblance.[2]

Among the many things and events which remind us by resemblance of others, only a small proportion are brought into existence by human agency; but these are the only ones which now concern us, because they are the only ones which have any relevance to a discussion of the relation between signs and symbols. A rock in an uninhabited valley may remind an explorer of a lion, by having a similar shape; but no one would be tempted to say that it signified a lion, unless he had reason to suppose that some human being had given it this shape, or at least had set it up in this particular place (as a warning, perhaps, that lions infested the locality). At this point inductive considerations already begin to be relevant. Sometimes

[1]See Chapters VIII and IX, below.   [2]Cf. ch. II, pp. 162-3, above.

we do actually observe someone bringing into existence the 'reminding' object—the *resemblant sign*, if we may call it so. With imitative gestures, of course, we always do; to observe a gesture is to observe someone making it. And sometimes we see someone actually drawing a picture or a diagram, or constructing a brass shape resembling a brush, and setting it up outside a shop. Very frequently, however, it is not present observation, but induction based on past observations, which assures us that this object before our eyes *is* a picture, or diagram, or some other sort of resemblant sign; not just a queer object which happens to resemble something else, but a sign produced by human agency.

This is not all. We also have to use induction to discover what in particular this sign is a sign of. Every such sign resembles many other things or situations; some in one way, some in a second way, some in a third way, some more closely, some less. So far as mere reminder by resemblance goes, it might remind us of any of them. And what a resemblant sign is a sign of is not necessarily the thing or event or situation which it resembles most closely. Indeed it cannot be. Consider for example a piece of dumb-show, such as making the motions of swimming with one's two arms. What this most closely resembles is another piece of dumb-show in which exactly similar motions are made. The relevant resemblance—the resemblance which it has to a breast-stroke actually made in swimming—is a much less close one than this, if only because the gesticulator is on dry land and standing up, instead of being in a semi-prone position in water. Again, a picture or diagram used as a resemblance-sign is often highly schematic. What a schematic picture of a teapot most closely resembles is not a teapot, but another teapot picture which is equally schematic and schematic in the same way. And if it be agreed that pointing is *inter alia* a resemblance-sign, because it resembles bodily movement towards the place pointed at, this resemblance (though it does exist) is a highly abstract one, not nearly so close as the resemblance which one act of pointing has to another, and also less close than the resemblance between pointing with a finger and pointing with a walking-stick. The brass shop-sign too, though rather like a brush, is not *very* like one, because this resemblance only exists when the sign is seen from certain points of view, not, for example, when it is looked at edgewise. What the brass sign most closely resembles is another brass sign made to the same pattern by the same firm in Birmingham; but this is not what it is a sign of.

How is it, then, that we are usually able to pick out the relevant resemblance-relation and ignore the irrelevant ones? By means of induction. A resembles B, C, D, E, etc., and so far as mere reminder by resemblance goes it might remind us of any of them. But we have learned inductively that B (not C, D, E, etc.) is the thing or situation or event with which A is as a matter of fact usually conjoined. And so A's resemblance to B is as it were accentuated or picked out. It is B which we are reminded of, and the tendencies which we also have to be reminded of C, D, E, etc., are inhibited. It is a B-ish object, event or situation which we are prepared for and led to expect, and not a C-ish, D-ish, or E-ish one. For instance, we have learned inductively that flat brass shapes like this are frequently set up outside shops; and that when they are, other objects are to be found inside, to which these brass shapes have a more or less schematic resemblance. And so this resemblance, schematic and rather distant as it is, is psychologically effective in determining our expectations, emotions and actions. In short, apart from inductive considerations, resemblance-signs would be so ambiguous that they would not serve as signs at all.

There is another curious point about the relation between resemblance-signs and inductive ones. On the face of it, there is a striking contrast between the two sorts of 'bringing to mind', the resemblance sort and the inductive sort. When A resembles B, the observation of A reminds us of B, provided we have experienced at least one B-ish object before. When A has been more or less constantly conjoined with B in our past experience, the observation of B also reminds us of B, this time inductively. But there is a remarkable difference between these two remindings. The inductive one arouses a belief, or at least an inclination to believe, in the actual existence of B. (I say 'at least an inclination to believe' because there may be conflicting inductive signs, as we have seen.[1]) But with the resemblance sort of reminding, there is no inclination to believe. When I see a rock resembling a lion or look at the statues of lions in Trafalgar Square, London, I do not believe and have no inclination to believe, that a lion actually exists in the neighbourhood. Indeed, so far as this experience goes I have no inclination to believe that

[1] Cf. pp. 109-12, above.

M

lions exist at all, though other experiences may have given it to me. This comes out more clearly if we alter the example. A cloud in the sky reminds me, by resemblance, of a dragon. The resemblance may be close and striking. The spectacle interests me greatly, and I attend to it carefully; but it gives me no inclination to believe that a dragon actually exists, or that any dragons exist. To use the terminology suggested in Chapter IV my concept of Dragon or of Lion—my capacity to recognize such an object when or if I encounter one—is certainly sub-activated; but not at all in the believing way.

Then how is it that humanly produced resemblance signs do very often induce belief, or at least an inclination to believe? As we say, they convey information, information about matters of fact. On seeing the brush-like sign, I do believe that somewhere in its near neighbourhood there are brushes on sale, or at least have a strong inclination to believe so. (The inclination may be inhibited by other observations, for example if I am in a part of the town which has been badly damaged by bombs, but it is certainly there.) Likewise, on seeing a man make the motions of raising a cup to his lips, I believe or have a strong inclination to believe that he is thirsty. There would be no way of explaining this if resemblance-signs operated purely and simply by resemblance, since resemblance by itself never arouses belief concerning matters of fact. But if there is also an inductive factor in the situation, the explanation is easy. I happen to have learned inductively that there is a pretty constant conjunction between brass objects of this sort and brush-selling shops, or between gesticulations of this sort and drink-seeking behaviour. At any rate, the object or event which I now observe is sufficiently analogous to those which have been found to have these constant conjunction relationships in the past.

It is true that humanly made resemblance signs do not always arouse belief or convey factual information. Consider for instance the actions which occur in a game of charades. If a man makes cat-like noises, moves about the room on hands and knees in a four-footed way, has a tail-like appendage attached to him and pipe cleaners glued to his face resembling whiskers, am I at all inclined to believe that there is a cat in the house or even (so far as this experience goes) that there are cats at all? I am not. I know, or am sure, that this peculiar behaviour is 'not intended seriously', is not to be taken as conveying information about matters of fact. But how do I know this? Certainly not *a priori*, but empirically, by induction. I have learned from past experience that behaviour like this, occurring in this particular sort of social context, is to be interpreted in a special way, as merely representing a possible state of affairs, not giving information about an actual one. On the other hand, if I had never seen or heard of a charade before, my state of mind would be very different. I *should* then have an inclination to believe that information concerning matters of fact was being conveyed and that some actual situation existed in which an actual cat was an important element. And this inclination to believe would again be aroused not by resemblance alone, but by a combination of resemblance and induction. For previous experience would have taught me that when a piece of human behaviour has a striking resemblance to some other situation or event, that other situation or event is often found to exist in actual fact. My observation of other forms of dumb-show would have led me inductively to this conclusion.

It follows from this discussion that the inconsistency there seemed to be in Miss Stebbing's account of Natural Signs was at least partly avoidable. On the one hand, she seemed to accept what I called the Sign Theory of Symbolization, which makes a symbol just a special sort of inductive sign, namely a humanly produced one. On the other hand, she also held that there are natural signs (e.g. imitative gestures, onomatopoeic sounds) which symbolize by pure resemblance; and from this it would follow that there is an important class of symbols which are not inductive signs at all. But it now turns out that even with these symbols the resemblance between symbol and thing symbolized is not a sufficient condition of their symbolic efficacy. Even imitative gestures, dumb-show, diagrams, etc., *are* after all inductive signs, though they do also have a resemblance (not always a very close one) to the things or situations they stand for. And even deictic gestures, which are also counted as natural signs in Miss Stebbing's terminology, turn out to have something inductive about them. The doctrine that meaning in the Symbol sense is just a special case of meaning in the Inductive Sign sense is not refuted by these examples, as it seemed to be at first. So far as we have gone, it might still be true that if X and Y are to be related as symbol and thing symbolized, an inductively established constant conjunction is a necessary condition of their being so; or at any rate a conjunction sufficiently frequent to make the one an inductive sign of the other.

But though we are not obliged to abandon the Sign Theory of Symbolization—at least, not yet—there is one thing which we shall do well to abandon; and that is the term 'natural sign' itself. The word 'natural' is too ambiguous to be useful; and the phrase 'natural sign', by its deceptive simplicity, conceals the very problems which have to be discussed, or even suggests that they are undiscussable. It may be added that the word 'conventional' which is used in this context as the contrary of 'natural' is not free from difficulties either, as we shall see presently. The whole antithesis of Natural Signs *versus* Conventional Signs had better be forgotten. Or if it cannot be forgotten, let it be treated as just a convenient traditional label for a group of epistemological problems. It certainly does not give us much help in solving them.

The Inductive Sign Theory Applied to Language.

We have now to consider whether the Sign Theory of Symbolization will apply to language. Can the verbal utterances and written marks produced by human beings be regarded as just a special sort of inductive signs? Up to a point, they can. But this conception of human language, when we work it out in detail, involves us in strange perplexities, and grows more and more paradoxical when we attempt to solve them.

First we must notice that the Sign Theory does not do itself justice when it maintains that words, or sentences, are *conventional* signs. It might even appear to refute itself by saying so. Its business is to emphasize the resemblances between words and (for instance) weather-signs, such as the black cloud which is a sign of rain. But the term 'conventional' serves rather to emphasize the differences. A very long philosophical tradition, going back to the ancient Greek antithesis of νόμος and φύσις,[1] impels us to draw a sharp distinction between mere human conventions and inductively discovered regularities. 'Fire burns both here and among the Persians,' as Aristotle remarks,[2] and the laws of meteorology are the same in all ages and countries. But human conventions vary from place to

[1] 'Convention' and 'nature'.
[2] *Nicomachean Ethics*, Book V, ch. 7. 1134 b. 26.

place and from time to time. Conventions are made by human beings, and are altered by human beings. The regularities which prevail in the physical world are not made, but discovered by induction, and no one can alter them. It is quite clear that the cloud-rain correlation has nothing conventional about it; and if we say that the correlation between the word 'rain' and rain *is* merely conventional, we suggest that induction has nothing to do with our understanding of the word. This suggestion is not only false in itself, but is the very contrary of what the Sign Theory is trying to maintain.

In any case, it is not true that words have meaning by convention, if a convention is an explicit agreement entered into by a number of human beings. As Lord Russell points out, 'we can hardly suppose a parliament of hitherto speechless elders meeting together and agreeing to call a cow a cow and a wolf a wolf'.[1] In this sense of the word 'convention', the only words which have meaning by convention are some of the technical terms used in the sciences, in law, and in practical arts like medicine and navigation. And even though these words did originally acquire their meaning by explicit and conscious agreement, that is certainly not the way in which they keep it. Later generations do not have to accede to the agreement by swearing an oath or signing on the dotted line when they reach the age of twenty-one. They just slip into the habit of using those technical terms in more or less the same way as their elders use them. No voluntary decision is required, as words like 'agreeing' or 'acceding to an agreement' would suggest. It is not at all like what happens when a man *decides* to adopt the vocabulary used by the upper-middle classes. Still less is any promise needed, as if the first-year student of physics said to his teacher, 'I undertake henceforth to use the word "heat" in the way it is used by the President and Council of the Royal Society.'

It will be objected, perhaps, that I have been interpreting the word 'convention' in a very narrow sense. Surely it covers customs as well as explicit agreements? When we say that something is a matter of convention (e.g. shaking hands with people when one meets them, taking off one's hat to female acquaintances) surely we often mean that it is a matter of custom or social habit, with the implication, perhaps, that customs differ in different societies? Cer-

[1] *Analysis of Mind*, p. 190.

tainly. But if custom is what we have in mind, it would be better to say so. This will remove the air of mystery—I had almost said of Mumbo-Jumbo—which attaches to the statement that 'words are conventional signs'. If we want to maintain that they are signs at all, let us call them customary signs, or socially conditioned signs if that phrase sounds more up to date.

This way of speaking has the further advantage of not suggesting an antithesis between verbal signs and inductive ones. What one learns about the customs of other human beings is plainly learned by induction. That all or most speakers in a certain tract of territory mean by the sound 'cat' any entity which resembles Pussy, Tabitha and Tiger Tim as closely as these entities resemble one another, is a generalization established by experience of more or less constant conjunctions. In its logical character, though not in its subject-matter, this proposition has the same status as 'all or most nightin-gales sing in May and early June' or 'when there is a cumulo-nimbus cloud there is often a thunderstorm'.

We must add that it is even more misleading to call words *arbitrary* signs than to call them conventional ones. No doubt the epithet 'arbitrary' was useful at one time, in order to free people from the superstition that there is some sort of intrinsic or necessary connection between (say) the word 'cat' and a certain familiar sort of domestic animal. But by calling the conjunction between them arbitrary, we suggest that it comes into existence by some sort of *fiat* or voluntary decision and is maintained in existence by the same means; as when Louis XIV sent someone to the Bastille by an arbitrary act, and kept him there by issuing the equally arbitrary order 'let him stay there !' on the first day of every succeeding month. This is not the way words usually get their meanings, nor is it the way they keep them.

But though the speech customs of our human neighbours are discovered by each of us inductively, though this may be the only method one has for learning that human noises have meaning and what in particular they mean, it would not, of course, follow that the notion of meaning itself (in the sense in which words have meaning) could be analysed in terms of the notion of an inductive sign. The word-object relationship, or the sentence-fact relationship, when once we have discovered it, might still turn out to be some-thing quite different from the relation between black clouds and rain, or squeaky brakes and defective lubrication. If we are to be shown that the meaning which words or sentences have is just a special case of the meaning which ordinary inductive signs have, some additional argument is needed. Let us see whether it can be produced.

It would be pointed out, to begin with, that speaking and writing are after all forms of human behaviour. Now human behaviour can be considered from many different points of view. From the point of view of Psycho-physical Dualism, it may be regarded as the overt and public effect of certain inward and private psychical processes, such as perceiving, thinking and wishing. This is not the way in which the Sign Theory of language regards it. From the biological point of view, it may be regarded as a series of physical responses, some learned and some unlearned, by means of which a complicated organism adjusts itself to a changing environment (the environment, of course, consists in part of other human organisms). This bio-logical way of regarding it is characteristic of Behaviouristic psy-chology, which either denies the existence of inward and private psychical processes altogether, or maintains on methodological grounds that if they do occur they are not a possible object of scientific investigation. An advocate of the Sign Theory of language (or of meaning) does not reject this biological conception of human behaviour, but neither is he specially interested in it. There is, however, still a third way of regarding human behaviour. The things which a human being does may be regarded as inductive signs of events or states of affairs other than themselves. Some of them are inductive signs of other events, past, present or future, in that same human organism. If I see someone turning pale and trembling, that is an inductive sign that he is about to run away. More important, many of them are inductive signs of events or states of affairs in that human being's environment. As I sit indoors, I see a man in the road outside putting up his umbrella. This is an inductive sign that it is raining, just as a pitter-patter sound on the roof would be. I see him getting into the driving-seat of a motor-car, and this is a sign that there is petrol in the tank, much as a petrolly smell would be if one had taken off the lid of the tank and sniffed. These signs are not, of course, infallible. The man may be putting up his umbrella just to test it, because the metal ribs and joints are old and rusty. He may be getting into the driving-seat just to wind up the clock. But few inductive signs, if any, are 100 per cent reliable.

Now among the human events which are inductive signs of environmental states of affairs, human utterances are the most important, and the next most important are the written signs which human beings produce. I can learn a very great deal about the environmental world by noticing the noises which other human beings utter, and the written marks which they make from time to time. A very large part of the knowledge or probable belief which each of us has concerning events and objects which he does not himself observe is acquired by attending to the *verbal* behaviour of other human beings. And can it be denied that this knowledge or probable belief is in the end inductive? By noticing the more or less constant conjunctions which there are between different sorts of human noises and different sorts of environmental situations, one learns to take these noises as inductive signs for those environmental situations, when the noises are again observed but the environmental situations are not. Moreover, by attending carefully to the noises people make, one is able to distinguish those which are correlated with states of affairs earlier than themselves, with contemporary states of affairs, and with later ones. In this way some human noises come to be inductive signs of past events, others of present events not observed by the hearer, and others of future ones. And so the knowledge or probable belief acquired from these inductive signs extends far beyond the range of one's present observations, not only spatially but also temporally.

It can now be seen how this way of regarding human behaviour differs from the other two which were mentioned before. On the one hand, the notion that such behaviour, and especially verbal behaviour, is the overt and observable effect of inward and private psychical processes is entirely disregarded. If the word 'mind' is interpreted in the traditional Dualistic sense, then the Sign-theorist has no need to attribute minds to other human beings at all. So long as their verbal behaviour is a pretty reliable inductive sign of various environmental happenings, it does not matter to him whether they have minds or not. On the other hand, the biological utility which verbal behaviour may have to the organism that behaves is also disregarded. It might, of course, be important if one were inquiring into the causes of such behaviour; indeed, even the inward and

private psychical processes which the Dualist speaks of might conceivably be important, if a causal explanation of human verbal
behaviour were our aim. But such causal questions are of no interest
to the Sign-theorist, no matter how we answer them. Again, it
does not matter to him that the environmental happenings which a
human utterance is a sign of, is sometimes itself a cause or part-
cause of that utterance; as when a fox running across the road in
front of someone is the cause or part-cause of his saying, 'Hullo!
A fox!' The whole causal scheme of environmental stimuli and
biologically useful responses is simply disregarded. Thus the conception of human nature with which the Sign-theorist is working
is not exactly a Behaviouristic one either, although the *methods* by
which he conducts his investigation of human utterances and writings
are certainly Behaviouristic ones, since he takes no account of anything which is not overt and observable.

What then is his conception of human nature? It is a strange and
unfamiliar one, which Mr. William Kneale has called 'The Thermometer View'. Human organisms are conceived on the analogy of
scientific instruments. From certain events which happen in them,
especially their utterances, I learn to infer what is going on outside
them, just as I learn to infer the temperature of a bowl of water by
noticing how the mercury rises when a thermometer is put into the
bowl; or as I learn to infer what the weather has been, is, or
probably will be by noticing the wavy line on the chart of a recording barometer; or as I learn to infer that the sun is at its zenith
(though quite obscured by clouds) when I hear the clock strike
twelve strokes in daylight.

Of course the analogy of a scientific instrument is by no means
perfect. For one thing, scientific instruments are themselves made
by human beings. There are other differences. Human speech and
writing is often a less accurate indication of environmental happenings than a good scientific instrument is; on the other hand, it is
also a less specialized one. The position of the head of the mercury
column in the thermometer is a very accurate sign of the temperature of the room, but it gives no indication at all about the height of
Popocatepetl or about the state of the stock market. A human talker
or writer is, so to speak, a multi-purpose thermometer. Indeed,
there is almost no limit to the inductive indications it can give me.
Once I have learned what kinds of environmental happenings its

various noises are correlated with, I am able to get inductive information about almost anything in heaven or earth, including the past and the future. Of course these inductive signs are not 100 per cent reliable, as has been remarked before. But this is not to be expected. Even a good clinical thermometer gives false indications at times. Again with human utterances, as with other sorts of inductive signification, one sometimes gets conflicting signs. Mr. A says, 'The London train will be here in two minutes'; Mr. B says, 'The London train left half a minute ago'. The path of one who puts his trust in inductive signs is never altogether smooth. But on the whole, can it be denied that human noises and written marks are by far the most valuable of all inductive signs for guiding one's expectations and one's conduct, and for extending the range of one's knowledge or probable belief beyond the very narrow bounds to which direct observation and memory would confine them?

We may get another clue to this curious conception of human nature if we try to imagine a kind of Physicalistic analogue of the Correspondence Theory of Truth. In the traditional Correspondence Theory, what corresponds with a fact is either something mental—a thought, or idea or set of ideas—or else it is a proposition considered as a timeless and subsistent entity; and so it is thoughts, or else subsistent propositions, to which the predicate 'true' and 'false' are to be assigned. In a Physicalistic version of the theory, there is no place for thoughts and still less for subsistent propositions. What corresponds to a fact, or discords with it, is a piece of verbal behaviour, either an utterance or the production of a set of written marks; and the correspondence itself has to be defined in terms of inductive correlations. If a certain human organism A makes the noise 'it is raining', this utterance is true, or corresponds with a fact, provided it is one which A and other organisms of A's social group are usually found to utter when rain is actually falling in their near neighbourhood.

I have called this theory of truth Physicalistic, rather than Behaviouristic, for the reasons already mentioned. It is not at all concerned with the biological utility which such an utterance may have for the organism which makes it, or for other human organisms which respond to it. From the biological point of view of Behaviouristic psychology, truth and falsity are only relevant in an indirect and secondary way, because of the indirect influence they have upon the welfare or survival of human organisms; and sometimes, of course, a false utterance may have more biological utility than a true one, as a Behaviourist student of psychopathology or sociology would be quick to point out. The 'Thermometer View' of human nature has just the opposite order of priorities. The inductively establishable correlation between utterances and environmental happenings is its primary concern; and considerations of biological utility are only relevant in an indirect and secondary way, when one is asking why it is that in particular cases the usual correlation between utterances and environmental situations breaks down. One is then making a second-order inductive inquiry to discover in what circumstances the first-order inductive signs are unreliable. We make similar second-order inquiries into the defects occasionally found in clocks, thermometers, barometers, voltmeters, etc.

Such is the conception of human nature and human language which we are committed to if we take the Inductive Sign Theory of meaning seriously. And a very strange conception it is. All the same, it is not so utterly absurd as it may look. Some of the objections which naturally occur to us when we first encounter it can be answered.

Let us consider one of the most obvious. It might seem that such a theory would only apply, at the most, to one part of human verbal behaviour, namely the production of indicative sentences concerning matters of fact. No doubt the term 'sentence' must be construed rather liberally. There are one-word sentences. A man sometimes says just 'fox' when a fox appears in his near neighbourhood, and this utterance is equivalent to a sentence, and is true or false. In spoken language, outside the nursery, such one-word sentences are not very common. But on notice-boards they are fairly frequent. The word 'Wolverhampton' written in very large letters on a board at a railway station, is equivalent to 'this town is Wolverhampton', and the word 'surgery' written over a door is equivalent to 'this is a surgery'. Still more frequently, descriptive phrases, without verbs, function as sentences and convey information about matters of fact: for example 'Third Class Refreshment Room' or 'Oxford 7 miles' or 'Dangerous Corner'. Such written phrases are equivalent to deictic sentences, and acquire their deictic function from the place where they are located. It may be noticed that they sometimes give information about the past or the future: e.g. 'Roman Amphitheatre' or 'First performance 7 p.m.' (read at 3 p.m.).

But making all allowances for the misleading grammatical form which indicative sentences may sometimes assume, it may still be objected that indicative sentences are certainly not the only utterances or written marks which have meaning. Surely it is plain, in the first place, that individual words have meaning, not merely where they are equivalent to whole sentences, but also in their ordinary usage, when they are only constituents of sentences? When the single word 'rain' is equivalent to a sentence, gives information and is true or false, it *could* perhaps be argued that this utterance is a sign of rain very much as black clouds are, or that when I hear a man make it, it is very much as if I saw him putting up an umbrella. But suppose that at breakfast I hear him say, 'There was heavy rain at three o'clock this morning'. In this case, the word 'rain' does not seem to be an inductive sign at all; and if there is anything which can be regarded as an inductive sign of an environmental state of affairs, it can only be the whole sentence. But no one doubts that the word 'rain' still has meaning. It is still a symbol, but it is not an inductive sign. It conveys no information and it arouses no belief, though the sentence as a whole does both.

Moreover, granting that the sentence as a whole is an inductive sign, surely the signifying power which it has is somehow derived from the meanings which its constituent words have individually? The sentence as a whole is an inductive sign, if you like; but only because its constituent words are *not* inductive signs. If sentences as wholes are to have meaning in the way inductive signs have, it would seem that they can only have it because their constituent words have meaning in some quite different way, for which this theory has made no provision at all.

Let us see whether the Inductive Sign Theory of language can make any reply to this objection. To begin with, we shall ignore 'logical' words and phrases, such as *if, not, there is,* etc. For the present, we shall only consider what it might say about 'object' words, standing for observable objects and events, and the observable qualities and relations which they have: such words as 'cat', 'red', 'above', 'shrill'—ostensibly definable words, as they are sometimes called.[1]

Many logicians have maintained that 'the unit of meaning is the sentence', that sentences are 'prior to' words, or that words are 'abstractions from' sentences. Anyone who holds the Inductive Sign theory of language must clearly accept this thesis in some form or other. But how is he to reconcile it with the notorious facts which appear to refute it: with the fact that individual words (i.e. individual object words) clearly do in *some* sense have meaning, and that in *some* sense the meaning of a sentence is derived from, not prior to, the meanings of the individual words which compose it? Surely one of the main advantages of verbal symbolism is that it enables us to use old words in new combinations, and thereby to say things (true or false) which have not been said before; and how could this be done unless each of the words which are combined already had some independent meaning of its own?

Perhaps the Sign Theory might answer as follows:—When one hears or sees the individual word 'rain', one learns that something or other is the case with regard to rain (or was, or will be), but one does not yet know exactly what. An individual object-word, then, *is* an inductive sign, but an exceedingly indefinite one. As further words are added, the inductive sign becomes gradually more and more definite, until at last a determinate piece of inductive information is acquired. And as to the belief which an inductive sign arouses, it is true that the hearing or seeing of an individual object-word does not arouse belief. Nevertheless, it does, as it were, give a direction to our believing tendencies. On hearing the word 'rain' we prepare ourselves to accept a belief of *some* kind concerning rain— rather than, say, a belief concerning hippopotamuses, or scarecrows. But just what belief it is to be is only settled when we have the complete utterance before us, for example 'rain fell heavily at three o'clock this morning'. Moreover (we shall be told) the individual word 'rain' only has this effect upon us because it has already occurred many times in sentences which were themselves inductive signs. These sentences differed from each other in various ways, but were all alike in this, that the noise 'rain' occurred in them all, and a downpour of water from the sky was always somehow involved

---

[1]The distinction between object words and logical words is borrowed from Lord Russell's *Inquiry into Meaning and Truth*.

in the environmental states of affairs with which those sentences were inductively correlatable.

Thus when we say that an individual object-word has meaning, we should be saying something like this: that it is a sound or mark which has been found to be capable of forming part of an indefinitely large range of alternative inductive signs. It is not an inductive sign independently and in its own right (apart from the exceptional cases where it functions as a complete sentence). But it does bring to mind an indefinitely large range of alternative inductive signs; it brings them to mind by being a possible constituent in any one of them. And so, indirectly and derivatively, it becomes an inductive sign itself, though an exceedingly indefinite one, and is able to give a direction, though again an exceedingly indefinite one, to our believing tendencies. Thus, according to the Inductive Sign theory of language, object-words do after all have meaning, but only in a derivative way. And when we are said to make up a new sentence by combining object-words, we shall not be allowed to suppose that this is at all like making up a new whole out of old bits. It will be argued that what we really start from, in this so-called 'combining', is two or more ranges of sentences, say the range of sentences from which the word 'cat' derives its meaning, and the range of sentences from which the word 'fat' derives its meaning. And the result of the operation is that these two or more ranges of sentences now have a common member. We have a new sentence which is, so to speak, the overlap of these two or more ranges of sentences. It will have to be admitted, I think, that a sentence which has never been uttered before is not in any strict sense an inductive sign, just because it is new. There cannot as yet have been any constant conjunction between this sentence and an environmental state of affairs. But the Sign Theory could still maintain that the meaning which this new sentence has is entirely derived from its relationship to other sentences which *are* inductive signs.

We may now turn to another very obvious difficulty. It would seem that the Sign Theory could only apply, at the most, to the descriptive factors in language. It has already been pointed out that the Sign Theory seems at first sight to apply only to indicative sentences concerning matters of fact, sentences which 'directly describe the world'; for these, it would seem, are the only ones which can plausibly be regarded as inductive signs. What account does it give of the *logical* factors in human language? There are differences of logical form between one utterance and another, and in a well-developed language these are indicated by the use of special logical words, such as *not, if, either-or, all, some,* etc. Moreover, there are sentences, and perfectly intelligible ones, which do not describe matters of fact at all: *a priori* sentences such as $2+3=5$, or $(x+y)^2=x^2+2xy+y^2$. Such sentences, we usually suppose, are true whatever the empirical facts may be. Their truth consists in their being logically necessary. And their contradictories are false not because they misdescribe the world, but because they are logically impossible or absurd. Here we must remember that not all *a priori* truths are concerned with *a priori* concepts, as in the examples just given. 'Red is a colour' is also an *a priori* truth, and 'some cats are not animals' is not just factually false, but absurd.

How is it that logical words have meaning on an Inductive Sign theory of language? How is it that sentences of different logical forms have different meanings? And how can *a priori* sentences have meaning at all? Let us reformulate the problem before we consider how the Inductive Sign Theory might try to solve it. No one really supposes that 'not' and 'all' have meaning in the way that 'cat' and 'black' have. It would be better to say that a logical word has a force or a function or a use, rather than a meaning. And the right question to ask is, what account does the Inductive Sign Theory give of the force or function of logical words, and of the force or function of the logical forms of sentences? Similarly with *a priori* sentences. If the word 'meaning' is interpreted in the way the Inductive Sign Theory interprets it, *a priori* sentences cannot be said to have meaning. But for all that, they might still have a function in human discourse, and an important function too, and there is no reason why an Inductive Sign Theory should deny it. And whatever theory of meaning one holds, however orthodox and respectable one is, can it really be supposed that '$2+3=5$' has meaning in at all the same way as 'it is raining'?

Let us first consider the part which logical words play in descriptive sentences concerning matters of fact. We have already seen that certain logical factors are involved in inductive signification itself.[1] They are already present in very simple and unsophisticated forms of sign-cognition, where the signs are not human utterances

[1] Cf. ch. v, above.

and writings, but simple, familiar things like black clouds, or clear skies on winter evenings, or the squeaking of the brakes of a bus. We have seen, for example, that the state of vigilance, which occurs in animals as well as in ourselves, has something disjunctive about it; it is a state of being prepared for either A or B, and the sign which evokes it is a disjunctive sign. It may accordingly be suggested that we can learn the force or function of logical words by noticing the situations in which sentences containing them are uttered, provided that the situations are themselves already sign-situations. Thus 'it will *either* rain *or* hail' is uttered when there is a very black cloud and a cold, gusty wind. And this situation is itself a disjunctive sign, a non-verbal one. 'Someone is at the door' is uttered in a situation where there is already a non-verbal sign which is general, rather than specific, for example when the front door-bell rings. Similarly with *not*. Let us suppose that we have already learned what the utterance 'it is raining' signifies, by noticing what environmental states of affairs it is regularly conjoined with. It will then be fairly easy for us to discover what difference the addition of the word NOT makes to this sentence. We already know what it is for an inductive sign to be falsified, and 'it is raining' is already an inductive sign for us. And so we can learn that 'it is not raining' is what people say when the inductive sign 'it is raining' is falsified.

In a similar way, we can learn to appreciate at least part of the force, or function, of the conditional form of sentence. As I have tried to explain, there is such a thing as conditional signification quite apart from the understanding of words. It may arise from a combination of strong and weak signs, where A is a weak sign of B, and B, *if* it were to occur, would be a stronger sign of C; or again, where A by itself is a weak sign of something, but *if* B were to occur as well, the two together would be a strong one. I have also tried to explain how there may be a state of vigilance, even in animals, which is conditional as well as disjunctive; one is prepared for either A or B, and for X *if* A happens and for Y *if* B happens. When I am already observing an environmental situation which puts me into such a state of conditional preparedness, I may notice that if-then sentences are uttered by human beings in my neighbourhood. And if this happens repeatedly I may learn to correlate such non-verbal conditional sign situations with utterances containing the word *if*; and thus I learn to appreciate the force or function of this word.

It will be seen that the Inductive Sign Theory is here drawing a distinction between two sorts or levels of verbal signs. The primary ones are those which a spectator or hearer could learn to understand without any previous experience of inductive signs. The understanding of them is similar in principle to the way Russell's object words are understood, though they are sentences and not single words. 'It is raining' is an inductive sign of rain, very much as black clouds are. The secondary verbal signs are those which can only be understood if one has some acquaintance with *non*-verbal inductive signs already. A perfectly empty mind, without any previous inductive learning, could learn to correlate 'it is raining' with a certain recognizable and repeatable state of affairs, and 'it is snowing' with another one. But such a mind could make nothing of 'either it is raining or it is snowing' unless it had had some previous experience of non-verbal inductive correlations.

Thus the Sign Theory can give quite a plausible account of the force or function which logical forms and logical words have in the descriptive use of language. The logical form which a given empirical sentence has does help to determine just what sort of environmental state of affairs the utterance of that sentence is a sign of; and how it helps to determine this, one could discover by an inductive study of the situations in which affirmative or negative sentences, categorical or hypothetical or disjunctive ones, are habitually uttered by the human organisms which come under one's observation. With all sentences except affirmative and categorical ones, it would be found that these situations are themselves already sign-situations. But there is no difficulty about this, if our account of non-verbal sign situations in Chapters IV and V was correct.

Nevertheless, the descriptive use of language is not of course the only one. Language is also used for reasoning. Indeed, one of the most important facts about verbal signs—assuming that they are signs at all—and the great advantage they have over gestures, diagrams, dumb-show and the like, is that long and elaborate trains of argument can be carried on by means of them; whereas one cannot argue at all in gestures or diagrams, or only in the very simplest way. Again, one of the most important functions which the logical form of a sentence has is that it helps to determine the part which the sentence can play in reasoning processes—what other sentences follow from this one, what other sentences it

N

follows from itself, what other sentences it is consistent with, or inconsistent with.

Thus one of the most important questions we must ask ourselves, if we want to hold an Inductive Sign theory of human language is this: what is ratiocinative discourse, and when one understands a piece of ratiocinative discourse uttered (or written) by some human organisms, what sort of understanding is it? Has it anything at all to do with the inductive sort of understanding, as when a clear sky on a winter evening is understood as a sign of a frosty night?

It is true that in some pieces of ratiocinative discourse all the constituent utterances are descriptive sentences which are true (or false) 'about the world'. A simple example is, 'It is either raining or snowing; it is not raining, therefore it is snowing.' We have seen that even the disjunctive sentence, with which this piece of discourse begins, can be regarded as an inductive sign; and so could the negative sentence. But what is to be made of the 'therefore'? Can an Inductive Sign theory of language make any sense of the fact that the third sentence is a *logical consequence* of the first two taken together? Or if it can, must it not first abandon the 'Thermometer' conception of human nature, and treat human utterances not just as signs of environmental states of affairs but rather as signs of acts of thinking?

Moreover, there are important pieces of ratiocinative discourse in which one or more of the constituent utterances are not descriptive sentences at all, but *a priori* ones: for instance, 'There are 14 men in this room; 14 is an even number; therefore the men in this room can be divided into two equal groups'. The sentence '14 is an even number' does not describe the world. It is true whatever the empirical facts may be. And whatever sort of meaning it has, it certainly does not mean by being inductively correlatable with observable states of affairs. Finally, there are pieces of ratiocinative discourse in which *all* the constituent utterances are *a priori* sentences; for example, the discourse which occurs when someone is working out a multiplication sum, either aloud or by making marks on paper. In whatever sense *a priori* sentences are 'understood', it is plain that they cannot be understood at all apart from the functions they have in deductive argument. If one may say so, their whole *raison d'être* consists in their deductive potentialities. Moreover, the *raison d'être* of even the humblest empirical sentence (e.g. 'it is raining') consists partly in its deductive potentialities; though not, of course, wholly, since it also has the function of describing matters of fact.

In this awkward situation, a holder of the Inductive Sign theory might perhaps argue as follows. Language, it might be said, has two different functions. In respect of one of its functions it is a means of describing the world, and this function can be analysed in terms of inductive signification. In respect of its other function, it is a kind of calculus, whereby one sentence or set of sentences can be transformed into another. But the sentences subjected to this process are still themselves inductive signs, and so are the sentences which result from it. That is why verbal signs (sentences) are more important than all other inductive signs. Verbal signs are so made that they fit, as it were, into a calculus. By manipulating descriptive sentences in a suitable way, human talkers—and writers—are able to derive from them other descriptive sentences, though the linguistic processes by which the derivation is carried out do not themselves describe anything. That this can be done, and by what linguistic devices it is done, is something one can discover by observing human verbal behaviour. Among these linguistic devices are logical words like 'if . . . then', 'therefore', 'is consistent with', 'contradicts'. It is the logical forms of descriptive sentences which make it possible to manipulate descriptive sentences in this remarkable way. They show us what other descriptive sentences can, or cannot, be derived from a given descriptive sentence, and from what other descriptive sentences it itself can, or cannot, be derived. And the function of logical words is to make the logical forms of sentences more manifest. Logical words are not absolutely indispensable. Instead of say 'not p' it might be the custom to utter p in a whisper, or with a shrug of the shoulders. Instead of saying 'p or q', people might say 'p' with a look to the right, and then 'q' with a look to the left. Instead of saying 'if p, then q' they might say 'p' with a pause after it, and 'q' after the pause. Contrary to the opinion of some philosophers, the logical word 'is', at least in its predicative use, can be more easily dispensed with than most others. Even in English one can say 'Dark night' instead of 'The night is dark'. Nevertheless, in written language, where we get no help from tones of voice or gestures, the ratiocinative manipulation of descriptive sentences is very difficult unless logical words are used to indicate the logical forms of the sentences manipulated.

These considerations about logical form and logical words may help us to understand the force or function (rather than 'meaning') of *a priori* sentences like '14 is an even number'. According to the Sign Theory of language, *a priori* sentences are just part of the machinery of the linguistic calculus itself; and this, it would be said, is the only function they have. They are just devices whereby one descriptive sentence is transformable into another; as the descriptive sentence 'There are 14 men here' was transformed into 'The men here can be divided into two equal groups'. Similarly 'There is a cat in the room' can be transformed into the more general descriptive sentence 'There is an animal in the room' by means of the *a priori* sentence 'All cats are animals'. The ordinary view is that this *a priori* sentence is an analytic truth. But according to the Sign Theory, it should not be called true at all (or, of course, false either). But we are not to conclude from this that it has no force or function, as 'Abracadabra is a second intention' has none. On the contrary; it is a linguistic device whereby cat-mentioning descriptive sentences may be transformed into animal-mentioning descriptive sentences.

Finally, when we come across a piece of ratiocinative discourse in which *all* the constituent sentences are *a priori* ones (e.g. a purely arithmetical argument) the Sign Theorist will say that this in itself is nothing but a series of moves in a complicated speech-game, played according to certain curious rules which we can discover by carefully observing the noise-making or mark-inscribing behaviour of the players. But the game is important all the same. By the observable procedures of counting and measuring, the game can be brought into relation with observable matters of fact, or with the descriptive sentences which describe them. Multiplying 252 by 763 ceases to be a mere game when we are provided with the descriptive sentences 'There are 763 bags here', and 'There are 252 potatoes in each bag'. By applying the rules of the game to these sentences we can derive the new descriptive sentence 'There are 192,276 potatoes here'. To alter the analogy: in the sort of ratiocinative discourse which occurs in pure mathematics it is as if a sausage-machine were operating idly, without any meat in it. But put in a lump of meat at one end, and you will find that a very acceptable set of sausages emerges at the other. Thus ratiocinative discourse, even when it is of a purely *a priori* sort, still has a function or use; and the importance of that function or use is in no way minimized by the Sign Theory, though we do, of course, have to abandon the metaphysical (and epistemological) theories which some philosophers have tried to extract from it.

On some such lines as these, the Inductive Sign theory of language could claim to make room for ratiocinative discourse, as well as descriptive discourse. And it is not just that we find an inductive-sign analysis will apply to only one of the functions of language, the descriptive function, and then by an after-thought tack on to this analysis another different analysis—consistent with our original one, but quite separate from it—to deal with the ratiocinative function of language. The 'calculus' conception of ratiocination, and the Inductive Sign conception of descriptive sentences are not merely consistent with each other, but connected; and both of them fit the conception of human nature with which the Inductive Sign theory of language began. For the 'calculus' aspect of language is not conceived as something self-sufficient, complete in itself, existing side by side with the descriptive aspect. On the contrary, the material to which the calculus is applied consists entirely of inductive signs; and the whole purpose which the calculus serves is to transform inductive signs into one another, to derive other inductive signs (empirical sentences) from the inductive signs we already have. It may, therefore, be claimed that the 'calculus' conception of ratiocinative discourse is not just an extraneous addition to the inductive-sign conception of descriptive discourse. And the curious conception of human nature, which assimilates human verbal behaviour to the behaviour of scientific instruments, is still retained. Human talkers are indeed multi-purpose instruments! Only the functions they perform turn out to be even more multiform than we thought they were when we considered only the descriptive aspect of human behaviour. These admirable thermometers are calculating machines as well.

CHAPTER VII

SIGNS, SYMBOLS AND OSTENSIVE
DEFINITIONS

ONE cannot judge a philosophical theory until it has been applied in detail. To estimate its merits and defects, one must watch the theory at work, so to speak. One cannot accept it or reject it merely by examining a brief formula. 'Symbols are a species of inductive signs, distinguished from others by the fact that they are produced by human beings.' We have a temptation to examine such a sentence in isolation. We go through it with a toothcomb and turn it inside out. This is a pleasant exercise for those who like that kind of thing, but it does not conduce greatly to the discovery of truth, or the increase of clarity, or whatever we think the aim of philosophical inquiry is. The results which we shall reach by such a method will seem to the onlooker to be purely verbal, academic in the bad sense of the word; and he will not be far wrong. Confronted with such a formula, one ought to see what can be *done* with it. To estimate its value fairly, one must first discover what degree of clarificatory power it has; and for this, one must apply it, in some detail, to the problems and puzzles which it was designed to solve, and perhaps also to some problems and puzzles which its inventors themselves overlooked. In the previous chapter I have tried to treat the Sign Theory of Symbolization in this way, by exhibiting it at work and showing what can be done with it. We should now be in a position to judge it.

The defect of the Sign Theory is its one-sidedness. From beginning to end, it confines itself to the spectator's point of view. It is a theory not of meaning as such, but of meaning for the looker-on or the listener, who observes and interprets the utterances, writings, gestures, diagrams, etc., produced by other people; it throws no light on meaning for the speaker, for the writer, the gesticulator, the one who draws the diagrams. It looks at symbolization entirely from the consumer's end, and not at all from the producer's.

This one-sidedness is inevitable. For Sign-cognition is an

observer's attitude. It is, of course, intelligent observation. Sign-cognition is a form of thinking, as we have already argued; it is one of the ways in which concepts manifest themselves. But what sort of thinking is it? One hesitates to appeal to use the distinction between 'passive' and 'active', because these terms have been so heavily charged with emotion by the way they have been exploited in manuals on the History of Philosophy. ('The Empiricists hold that the human mind is passive.' How degrading! 'The Rationalists hold that it is active.' This was splendid.[1] But if we can treat the distinction between passive and active as a distinction of degree, and disinfect it of its emotional aura, then we have to say that sign-cognition is a *relatively* passive attitude, *less* active than other forms of thinking. A being who could understand signs, but could get no further, would certainly be thinking. But yet we should hesitate to call him 'a thinker'. This is because his thinking is something imposed upon him from without, dependent on perceptual cues. He thinks, but he does not think for himself. The initiative is not in his hands. He remains at the level of tied ideas, and has not yet risen to free ones. And all this is still true when the signs happen to be the sounds, gestures, marks on paper, diagrams, etc., produced by other human organisms. Certainly the information I get from these signs (allowing for the moment that they *are* signs) is vastly wider and more varied than what I get from thunder-claps or cirrus clouds, or bird-songs, or autumnal smells, or other signs which 'just happen' without human agency. All the same, this information just comes to me, without any initiative on my part, once I have performed the basic inductions which correlate human noises, gestures, etc., with various sorts of environmental happenings. I am still dependent on perceptual cues. My thinking is still 'tied' and not 'free'. To use the same paradox as before, I am thinking but I am not yet a thinker. The Sign Theory, then, cannot give

---

[1]It is, of course, historically false that the Empiricists thought the human mind passive. It would be more just to criticize them for making it more active than it can possibly be. It is the Rationalist Mind, if either, which is the passive one, or at least the lazy one, equipped from the start with a complete outfit of basic ideas; born, if one may say so, with a silver spoon in its mouth. The Empiricist Mind has to acquire these basic ideas for itself (e.g. the idea of Thing or of Physical Space) by its own effort and initiative; and according to the Empiricist account of them, they are enormously complex. The Empiricist does too much honour to human nature, rather than too little.

an analysis of meaning for the thinker, but only at the most of meaning for the onlooker or the listener.

Yet, from the epistemological point of view at least, it is meaning for the thinker which is important, the function which words, gestures, diagrams have (and mental images too) in autonomous or free thinking. Indeed, it is the fact that we have these thought-instruments at our disposal, these multifarious sorts of symbols or symbolic particulars—it is this that makes free thinking possible. The autonomy of rational beings depends upon the use of symbols, and especially on the use of words; on the using of them, not just the listening to them. This is what makes such beings independent in some degree of their physical and perceptually presented environment; free, within quite wide limits, to think about what they like and where they like, with all the advantages, and, of course, the dangers, which such freedom gives. Men have written learned books in prison; and Archimedes, while Syracuse was being captured, could think about geometrical problems.

Such autonomy is beyond the reach of even the most accomplished sign-cognizant. And here, if anywhere, is the difference of kind between men and the lower animals. As we have seen, it is not true that the lower animals lack intelligence. Despite the authority of Locke, it is false that 'brutes abstract not'. Concepts or abstract ideas are manifested in their actions and their prepared-nesses to act. And animal learning, with the responsiveness to signs which results from it, is a primitive form of induction, as Hume noticed. But the lower animals do not seem to rise to the inde-pendent or autonomous thinking which the use of symbols makes possible. Their thinking always remains 'tied'. And so, though we must not deny that they think, we hesitate to call them thinkers.

If there is any truth in these considerations, a theory which reduces symbols to signs is bound to be one-sided. It can make no room for the distinction between tied thinking and free. Indeed, if symbolic cognition is just a special case of sign-cognition there can be no free thinking at all. All thinking will be tied to percepts (by the very nature of the sign-situation) and the fact that some of these percepts are human noises which we hear, or humanly produced marks or gestures which we see, makes no essential difference.

Let us put this in another way. Utterances, gestures, writings, diagrams have meaning for me when I produce them for myself, when I am *using* them as instruments of my own autonomous thinking, and not merely when I observe them being produced by others. But when I am using them for myself, they certainly are not functioning as signs; at any rate, they are not signs for me, even if they are signs for others who hear what I say, or see my writings or gestures. When I say 'the cat is in the cupboard' this set of sounds is not *for me* a sign of the cat's being in the cupboard. It evokes no belief in me that the cat is indeed there. My belief has quite other grounds: that I saw the cat go in two minutes ago and have not seen it come out, that I hear a mewing or a scratching noise from behind the cupboard door. It is only a lunatic or a dictator who makes the claim 'It is so because I say so'. Yet if the Sign Theory were right, we must all be making this claim whenever we say anything. Indeed, it may be that in making this remark about the cat I have no belief at all. I may have uttered the words playfully, or merely as a philosophical example (which was my reason for writing them down just now). Yet I still understand them perfectly well. In the terminology we are using, these sounds are symbols for me, something that I *think* with; but for me they are not signs, at any rate on this occasion of their occurrence.

The point is still more obvious if I do not utter the words aloud, but merely have the kinaesthetic sensations of incipient utterance; and it is most obvious of all if I think this proposition by means of mental images, verbal or pictorial. These sensations or images must certainly be counted as symbols, according to our present terminology. They are particulars 'in' which or 'with' which I am thinking. But they are not signs in any way at all, not even for onlookers; for no one else can observe my kinaesthetic sensations or my images. Messrs. Ogden and Richards must surely be mistaken in regarding images as a species of signs.[1] Yet images are certainly symbols. Whatever views we hold about image-thinking, and however sceptical we are about it, we cannot deny that the term 'symbol'—in the wide sense which it has in the present discussion—must cover verbal imagery at any rate. (The type-word 'cat' has *imagy* tokens as well as overtly perceptible ones.) Similarly, if pictures and diagrams drawn on paper be counted as symbols, mental pictures and

[1] *The Meaning of Meaning*, p. 23.

'imagy' diagrams must be counted as symbols too; and it is perfectly clear that they are not signs.

There is, however, one exceptional case which is familiar to students of psychical research and psychopathology. Symbols, even long and complicated concatenations of symbols, are sometimes produced without any conscious intention or control. Automatic writing is the best-known example. Automatic drawing also occurs, and so does automatic speech. Here the symbols sometimes *are* signs even for the person whose hand or vocal organs produce them. With certain people, it is found that these automatic writings or utterances are inductively correlatable with states of affairs outside their own organisms, states of affairs of which they have no 'normal' knowledge. This is one of the ways in which telepathic or clairvoyant impressions are sometimes manifested. It is also one of the ways in which repressed memories and wishes are manifested (cf. the slips of the tongue and pen studied by Freud).[1] Such automatic symbol-producings, then, *are* inductive signs—though not very reliable ones—and may even be signs for the person who is producing them; or rather for the person whose bodily organs produce them, for there is a sense in which 'he' does not do it at all. Similarly mental images, whether verbal or representative, may occur automatically. This is another way in which telepathic or clairvoyant impressions may manifest themselves, and repressed wishes or emotions likewise. In this one exceptional case, we may admit that even mental images are signs. But it is a case which Messrs. Ogden and Richards would probably refuse to contemplate; and it is certainly not the one they had in mind when they classed images as signs.

So far, I have been trying to show that the Inductive Sign Theory of Symbolization can give no account at all of meaning for the speaker, or the writer or other symbol-producer, even though it can give some account of meaning for the onlooker. And this amounts to saying that it can give no account of meaning for the thinker, that is, for one who *uses* symbols himself, freely and autonomously. It is the function of words, gestures, images, diagrams, ritual actions, etc. in 'free' thinking which the epistemologist wishes above all to analyse. And if we class all these diverse particulars together under the term 'symbol', then the important epistemological problem is, how symbols function in free thinking, when

[1] S. Freud, *The Psychopathology of Everyday Life*, chs. V and VI.

one thinks 'on one's own' or 'for oneself' either privately or publicly. On this problem, the Sign Theory of Symbolization throws no light at all.

Will it be replied, perhaps, that the sense in which my words, etc., have meaning for me when I use them myself is a purely dispositional one, equivalent just to saying that I *should* understand them, in the sign-cognitive way, *if* I were to hear or see them produced by other people? In that case, I understand my own utterances at the time when I make them in much the same way as I understand cricket when I am asleep or taking a bath. Let us agree for argument's sake that sentences like 'X understands S' and 'S has meaning for X' are statements about X's dispositions or capacities, and are not to be taken as descriptions of occurrences actually going on in him. It certainly sounds odd to say 'X is engaged in understanding S now' or 'S was having meaning for X at 12.10 p.m. yesterday'. Nevertheless, these dispositions are sometimes actualized, even though the actualizations cannot be described by using over again the words which describe the dispositions. And can it really be maintained that my understanding of the sentence 'the cat is in the cupboard' is actualized *only* when I hear or otherwise observe other people using it, and remains wholly latent and unactualized when I am using the sentence myself? On the contrary, the way I use the sentence myself is one of the most important and obvious criteria for deciding whether I understand it or not, for deciding whether it has meaning for me and what meaning it has for me. It is one of the most important and obvious ways in which an understanding-capacity is exercised or actualized. And this actualization of an understanding-capacity is just the one upon which the Sign Theory can throw no light.

But the Sign Theory does not really give an adequate account even of meaning for the hearer (reader, gesture-observer, etc.). It is true, of course, that many of the utterances, writings, etc., of my neighbours *are* among other things inductive signs. The fact that Mr. A says 'p' does usually give me fairly reliable inductive grounds for thinking that p is indeed the case. It is an important truth, and a truth too much neglected by epistemologists, that testimony is for each of us one of the chief sources of his information about the world. The Sign Theory deserves credit for insisting on this. All the same, it gives a one-sided and distorted account of what testimony is.

Receiving testimony (or indeed any sort of communication) is something more than acquiring information. It is acquiring information from another intelligent being; and not only so, but from an intelligent being who is actually exercising his intelligence in producing these words, gestures, diagrams or whatever they may be. If he were talking in his sleep, I should not be receiving a communication from him. His words would not be testimony, even though I might be acquiring most valuable information from them, say about a murder which he had witnessed but had hitherto kept concealed. Again, if he were writing automatically, I should not be receiving a communication from *him*, though I might conceivably be receiving a telepathic communication from someone else, which was manifesting itself through the automatic movements of the writer's hand-muscles. This amounts to saying that if we are to receive testimony from someone, the person who produces the words, gestures, etc., must himself be using them as symbols. It is not enough that he should just produce them; a parrot might do that. He must produce them in an understanding way. In short, in producing them he must be *thinking*—overtly and publicly, of course — just as I myself do when I use uttered words or overtly written marks understandingly. Thus the one-sidedness of the Sign Theory, its neglect of what I called 'meaning for the speaker', distorts the account which it gives even of the receiving of communications. For if something is to be a communication, it has to be *made* as well as received, and the making of it requires that the words, etc., have meaning for the person who produces them; and not merely in the dispositional sense, that he has the capacity of understanding them (this would be true of him if he were talking in his sleep) but in the sense that this capacity is being actualized or manifested in his present utterance.

This still holds good, *mutatis mutandis*, even if one insists upon regarding other human beings as superior thermometers. The whole point of a recording or measuring instrument (as also of a calculating machine) is that it does fulfil *some* of the criteria for being intelligent. When I look at the dial and see where the pointer stands, or how it is moving, this does in some degree approximate to receiving a communication. And for just this reason the instrument itself is not in a state which is analogous to sign-cognition, but in a state analogous to symbol-using. It approximates in some degree to a being who *makes* a communication, and who thinks in so doing. For the machine itself (if we may use the word 'for' in a stretched and analogical sense) the movement of the pointer is not a sign that the voltage is rising, but is analogous rather to a perceptual statement announcing something which the speaker himself observes. It is as if the voltmeter said, 'I feel the voltage rising' and *not* as if it said, 'I have inductive grounds for inferring it'. The analogue of sign-cognition, for the instrument itself, would be, for example, the setting in motion of a mechanism for switching off the current when the voltage rises above a certain point. (This would be something like the sign-cognition of animals, where the cognition is not separate from appropriate action.)

Thus the more the Sign Theory insists on the analogy between human beings and thermometers, the more it is obliged to misrepresent what thermometers and other such instruments do. It just takes the spectator's attitude to them, omitting to consider the function these pointer-readings have for the instrument itself; but this is just what must not be omitted, if—or to the extent that—the analogy between scientific instruments and intelligent beings is a valid one. If one may say so, the Sign Theory fails to take the thermometer's own point of view. Yet that is what must be done, if we are to assimilate human beings to thermometers and conceive ourselves as receiving *communications* from these thermometer-like objects.

The last criticism I shall offer is this. It could be argued that the utterances of other people (considered now from the listener's point of view) are only signs for me because they are *already* symbols. If so, of course the Sign Theory of Symbolization would be circular. In this connection, we notice first that we can perfectly well understand someone else's statement without at all believing it. How then can such an utterance (writing, gesture, etc.) be an inductive sign? Even if we confine ourselves entirely to the onlooker's point of view, and do not ask ourselves whether or how it can be an inductive sign for the person who makes it, can it be an inductive sign even for the onlooker? True enough, he knows what he would have to expect if it *were* an inductive sign. When someone says, 'there is a crocodile in the bathroom', I know just what I should have to expect, if the fact of his uttering it were a reliable inductive indication of the actual existence of the state of affairs described. But the difficulty is in the phrase 'the state of affairs described'. Some conceivable state of affairs *is* for me described by his utterance, and pretty unambiguously too, so that I know very well what it would be like, supposing it existed.

This suggests that even when I do believe what is said to me (as no doubt I do much more often than not) the describing function of the words is at least distinguishable from their inductive-sign function, even though both functions are in fact being performed. Moreover, their describing function, which they would have whether believed or not, appears to be logically prior to their belief-arousing functions which they have in their capacity of inductive signs, and to be a necessary condition of it. I have to understand what is said, *in order* to believe it, though usually there is no temporal interval between the understanding and the believing. If this is right, the Inductive Sign analysis of Symbolization is circular; and words, gestures, diagrams, etc., can only be inductive signs because they are already symbols. To be understood in the Inductive Sign sense of the word 'understand' (as when the doctor 'understands' the symptoms he observes) they must already be understood in the Symbol sense of 'understand'. Knowing what your words mean cannot just consist in knowing what to expect, if I must already know what they mean in order to know what to expect; whereas knowing what a red sky at sunset means *is* just knowing what to expect.

These criticisms of the Sign Theory will not, however, satisfy the reader unless we can also explain why the theory is so plausible. In spite of all, he will say, there must surely be something in it? There is. But to state clearly what there is in it is not an easy task.

The starting point of the theory is the pretty regular and reliable correlation between human utterances, gestures, etc., on the one hand, and environmental states of affairs on the other. These more or less constant conjunctions do have an important bearing on the analysis of meaning in the Symbol sense, though the Sign Theory gives a misleading account of what that bearing is. The important fact is that unless we did observe these more or less constant conjunctions, we should never come to *use* these sounds, etc., for ourselves, as instruments to think with.

Does this amount to saying that unless the majority of human utterances were true, no human utterance would have meaning in the Symbol sense? There is an air of paradox about this suggestion. (Surely an utterance, gesture, etc., must *already* have meaning in the Symbol sense, in order to be true—or false either?) But let us consider the suggestion all the same.

There does seem to be some close connection between meaningfulness and veracity. It certainly does appear that if all the sentences we ever heard were false, none of them could have meaning for us, though they would still have it for the speakers of them. But the word 'false' here is not sufficiently explicit. If they were *systematically* false, these statements would still have meaning for us; only it would be different from the meaning they had for the speakers of them. Imagine that whenever there was a black cat in the room our neighbours always said, mendaciously, that it was a white one. Their statements would be false. But we should attach meaning to them all the same. We should take 'white' to mean the quality which other people call 'black'. The first few times we heard the sentence 'this is white' it would be for us the ostensive definition of the word 'white' (or of the sentential function '*x* is white'), and so would be neither true nor false. But afterwards, if they went on saying, 'this is white' whenever a black object was before them, the statement would come to be, for us, true; though false, and even mendaciously false, for the utterers of it. It would be true for us, because it would be in accordance with the way in which the word 'white' had been, for us, ostensively defined. Likewise, if they systematically said 'the dog has eaten the fish', 'the dog has drunk the milk', etc., whenever the cat had done it, the sound 'dog' would have meaning for us, and we could use it in our own thinking, though it would mean for us what 'cat' means now. And after a time the statement 'the dog is mewing outside the door' would be true for us, though false for the speaker of it.

The fatal thing, which would prevent a sentence from having meaning for us, would be random or unsystematic falsehood. Or rather it would be random or unsystematic mendacity. For it is observation-statements which make ostensive definition possible; and it would be necessary that the object or situation misdescribed should be perceptually present both to speaker and hearer, so that the speaker would have to make his false statement consciously, well knowing what the true one would be. If our neighbours sometimes said 'this cup here is full of water' when there was ink in it, and sometimes when there was sand in it, and sometimes when it was empty, and sometimes when there was no cup at all, we should never learn to attach any meaning to these human noises. To be sure, we should suppose that they probably did have meaning, on grounds of analogy, because they are similar in sound-quality and audible pattern to other human utterances which have. But if *all* the human utterances we ever heard were uttered in this randomly false way, none of them would have meaning for us, neither in the Symbol sense nor even in the Sign sense. For us they would just be strange noises. We could not use them to think with, as we use words and sentences now; and they would not even have an effect upon us as signs, in determining the direction of our inductive expectations.

Let us look at this in another way. Understanding a sentence, it has been said, consists in knowing what it would be like for the sentence to be true (not necessarily in knowing how to verify it; that is a more stringent criterion of understanding than this traditional one). Now could it be argued that we only know what it *would* be like for S to be true, if we know what it *has* been like for S to be actually true? This would be another way of formulating the thesis we are discussing, that meaning for us depends upon the general veracity of other people. We can now see that the thesis is over-stated. For often, of course, we do know what it would be like for a sentence to be true without ever having experienced any situation in which the sentence was in fact true. I know quite well what it would be like for 'there is a crocodile now in the bathroom' to be true. I have never in my life observed such a situation, but I should recognize it if I did observe it, and should recognize too that the sentence is a correct description of it. A very young student of economics in the year 1951 knows what it would be like for the sentence 'there is a general fall of prices' to be true. He does not know what it *has* been like for the sentence to be true, because no such situation has occurred in his lifetime and he has never had a chance of observing it. All the same, he would be able to recognize such a situation, if by any chance it were to occur in future.

Phrases such as 'crocodile in bathroom', 'general fall of prices' are traditionally said to stand for *complex ideas*. And it is plainly true that one may possess a complex idea without ever having experienced an instance of it. Indeed this is a fundamentally important fact about human cognition, whatever scruples we may have about the way the 'idea' terminology formulates it. But with simple ideas it is very different (if we may continue to use the traditional terminology for the moment). A simple idea can only be possessed by someone who has actually experienced instances of it. We may have our doubts about the term 'simple'. But there is no doubt that there are complex ideas, in some good sense of the word 'idea'; there is no doubt either that they are analysable into ideas which are simpler than themselves; and that at some stage of the analysis we come down to simpler ideas (whether absolutely simple or not) which we only possess through having had experience of instances of them.

To translate this into a terminology of sentences: the principle suggested just now, that we should not know what it would be like for a sentence to be true if we did not know what it has been like for the sentence to be actually true, was certainly too sweeping. It certainly does not apply to all the sentences which we understand. But surely there must be *some* sentences to which it does apply, if any sentences at all are to be understood? (So, too, *mutatis mutandis*, if we substitute other examples of human symbolic behaviour for sentences—e.g. gesture, dumb-show, diagrams, ritual actions, and even telepathically communicated images). There must be basic or primary or 'ground floor' symbols which are directly connected to the world, tied to observable things and qualities and situations, if anything is to be for us a symbol at all. And the tie or connection can only be provided if these symbols are used veraciously by our neighbours, at any rate much more often than not. With these basic symbols, the general truthfulness of our neighbours really does seem to be a necessary condition of understanding in us. Sentences referring to sensible qualities and relations, such as 'green', 'squeaky', 'in', 'above', can only get their meaning in this way. Or at least, in uttering these sentences in our presence our neighbours must be either truthful or else *systematically* (not randomly) mendacious.

Yet the thesis 'no meaning anywhere without truth somewhere'

G

(to formulate it roughly and briefly) is still not altogether free from paradox. There is the difficulty mentioned earlier that meaningfulness seems to be prior to truth. Surely an utterance must already have meaning, in the Symbol sense of 'meaning', in order to be true? Moreover, if a sentence is true, it must be conceivable that it might have been false instead; at any rate if it is an empirical sentence, and it is empirical sentences with which we are at present concerned. Is it seriously suggested that some empirical sentences are necessary truths?

The paradox arises from a failure to distinguish between the point of view of the hearer and the point of view of the speaker. When we do distinguish them, we notice that some utterances have a dual status; they are as it were double-faced. They may function either as truths or as ostensive definitions. The very same utterance may be a truth for the speaker and an ostensive definition for the hearer. Indeed, any statement which truly describes an observed matter of fact is capable, also, of being an ostensive definition; or rather perhaps of being a contribution towards an ostensive definition, for normally ostensive definition requires a series of similar utterances uttered in the presence of a series of similar situations. 'This is green,' said in the presence of an unripe apple, is true. But it could also be (or contribute towards) an ostensive definition of 'green', or, if it be preferred, of the sentential function 'x is green'. By hearing such an utterance repeatedly made in the presence of unripe apples, fresh grass, cucumbers, etc. I learn to attach meaning to the word 'green'. Or rather, the *sound* 'green' comes to be for me a *word*. It comes to have meaning for me in the Symbol sense. But if that is the way I take the utterance 'this is green', it is not for me true. This does not, of course, entail that it is for me false. The point is that for me the disjunction 'true or false' does not yet apply to it. For me, it is not a meaning-using utterance, but a meaning-giving one. For the speaker, on the contrary, it is a meaning-using one, and for him it is either true or false; true in this particular instance, but capable on other occasions of being false, and it is conceivable (though not in fact the case) that it might have been false this time.

Thus it is not really being suggested that in these basic empirical sentences 'truth is prior to meaning'. That would be a gross over-simplification. What is being suggested is only that truth for the speaker is prior to meaning for the hearer. In the speaker's case the priority is the other way about. For him the utterance is already a symbol, and naturally its meaningfulness is a necessary condition of its being either true or false. And the speaker does have to speak the truth, at least in these basic or 'ground-floor' sentences, usually even if not invariably, if his utterances are to function as ostensive definitions for the hearer. Or at any rate, if his utterances are to be ostensive definitions for the hearer, they must be at least systematically false (not randomly false); though if they are, the ostensive definition which the hearer acquires will be different from the one accepted by the speaker himself.

This distinction, between the function which an utterance has for the speaker and the function it has for the hearer, goes some way towards solving the paradox which troubled us, but not all the way. There is also the fact that the very same (type) utterance, which is an ostensive definition for me now, may later be a true sentence for me also, as well as for others. Next week, having acquired my ostensive definition of 'green' (or of 'x is green') by hearing 'this is green' repeatedly uttered in the presence of leaves, grass, unripe apples, etc., I shall myself be using the very same (type) utterance to make true statements; and conceivably to make false ones too— at any rate, the utterance 'this is green', as I shall *then* use it, will always be capable of being false even when it is in fact true. This perplexity is likewise resolved by distinguishing between two points of view; in this case, the different points of view which the same person may have at two different stages of his mental history. The very same (type) utterance has different functions at different times even for the same person. At t_1 it is an ostensive definition, at t_2 it is a truth.

We can now begin to see what is right in the Inductive Sign Theory of Symbolization, whatever mistakes it may have made. In an oblique and half-conscious manner, it does draw our attention to the fundamental importance of *ostensive definitions*. There really is something inductive about ostensive definitions. These inductively reliable correlations between human utterances and environmental matters of fact, on which the theory insists so much, are just the more or less constant conjunctions by which ostensive definitions are acquired; and that is what makes them so important in an analysis of symbolization. It is through these constant conjunctions that the basic symbols get their meaning for the listener. Or rather, it is these constant conjunctions which turn these observed noises, gestures, marks, etc., into symbols, and enable us to use them for ourselves as instruments to *think* with.

Thus sign-cognition and symbolic cognition do have something in common. The experiences of constant conjunctions is fundamental to both, and neither could have existed in a perfectly random or chaotic world. The difference between these two sorts or stages of cognition comes from the different use to which the constant conjunctions are put. In sign-cognition, they guide our expectations and our actions. A-like events have been pretty constantly accompanied by B-like ones in our experience; when a new A-like event occurs, we are 'prepared for' another B-like event, both cognitively and practically. In an earlier chapter I have discussed this preparedness and have argued that it deserves to be called a form of thinking.[1] But it is a low-grade and undeveloped form of thinking, because it is always tied, more closely or less, to sensible cues. In symbolic cognition, on the other hand, observed constant conjunctions are put to a different use. This time they are more or less constant conjunctions between human utterances, etc., and environmental states of affairs. And now we use A to think of B not merely when a new A-like particular is presented to us, for instance when we hear someone say 'green' again, but by *producing* new A-like particulars for ourselves; whereas it is beyond our power to think of a thunderclap by producing a lightning-flash. Or if we can do something which faintly approximates to this, by producing a visual image of a lightning-flash, or drawing a zigzag line on paper with a reddish-yellow pencil, to that extent the particular which we produce *is* being used as a symbol.

Consequently, it is only certain sorts of particulars, not all, which are capable of becoming symbols. They have to be particulars which we can learn to produce for ourselves. But what particulars these are depends upon the constitution which the human mind and body happen to have. There might conceivably be intelligent beings which do use actual lightning flashes as symbols, as instruments for their own autonomous thinking. They might have the same control over meteorological occurrences that we have over

[1]Cf. pp. 93-104, above.

our utterances, gestures, writings and mental images. Again, in our case it so happens that quite a large part of the human brain is concerned with the activation and control of the speech muscles, and another large part is concerned with the control of the hand and finger muscles. There might conceivably be intelligent beings whose organisms are arranged quite differently, or who do not have organisms at all in the sense in which the human body is an organism, with a vast variety of organs all packed together in a clearly delimited region of physical space. The mind-matter linkage, whatever its nature is, might conceivably subsist not between a mind and a single compact piece of matter, but between a mind and many scattered bits of matter separated from each other by dozens of miles. Such a mind would have a kind of diffuse body without anything that could be called a shape. The question 'where is it?' would not have the same sort of straightforward and unambiguous answer which it has when asked about a human being. All the same, if such an intelligence could control events in these scattered bits of matter in the kind of way we control our speech movements and finger movements and gestures, such events could be used by it as symbols.

It is useful to consider these fanciful possibilities, because they bring out what properties it is necessary for a particular to have in order to be a symbol, and enable us to distinguish them from other properties which are irrelevant. It does not matter what sort of sensible (or imagable) properties these particulars have, though they must, of course, have some sensible properties or other. Such a particular need not be a vocally uttered sound, or a visible mark, or a gesture or an image of any of these, or a kinaesthetic sensation attending the production of any of them. That entities of these sorts are for human beings the most important symbols is a contingent fact, dependent on the constitution which the human organism happens to have. The property which an entity *must* have, in order to be a symbol, is the property of being easily produced and controlled by the mind which uses it to think with. It is also necessary, with basic symbols at any rate, that the symbol-to-be should have entered into constant conjunctions whereby it is linked to something other than itself, and that the mind which is to use it as a symbol should be capable of observing these conjunctions and retaining memory-traces of them.

It may be noticed in this connection that the sign-relation is often reversible. When A is a sign of B, it is often true that B is also a sign of A; consider for example, the relation between smoke and fire, or rain and wet streets. But when A is a symbol for B, the relation is irreversible. The sound 'rock' is a symbol for a certain familiar sort of object, whereas the object is not a symbol for the sound. This is because we cannot *use* the object for thinking of the sound, as we can use the sound for thinking of the object. And this in turn is because rocks are not producible at will (at any rate not by us) whereas sounds are.

Before we go further in our evaluation of the Sign Theory, it may be well to free ourselves from certain current superstitions about ostensive definition. These superstitions tend to obscure the close connection which there is between ostensive definition and induction, and thereby prevent us from doing justice to the Sign Theory. (If the reader prefers to restrict the word 'definition' to its traditional meaning of *inter-symbolic* definition, where one word is defined in terms of other words, he may substitute 'ostension' or 'ostensive process' for 'ostensive definition').

In the first place, ostensive definition need not have the ceremonious or ritualistic character which some philosophers have attributed to it. It is supposed that one takes the child or the foreigner by the hand, points to a tomato or a piece of sealing-wax, and says in a solemn and impressive tone of voice 'red' or 'this is red'. But this only happens when the hearer understands a number of other words already. He must already be familiar with the situation of being talked *to*, addressed by someone else; and for this, he must already have passed the stage in which words are just queer noises whose occurrence he observes from time to time. He already knows what discourse in general is. What he does not know, and is now to be taught, is what this particular bit of discourse, the word 'red', refers to. Thus the ceremonious sort of ostensive definition is only a way of adding to his vocabulary, not of providing him with one *ab initio*. Moreover, if we were right in suggesting that our understanding of deictic gestures has something inductive about it,[1] the meaning of pointing itself could not be taught by any such ceremony. The ceremony could only be effective if pointing is understood already. And thirdly, though ostensive definitions do have

[1] Cf. ch. VI, pp. 172-3, above.

to be learned, they are very seldom taught. Far more often, I acquire my ostensive definitions just by noticing what noises people make, and where. I learn, but I learn for myself, without being taught.

Again, deictic gestures need play no part in the process, and deictic words ('this', 'here', 'over there') need not occur. Deictic sentences like 'this is a cat' are much more common in philosophical books than in ordinary life and discourse. It is sufficient if a certain recognizable sound, gesture, mark, etc., repeatedly occurs from time to time (and there may be quite long intervals between the times) in such a way that I can correlate it with some other recurrent and recognizable item in the observable world. Moreover, the utterances which are to provide me with an ostensive definition of 'cat' need not be similar in respect of every one of their constituents, as when the very same type-utterance 'this is a cat' is repeated over and over again in the presence of cats. It is sufficient if the sound 'cat' recognizably occurs in all of them, and there is a recognizable common element in the perceptible environments in which they are uttered. The other sounds which are uttered along with this one may be different in each case. Indeed, it will be better if they are, because the one sound which is common to all these utterances will then be more easily noticed. 'Black cat,' 'cat at the window,' 'the cat has come in,' and even 'cat, go away!' would be quite a suitable series for the purpose. The last of these utterances might appear to infringe our principle that an ostensive definition must be for the speaker a true sentence, though the first two, if uttered in the presence of the object, may be counted as true sentences. But 'cat, go away!' though not true or false, cannot be properly said by the speaker unless he actually sees or feels or hears a cat very close to him. He must, therefore, be *ready* to utter the true sentence 'this is a cat'. And indeed there is something deictic about the use of the vocative case ('O cat, go away!').

The truth seems to be that certain recognizable sounds gradually sort themselves out from the different complex utterances in which they are constituents. And the common factor, e.g. 'cat', in these otherwise unlike utterances is gradually correlated with a common factor in observed environmental situations which are otherwise unlike. Similarly 'black' gradually sorts itself out from another range of utterances which are otherwise unlike, and is correlated with a visible quality experienced in otherwise unlike situations.

It is important to notice that such ranges of utterances may overlap. (In our example 'black' occurred once in the 'cat' series.) In this way, we acquire our first glimmerings of the syntactical properties of words. We find out, by an ostensive process, what other sounds a given sound is capable of being conjoined with, and how complex utterances are compounded out of simpler ones, where the simpler ones in their turn are correlated with *different* features in the observable world.

Nevertheless, the 'ceremonious' account of Ostensive Definition is not entirely wrong-headed. Whatever weaknesses it may have, it is an attempt, though not a very successful one, to solve a real difficulty. I have been speaking throughout of 'constant conjunctions' between human noises, gestures, etc., on the one hand, and environmental objects or situations on the other. But are there in fact such constant conjunctions, even if we take the word 'constant' in an elastic sense to mean 'much more frequent than not'? When I hear the sound 'cat' uttered by someone, of course there is sometimes a cat in the immediate neighbourhood of the speaker. But is it really true that this sound-and-object conjunction is usual, or even frequent? The fact surely is that words, and other symbols too, are far more often used *in absence* than in presence. Indeed, as we shall see later, this is perhaps the most important property that symbols have. By their means we contrive, somehow, to have in mind what is not now being perceived, to adjust our conduct with reference to it, and to bring about such adjustments in other people with whom we communicate. If you are hunting for a lost pencil, communications including the word 'pencil' are useful when you do *not* yet see the object and are still looking for it; and that is the time when you will most need this symbol in your own thinking too. Once you do see the object, there is no more need for words.

Thus (it may be objected) it simply is not true that when I hear the utterance 'cat' there is usually or even frequently a cat in the immediate neighbourhood. Nor is the converse proposition true that when there is a cat in someone's immediate neighbourhood, the sound 'cat' is usually or even frequently uttered by him. If he talks at all, he is just as likely—indeed more likely—to talk about something utterly different, something 'absent', such as the prospects of tomorrow's weather, or Mr. Jones' new motor-car, or the news in this morning's copy of *The Times*.

To meet this difficulty, it is quite naturally supposed that ostensive definition can only occur if words are sometimes uttered in a rather special and 'out of the way' manner—uttered in a specially emphatic tone of voice, repeated two or three times, accompanied by deictic gestures and by other actions designed to attract the hearer's attention (e.g. taking him by the hand, gazing fixedly in his direction). It is supposed that if a sound of this special kind, with these special accompaniments, is uttered in the presence of a certain environmental object, then—but not otherwise—the sound will have a chance of becoming a symbol for the hearer; whereas he would never learn what sort of object it referred to, or even that it referred to any object at all, if he were confined to observing the way it occurs in everyday life and discourse, where it is far more often used in absence than in presence. This is the line of thought which leads very naturally to the 'ceremonious' theory of ostensive definition; and if we reject that theory, we must find some other solution for the difficulty it is intended to meet. The phrase 'constant conjunction of noises and objects' clearly needs further analysis, and still needs it even when we explain that the constancy we have in mind is not absolute invariability.

As we have seen, it is not at all necessary that my neighbour should point at the object when he utters the word; it need not be uttered in a special tone of voice, nor need it be accompanied by a deictic word such as 'this', 'that', 'there', nor yet by an action designed to attract the hearer's attention. But it *is* necessary that he should show what I will call 'perceptual concern' with the object when he utters the word. (The word might, of course, be part of a much longer utterance.) He must direct his gaze at the object, or walk towards it, or touch it or handle it. Perhaps he picks the cat up and strokes it, and then lifts it out of the arm-chair and sits down there himself. Or he goes off to the kitchen, brings back a saucer of milk, puts it down on the floor, and gently propels the animal in that direction. And in the course of doing those things he makes an utterance, perhaps quite a complex one, in which the sound 'cat' is included. The phrase 'perceptual concern' must be understood, at this stage of our analysis, in a Behaviouristic sense. The man who utters the sound 'cat' *does* something about a certain object, and applies his sense organs to the object in so doing. The degree of perceptual concern which he shows may of course be small.

While making the utterance in which the sound 'cat' occurs, he may just glance at the creature and then return to his newspaper. But there must be some degree of overt perceptual concern on the speaker's part, and if it were always as small as this, the hearer would have difficulty in discovering what object the utterance 'cat' referred to. Fortunately, our neighbours do from time to time show a very considerable degree of perceptual concern with the objects around them, and in the course of showing it they do frequently utter words referring to those objects. If I had always lived among very taciturn and very absent-minded philosophers, who took little or no notice of their physical environment and talked only of the works of Fichte and Hegel when they did talk, I should acquire no ostensive definitions and should never learn to think in words at all. I might learn to expect that the sound 'dialectical' would probably occur pretty soon when the sound 'Hegel' had been uttered. But this would only be a special case of sign-cognition, like expecting the sound 'puff-puff-puff' when you hear a steam-engine whistling.

It comes to this, then. The relevant conjunctions are between the noises, etc., which my neighbours produce and the environmental objects or situations in which they show perceptual concern. To say that they are conjunctions between noises and objects is true, and convenient for brevity's sake, but in some contexts it is not sufficiently explicit. The 'ceremonious' account of ostensive definition is an attempt to remedy this inexplicitness, but a misguided one. The cure is worse than the disease.

The acquisition of ostensive definitions resembles induction in another way. It proceeds by trial and error, indeed by the unreflective application of something like Mill's Inductive Methods, as Lord Russell has pointed out.[1] In this respect again, the way we acquire symbols has something in common with the way we learn inductive signs. If we have only heard the word 'cat' used in the presence of black cats, we may easily take it to mean 'black'. But we correct this assumption later, when we find the word 'cat' being uttered in the presence of white or tabby or ginger-coloured creatures. To call it an assumption is not, of course, strictly accurate. It is something less conscious and explicit than an inductive hypothesis. It is rather that we acquire a habit of expecting a black thing

[1] *Inquiry into Meaning and Truth*, ch. 4, p. 76 (English edition).

when the word 'cat' is heard; then one day we see a white thing instead, and we suffer a shock of disconcertment and surprise. We cannot literally say that the habit is falsified, as an ordinary inductive hypothesis is falsified, in the textbooks, by the falsification of a prediction which follows from it. A habit is not the sort of thing which can be literally true or false. But we can say that our habit has 'let us down' or misled us or deceived us, much as an erroneous inductive hypothesis might. Again, the correcting of this habit is not the explicit and conscious adoption of a new hypothesis about a word-to-object correlation. It is simply that the old habit of expectation is broken down, as a result of this disconcerting experience, and a new habit of expectation begins to grow up in us instead. All this is very like what happens when an inductive sign 'lets us down'. The state of preparedness, cognitive and practical, which the occurrence of the sign puts us into, turns out to be inappropriate to what actually happens. We saw a familiar-looking sort of footprint, and round the corner we found not a dog but a wolf. Our state of preparedness will be different next time the sign occurs.[1]

It is clear from what has been said that ostensive definition is not necessarily the smooth, well-oiled process it is often represented to be. On the contrary, it is often slow, hesitant and gradual, with false starts and wrong turnings which have to be painfully corrected. No doubt those who offer the 'ceremonious' account of it, already criticized, would admit that the ceremony has to be repeated two or three times, if it is to be effective. But after that, it is supposed, the process of ostensive definition is over and done with, and the pupil understands the word once for all. This account of the matter, apart from its other defects, is much too clear cut. There is such a thing as half-understanding or incomplete understanding. Even when one has been subjected to the ceremony, one may get only part of the way towards an ostensive definition and not all the way. This state of half-success is still more frequent when one has to acquire an ostensive definition for oneself, without any teaching, merely by observing the utterances of other human beings and the circumstances in which they occur. And this is the way one usually does acquire them. Indeed, one's earliest symbols *must* be acquired in this untaught way. As we have seen, the ceremony is only effective

[1] On disjunctive preparedness, see pp. 119, 129, above.

if one understands some symbols already. Accordingly, one often has to be content with what may be called a 'working' ostensive definition, as one has to be content with 'working hypotheses' in other inductive procedures. It is not final, but we accept it *faute de mieux*; and we are prepared to modify it if need be, knowing from experience that other ostensive definitions have had to be modified. I myself am prepared to modify my provisional ostensive definitions of 'puce' and 'gibbous' at any time.

Of course a crucial state is reached when we begin to *use* the word or gesture or mark for ourselves in our own thinking. Then, but not till then, it has become a symbol for us. We have now acquired a working ostensive definition at least—'working' in the sense that it is actually put to use. But this does not exclude future modifications, even drastic ones. The status which the sound or mark now has as a symbol for us may still be incomplete and insecure. Our capacity to use it in our own thinking (in other words, our understanding of it) is something which may vary in degree, as has been said already; and the degree of it may easily be less than the maximum. Perhaps we do use this sound or mark in our own thinking, but our use of it will be hesitant and fumbling. We are prepared to use it in some sorts of discourse but not in all; privately perhaps, but not publicly, or among laymen but not among experts. We are willing to use it in absence, but we hesitate sometimes to use it in presence, when we are confronted with a 'difficult' or 'border-line' instance. Most people, other than biologists, acquire their understanding of the word 'insect' ostensively. In the presence of a bee or a horse-fly, they apply the word without hesitation. But they may hesitate whether to apply it to a spider or not.

Finally, it must not be supposed that we always learn the meanings of words or other symbols one at a time. Quite often, perhaps usually, our observation of human utterances and their circumstances gives us a more or less vague understanding of several words at the same time; and we then make use of our less vague understanding of some to improve our more vague understanding of others. Thus I may be much nearer to a full understanding of the word 'table' than to a full understanding of the word 'aspidistra'. When I hear someone say 'there is an aspidistra on the table', my already fairly firm grasp of what 'table' means will enable me to locate the object to which the word 'aspidistra' refers, and so my ostensive definition of this word too will become less tentative and more adequate. This is the kind of way in which the ceremonious sort of ostensive definition works, when it does work. I have already acquired some ostensive grasp of the sort of circumstances in which the deictic word 'this' or the deictic gesture of pointing occurs in the behaviour of my neighbours. I have a much weaker ostensive grasp of the circumstances in which the word 'green' is uttered, though I am fairly sure that it is visible (rather than tangible or audible) circumstances which are relevant. But for all I know, the word may be applicable to almost any visible quality, perhaps to the shape which a blade of grass has or the shimmery quality of water in a pond. If that is my situation, the ceremonious utterance of 'this is green' together with a deictic gesture pointing to an unripe apple, may really help me towards a better ostensive definition of 'green', though the ceremony will have to be repeated several times, in the presence of objects with different shapes and sizes and locations.

But whatever defects there may be in the current accounts of ostensive definition, and however difficult it may be to amend them, the point to be insisted on is the fundamental importance of the process. It would be an exaggeration to say that without ostensive definition there could be no thinking at all, or no conceptual cognition. There would still be the sort of thinking which occurs in sign-cognition. Concepts do operate in this, as I have tried to show. There would also be image-thinking, which I shall discuss later, and the analogous sorts of thinking which may be conducted with physical replicas of various kinds, such as diagrams and dumb-show. But *verbal* thinking really would be impossible without ostensive definitions. And no one will deny that verbal thinking is the most highly developed form of thinking. If the characteristic of 'being conceptual' admits of degrees, as we have seen reason to say it does, then verbal thinking is the *most* conceptual form of cognition that there is, in human beings at least.

These remarks about the importance of ostensive definitions may appear platitudinous; and indeed I hope that they are. Nevertheless, some philosophers would boldly deny them. Let us consider the grounds they would give. They would not, of course, deny that ostensive definition is as a matter of empirical fact the procedure by which an understanding of many words is acquired. But this, it is said, is merely a matter of psychology, entirely irrelevant to the philosophical analysis of what understanding is. Accepting the wide use of the term 'symbol' which has been adopted in the last two chapters, it would be maintained that a philosopher is only concerned to ask what symbolization is, or what it is for something to be a symbol; and that the psychological or psycho-social process by which something *becomes* a symbol for such and such persons throws no light on this question. Surely it is logically possible that this process might have been quite different from what it is? It is logically possible that there might still have been symbolic cognition even though the capacity to use symbols was acquired in some other way. Indeed, is it not logically possible, however improbable, that someone might have this capacity without having *acquired* it in any way at all? At birth, or some fine day, we might just find ourselves possessed of the power to use various words or other symbols understandingly, without any preceding ostensive process. Of course, if we take this suggestion as an empirical hypothesis, it is incredible. But surely it is not self-contradictory, and it could not be incredible if it were. And if it does make sense to say that there could, logically, have been verbal thinking and intelligent speech without any ostensive definitions, surely that settles the matter? The purely historical characteristic of having been learned in the way it was, or indeed in any other way, cannot be what we *mean* by 'understanding', when we say that in verbal thinking we understand the words we use, or use them understandingly.

There is a disquieting air of *Wesenschau*[1] about this argument, though the philosophers who propound it would reject that alleged activity with horror. Can we really just 'see' that verbal thinking would still have been the same thing, even though our understanding of basic words, 'ground floor' verbal symbols, had been acquired non-ostensively, or just possessed, somehow, without ever being acquired at all? Can we just 'see' that in *all* cases questions of philosophical analysis are wholly separable from questions of psychological origin? And more generally, can we just 'see' what truths are logically necessary and what other truths are merely empirical or contingent? When they were asked whether propositions like 'all cats have fur' and 'gold is soluble in *aqua regia*' are empirical or

[1] 'Intuition of Essences,' a term used by philosophers of the school of Husserl.

logically necessary, some people have felt the gravest doubts about the right answer.

What we are now discussing is our knowledge of word-to-object relationships. With basic words, I have said, this knowledge is acquired by the quasi-inductive process of ostensive definition; and certainly I have suggested, by implication at least, that the ostensive way in which the knowledge is acquired does have some relevance to the philosophical question, what kind of knowledge it is. Now if it is logically possible that this knowledge of word-object relationships might have been acquired in some other way, or just possessed without being acquired at all, it is also logically possible, I suppose, that human beings might have known all sorts of other regularities without doing any inductions; someone might conceivably know that ice floats in water without doing any inductions and without receiving the testimony of anyone else who had. But is it irrelevant to the analysis of scientific knowledge that we do in fact acquire it inductively? Is this merely a matter of psychology? Certainly not; because its inductive origin is not only the cause of it, but also the ground or reason for it, what justifies us in accepting it as knowledge. Its inductive origin, the fact that it is acquired in this way and not in some other way (e.g. by direct intuition or by revelation from Heaven) makes it the *sort* of knowledge that it is. And if someone did know that ice floats in water without acquiring his knowledge inductively or receiving the testimony of others who had, it would be a different sort of knowledge from ours, different not merely in its origin but in its nature; and the difference would still be there, even if he formulated his knowledge in the very same sentence 'ice floats in water' which we use to formulate ours.

Why should we not say the same about our understanding of basic symbols? The ground, and not merely the origin, of taking 'cat' to mean objects like Pussy and Tabitha and not objects like Fido or Tray, is the ostensive process of noticing the objects in whose presence this sound is commonly uttered by our neighbours, and generalizing inductively from what we have noticed; it is the observation of constant conjunctions, as it is also the observation of constant conjunctions which is our ground for thinking that ice floats in water. Will it be objected that in other nations or ages the sound 'cat' does not mean this and perhaps has no meaning at all, that word-object relationships are 'conventional', and not 'natural' like the properties of ice? Then the reply is that our knowledge of conventions is itself inductive knowledge, as it is also induction which informs us that different conventions prevail in different societies. What else can it be? Are we to suppose, as the reverential attitude of some modern philosophers towards conventions might suggest, that we know about them by Divine Revelation?

But though there is an inductive factor in our understanding of the basic verbal symbols—in that understanding itself, and not merely in its psychological origin—this is not, of course, a complete account of the matter. If it were, there would be no difference between symbols and inductive signs. In addition, these inductively discovered correlations (between noises and objects, written marks and objects) become *rules* for our own use of these noises, etc., in our own thinking. I do not mean that we consciously and voluntarily accept them as rules, any more than we voluntarily and consciously obey them thereafter, when they have established themselves in our minds or psycho-physical organisms. It is not like what happens when a grown-up man decides consciously and voluntarily that he will henceforth adopt the vocabulary which is customary in 'good society'. It is rather that we just slip into accepting these observed correlations as rules for our own use of these noises or marks in our own thinking. But this 'slipping into' is a crucial stage in our mental development all the same. Until it happens, the noise is not yet for us a word or a sentence, the bodily movement is not yet a gesture, the marks on paper are not yet a piece of writing, and the process of ostensive definition is not finished but only begun. The final state of the ostensive process is the establishment of ostensive rules. Such a rule, if it were itself put into words (which of course it cannot be at the stage of mental development we are considering) would be of the form 'If an object or situation of sort A is experienced, the word W is to be applied to it'. Henceforward our use of the utterance 'W' for thinking with, both in the presence of A-like objects and in their absence, is governed by this rule, though the rule is neither consciously adopted, nor formulated, nor consciously obeyed.

The critics I have in mind seem to have fixed their attention on the 'rule' aspect of ostensive definitions and averted it from the ostensive aspect. They might perhaps agree that some words must be basic or 'ground-floor' symbols, if any words are to be understood, and that the rules for the use of these basic symbols must relate them to experienceable objects and situations. But, they would say, it is logically possible that these word-object rules might not have an ostensive origin, even though as a matter of empirical fact they did; and if they had had a different origin, or no origin at all, they might still be the sort of rules they now are and have the function in our thinking and discourse which they now have.

Let us try to conceive what such *un*ostensive word-object rules might be like. Two suggestions may occur to us. First, it sometimes happens, even now, that a particular thinker invents a word for himself, and even occasionally a basic or 'ground-floor' word, applying directly to experienceable objects or situations. He suddenly begins to use the sound 'squongle' for objects with bristles on them, such as hairbrushes, toothbrushes and hedgehogs. He has never heard other people utter this sound in the presence of bristly objects; indeed he has never heard them utter this sound at all. Yet he now proceeds to use this sound, understandingly, in his own thought and discourse. It is what is sometimes called a 'private' symbol; not because other people cannot hear him utter it, nor yet because they cannot discover what he means by it (they could, by noticing carefully the circumstances in which he utters it), but because he has *given* it the meaning which it has for him. Many children, it is said, use some words which are 'private' symbols in this sense; and even adults occasionally do, thereby winning the enthusiastic commendations of the more advanced literary critics. Such a symbol is used in accordance with a word-object-relating rule. But surely this rule is not an ostensive one? Now is it not logically possible, however unlikely, that *all* basic words might have been used in accordance with such 'private' rules? And if they were, the rules would still relate them to observable objects (as 'squongle' was related to observable objects in my example) but would have nothing ostensive about them.

This suggestion, however, does not really help us. In the first place, such 'private' words seem to be essentially parasitic, as it were. They are only invented by people who have already acquired an understanding of many other words in the ordinary ostensive way. The rules for their use are not sheer inventions, products of

P

untaught original genius; they are modelled on the analogy of ordinary humdrum ostensive rules with which the speaker has long been familiar. He can only *give* meaning to 'squongle' because he has already *taken* the meanings of many other words from his neighbours, by noticing the occasions on which his neighbours uttered them; that is, by the ordinary process of ostensive definition.

Secondly, is it after all true that these 'private' word-to-object rules are entirely non-ostensive? Such a rule cannot be established by a mere *fiat* of the will. A process of learning or accustoming is still needed. I must repeatedly utter this sound 'squongle', or image it, or pronounce it sub-vocally, in the presence of a certain sort of observable objects, bristly ones. Thus here too there must be a more or less constant conjunction between sound and object before I can use this sound understandingly; and this is very like what happens in ordinary ostensive definitions. The difference is that in this case the constant conjunction is brought about by myself and not by my neighbours. But it still has to be there, and it still has to lead to the same sort of psychological result, an associative linkage between sound and object; or rather, between a class of mutually resembling sounds and a class of mutually resembling objects. In short I still have to *learn* to use this 'private' word of mine, and I learn it by means of a constant conjunction. If this is not an ostensive process, it is at any rate very like one. It might fairly be called quasi-ostensive.

Thus the fact that there are so-called 'private' words does not really help us to conceive what it would be like if the word-object rules for all our basic words were non-ostensive. Let us consider another suggestion. Would such non-ostensive rules be like the rules we have now for the use of 'complex idea' words, such as 'dragon'? (If not, I cannot think what else they could be like.) There are, of course, rules for applying complex idea words to objects, *if* objects satisfying the rules should happen to turn up. We do know what a dragon would be, if there were any dragons. If we ever saw a dragon, we should recognize it to be one. We know what sort of an object, supposing we were ever to observe it, would properly have the sound 'dragon' applied to it, where 'properly' means 'in accordance with the relevant word-object rule'. Here surely we have a word-object rule with nothing ostensive about it? For if it were ostensive, we must have observed several dragons, or the same one several times, and noticed the sounds other people uttered in the presence of such an entity. But this particular sound-object conjunction has never in fact been observed. It is true that we may have seen pictures of dragons. Yet people can understand the word quite well without having seen any. Moreover, the man who first drew or painted a dragon-representing picture must have known already what a dragon would be like, in order to make his drawing or his painting. Perhaps then what these philosophers are maintaining is that all our ideas might conceivably have been complex ideas in the sense in which the idea of Dragon is; or rather (to formulate it in a terminology which they would like better) that all our rules for applying words to objects might conceivably have been like what our word-object rules for complex idea words are now.

But is this really conceivable? It is true, of course, that a complex idea word, such as 'dragon', does not itself have an ostensive definition. But is our understanding of it completely independent of ostensive definitions? Let us first consider the facts, and then the might-have-beens, which these philosophers are so skilful in exploiting.

As to the facts: when a complex idea is the idea of something which might in principle be observed (even though it never has been) our rule for applying the complex-idea word to an object, if and when a suitable object turns up, is a derivative rule and not an ultimate one. A complex-idea word, such as 'dragon', always has a definition. This is not, of course, an ostensive definition, but an inter-verbal definition, saying what combination of other words the given word is equivalent to. 'Dragon' means the same as 'winged, fire-breathing lizard'. (There might be some doubt as to the size a creature would have to have, in order to be counted as a dragon; and to that extent the idea of Dragon, or the word-object rule for the word 'dragon', is a vague one. If we saw a creature no larger than the common English lizard with wings and breathing fire, perhaps it would not be large enough to be a dragon; or perhaps it would.)

But what of the words which constitutes this inter-verbal definition? They are themselves *ostensively* defined. Or if any of them, for a particular speaker, are not (perhaps he has never seen a lizard) these words in turn must be inter-verbally definable in terms of other words which do for him have ostensive definitions. 'Lizard' means the same as 'elongated four-footed reptile with a tail'. Perhaps this might not satisfy a zoologist, but it is a sufficiently accurate analysis of the way most people use the word. And the words 'elongated', 'four-footed', etc., do have ostensive definitions. Whatever might-have-beens may be conjured up by ingenious philosophers, in actual fact we only know what a dragon would be like (have 'the idea' of Dragon) because we have actually observed winged things, four-footed things, breathing things, and fires. In actual fact, we only understand the word 'dragon' because we understand the words 'winged', 'reptile', etc.; and these latter words in turn are understood ostensively, and the rules for applying them to objects are ostensive rules. The parallel to this in the traditional terminology is the doctrine that complex ideas are reducible to combinations of simpler ones, and that these simpler ideas themselves have been directly abstracted from actually observed instances.

To turn now to the might-have-beens. Is it indeed logically possible that *all* our ideas might have been complex ones; that all our word-object rules might have been what our word-object rules for complex idea words are now; that with *all* words applicable to objects, we might have been capable of recognizing the objects to which they apply, without having had ostensive definitions of *any* words?

To suppose that this is logically possible is in effect to change the meaning of the phrase 'complex idea', of the word 'idea' itself, and of the expression 'word-object rule' or 'rule for applying a word to observable objects'; or rather, not so much to change their meaning as to abolish it, and use these expressions for we know not what. For if we use these expressions in their ordinary sense, we cannot describe without contradiction what this alleged logical possibility would be. A complex idea which was not analysable in terms of simpler ones, themselves 'cashable' by experienced instances, would not be a complex idea at all. At any rate it could not be a complex idea applicable to objects, and it is complex ideas of this sort, capable of being applied to objects even though there are, in fact, no objects to apply them to, which we are considering at present. (We are not considering the complex ideas which are met with in the *a priori* sciences, such as formal logic and pure mathematics.) Likewise a complex idea word for the use of which there was a word-object rule, but a rule entirely independent of ostensive definitions, not in any way derivable from the ostensive rules for the use of other words, would not be a complex idea word at all; that is, it would not be what we *mean* by the expression 'complex idea word'. If there is a rule for applying a given word to objects, it must either be itself an ostensive rule, or else it must be derivable from other word-object rules which are themselves ostensive. (In Logic and Pure Mathematics there may be words without any word-object rules for their use, words or other symbols such as '+' '∼' or '√‾' which are not applicable in any way to the world, with no rules for their use except rules of inter-symbolic transformation. But these are not the sort of symbols we are now considering.)

If this argument is valid, it is not after all a mere psychological accident that our basic symbols are ostensively defined and the word-object rules for their use are ostensive rules. And that there *are* basic symbols is not a mere psychological accident either. It is a psychological accident, if you like, that there happen to be symbol-using creatures. At any rate, it is logically possible that there might not have been any. But if there are some, they must possess some symbols which are directly linked to the observable world by the process of ostensive definition.

This long and complicated discussion of ostensive definition may well have distracted the reader's attention from the main topic of the present chapter, the evaluation of the Inductive Sign Theory of symbolization. But these complexities were unavoidable. What is right in the Sign Theory, I said earlier, is that it draws our attention to the importance of ostensive definitions, though in an oblique and one-sided way. To justify this estimate, it was necessary to show that ostensive definition is indeed a fundamentally important process, despite the opinion of some philosophers to the contrary. Without it, there would be no basic or 'ground-floor' words, linked directly to the experienced world, and in that case there would be no words at all. The sounds and marks which we now use as symbols, to think with, would not in that case have been symbols; for there can be no symbols unless *some* symbols are empirically cashable. It was also necessary to clear out of the way certain distorted and superstitious views of what ostensive definition is and how it works.

Now at last we may return with a good conscience to the Sign Theory.

As we have seen, our basic symbols really do have something in common with inductive signs. Ostensive definition is in part an inductive process. The first stage of it is an experience of constant conjunctions between human noises and other sorts of occurrences or situations. It is true that there is also a second stage, equally indispensable, where we begin to use these noises, etc., for ourselves in thinking 'freely' (not merely in the 'tied' sign-cognitive manner) of the things with which they have been thus conjoined. No doubt the two stages may overlap in time. When the induction is as yet only partially achieved and is still subject to revision by later experience, we may have already begun to use these noises in a hesitant and provisional way in our own free thinking. But despite this possible temporal overlap, these two stages of the ostensive process must, of course, be distinguished; and without the second, the using as distinct from the correlating, these noises, marks, etc., would not be for us symbols at all. What is right in the Sign Theory is that it insists on the indispensability of the first stage. The basic symbols would not be symbols for us, at any rate they would not be basic ones, unless they had first been signs. What is wrong in the Sign Theory is that it neglects the second stage altogether. It supposes that because our basic symbols began by being inductive signs, that is all they ever are.

This is because it sticks one-sidedly to the spectator's or hearer's point of view. Its outlook is altogether too sociological. The Sign Theorist is interested only in other people, and not at all in himself. This altruism would be laudable, if it did not lead him to forget that his neighbours are selves too, and not just high-grade thermometers. The Sign Theory overlooks the glaringly obvious fact that each of us, individually, uses words and other symbols for himself, in his own autonomous thinking, both public and private. And thereby its sociology is itself distorted. For a society (though nowadays we all forget the fact) is nothing but a group of conscious individuals who communicate with one another and co-operate in the ways which communication makes possible. And unless each of these individuals was a thinker, able to use symbols for himself, they could not receive communications, though they might listen to noises and form inductive expectations about the consequences which were likely to follow. They could not make communications either. For in making a communication I am myself using the noises which I produce as instruments to think with, and I am assuming that my neighbour will use them in the same way in the act of hearing them. If he cannot, he does not 'follow' my utterances.[1] He fails to understand them in the symbol-cognitive way, and no communication has taken place. To understand my utterances, in the Symbol as distinct from the Sign sense of the word 'understand', he has to think with them himself in the act of hearing them, just as I think with them myself in the act of uttering them.

What is right in the Sign Theory, and what is wrong with it, may also be formulated in a more psychological way. What links a basic symbol to the world, and thereby makes it a basic symbol, is from the psychological point of view a habit; or if it be preferred, it is an associative linkage. Traditionally, it would be described as an associative linkage between a sound, mark, etc., on the one hand, and an idea on the other. It would be said that the sound 'cat' is for me associated with the idea of an entity resembling Pussy, Tabitha and Tiger Tim as closely as they resemble one another; whereas for an Italian it is the sound 'gatto' which is associated with the idea of such an entity. This account of the matter needs amendment. For 'idea' it would be better to substitute 'recognitional capacity'. And what is associated with this is not just a sound or mark, but another pair of acquired capacities: the capacity of recognizing a given sort of sound or mark, and even more important, the capacity to *produce* a sound or mark of that sort either overtly or in an imaged form.

From the psychological point of view, ostensive definition is just the process by which associative linkages of this special kind come about. And the 'rule' aspect of ostensive definition (cf. p. 224 above) from the psychological point of view just a way of describing the fact that these associative linkages remain constant when once set up, and continue thereafter to manifest themselves repeatedly in our thinking and discourse. This is not, of course, an exhaustive account of the 'rule' aspect of ostensive definitions, though it is a true one as far as it goes. It is not exhaustive, because these ostensive rules have a *sanction*, and that is why we call them rules and not

[1] See ch. xi, pp. 351-3, below.

merely regularities displayed in our thought and discourse, although they are in fact thus displayed. The sanction is that unless a symbol retains a pretty constant meaning for a given thinker over a period of time, it ceases to perform its function as a symbol. Obviously if the word 'red' had a different meaning for me every time I uttered it, I could no longer use it to think with, either publicly or privately. If you are to talk sense, to yourself or to others, your words must retain at least a relative constancy of meaning.

But we should be careful not to misunderstand the force of this 'must', lest we attribute to these ostensive rules, or to other linguistic rules, a sacrosanctity which they do not possess. The 'must' is hypothetical, not categorical. It is only that *if* you are to go on using these sounds, etc., to think with, then they must retain for you a relatively constant meaning. But there is no categorical necessity that you will go on using them to think with and to talk sense with. It is logically possible, and indeed causally possible too, that you will cease to use them in this way and will start talking nonsense instead. It is, however, an empirical truth of human psychology, true about most people at most times, that when they have learned to understand a sound, mark, etc., they do go on using it thereafter to think with and talk sense with. And this is just a restatement of the psychological fact mentioned just now, that the associative linkages set up by ostensive definitions remain constant—in most people—thereafter, and manifest themselves repeatedly from that time onwards in the thinking and the discourse of these people.

This psychological account of symbolization is relevant to the Sign Theory in the following way. From the psychological point of view, the process by which one occurrence becomes an inductive sign of another is also an associative one, as we have already noticed.[1] The dispositional sign-statement that X is for a given man or animal a sign of Y describes an associative linkage, psychical or psychophysical, between the X-recognizing capacity and the Y-recognizing capacity in that man or animal; while the occurrent statement that a particular instance of X is at a particular moment signifying Y to him ('bringing Y to mind' in the sign-cognitive way) describes an actualization of this associative linkage. Thus it could be argued that from the psychological point of view signification and symbolization have an important feature in common; both of them, from this

[1] Cf. ch. v, p. 136, above.

point of view, are acquired associative linkages. But true as this may be, we must not forget the differences between them either. In symbolic cognition these associative linkages are *used* in a way that they are not used in sign-cognition. When an associative linkage has been set up in me between the three capacities mentioned—my capacity to recognize an object of sort A, my capacity to recognize a sound or mark B, and my capacity to produce a sound or mark B (overtly or privately), then I am able to use that sound or mark for myself as a means of thinking 'freely' of the object A; and the sound or mark is then something more than it was for me at the level of mere sign-cognition, when I had to wait until I happened to perceive it again, if it was to bring the object A to mind.

CHAPTER VIII

THE IMAGIST THEORY OF THINKING

AFTER listening to a lecture on Imageless Thinking, a lady in the audience came up to the lecturer and said with a puzzled air, 'But, Professor, you can *think*, can't you?' The view that thinking is some kind of operation with mental images, though nowadays out of favour with philosophers, is still widely held by the general public, and the lady was only unusual in the candour and courage she showed in admitting it. Indeed, at one time it was accepted by many philosophers, especially philosophers of the Empiricist tradition. That is why there was a 'problem of Abstract Ideas'. It was assumed that an idea *ought*, somehow, to be a mental image; if some of our ideas appeared not to be images, this was a paradox and some solution must be found for it. The theory that thinking consists in operating with mental images (especially, but not exclusively, visual ones) has no generally accepted name. I am going to call it 'Imagism'. This is a horrid word, but it is needed. Because it did not exist and no one had the enterprise to invent it, the philosophers who hold this theory have been grossly misunderstood. In text-books on the history of thought, Berkeley and Hume are nearly always classed as Nominalists, and even Locke is sometimes thought to have been a Nominalist. The ground for this opinion presumably was that all three of them rejected what I have called the Philosophy of Universals, and accepted the Philosophy of Resemblances. That being so, they were also compelled to reject the Realist epistemology, which holds that thinking is the inspection of objective universals and of the relations between them. And it was assumed, quite erroneously, that anyone who was not a Realist must, of course, be a Nominalist. In fact, however, Berkeley is an Imagist; Hume's theory, in the section 'Of Abstract Ideas', is a mixed one, partly Imagist and partly Nominalist; while Locke is a Conceptualist, though some passages in the *Essay* will perhaps bear an Imagist interpretation, and others, perhaps, a Nominalist one.

We can agree at once that the philosophers of former days over-

234

estimated the importance of mental images in thinking. But the philosophers of our own time seem to underestimate it. Some of them write as if images did not exist at all. They are like one of Francis Galton's correspondents, who replied to a questionnaire about his memory-images as follows: 'These questions presuppose assent to some sort of a proposition about the "mind's eye" and the "images" which it sees. . . . This points to some initial fallacy. . . . It is only by a figure of speech that I can describe my recollection of a scene as a "mental image" which I can "see" with my "mind's eye". I do not see it, any more than a man sees the thousand lines of Sophocles which under due pressure he is ready to repeat.'[1] When people write like this, we may suspect that they themselves have no mental images, or at any rate no visual ones. As Galton's researches show, there are very great differences between the imaging powers of different individuals; and it would appear that some very clever people do their thinking, and their recollecting too, almost exclusively in words. But it is a misfortune for a philosopher to be too clever. It is the human mind in general, and not just the minds of highly intellectual persons like himself, which he is supposed to be studying.

Other contemporary philosophers do not go as far as this. They do not deny the existence of mental images altogether. But they lose no opportunity of telling us how uninteresting and unimportant mental images are. The study of images, we are assured, is a matter of 'mere psychology' in which philosophers are not all concerned; or if they are, their only concern is to clear away the confusions which have made other philosophers suppose that imaging and thinking have something to do with one another. Of course images may sometimes occur in our minds when we are thinking. But, we are told, they are merely irrelevant accompaniments of the thinking process. Indeed, they are worse than irrelevant, because they distract our attention from what we are about; your business as a thinker is to talk understandingly, to yourself or to others, in private or in public, and instead you lapse into mere day dreaming.

Against this, it is important to insist that some of us do *use* images in our thinking. We use visual images rather as we use maps or sketch-plans to find our way about a piece of hilly and wooded country; and when someone else asks us the way to Little

[1]Francis Galton, *Inquiries into Human Faculty* (Everyman edition), p. 59.

Puddlecombe, we refer to this mental map and read off the answer. An engineer engaged in inventing a new machine, a garage-mechanic considering how to take an old one to pieces, a surgeon planning a difficult operation, a housewife wondering how that new picture would look over the mantelpiece in the spare bedroom, or even a student of elementary geometry who is told by his teacher to bisect an angle—all these people, whose thoughts are concerned with the spatial relations of things, with their shapes or their colours, use visual images to solve their problems, and some of them would be completely at a loss if the power of visual imaging suddenly deserted them. If such problems could only be solved by producing long and complicated verbal rigmaroles for oneself or scribbling screeds on paper, they would become, for these people, insoluble. With a visual image, one can quite often 'see at a glance' what the solution is; and if one cannot, one's best method often is to produce a series of different visual images. Very likely there will be a few scrappy words as well, since human beings are word-using creatures. But it is far from being true, in these cases, that the images are mere irrelevant accompaniments of the words. The truth is almost the other way round. The words, here, are only relevant in so far as they help us to summon up the images. What is more, images often play a part in the understanding of words themselves. Ask the ordinary man (not a philosopher) what he means by the word 'butterfly' and he will very likely have a visual image representing the common Cabbage White. Say to him 'there is an elephant coming down the street' and he will very likely have a visual image of this unlikely spectacle, perhaps a vivid and detailed one. Our understanding of a word, and our knowledge of what it would be like for a sentence to be true, are no doubt persistent dispositions or capacities, and not just occurrences, neither imagings nor any-thing else. But they do manifest themselves by occurrences. And with many people (though with few modern philosophers) the production of a mental image is *one* of the ways in which such dispositions are manifested, and even the most striking and obvious way.

The ordinary man is so much concerned with the visible aspects of the world that visual images are the ones he uses most (unless he is *too* clever to use images at all). But he does use others as well. If someone tells me that Jones has a voice like a crow with a sore throat, I can accept or reject this description, or amend it, by summoning up auditory images of Jones' utterances. If someone describes the sound made by starlings congregated at their roosting place in winter, he may say that it is like the noise of a waterfall. I check his description by means of an auditory image representing what starling-roosts have sounded like to me when I have been there; or if I have never visited a starling-roost, I understand his sentence (unbelievingly perhaps) by means of an auditory image of the sound of a waterfall. If told that the grass on an old-fashioned English lawn is as soft as velvet, people who have never been to this country can 'bring home to themselves' what is meant, by having a tactual image of the feel of velvet. I myself could never be a golfer, because I am quite unable to follow the complicated descriptions of successive and simultaneous muscular adjustments which golf instructors give. My kinaesthetic imagery is very defective; I can only make any sense at all of these descriptions by trying to visualize what my body would look like from outside if *per impossibile* it were executing these complicated movements and postures, and am quite unable to image to myself what the 'feel' of them would be. A good pupil at golf, I suppose, has clear and detailed kinaesthetic images; and so he can plan a complicated series of muscular adjustments before he executes them, and can go over them 'in his head' afterwards and discover where he went wrong.

It begins to look as if this extreme view about the total irrelevance of images in thinking were just academic in the bad sense of that word: a superstition engendered in the minds of highly intellectual persons by their ignorance of what happens in ordinary unintellectual mankind. It does not, of course, follow that the Imagist theory of thinking is correct either. It is an extreme view too, though its extremism is in the opposite direction. But it is not an utterly silly theory; at any rate it is no sillier than the purely Verbalistic theory which is at present fashionable. We may well have something to learn from it.

In the last two chapters the term 'symbol' has been used in a very wide sense, to mean roughly 'whatever we think with'. It would seem that there is no such thing as pure or naked thinking; or if conceivably there could be, it is beyond the reach of human frailty, even though superhuman intelligences may be capable of it.

The human mind, it seems, must always have sensible or quasi-sensible particulars to 'carry' its thought, sensible or quasi-sensible media 'in' which we think.

In primary recognition,[1] of course, it is not so. What I recognize to be red is *ex hypothesi* an instance of the concept Red. Now suppose that we take primary recognition as our model or standard of what thinking ought to be, as perhaps some philosophers have. It will then appear to us that there is something paradoxical and as it were radically defective about the thinking which actually occurs in human beings, precisely because the particulars we think 'in' are non-instantiative ones. But perhaps it is a better policy to start with what we actually find thinking to be, and not with what we suppose it ought to be. If so, we look at the matter the other way round. It now appears that primary recognition is, not indeed a paradox, but a limiting case. And though it is certainly an exercise of intelligence, we are reluctant to call it thinking. For if we do, we have to say that here what we think *in* and what we think *of* coincide, the one being an instance of the other; whereas in what is ordinarily called thinking, the particulars which are present to our minds are always non-instantiative ones.

This is already true of the 'tied' thinking which occurs in sign-cognition. The footprint we see is not an instance of the concept Human Being, and the pitter-patter sound we hear is not an instance of the concept Rain. But still we think in or with these non-instantiative particulars, and it is only through their means that the significate is brought to mind. Only we do not produce them for ourselves, as we do in the 'free' thinking which is our present concern; we must wait for the environment to produce them for us.

In free thinking we think 'in' all sorts of sensible and quasi-sensible particulars, and indeed in principle there is no limit to their variety. We think in words, in images, in gestures or incipient gestures, in pantomimic actions, with models or sketches or other sensible replicas. None of these are instances of the concepts thought of by means of them (though some of them, as we shall see, come closer to being so than others do). Thus the sound 'red' is certainly not itself red; and the written mark 'dog' is not itself an example

---

[1]On the distinction between primary and secondary recognition, see ch. 11, above.

of the concept Dog, and neither barks nor bites. The peculiarity of thinking, as opposed to other forms of cognition—the paradox of it, if you like—consists in this: on the one hand, we have to use non-instantiative particulars to think in, and cannot think without them; on the other hand, we manage perfectly well with them, and they serve us almost as effectively as if they *had* been instances of the concepts thought of.

It is these non-instantiative particulars, used in free thinking, which have been called *symbols* in the last two chapters. If we may continue to use the term 'symbol' in the same wide sense, the thesis of the Imagist philosophers may now be formulated as follows: Mental images are the primary symbols, and all other symbols are secondary and derivative. In particular, words are secondary symbols. Of course, the Imagist does not deny that words have meaning, but he holds that they have it only indirectly, as substitutes for images. These substitutes are needed, because words can be manipulated much more quickly and easily than images can. Hence they are normally used in an *uncashed* manner; indeed that is precisely their function. Berkeley says this clearly. 'It is not necessary (even in the strictest reasoning) significant names which stand for ideas [i.e. for images] should, every time they are used, excite in the understanding the ideas they are made to stand for; in reading and discoursing, names being for the most part used as letters are in algebra, in which though a particular quantity be marked by each letter, yet to proceed right it is not requisite that in every step each letter suggest to your thoughts that particular quantity it was appointed to stand for.'[1] But just for that reason, a philosopher must constantly bear in mind Lord Bacon's epigram 'Words are the counters of wise men, but the money of fools.' The whole Imagist epistemology, both on its constructive and its destructive side, could be extracted from that remark.

But this is only a rough statement of the theory. It would be admitted that there are two sorts of words which are not just substitutes for images. There are logical and syntactical words such as 'if' and 'than', whose function (rather than meaning) is to tie other words together. There are also emotive and evocative words, as Berkeley pointed out, whose function is 'the raising of some passion, the exciting to or deterring from an action, the putting the

[1] *Principles of Human Knowledge*, Introduction, Section xix.

mind in some particular disposition.'[1] But all those words which we have hitherto regarded as basic symbols, whose meaning is supposed to be given by ostensive definition, are according to the Imagist merely substitutes for images. And so they are not basic symbols after all. They only come as near to it as words can. Among words they are basic, if you like, as Achilles in the *Odyssey* was king among the Shades, because unless we understand them we could not understand any other words. But though basic in this relative sense, they still symbolize only indirectly and as it were at second hand, as deputies for images; and images, according to this theory, are the only symbols which can be called basic without qualification.

So far from its being true, then, that images are mere irrelevant accompaniments of thinking, as our modern denigrators of images suppose, the truth, according to the Imagists, is the other way round; unless our words were cashable by means of images, we could not think in words at all. We could indeed still write or talk, in private and in public. But our writings and talkings would be devoid of meaning. In Berkeley's view that was just what was wrong with the talk and writing of the scientific philosophers of his own time. They used uncashable words like 'matter' and 'material substance' which are not substitutes for mental images, and in so doing they were talking nonsense. It is also true, of course, that the vulgar use material-object words like 'tree' and 'house'. But *they* use them in a cashable manner, as substitutes for images, and therefore meaningfully. The two sides of Berkeley's thought—his attack on the Materialistic and Dualistic metaphysicians, and his defence of Common Sense—are in no way inconsistent with each other. Both follow directly from his Imagist conception of thinking. And his embarrassment concerning 'notions' also follows from it. For the words we use for referring to introspectible occurrences do not seem to be cashable by images.

If we now compare the Imagist theory of symbolization with the Sign Theory, we see that they start as it were from opposite ends. The Sign Theory starts from the thinking which is public and overt, from the perceptible occurrence of meaningful utterances, gestures, writings, diagrams and other public symbols. This

[1] *Op. cit.* Introduction, section xx.

is what makes it plausible to assimilate symbols to signs, such as footprints, clouds, pitter-patter sounds on the roof, since these also are public objects or occurrences in the perceptible world. Hence too the 'Thermometer' conception of human nature, to which the Sign Theory, we saw, is committed. The disadvantage of this starting point is that the very existence of private thinking becomes a grave embarrassment. Even the 'tied' private thinking which occurs in sign-cognition itself is something of which the Sign Theory can give no adequate account. It forgets, and is obliged to forget, that there must be an observer to perceive, and to interpret, the signs which these human thermometers produce; and he cannot be just a thermometer himself, even if that is all his neighbours are.

The starting point of the Imagist theory, on the contrary, is private thinking, and private thinking of the 'free' symbol-using kind. It is overt and public thinking which is now an embarrassment. The Imagist is obliged to suppose that it is not thinking at all, but is just an effect of private mental activities which alone deserve the name; whereas each of us knows from his own experience that this account of the matter is true only sometimes and not always, since we often find ourselves thinking in the act of speaking or writing or gesticulating. And here the particulars in which we think are just the publicly perceptible symbols which we overtly produce. It is true, of course, that sometimes our overt symbol-productions are effects of private rehearsals which precede them: first we 'think out' privately what we are going to say or write, and then, and in consequence, we say it or write it. But this certainly does not happen always.[1]

Again, the starting point of the Imagist theory leads to a conception of human nature which is very unlike the 'Thermometer' conception. Minds are now regarded as something irreducibly different from behaving bodies; and still irreducibly different from them, even if bodies are resolved into classes of sense-data, as they are in Berkeley's own metaphysics. And now the traditional problem of 'Other Minds' is very much on our hands. We escape from Behaviourism only to fall into the danger of Solipsism.

All the same, if we were compelled to choose, we should have to admit, I believe, that the Imagist starting point is the better, at any rate so long as we are concerned with the epistemology of

[1] Cf. pp 158-9, above.

Q

thinking. From the point of view of the theory of cognition in general, and the theory of conceptual cognition in particular, the most important fact about symbols is that each of us uses them for himself in his own thinking; and this fact is most obvious when he uses them privately. It is then quite manifest that symbols are not just signs. It is true that for the user himself they are not just signs when he uses them publicly either. But it could be argued with some plausibility, as we have seen, that they are so for other people, and this might lead us to overlook the function they have for the speaker or writer himself. The Imagist is in no danger of overlooking it; and so far, his starting point does enable him to put first things first.

The conclusion which emerges from this comparison is a very tame and obvious one. Somehow we must avoid choosing between the two starting points. We must contrive to start from both at once. We must admit, what we cannot candidly deny, that some thinking is private, inaccessible to outside observers; image-thinking is the most obvious example of this, though not the only one. We must also admit that much thinking is public; that each one of us—and not merely his neighbours—often thinks 'in' publicly uttered sounds, public gestures, overt and publicly observable acts of writing or drawing or dumb-show or ritual behaviour. And as to the traditional problem of Other Minds, we must try somehow to 'have it both ways'. The current Behaviouristic views, which appear to explain the problem away altogether, are just as one-sided as the traditional Dualistic views, which appear to make it insoluble. A mind, whether it is another mind or my own, is something which is neither wholly public nor wholly private, but partly both. Some mental processes, and in particular some thinking processes, are accessible only to the person who experiences them; others are accessible to his neighbours too. And somehow there is a 'solidarity' between the public mental processes and the private ones; they are continuous with one another, or interlock with one another.

It is this relation which I have called 'solidarity' which gives the traditional analogical argument for the existence of other minds such force as it has. But the traditional argument starts off on the wrong foot, so to speak. The datum it should start from is not just observed bodily movements, but bodily movements which are already mental;

not just noise-making, but thinking aloud; not just hand-shiftings, but gestures; acts of writing or drawing, and not mere movements of fingers or pencils across pieces of paper. It is, or it ought to have been, not an argument from matter to mind, but from public mind to private mind, from public and overt mental processes to inward and private ones.

The private ones, moreover, are publicly describable even though not publicly observable. Other people can understand my introspective reports, and I can understand theirs. Each of us can understand those dreary reports about our neighbour's toothaches and headaches which contemporary philosophers find so exciting; and each of us can understand the much more interesting things our neighbours tell us about their mental imagery, their dreams, their private emotions and wishes. An introspective autobiography is not a closed book. The reader knows, at least in some degree, what it would have been like to live through the queer experiences described in it.

This way of solving the problem of Other Minds is easy enough to state in general terms. Is it not just the common sense solution, which all of us in our hearts believe in? To work it out in detail would, of course, be a difficult and perplexing task, and one which is fortunately irrelevant to the main theme of this book. I have only mentioned the problem of Other Minds at all, in order to make clear to the reader what kind of a theory the Imagist theory of thinking is, by showing what its wider bearings are. And perhaps it is just as well to remember that one's theory of thinking does have a bearing on one's theory of human nature or human personality. A philosopher may commit himself to an answer to the old question 'What is man?' even when he professes to be unable to say anything about it.

So much for the starting point of the Imagist theory. Before we go further, we must consider a topic about which there may be some confusion: verbal images. The Imagists, we have seen, draw a sharp distinction between image thinking and verbal thinking. But is there not a sense in which some verbal thinking is itself image thinking? Certainly we do often think in or with verbal images—visual, or auditory, or kinaesthetic.

But these are not the sort of images with which the Imagist is concerned, and this sort of thinking is not what he means by 'image thinking'. Words, he says, are substitutes for images. But a word overtly uttered or written is not a substitute for an imaged word (if anything, it is the other way about) and no one would suggest that overt words need to be, or could be, 'cashed' by imaged ones. When people distinguish between verbal thinking and image thinking, thinking in verbal images must be classed under the first head, not under the second. Verbal images, at least from the epistemological point of view, are just one sort of token words or word-tokens; and the function they perform in our thinking, the way in which they symbolize, does not differ at all from the function which overtly uttered words perform. I may quite well do my private thinking aloud or by writing on bits of paper; equally well, I may do it by means of verbal imagery of one sort or another. It will be said, perhaps, that only overt words can be used for communication. But this is not certain. Verbal images do seem to be used sometimes for telepathic communication. In any case it is private thinking rather than communication which now concerns us.[1]

It comes to this. A given type-word, such as 'house', has a very large variety of different tokens: overtly spoken ones, whispered ones, sub-vocally spoken ones, some written in pencil, some in ink, some printed, some perhaps delineated in the air with gestures. Among the many different tokens of the same type word, *imagy* tokens must be included (visual, auditory or kinaesthetic). Thus thinking in verbal images is just one way among many of thinking in words. It differs from other sorts of verbal thinking only socially, not epistemologically. If I do my private thinking in verbal images, my thoughts cannot be overheard or overlooked by other people, not even with the aid of scientific instruments which conceivably might enable them to observe my sub-vocal speech.

In discussing the Imagist theory, then, or indeed in any epistemological discussion of image thinking, the term 'image' must be taken to mean *non-verbal* images only; as when I think of dogs not by means of the word 'dog' (not even the imagy word 'dog') but by means of a dog-like image of some kind, usually a visual one, but possibly tactual or olfactory, or by an auditory image resembling a dog's bark or growl. If we want an adjective to distinguish these

---

[1] On the distinction between 'private' and 'public' symbol-using, cf. ch. VI, pp. 153-5, above.

images from verbal ones, they might perhaps be called 'representative' or 'reproductive'.

There is another confusion, or perhaps rather ambiguity, which involves us in much greater perplexities. The Imagists have not always distinguished clearly enough between *occurrent* images and image-*dispositions* (or image-producing dispositions). They speak sometimes as if an image were something we carried about with us permanently. Indeed, we all speak in that way at times. Almost any Oxford man, we say, is likely to have a pretty clear image of Magdalen Tower. Here the image of Magdalen Tower, which Smith is said to 'have', is regarded as a permanent possession of his, acquired in his undergraduate days and remaining continuously in his mind thereafter. Again, when Locke speaks of 'precise naked appearances in the mind (which) the understanding *lays up* as the standards to rank real existences into sorts',[1] these appearances seem likewise to be thought of as permanent images, which—once acquired—are always there, in the margin of consciousness at least.

Now it is conceivable that there are such permanent images (they need not, of course, be everlasting; they might fade away after a time, and some might last for many years, while others lasted only for a week or two). If Smith at a particular moment pictures Magdalen Tower to himself 'in his mind's eye', it is conceivable that this occurrent visual image is just a short phase in the history of a permanent image or image-continuant which somehow persists in his mind for many years. Such a conception may have its uses, as a stopgap at least, both in abnormal psychology and in psychical research. But if there are such permanent images, it is at any rate certain that the greater part of their life-history is passed 'in the unconscious' or 'beneath the threshold'. Indeed, the postulation of them is just one way (a very speculative one) of trying to conceive what the unconscious stratum of our minds may be like, and what kinds of contents it may have. But whatever value such speculations may have in their proper place, they are irrelevant to the epistemology of thinking. For our present purposes, all we need to suppose is that *something* persists in the mind or the psycho-physical organism of our Oxford man; and all we really know is that because it is

[1] *Essay*, Book II, ch. 11, section 9; my italics. In this passage Locke seems to be an Imagist; at any rate, the word 'appearance' suggests so.

there, he has the permanent capacity to produce an *occurrent* image resembling Magdalen Tower whenever he is suitably stimulated. The required stimulus might be just a wish of his own. He might be able to produce an occurrent image of Magdalen Tower whenever he wanted to. Or he might only be able to do it when reminded in some way, for instance by being shown a photograph of the late President of Magdalen College, or by having suitable words addressed to him in a psycho-analyst's clinic.

But whatever doubts may be aroused by the conception of a permanent image, we must not let them run away with us. We need not regard an image as a persistent particular, a kind of continuant. But we go too far in the other direction if we conclude that it is not a particular at all. And this is the conclusion which the Anti-Imagist philosophers do draw. They repeat *ad nauseam* that a mental image is not like a picture; and then they proceed to tell us that the entity-word 'image' ought not to be used at all, and we should speak instead of the process or activity of 'imagining'. But whatever way we should speak, this way at any rate is certainly the wrong one. If a process-word *must* be used, it should be 'imaging', not 'imagining'. The verb 'to imagine' is radically ambiguous. It does sometimes mean imaging. But also, and far more commonly, it means imagining *that* so and so is the case. If I ask you now to imagine that there is a crocodile in the bathroom, you can carry out my instructions without having any images at all. You can entertain this proposition in a purely verbal way. When we call Shakespeare a great imaginative writer, we do not mean that he was specially good at having mental images, though very likely he was. We mean that he was specially good at inventing factually false but aesthetically moving propositions, or aesthetically moving propositions whose factual truth or falsity is irrelevant to their aesthetic properties. We are saying nothing at all about the way in which he entertained these propositions—whether by means of words, or by means of images, or somehow else. When we say that imagination is needed for making scientific discoveries, we are certainly not saying that imaging is needed. Indeed, there is some evidence to suggest that eminent practitioners of the more advanced sciences, such as physics, have less imagery than ordinary people rather than more, and conduct their thinking almost entirely in words or in the technical symbols of mathematics. The imagination which the scientist needs is just the power of inventing empirically testable hypotheses which explain a large and varied range of empirical facts; and this is quite a different thing from imaging, even though the two may sometimes go together.

Thus if the entity-word 'image' is to be forbidden, and a process-word is to be substituted, 'imaging' and not 'imagining' is the process-word which we must use. The argument then proceeds as follows. Imaging is something which certainly does occur. Most of us know what it is to image a house or a dog, or the sound of someone's voice; and some people can image a smell, say the smell of burnt castor oil. But, it is said, this imaging process, which undoubtedly occurs, has been quite wrongly analysed by philosophers. They have analysed it in a three-term manner, into (1) an act of immediate awareness or intuitive apprehension (2) an entity called 'an image' which is what we are supposed to be immediately aware of (3) a material object or physical event or part of one, which this entity resembles and represents. This analysis, we are told, is mistaken. There are not three terms, but only two. There is the imaging, and the thing imaged, and there is no intermediate entity ('an image') coming between them. What we image is just a house or a dog or a sound or perhaps a smell. And this is not something immaterial and private and intra-mental. It is something physical and public. To be sure, it need not actually exist, nor need it ever have existed. One may image a dragon, or a cat with green spots, or a voice issuing from the clouds. But still *if* the thing imaged did exist, it would be a member of the ordinary, public, physical world.

Put briefly, then, the contention is this: there is imaging, but there are no images. There is mental picturing, but there are no mental pictures. There is 'hearing in the mind's ear', but there are no intra-mental quasi-sounds.

Now doubtless there are dangers in using the entity-word 'image'. We may be led to suppose that an image is a persistent intra-mental *thing* or continuant, as explained already. Almost any choice between terminologies is a choice of evils. But in this case, I believe, the traditional terminology is much the lesser evil of the two.

First, we observe that these philosophers do not scruple to talk about *words* as if they were entities. If they insist that there are no images, but only imaging, ought they not equally to insist that there are no words, but only speaking and writing? Indeed, a token-word is far less 'like an entity' than an occurrent image is. And as for type-words, to talk about a type-word as if it were a quasi-continuant, sitting somewhere permanently like a screwdriver in a box, ready to be 'used' by anyone who needs it, is surely a very misleading way of speaking—if we choose to be misled by it. The grounds for supposing that the type-word 'cat' is a persistent sub-stance (or should it be a timeless one?) are far weaker than for sup-posing that my cat-image is a persistent substance. Why then do these philosophers choose to be misled when images are spoken of as entities, even as very short-lived particulars, whereas they do not choose to be misled when words are spoken of in the same entity-like way? The answer is what the cobbler said, 'There is nothing like leather'. It is simply because they are not at all interested in the phenomenology of imaging, whereas they are passionately interested in the phenomenology of talking.

In any phenomenological inquiry, it is all but impossible to avoid using an 'entity' language to describe what you are studying and to distinguish one type of phenomenon from another. It is all but impossible to talk about the phenomenology of perception, normal and abnormal, without using a language of 'sense-data' or 'sensa' or 'appearances' or some other entity-like term. Whatever my par-ticular fancy is, whether I am a pigeon-fancier, or a weather-fancier, or a colour-fancier, or a taste-fancier, or a word-fancier, you may be sure that I shall speak of my favourite subject in an entity-terminology. I can do no other if I want to go into detail about it—as opposed to telling other people not to talk about it. A weather-fancier talks of warm fronts and cold fronts as if they were *things*. How very misleading! I recall a meteorological forecast in *The Times* newspaper in which it was predicted that 'a thundery tendency would move across England in the course of the day'. The colour-fancier will speak of colours as if they were things. But these ways of speaking mislead nobody, because nobody chooses to be misled by them.

To turn from these general considerations to the special features of imaging itself: if we care to study these special features (instead of just telling other people not to) we cannot help noticing that in imaging we seem to be confronted with something, to have some-thing over against us or presented to us—and something other than the material object or physical event, real or fictitious, which we are trying to envisage. And it is natural to say that we are aware of an entity, to use the entity-word 'image' for what we are aware of, because we are experiencing something which behaves in an entity-like way. It shows a certain independence of us, a certain obstinacy or recalcitrance, almost as if it had a will of its own. Often it will not come when we summon it. It obtrudes itself on us when we do not want it, changes when we would like it to 'stay put', vanishes when we try to retain it, stays when we try to get rid of it. It may even intrude upon us and stay with us to the point of becoming an obsession. The horrid picture of a street-accident we have witnessed continues to haunt our minds for hours, growing fainter at times but still renewing itself, and it will not go despite all our efforts to get rid of it; and then at last it suddenly fades away of itself. What behaves in this way is naturally described as an entity, a particular. A noun substantive, such as 'image', is just the sort of word that fits it.

Modern philosophers are never tired of telling us that mental images are not at all like pictures. But they are. It is true that a visual image cannot be handed round the table at a party, as a photograph can, to fill a gap in the conversation. It cannot be torn up or put in the fire (sometimes we may wish it could). It cannot be touched, nor seen simultaneously by different people from different points of view. All the same, in some ways it is very like a picture, and these likenesses are not unimportant. I am now imaging the Front Quadrangle of my college. I am aware of something which changes shape and colour quite rapidly, flickers, fades, becomes vivid again. But I do not for a moment suppose that these changes occur in the Front Quadrangle itself. And if it is a past event which I am visualizing, it even makes no sense to say that this changes. What changes is not the material object or event which is visualized, but that presented and inspectable something by means of which the visualizing is done. And this something, the visual image, does have a good deal in common with a picture. As to its origin, a picture is dependent in one way or another upon the object or event depicted. But once it has come into existence this dependence ceases, and it has as it were an independent career of its own. It changes when the object does not change, or remains unchanged when the object does change. It continues to exist when the object has ceased to exist; or conversely, it is torn up and put in the fire while the object remains in existence. In these ways, in having a history independent of the history of its original, a mental image *is* like a picture. It is also, of course, like a picture in having a more or less close resemblance to the object 'of' which it is an image; and it is like a picture, again, in being a means by which we think of its original.

All things considered, the expression 'mental picture' is about as good a phrase for describing visual images as the poverty of ordinary everyday language permits. Of course if we try hard enough to be misled by it, we can be. With sufficient effort and ingenuity, we can contrive to be misled by almost any expression under the sun. But the adjective 'mental' ought to be enough to insure us against supposing that these pictures are material objects. The defect which the term 'mental picture' does have is quite different from the one the Anti-Image philosophers attribute to it. It may tempt us to think that *visual* images are the only images there are.

The doctrine that there are no images but only imaging is sometimes supported by another argument. It is objected that if images are particulars they must be *somewhere*; at any rate visual and tactual images must be somewhere. And where can they be? To say that they are 'in one's mind' is no answer, for that is a metaphorical use of the word 'in'. To this I am tempted to reply, they are where they are, and have the spatial relations to other entities which they are empirically found to have. But such a reply will not, of course, satisfy the critic. We must first uncover the tacit assumption upon which his objection is based. He is assuming that if an entity is somewhere, it must be somewhere in physical space. This is no doubt a logically possible assumption. It might have happened to be true. But there is no sort of logical necessity about it, and in fact it happens to be false. My visual image of the Front Quadrangle is not anywhere in the physical world at all. It is spatially extended. Its parts are spatially related to each other by relations of location, and also by relations of larger and smaller. But as a whole it has no size, though its parts have sizes in relation to one another. And as a whole it is nowhere; or if you prefer, it is its own 'where'. It is a spatial world of its own, though a very poverty-stricken and short-lived one.

Will it be suggested that it is in my head? (In that case, of course, it would after all be quite comfortably situated in the space of the physical world.) But if it is in my head it must be two and a half inches from my left ear, or some other number of inches; and the middle part of it must be south-west of the tip of my nose, or in some other direction from the tip of my nose. We could properly enquire whether it is a quarter of an inch high, or smaller, or larger. And these suggestions do not make sense. It is not false, but absurd, to say that a visual image of mine is two and a half inches from my left ear. No doubt the physiological processes which are the causes or part-causes of the image's occurrence really *are* in my head, though physiologists may not yet have discovered exactly where they are. But the image itself is neither in my head nor out of it. It is in a space of its own, and has no spatial relations to anything in the physical world, though doubtless it has causal ones.

But the matter is more complicated than this. Some images, though not this present one of mine, are 'projected', and do have a place, not indeed in physical space, but in the space of the percipient's visual field. This is one of the characteristic features of eidetic images (the other is their quasi-sensory vividness and richness of detail). Eidetic images are rare. But many people have the power of projecting their visual images in some degree. For example, a visual image of a black cat can be projected on to the hearth-rug. Here the image *is* 'somewhere'; at least it is somewhere in the percipient's visual field. Even so, it is 'there' in a peculiar way. It is not, as it were, visually impenetrable. Although it is on the hearth-rug, no part of the hearth-rug's top surface is rendered invisible, as it would be if a real live cat walked in and sat there.

It comes to this. Some images do have spatial properties. But their spatial properties are peculiar, and not what might have been expected *a priori* by learned persons whose own imagery (other than verbal imagery) is commonly very deficient. We must just take the phenomenological facts as we find them, and we cannot settle the matter off-hand by the mere dogma that all extended entities must be somewhere in the space of the physical world. I repeat what was said before. Images are where they are, and have such spatial relations (or lack of spatial relations) to other extended entities as they are empirically found to have.

It was necessary to go into these points if the Imagist theory of thinking is to get a fair hearing. The Imagist is, of course, committed to the view that there *are* images, or that images are particulars of a special kind. His analysis of the imaging-process is the three term one. Imaging, he holds, is the experiencing or awareness of an image-entity, an actually occurrent particular, which in turn resembles some object or event or situation other than itself. It was necessary to show that these ways of speaking are not just silly confusions, but are dictated by the phenomenology of the imaging-process itself. I have often thought that if rainbows, reflections, mirages and the like had been less common than they are, philosophers would have denied their existence on *a priori* grounds. For how can there be entities which are at once physical and non-physical, in the physical world and yet not of it, existing from some points of view in physical space but not from others, spatial but lacking backs or insides? The fate of mental images, in these latter Verbalistic days, has been somewhat similar. We have the misfortune to live in the most word-ridden civilization in history, where thousands and tens of thousands spend their entire working lives in nothing but the manipulation of words. The whole of our higher education is directed to the encouragement of verbal thinking and the discouragement of image thinking. Let us hope that our successors will be wiser, and will encourage both.

We are now ready to consider the central doctrine of the Imagist theory concerning two layers or strata of symbols. As we have seen, the theory holds that images are the primary symbols, and all other symbols are secondary and derivative. Words in particular, and even ostensively defined words, which are commonly supposed to refer directly to objects, are only substitutes for images. They have no meaning in their own right, so to speak, and can only be used understandingly if we are able, on demand, to 'cash' them by calling up the images for which they are substitutes.

Now why is this primacy given to images? And why is cashability by means of images thought to be so crucial? Of course, in any Empiricist theory of thinking, indeed in any theory which allows that thought is *cum fundamento in re* and refers in some way or other to the objective world, there has to be a doctrine of cashability. But one would have supposed that cashing by means of actually observed objects and events, not by means of images, is what is needed. And among words, and other symbols which the Imagist calls derivative (e.g. signals, gestures), there are some which are cashable in this direct perceptual manner. Thus the word 'yellow' can be cashed by actually seeing something yellow, and the word 'bump' by actually feeling a bump or hearing one.

Yet it is true that we do sometimes cash our words by means of images in the way the Imagist describes, and perhaps if we did it more frequently we should talk less nonsense, both publicly and privately. When I utter a sentence to myself or to others, I am only using my words understandingly if I know what it would be like for the sentence to be true. Similarly I can only understand another man's sentence which I hear or read, if I know what it would be like for that sentence to be true. This knowledge is dispositional. It is a capacity for recognizing situations which would render the sentence true and for distinguishing them from situations which would render it false. If in a particular case I am doubtful whether I possess it, what shall I do? Sometimes I shall do just what the Imagist describes. I shall try to cash the sentence by means of images. I shall try to 'envisage', to 'picture to myself', an example of the kind of situation there would be if the sentence were true. I might try to do this if someone told me that there is a gibbous moon in the sky this evening. If I can form a tolerably clear visual image of what a gibbous moon would look like, I shall be satisfied that I do understand him. The reader might do the same if I told him that I had seen an osprey this afternoon, assuming that he is an ordinary person and not a very learned philosopher who is too clever to be able to form visual images at all. It is possible, of course, that the reader's image might mislead him. The image which the word 'osprey' suggests to him might be the image of a kind of octopus, like a lamprey, and not the image of a large fish-eating hawk. He would then be misunderstanding me. But misunderstanding is different from sheer absence of understanding. The reader would be attaching a meaning to my words, although it would be a private meaning. He would be able to claim that my words were not 'mere words' for him, as an article in an economic journal might be.

We can now see what the importance of image-cashing is. It is something which we do in the *absence* of the object or situation described. One of the most striking characteristics of symbolic cognition is that it is cognition in absence. In thinking we are somehow referring to, in cognitive touch with, what we do not at the moment see or feel. (Indeed, this is already so in sign-cognition, the most humble and primitive form of thinking.) Such reference to the absent is, of course, conceptual. I am not suggesting that symbolic cognition is a kind of clairvoyance of absent particulars, though it may be just as useful to us as if it were. When we think of an absent object by means of symbols, we cognize it not *in concreto* but *in abstracto*, as something satisfying this concept or that; as a member of this class or that, or of several classes at once; as characterized by such and such qualities or such and such relational properties. Accordingly, in saying that symbolic cognition is cognition in absence, we are only repeating in another way what was said before: that in thinking concepts are brought to mind by means of particulars which are not instances of them—such particulars as (occurrent) words, images, gestures, dumb-show, diagrams, etc. A 'symbol', in fact, in the wide sense the term has had in our discussion, is just another name for a non-instantiative particular used in 'free' thinking, as opposed to the 'tied' thinking which occurs in sign-cognition.

Now although images are non-instantiative particulars, they have this superiority over words: they come *nearer* than words do to being instances of the concepts brought to mind by means of them. A visual image of a dog is not an instance of the concept Dog, but it is much nearer to being so than the word 'dog' is. It is in many ways like what an actual instance of the concept would be. And if I cash the word 'yellow' in absence by means of a visual image, or the word 'squeak' by means of an auditory one, it might even be claimed that the image actually *is* an instance of the concept in question. An image of a yellow patch, it might be said, is actually itself yellow, as a buttercup seen in full daylight is, and an image of a squeak is actually itself squeaky. This claim, I think, is not altogether justified. The image does not seem to me to have the characteristic of intrusiveness or sensible forcefulness which the actual percept has. But the point now is that the claim is at any rate plausible. Some images come so very close to being instances of the concepts brought to mind by their means that it is at any rate not utterly absurd to say they actually *are* instances.

In this connection, let us ask ourselves how or in what sense an image is *recognized*. When I have an image of a dog, it is through the concept of Dog that I recognize it. It does not, of course, fully satisfy the concept—it is not a material object, it cannot be touched, it does not bite—but still this is the concept which applies, though it does not apply perfectly. When the word 'dog' comes into my mind, I recognize that too. But the concept through which I recognize it is certainly not the concept of Dog. It is the concept of the type-word 'Dog'. Through this, and not through the concept of Dog itself, I recognize any particular token of that word which I may meet with. It is even possible that I might be able to recognize the word without having the concept of Dog at all; as I can and do recognize the word 'dicotyledon' though I have quite forgotten what it is like for a plant to be dicotyledinous. As a matter of fact, of course, the concept of the type-word 'Dog' is linked in my mind with the concept of Dog, which I do also happen to possess, and that is why this type-word has for me the meaning that it has. But the link in this case is associative, established by a process of ostensive definition, whereas the link between the concept Dog and the dog image at any rate approximates to the link between the concept of the type-word and one of its tokens, or between the concept Dog and an actual dog which I see in the street.

We may sum this up by saying that images are at any rate *quasi-instantiative* particulars, whereas words (except for onomatopoeic words like 'cuckoo') are completely non-instantiative particulars. Thus when we think in images, thinking in absence comes much nearer to perceiving in presence than verbal thinking can. And this is the way in which words are cashed by images. By means of images, a kind of cashing in absence is made possible. We can make sure that we understand what we are talking about without the need to go and look. On the face of it, this may sound like a contradiction, as if the thing talked about (say a gibbous moon) were present and absent at the same time, or as if we were both perceiving and not perceiving an actual instance of some concept. If we have no images, or only verbal ones, or non-verbal images so faint, unclear and fugitive that we do not notice them, we shall probably think that it *is* a contradiction; and the remarks which some very learned men make about image-thinking suggest that they do think so. But contradictions have no power against empirical fact. It is useless to tell us that something which we actually experience is *a priori* impossible; in saying so, all you have done, at the most, is to warn us to be more careful in the way we describe it. Whether we like it or not, and scandalous as it may appear, the process of cashing in absence does occur in some people, and does sometimes help to assure them that they understand what they hear or read, or what they say themselves. To avoid the appearance of contradiction, we have only to say that images are quasi-instantiative particulars, which approximate to being instances of the concepts brought to mind without actually being so; and that cashing in absence approximates to, but is not, cashing in presence. But we must insist on the approximating, as much as on the falling short.

To placate the Anti-Image philosophers, we now turn to an important point which the Imagists have completely overlooked. Although mental images are quasi-instantiative particulars, they are not the only ones. Perfectly good perceptible objects, denizens of the public material world in which the Anti-Imagists feel so much at home, may have this quasi-instantiative function, and may cash our words in absence, or approximate to cashing them, in very much the same way as mental images do. Models, diagrams, pictures drawn publicly in the light of day with nothing 'mental' about them, dumb show, pageantry, acting on the stage or public cinematographic reproductions of it—all these entities and occurrences have the same quasi-instantiative function as images have. A clay model of a crocodile will cash the word 'crocodile' for me, in the absence of the actual beast. To convince myself or others that I do understand the word 'gibbous', I may draw a sketch of a gibbous moon on the blotting paper.

If it be objected that one has to have a mental image first, in order to produce a model or drawing, we must reply that this is both false in fact and vicious in principle. It is false in fact. If I am asked to draw a hexagon, I may have an image first, especially if I am somewhat uncertain what a hexagon looks like. But it is not true that I *must* have one. I can perfectly well draw a hexagon 'straight off' without having an image at all. And if there is something wrong with my drawing, as very likely there will be—if one of the sides, for instance, is curved instead of straight—I can detect my mistake, and correct it more or less adequately, without having to compare it with a mental image of a hexagon. And if such comparison with an image blueprint were indeed indispensable, how about the production of the image blueprint itself? Should we not be driven to say that it too could only be produced if we have a super-blueprint to copy it from, and to guide us in detecting and correcting any defects if may have? In actual fact, of course, I produce my image of a hexagon 'straight off', just as I produced the drawing 'straight off'. I do not need a previous mental image to copy from or to serve me as a blueprint for correcting the defects of this one. And if I did, there would be a vicious infinite regress. For how would the supposed pre-image itself be produced? By having a pre-pre-image to copy from? Then the same question arises again. Or if it is allowed that this (hypothetical) pre-image can be produced 'straight off', without being copied from anything, then why should not an ordinary image be produced 'straight off', as in fact it obviously is?

All these different sorts of quasi-instantiative particulars which I have mentioned, both imagy ones and public and physical ones, may be called 'replicas' if the reader pleases. We do sometimes think by means of replicas. And we do sometimes cash our words by means of replicas, either by producing the replicas for ourselves (whether images or physical ones) or occasionally by finding them ready made —as I may look up the picture of a mastodon in a zoological treatise, if I suspect that I am using the word 'mastodon' without understanding. So far as our inquiry has yet gone, it would appear that image-thinking differs from thinking with other sorts of replicas not in respect of the kind of thinking it is, but in being, for some people, easier and less at the mercy of external circumstances. To produce a model, one needs clay or plasticine; to produce a picture or diagram one needs pencil and paper. One can produce neither unless one has the free use of one's hands; and to enact a piece of dumb-show or of ritual behaviour, one may need the free use of all one's limbs. Image replicas require no external materials, no tools or instruments, and no use of the limbs. In so far as their production depends on anything physical at all, it depends only upon the integrity and healthy functioning of certain parts of the brain. These conditions for image-production may, of course, be destroyed or impaired, either by disease or by physical injury, but they exist in most men at most times.

Do mental images have the compensating disadvantage that they are less under our voluntary control than drawings or clay models

R

and other material replicas, even though they are also less dependent on physical circumstances? The answer would seem to be, yes and no; yes, for some people, no for others. Despite the authority of the Imagist Berkeley, we may doubt whether many people's images are completely under their voluntary control, though possibly Berkeley's own were.[1] The causes of their production, and of their vanishing, are within one's own personality; except, indeed, in telepathy, and it is possible that many of our images are partly telepathic in origin though few are wholly so. But even assuming that these causes are wholly within us, and even if those causes were purely psychical and not at all physiological, it would not, of course, follow that our images were wholly under our voluntary control. The psychic cause-factors on which their production depends are at least partly in the 'unconscious' stratum of our personalities, and not very much can be done by voluntary effort to influence what goes on there.

Some people, then, when they need quasi-instantiative particulars to think with, or to cash their words in absence, may find it better to produce a clay model or a drawing or a piece of dumb show. And this applies not only to people whose imagery is very defective, but also to some in whom it is copious and vivid. Their imagery, though abundant, may be chaotic and largely uncontrollable; the relevant image will not come at need, and irrelevant ones come instead, which are not only useless but worse than useless. On the other hand, some people are almost incapable of drawing. They cannot model in clay, nor imitate sounds, and are very bad at dumb show. Such people must use mental images, if they are to use quasi-instantiative particulars at all. And if in very learned circles there are some who can neither image nor draw, who have no power of producing either image-replicas or physical ones, their plight is sad indeed. They can only cash their verbal symbols by going and looking. And when they use words in absence, it will not be surprising if they sometimes rise to heights of nonsense of which the Vulgar are quite incapable.

It would seem then that the Imagist philosophers have mis-stated their own distinction between two layers or strata of symbols,

---

[1] Cf. *Principles of Human Knowledge*, section xxviii. The contention that images are under our voluntary control, whereas sense-data are not, is the basis of Berkeley's argument for the existence of God.

the primary symbols which symbolize directly, and the secondary symbols which are only substitutes for these. If the distinction is valid at all, the honourable title of 'primary' should not be reserved for images alone, but should be extended to replicas of all sorts, mental or physical, private or public. Images may be much the most useful replicas, for many thinkers at any rate, and the most readily available, but they are not the only ones. Accordingly, the doctrine we are to examine should be reformulated as follows: quasi-instantiative particulars or replicas, whether images or others, are the primary symbols; while the completely *non*-instantiative particulars, especially words, which we also use in thinking, symbolize in a secondary and derivative manner, and are only substitutes for these primary ones, made use of, as Berkeley says somewhere, 'for quickness and despatch'.

We can now reformulate the consideration which makes this doctrine plausible. It is a certain tacit assumption which turns up in different forms (as we shall see) in different philosophical theories of thinking. Thinking is cognition in absence. What is thought of is not itself present to our minds. We tend to suppose that there is something paradoxical about this 'absence', as it were something wrong about it. Surely cognition in all its forms *ought* to be some sort of direct inspection? And that is just what thinking is not. The only inspectables which are present to the mind in thinking are the various sorts of particulars which we have been calling symbols. Nevertheless, image-thinking (or other thinking by means of replicas) comes much nearer to direct inspection than verbal thinking does, because the particulars we then use to think with are at any rate quasi-instances of the concepts brought to mind. To put it very crudely, the assumption is that thinking *ought* to be a sort of seeing; or if this is too much to hope for, at any rate it ought to be as like seeing as possible. And image-thinking, or other replica-thinking, is very much more like seeing than verbal thinking is. We, therefore, conclude that verbal thinking, however useful 'for quickness and despatch', can only be a second best, and even perhaps, that it is not 'really' thinking at all. What more can it be than a skilful manipulation of substitutes, when we do not at the moment know what we are talking about, though we may hope that 'it will all come right in the end', and quite often it does? If we insist on knowing all the time what we are talking about, we must continually cash our words with images or other quasi-instantiative particulars. Of course life is too short for that, in practice. The need for 'quickness and despatch' is too urgent. But still, we should be wise to cash our words with images or other quasi-instantiative particulars much more often than we do. And we remind ourselves once again of Lord Bacon's menacing dictum 'Words are the counters of wise men, but the money of fools'.

The point may be put in another way if we regard concepts as recognitional capacities. Then the essence, and the paradox, of thinking consists in the fact that recognitional capacities can be sub-activated in the absence of the *recognoscenda*. My capacity for recognizing yellow things is only fully activated when I see something yellow. But it is sub-activated when I think about yellow things, in absence, by means of symbols. Now the Imagist holds that this indirect and derivative exercise of recognitional capacities ought to come as close as possible to full-blooded perceptual recognition, and in image thinking it does come very close to this. We cannot quite say that a visual image of a buttercup is actually an instance of yellow or is actually recognized to be so. But it is very close to being so, and when it is before our minds something very close to recognition occurs; whereas in verbal thinking nothing even approximating to recognition occurs, apart from the recognition of the words themselves. And so it is concluded, as before, that the kind of understanding which is manifested in verbal thinking must be something quite different from and inferior to the kind which is manifested in image thinking or other replica-thinking; and that it consists in the skilful manipulation of counters or substitutes, together with the readiness to cash them with images or other quasi-instantiative particulars at need.

But is it true that thinking ought to be a kind of inspection? And is it true that when we are 'really' thinking, as opposed to manipulating substitutes, the particulars we think with must be quasi-instantiative ones, either images or other replicas? It is true, and important, that in thinking, in using symbols understandingly and not like a parrot, we are somehow 'in touch with reality'. Thought, to be thought at all, must be *cum fundamento in re*, as has been remarked already. In other words, thinking is after all a form of cognition.

This truth, or rather platitude, was emphasized in all the traditional non-Nominalist theories of thinking, from Realism at the one extreme to Imagism at the other, and even perhaps in some traditional versions of Nominalism. But it is strangely forgotten, or ignored, by some of the Linguistic Analysts of today, who talk as if thinking were just a queer game which we play with our tongues or pens or typewriters, without any reference to the real world at all. And it is just this forgetfulness which prevents them from making any sense of all this strange talk about universals, abstract ideas, concepts and even images. But the fact is that these 'queer entities' were not just invented for fun, or out of sheer metaphysical perversity. People introduced them because they wanted to make clear to themselves how it is that thinking, though conducted in absence, could nevertheless be a form of cognition, in touch with the real world. The point of the Realist's universals was that they were abstracted from real objects, or at any rate were supposed to be analysable into universals thus abstracted. The point of the Conceptualist's occurrent abstract ideas was that they were 'founded on the similitude of *things*'[1]—on objective resemblances independent of us and of our talking. By saying, however misleadingly, that thinking is the awareness of such 'queer entities' and of the relations between them, philosophers did at least secure this much, that in thinking we are somehow in touch with realities outside our own minds. As for the images of the Imagists, they are not 'queer entities' at all, or if they are, their queernesses are just matters of phenomenological fact; and no one can say that they are 'invented', because they actually do occur. Nevertheless, the Imagists' motive for making such a fuss about them is fundamentally the same as the motive the Realists had for making such a fuss about subsistent universals, and the Conceptualists had for making a fuss about occurrent abstract ideas. The Imagist is aiming at just the same result as the Realist and the Conceptualist whom he criticizes, though he hopes to achieve it by more empirical and more economical means. He wants a theory which will secure that thought is *cum fundamento in re*. And this aim, so far from being a silly aberration, is one which any tenable philosophy of thinking must try to achieve.

But however respectable the Imagist's purpose may be, we must still ask whether he goes about his task in the right way. As I have

[1]Locke, *Essay Concerning Human Understanding*, Book III ch. 3, section 13; my italics.

said, he tacitly assumes that thinking can only be in touch with reality if it is a kind of inspection, or at any rate approximates as closely as possible to inspection. To put it another way, he assumes that cognition in absence can only be cognition if it is somehow not 'in absence' after all, or not wholly in absence. In image-thinking he finds what he wants, and he ought to have found it in other sorts of replica-thinking too. For when we think by means of images or other replicas, we can at any rate claim that quasi-instantiative particulars are present to the mind, even though real-life instances are not.

But we must ask again whether his initial and tacit assumption is right. Is it true that thinking ought to be a sort of inspection— 'ought' to be, in the sense that otherwise it cannot be in touch with reality, *cum fundamento in re*? On reflection, it does not seem to be true at all. (I use the vague phrase 'in touch with reality' on purpose, to avoid begging questions.) Nor does it seem to be true that verbal thinking, or other thinking in which completely non-instantiative particulars are used, is necessarily inferior to image-thinking. Verbal thinking is kept in touch with reality by means of ostensive definitions. It is, of course, true that words are sometimes 'the money of fools', and this sort of folly is not uncommon among very learned persons, as Berkeley pointed out. But the folly consists in talking and writing *without* ostensive definitions. And it is not true that words, for wise men, are only counters. A counter is something which one manipulates according to the rules of a game or of a calculus. No doubt the technical symbols of Mathematics and Formal Logic are used in this way, and really are analogous to counters. But basic-symbol words, like 'yellow' and 'bulgy' and 'above', are certainly not just counters in this sense. They are tied firmly to the real world by ostensive definitions. It is more likely, however, that Bacon was thinking of the use of counters in gambling, where the counters are exchanged for coin of the realm when the gambling-match is finished. But if words, for wise men, are counters in this cashable sense, it is real-life instances, and not only images, which cash them. This cash is better, not worse, than the cash provided by images and other replicas. For they, at the best, are only quasi-instantiative particulars; and that sort of cash is only an approximation to the real thing, though doubtless it is much better than no cash at all.

The trouble with the Imagists is that they will not trust their memories; or rather, they will not trust them enough. As has been said before, thinking is in the last resort a function of memory, or of retentiveness if that term be preferred. One of the ways in which memory manifests itself is by the production of quasi-instantiative particulars, both images and others. I remember what a crocodile is like (which is just another way of saying that I possess the concept of Crocodile); and this memory manifests itself sometimes by the production of visual images which resemble, but are not, crocodiles— and also by the production of pencil sketches and clay models which resemble crocodiles, and by crocodile-like actions and pos- tures when I am acting in a charade. But these are not the only ways in which this memory of mine is manifested. It is manifested when I actually find a crocodile in the bath or in the Zoo and recognize it to be one. Not only so; it is manifested in still another way when I used the word 'crocodile' understandingly in private or in public, or listen understandingly to other people using it. This happens because my capacity to utter that sound, and to recognize it when uttered by myself or others, has been associatively linked with my memory of what a crocodile is like. Because of this associative link- age, I can talk sense about crocodiles in their absence and can detect the nonsense talked about them by myself or others, without going to the trouble of producing a crocodilish image, and even if I am one of those unfortunate people who cannot form images at all. And if the image comes of itself while I talk or listen, as it easily may, I can quite well get on without it, though it is quite a pleasant thing to have. I need not attend to it carefully to make sure that I am talking sense or that my neighbour is. My memory of what a crocodile is like is already operating in another way, because my word-producing and word-recognizing capacity is firmly linked to it.

The Imagist, in short, has too narrow a conception of the many and varied ways in which memory operates; and this is what makes him say that words are only substitutes for images. In his polemic against verbal thinking he is therefore mistaken, and is trying to deprive the human mind of the most valuable power, perhaps, that it possesses. Ostensively definable words, and other words whose meanings are analysable in terms of these, are symbols in their own right and are not substitutes for anything. I have said already that

Imagism is an extreme view, and this is where its extremism lies.

But the polemic against verbal thinking is not the whole of the Imagist theory, nor even the most interesting part of it. There *is* after all such a process as image-thinking. And in the constructive, as opposed to the polemical, part of their theory, the Imagists offer an account of what image thinking is.

In the next chapter, we shall consider what they have to say. In saying it, they get into great difficulties; and when we examine the solutions which various Imagists have proposed for them, we shall be involved in great perplexities ourselves. We must not blame the Imagists for this. The subject itself is difficult, if only because so few philosophers have applied their minds to it. We ought to give full credit to the very few who have.

CHAPTER IX

IMAGES AS GENERAL SYMBOLS

The reader may recall our criticism of the doctrine of Natural Signs in an earlier chapter. One form that doctrine takes is to maintain that there are signs which signify by pure resemblance. I tried to shew that though there is sometimes a resemblance between a sign and its significate, this resemblance is never by itself sufficient to make the one a sign of the other. There are parallel difficulties in the Imagist theory. Of course the Imagist is not himself propounding a doctrine of natural signs, nor talking about signs at all. It is 'free' thinking which he is concerned with, not the 'tied' thinking which occurs in sign-cognition. But he *is* propounding a doctrine of natural symbols, in that sense of the word 'natural' in which it is equivalent to 'unlearned' or 'independent of acquired associative linkages'. Images, he says (i.e. non-verbal images), function as symbols, as something in which or with we think, because they are quasi-instantiative particulars; and he ought to say the same of other quasi-instantiative replicas. It is true that this sort of symbolization is not wholly independent of learning and experience. One must already have acquired the concept of which the image or other replica is to be a quasi-instance. But granted that one has acquired it, no further learning is required to enable the image or other quasi-instantiative replica to function as a symbol. Once we possess the concept of Dog, a dog-like image or model or picture will bring the concept to mind 'straight off' without the need of any further process of learning or habituation. How does it do this? By resemblance. Not, of course, because the image or model resembles the concept itself. It makes no sense to say that an actual occurrent, such as an image or a piece of dumb show, or an actual object such as a picture or a clay model, can resemble a disposition—or fail to resemble it either. But what an image or other replica does resemble is an *instance* of the concept. Such entities symbolize by being quasi-instantiative particulars. And to be a quasi-instance is to resemble an actual one.

How close does the resemblance have to be? That is the first question which naturally occurs to us. How closely must my image resemble an actual crocodile, if it is to be for me a natural symbol with which I think about crocodiles? Again, how clear and detailed must the image be? Will a very faint and hazy image suffice, provided it has *some* likeness to the way an actual crocodile would look if I saw one? Will something so wretchedly feeble and poverty-stricken be enough to cash the word 'crocodile' for me in absence, and to assure me, in case of doubt, that I do understand the word when I use it or hear it used by others?

But perhaps we should not expect hard and fast answers to these questions. Perhaps the difficulty here, so far as there is any, is a difficulty not in the Imagist theory but so to speak in the nature of things. Being a quasi-instance might be a matter of degree. We have already noticed that in the *Ante Rem* version of Realism being an *actual* instance is a matter of degree.[1] Your penny is a better instance of circularity than the back wheel of my bicycle. Indeed, nothing in this world is a perfect instance of circularity, according to the *Ante Rem* theory, though there is a transcendent world, studied by mathematicians, in which they are very abundant. There is a similar doctrine in some versions at least of Conceptualism. My concept of circularity, it would be said, is satisfied in different degrees by this object and by that. And plain men, who hold no particular philosophical theory, are quite familiar with the distinction between good instances of such-and-such and bad ones, better ones and worse ones. I do not see why we should scruple to allow that being a quasi-instance of a concept is a matter of degree, if we admit that being an actual instance of a concept is a matter of degree.

Thus we might be quite sure that a very clear, vivid and detailed image does sufficiently resemble an instance of the concept Crocodile; that it does activate our crocodile-recognizing capacity almost, though not quite, as an actual instance would; that it does suffice to cash the word 'crocodile' in absence, when no actual crocodile is being perceived. At the other extreme, there might be images so faint and poor that we could not use them in our thinking at all. And there might be intermediate cases where we could just manage to think with them and cash our words by means of them, but only in an imperfect and hazy manner. After all, though we may rightly

[1] Cf. pp. 18, 28, above.

reject the polemical side of the Imagist theory, and hold that words and other associative symbols are symbols in their own right, not merely substitutes for images, we still have to admit that verbal thinking too can be pretty hazy. Even basic words, susceptible of ostensive definition, such as 'magenta' and 'gibbous', have for some of us a meaning so vague that it is hardly meaning at all. And this is true *a fortiori* of many of our complex-idea words; we could make only the feeblest attempt to analyse their meaning in terms of basic or ostensively definable words. Consider the complex-idea word 'oecumenical', and suppose it occurs in a sentence in which the meanings of all the other words are known, for example 'An oecumenical council is now meeting in Valparaiso'. Do we or do we not know what it would be like for this sentence to be true? Some of us do, some do not, and many are betwixt and between. If this is admitted, we cannot fairly object to the Imagist on the ground that no hard and fast line can be drawn between the images which are good enough to count as quasi-instantiative particulars and those which are not. For this difficulty, if it be one, occurs in one form or another in all theories of thinking. Is the word 'oecumenical' good enough to think with, supposing you only half understand it?

We may notice also that this question about 'drawing the line' does not arise about mental images only, but about quasi-instantiative particulars in general. We can ask about any sort of replica, mental or physical, private or public, whether it is close enough to an actual instance to be counted as a replica. My plasticine model of a crocodile may have some resemblance to an actual crocodile, but so little that you are doubtful whether it should be called a crocodile-replica at all; you are inclined to say that it is just a shapeless lump. As there are 'bad' images, there are also 'bad' models in clay or plasticine, pictures so poor that we hardly know whether they are pictures or not, vocal imitations of a nightingale's song which are so little like the real thing that they might be just emotive noises, dumb show so feebly executed that it might as well be just random gambolling. With these overt and public replicas, everyone would admit that being a replica was a matter of degree. The Imagists may fairly claim that the same is true of image-replicas too.

A more serious difficulty in the notion of symbolization by

resemblance is not that there may be too little resemblance between an image and an actual instance, but that there is often too much. And this in two ways. On the one hand, the image may resemble too many things; on the other, it may resemble some one thing too closely. Let us begin with the first, which is the more obvious of the two, and the easier one to solve.

I have before my mind a visual image of a crocodile, that is, an image-particular which is crocodile-like. We will suppose that it is a 'good' image; clear, detailed and fairly steady. It does resemble an actual crocodile quite closely, or at least it quite closely resembles what an actual crocodile would look if seen from the side with its nose pointing to my left. I can quite well cash the word 'crocodile' by means of it; and it may well be useful to me for this purpose, because I so seldom have an opportunity of seeing the beast itself. So it is quite good sense to describe this image as a quasi-instance of the concept Crocodile. But unfortunately that is not all that it is. It does resemble a crocodile, but in so doing it also resembles a lizard, a reptile, an animal, an organism of any sort you please. So it is a quasi-instance of these concepts too. It is indeed a quasi-instance of any concept which comes above Crocodile in the determinable-determinate hierarchy. If it is a natural symbol for crocodiles, as the Imagist claims, why is it not equally a natural symbol for lizards, or for reptiles in general, or even for organisms in general? Perhaps he will say that it is. But if so, what determines that on this occasion I use it for thinking of crocodiles, whereas on others I might use it (or another image just like it) for thinking of reptiles, or even for thinking of organisms in general? It looks as if an image-symbol had a kind of systematic ambiguity within the determinable-determinate hierarchy it refers to. By being a quasi-instance of a determinate concept, it is *ipso facto* a quasi-instance of all the less determinate concepts under which that determinate one falls. It is as if the word 'scarlet' could mean either Scarlet, or Red, or Coloured, or even Visible Quality in general.

Some Imagists might reply that the meaning which the image has for me (within this range) depends upon the particular mental 'set' I have at the time, the particular problem, theoretical or practical, which I happen to be concerned with at the moment. (This is in effect Berkeley's solution, though his terminology is different.) But then we are naturally inclined to ask another question. How is this 'set' itself determined? Very often, by previous verbal thinking, either my own or someone else's whose words I hear or read; the *word* 'crocodile', already in my mind, determines which of these resemblances will be the psychologically effective one. Sometimes, on the other hand, my mental 'set' is determined environmentally. Perhaps I am beside the River Nile, or seeing a film of it in a cinematograph theatre, and this explains why the image means Crocodile and not just Reptile. In the former case, it cannot be true that image-thinking is wholly independent of verbal thinking, as the Imagist (in his polemical mood) tries to maintain. In the latter, image-thinking is not the 'free' thinking which the Imagist professed to be discussing, but is 'tied' to environmental stimuli.

But this criticism, I think, goes too far. We have already agreed that the polemical side of the Imagist theory must be abandoned. We are concerned only with the constructive side of it, its constructive account of what image thinking is. That being so, it does not matter if the images we have, and the way we use them, are sometimes influenced by the words which are already before our minds. And in point of fact the influence is reciprocal. Images sometimes bring words into our minds, as words sometimes bring images. And where a word is ambiguous (and after all, a great many words are) it is sometimes the presence of an image that determines which meaning, out of several, the word is to have for us in that particular piece of thinking. The cat-like image in my mind determines that I shall now use the word 'cat' to mean an agreeable domestic animal, and not a very horrible instrument of corporal punishment. As to the alleged 'non-free' character of image-thinking, it might be enough to say that the 'free', as distinct from 'tied' character, of thinking is a matter of degree. A piece of thinking which is initiated by environmental stimuli (as in the example about the Nile just now) may continue for many minutes or even hours in complete independence of them. And that, surely, is 'freedom' enough.

It may, however, appear that images suffer from another sort of ambiguity which is much more damaging because it is not in this sense systematic. A dog-image is quite like a jackal, and also quite like a wolf. My crocodile-image is dull yellowish green in colour. In that way, it resembles a muddy river; it also resembles various other creatures, such as tortoises, which live in muddy rivers and are protectively coloured (according to the usual principles of natural camouflage) so that it is not easy to distinguish them visually from their surroundings. In shape, too, my crocodile-image is not very unlike those long loaves of bread, pointed at both ends, which are to be met with in France. Moreover, I can make its tail switch if I like, and then it has a considerable resemblance to an angry lion as well as to a crocodile. Again, Jones' image of a dachshund may resemble a sausage about as closely as it resembles the actual dog.

It would seem then that any image symbol, or indeed any replica whether physical or mental, is bound to be ambiguous. It suffers from a kind of *embarras de richesse*, because it cannot help having too many resemblances. In this respect, surely, the particulars which symbolize by resemblance are greatly inferior to words and other non-resemblant symbols. As Lord Russell remarks somewhere, 'words differ more than objects do'. The word 'crocodile', for example, is not at all like the words 'tortoise' or 'muddy river' or 'French loaf'; nor is the word 'dachshund' at all like the word 'sausage'. It may be said, no doubt, that an actual crocodile does resemble an actual tortoise or muddy river in colour, or an actual French loaf in shape, and that a real dachshund is after all quite like a real sausage. So if my image is closely similar to an actual crocodile, we should naturally expect that it too would resemble a muddy river in colour or a French loaf in shape. To the extent that it shares the characteristics of the object symbolized, of course it resembles the other objects which that one resembles. Quite so, but is not that just where the trouble lies? It would seem that a symbol which symbolizes by resemblance *must* be ambiguous, just because it does symbolize in that way.

Let us now consider this difference between words and images a little more closely. Two objects A and B may be very like each other in their immediately perceptible characteristics—colour, shape, hardness, texture, taste, smell. And then a mental image or physical replica resembling object A will also resemble object B, since it is only the immediately perceptible characteristics which an image or other replica can reproduce. Yet A and B may differ greatly in their causal properties and their mode of behaviour. A snake often looks very like a stick, but it has very different causal properties. Cheese often looks like soap, feels like soap to the touch, and even tastes like soap. But its effects upon the human organism are very different. If we think in words, we shall not be misled by these 'superficial' likenesses—perceptible likenesses accompanying unlike causal properties. We take care that the *word* 'cheese' is very obviously unlike the *word* 'soap'. Or rather, it is not a matter of deliberate devising. Language has just grown up in that way as a result of practical exigencies. If there ever was a time when the words for cheese and for soap were indistinguishable, that speech-habit has failed to survive and perpetuate itself. There is a kind of Natural Selection among speech-habits which ensures that only the fittest will survive; the fittest, that is, for directing attention to those properties of objects (especially their causal properties) which are important for the guidance of our expectations and our conduct. But with images and other replicas no such principle can operate, just because they *have* to reproduce the immediately perceptible characteristic of the objects which they mean. It is rather as if all words had to be onomatopoeic, like 'cuckoo' or 'gong'.

Yet there is something wrong with these objections. They prove too much. If they were wholly right, we should have to conclude that images and other quasi-instantiative replicas could never be used at all for thinking with; they would be so ambiguous that they would be useless. And this conclusion is certainly false. Let us consider physical replicas for a moment, since images, in philosophical circles at any rate, are viewed with so much suspicion. In actual practice, *are* we so very much misled by the 'ambiguity' of physical replicas? Sometimes no doubt we see a picture or model with a word attached to it. A queer-looking statue in a museum, the Corbridge Lion, for instance,[1] may have the word 'lion' inscribed on its base; and then we know that it *is* a statue of a lion, however many other things it resembles. (Indeed, the face of the Corbridge Lion resembles a man's face quite as much as a lion's.) But we do not always have the aid of words to protect us from the 'ambiguity' of physical replicas, and we seldom need it. The china object on the cottage mantelpiece is quite clearly a china dog, though there is no label on it saying 'dog'. An Ancient Egyptian statue, used in

---

[1]This celebrated object was discovered at Corbridge, near the Roman Wall in Northern England. It is a product of Romano-British art, and is dated to the second century A.D.

the worship of the Goddess Pasht, is clearly a statue of a cat, though no one tells us so, and we may never have heard of the cat-goddess Pasht. Almost anyone can draw a tolerable picture of a snake, and almost anyone else can recognize it to be a picture of a snake, without being told what it is. No one would think that my plasticine model of a dachshund was a representation of a sausage, though it is quite like a sausage.

If the 'ambiguity' of physical replicas does not in practice mislead us, why should the 'ambiguity' of mental images mislead us either? In actual fact it does not. Let us consider the example about cheese and soap. Assume that all the cheese I have ever eaten did look and feel and taste very like soap. It does not follow that I shall be liable to use my cheese-images for thinking about soap, or my soap-images for thinking about cheese. Nor is it true that the perceptible characteristics of cheese and soap have been indistinguishable, even in my very limited perceptual experience. For after all, the difference in their causal properties is a matter of perceptual experience too. And so is the difference between jackals and dogs, or between crocodiles and loaves of French bread, or even between crocodiles and alligators, which really *are* pretty much alike in their causal properties and mode of behaviour.

This bring us to the crucial point which is neglected in the Anti-imagist line of thought we are considering. (Some Imagists have neglected it too.) When I think about some object or class of objects in an imagy manner, I am not restricted to using just one single image. I might use a series of different images. Again, the image which I use need not be static. It might be, as it were, a working model, cinematographic rather than static. It might change in such a manner as to represent the characteristic behaviour of a crocodile, as opposed to the static 'look' of one at a particular moment. A man who has eaten a piece of soap can remember very well what experiences followed, and how they differed from those which usually follow after eating cheese; and if his imaging powers are good, he can reproduce this series of experiences by means of a series of images. (He would, of course, need to have images of organic sensations among others, but presumably some people do have them.)

In practice, a single image usually suffices, and very often it is a static one. It is enough if we have the *capacity* to produce other suitable images at need, or to make the static one alter in a suitable way, and the capacity does not have to be actually exercised. Later, I shall have to discuss Hume's distinction between the image which is 'present in fact' and other additional images which are 'present in power'. As we shall see, it has a wider application than Hume himself realized, and this is already a case in point. When an image-symbol would otherwise be ambiguous, because it has too many resemblances, it may be saved from ambiguity if other images (or alterations in this one) are 'present in power' even though not 'present in fact'. This is only another way of looking at the suggestion made in an earlier chapter that thinking is a function of memory or retentiveness.[1] If I really do remember what a crocodile is like, I have the capacity of producing not just one crocodile-image, but many different ones; not just one static image resembling the look of a crocodile at one particular moment, but a changing or cinematographic image reproducing the way the creature moves about in the water, swishes its tail, snaps its jaws, climbs out on the bank. So long as I do have this multiform image-producing capacity, it will be enough if only one image is actually present in fact. Again, if I really do remember what a crocodile is like, I shall be able to produce a great variety of physical replicas of crocodiles, not just one clay model or drawing, but a good many different ones, even though in actual fact I produce only a single one on this particular occasion.

This same distinction of Hume's may also be used to elucidate the rather mysterious conception of a mental 'set', which was mentioned a few pages back when we were discussing the other and more systematic sort of ambiguity which images are alleged to have.[2] What determines whether a crocodile image means Crocodile, or Reptile, or Organism in general, it was said, is the mental set which the thinker has at the time. But how does such a mental set manifest itself in consciousness, and how do its manifestations differ from those of a different mental set? There may be no difference if we consider just one single image, especially if it is a static image. But there is a great difference if we consider what *other* images we produce, or have a tendency to produce, along with or after this one. If I am using my crocodile image for thinking of crocodiles, the other images will also be crocodile-like and will differ only in minor

[1]See pp. 58-9, 73, above.   [2]See p. 268, above.

S

details from this one. If, on the other hand, I am using it for thinking of reptiles, these other images will be, for example, images of
common English lizards, or snakes, or frogs. And if I am using it
for thinking of organisms in general, the subsequent images
will differ from each other very widely indeed, as much as
crocodiles differ from lions, or from fishes, or wasps or buttercups
or amoebas.

Here again these additional images need not be 'present in fact'.
It will be enough if they are 'present in power'—one series of additional mental images for this mental set and another for that. It
will be enough if the thinker is *ready* to produce them (or the
corresponding physical replicas). I am inclined to say that this readiness manifests itself in consciousness, and as it were colours the
image which is 'present in fact'. To put it another way, the crocodile image, which is the only one present in fact, feels somewhat
different according as the additional images I am ready to produce
are of this sort or of that. When I am in such a state of directed readiness, it is not merely that I have the capacity to produce other
images to follow this one, though certainly I do have it. The
capacity, after all, is permanently there. I have had it continuously
ever since I first learned what a reptile (say) is like. But if I am *ready*
to produce these other images now, this capacity is sub-activated;
even though I do not in fact produce them, I am on the verge or
on the brink of doing so. The capacity is no longer wholly latent,
as it is at other times. And this sub-activation shows itself in consciousness by imparting a characteristic 'feel' to the image which is
actually present. It is on the point of spilling over or proliferating
itself in this direction rather than in that. Again, if I am using physical
replicas, sketches on paper for instance, instead of mental images, I
may only draw one sketch to bring the concept of Reptile to mind
or to bring it to the mind of the spectator—just one very rough
sketch of a crocodile. All the same my fingers are itching, as we say,
to draw other sketches, of lizards, frogs, snakes, etc., even though I
do not actually draw them.

Something rather similar happens with words. When a word,
such as 'bank', has several different meanings, the meaning which
it has for me at a particular moment (the way I am now using it)
is made manifest by the other words I utter directly afterwards. If
I am using 'bank' to mean what an aircraft does when it flies in a

curve, the words I shall say afterwards will be different from those I should say if I were using it to mean a steeply sloping mass of earth, or an economic institution. Yet I need not actually say these additional words, and even if I intended to, I might be shot or struck dumb before I could get them out. It is enough if it is 'on the tip of my tongue' to say them. And the utterance 'bank', I think, has a different feel for me according as the additional words on the tip of my tongue are appropriate to this sense of the word 'bank' or to that.

So much for the difficulty about too many resemblances, and the consequent objection that all images symbols are ambiguous. But though the difficulty about 'too many' seems to be soluble, we are now in another difficulty about 'too much'. It would appear that by resembling one crocodile too closely, my image may be prevented from performing its main function, which is to be a symbol for crocodiles in general. From this point of view it would almost seem that a 'bad' image—schematic, sketchy, lacking in detail—is better than a 'good' one. By not being very like some one crocodile, it will have some resemblance to *any* crocodile.

The difficulty which we have now encountered is a very familiar one, and might almost be called classical. It comes to this: how can an image be a general symbol? Words, other than proper names and demonstratives, manage it quite easily. At least we ordinarily suppose that they do. The word 'yellow', for example, is a general symbol because it applies to, and could be cashed by, *any* yellow object, no matter what.

Let us return for a moment to the polemical side of the Imagist theory. In his polemical mood, the Imagist tells us a word such as 'yellow' is only a secondary symbol; not a symbol in its own right, but only a substitute for an image. Would it not be very surprising if a mere substitute had this property of generality, while the thing for which it is a substitute has not? For this is not an irrelevant or trivial property (as my deputy may have red hair while I have not). It is a crucial one. If verbal symbols, though mere substitutes, have this property of being general, then *a fortiori* images—or some images—must have it. And how do they manage to have it?

The difficulty is still there if we ignore the polemical side of the Imagist theory, as we have resolved henceforth to do, and confine ourselves to its constructive side, the analysis of image-thinking as such. For the problem now is, how there can be such a thing as image *thinking* at all. It would seem that there cannot be, unless images can somehow function as general symbols. The Imagist has to explain how a crocodile-like image can be a symbol for any crocodile, no matter which. This is not going to be an easy task.

Before we examine the suggestions which Imagist philosophers have made for solving this problem, we may pause and consider the Imagist theory as a whole in another light. What do the Imagists say about concepts? According to the books, they are trying to abolish concepts altogether. Surely the whole point of their theory is to 'get rid of universals'; not merely the extra-mental universals of the Realists, whether *in re* or *ante rem*, but also the intra-mental abstract ideas which Conceptualists like Locke have substituted for them? Now certainly the Imagists do reject what I have called the Philosophy of Universals, and accept the Philosophy of Resemblances instead. All the functions which subsistent universals, whether *in re* or *ante rem*, have been supposed to perform, could be performed equally well, in their view, by classes of mutually resembling particulars; equally well, or indeed better, because such universals, they would say, are only postulated 'metaphysical entities', whereas it is quite certain that there are classes of mutually resembling particulars.

But though they do wish to abolish extra-mental universals, it is not so clear that they wish to abolish concepts altogether—despite Berkeley's fierce and brilliant polemic against abstract ideas. For the term 'concept', or 'abstract idea', may have a dispositional as well as an occurrent interpretation. What the Imagist objects to is *occurrent* abstract ideas. He objects to them on the very cogent ground that they are not actually found to occur. The concepts he wishes to abolish are concepts which are alleged to be objects of inspection, inspectable or introspectible bits of intra-mental furniture. But if the term 'concept' be interpreted in a dispositional way, as it has been in this book, the Imagist philosophers do not abolish concepts at all, but offer an analysis of what a concept is, or of what it is to possess one. A man who possesses the concept Dog ('knows what a dog is like' is the ordinary phrase) has the capacity for doing two things which a man who lacks it cannot do. When he is actually perceiving a dog he can recognize that it is one, and he can think about dogs when he is not perceiving any dog. These two sorts of occurrence, recognizing instances in presence and thinking of them in absence, are the two fundamental ways in which a concept (or the fact that one possesses it) is shown or manifested. A concept is a recognitional capacity which manifests itself also in thinking in absence. It will be observed that the *objects* of cognition in either case are particulars. It is dogs, and not the concept Dog, that we recognize; and it is dogs, not the concept Dog, that we think of in absence. The concept is that which *enables* us to recognize them or to think of them, but neither in recognizing nor in thinking does it present itself to the mind as an inspectable or an introspectible entity. If we say, as I have myself, that it is 'brought to mind' on such occasions, this must not be taken to mean that we have a look at it, so to speak, but rather that it is operative in our minds (indeed psycho-physically also), being aroused from the state of latency in which it is at other times. What does present itself to the mind, and is inspectable, is in recognition a perceived particular. In thinking, even the particulars which we think *of* do not present themselves to the mind, still less does the concept itself. What do present themselves to the mind are the non-instantiative particulars which we think *with* (or 'in'), the particulars which we have been calling symbols: either completely non-instantiative particulars such as words, or quasi-instantiative particulars, whether mental images or other replicas.

It follows that there are two possible forms of Imagist theory, one moderate, the other extreme. The moderate form is not concerned with recognition at all, but only with thinking. The extreme form offers an analysis of recognition as well. It says that when I perceive a dog and recognize it to be one, I am comparing the perceived object with a dog-image which I have before my mind, and noticing that the two are alike, or sufficiently alike.

I do not know whether anyone has ever held the extreme form of the theory, though some of the Anti-image philosophers of the present day seem to suppose that all Imagists must have held it. The only example I can think of is, oddly enough, Locke, whose official theory is not Imagism at all. There is a passage in the *Essay* where he speaks of 'precise, naked appearances in the mind (which) the understanding lays up . . . as the standards to rank real existences into sorts'.[1] It looks as if these 'appearances in the mind' might be images. If so, Locke is suggesting an Imagist theory of classification, in which images function as exemplars. Anything would be a dog if it sufficiently resembled my dog-image. From this an Imagist theory of recognition would naturally follow. To recognize something as a dog, I should have to compare it with my exemplary dog-image. These exemplary images, presumably, would be permanent images, which I somehow carry about with me always, ready for use whenever they are needed.

Such a theory is suggested, perhaps, by the fact that we do sometimes recognize things by means of pictures or models. During the late war, aircraft recognition was taught by means of silhouettes and wooden models. A rare bird, which one has never seen before, might be recognized as a marsh harrier by comparing it with a picture in a bird book. So too with recognition of individuals. You have never seen the Prime Minister before, but when you do see him you recognize him from photographs in the newspapers.

But this is a provisional and second-hand sort of recognition; 'recognition on authority,' it might be called. What makes a bird a marsh harrier is not its resemblance to a picture, but to other actual birds. To know that this hawk which I see is a marsh harrier, as opposed to merely believing it to be one on the authority of the bird book, I must know that it sufficiently resembles certain other birds which I have seen for myself. And the artist who made the picture must have seen some of the actual birds for himself and noticed their resemblance to each other, or else he must have painted his picture under the supervision of someone else who had. Similarly, the sergeant who teaches aircraft recognition to recruits by means of silhouettes or wooden models must himself have seen actual Wellington bombers, or else he must have been taught by someone who had. At some stage or other, we come back to someone whose recognition is direct and perceptual and not by means of models or silhouettes. And the pupil, on his side, must begin with an act of mere faith. He must begin by believing, what he does not know, that the wooden model or silhouette is a sufficiently accurate replica of the actual aircraft. Similarly with recognition of individuals. One must begin by believing on the authority of the editor or the

[1]*Essay Concerning Human Understanding*, Book III, ch. 11, section 9.

photographer that the picture in the newspaper is a sufficiently accurate likeness of the Prime Minister.

But suppose that I had just invented the picture or model out of my own head. Obviously it would be useless to me for purposes of recognition. It would be equally useless if the bird-book artist had just invented the picture of a marsh harrier out of *his* head, or if the sergeant had just invented the aircraft silhouettes, or if the newspaper photographer had just faked the photograph in the studio. Now suppose that I try to use a mental image instead of a picture or physical model. This will be equally useless if I just invent it on the spur of the moment, no matter how 'precise and naked' it is. For then the most I could discover is that the object I perceive (the hawk or aircraft in the sky) does happen to resemble my image closely. To be of any value for purposes of recognition, the Image must be a *memory*-image and known by me to be so. It must be already known to be a sufficiently faithful likeness of one or several marsh harriers or Wellington bombers which I have previously seen for myself. Only then can I use it to decide whether this perceived object in the sky is or is not a member of the class of marsh harriers or Wellington bombers. In other words, the image itself must be recognized, in the sense of the word 'recognize' which is appropriate to replicas. It must itself be recognized as a quasi-instance of the concept in question, if it is to be of any use in settling the question whether this perceived object is an actual instance.

Now how is the image itself recognized? By comparing it with some pre-image or super-image, and finding that it sufficiently resembles this? Obviously not. No such pre-image or super-image is actually found to exist. Nor is it needed. The ordinary image, the one we do actually have, is recognized 'straight off', without being compared with anything. And if a super-image *were* needed, the same problem would arise over again. We should have to ask how it in its turn was recognized; and an infinite series of pre-recognitions would have to be completed before anything could be recognized at all. If, on the other hand, we are able to recognize an image 'straight off' as marsh-harrier-like or Wellington-bomber-like, without comparing it with a pre-image or super-image, why cannot we equally recognize the perceived object 'straight off' without comparing it with any image, as in fact we obviously do?

If we suppose that the image which we are to use for recognizing perceived objects is a permanent one, a kind of intra-mental continuant—and this, presumably, is what Locke's 'precise naked appearances' were[1]—we are confronted with another difficulty, or another form of the same one. It is not sufficient that my dog-image is *in fact* permanent (assuming that it could be). I should have to *know* that it is permanent, that it has remained unchanged, or unchanged in all relevant respects, ever since I first set it up, many years ago perhaps, as my exemplar for the class of dogs. In other words, I must recognize that this present phase of its history is sufficiently similar to its past phases, which at the moment I am not experiencing. I must recognize it as being, so to speak, a faithful copy of its past self. This amounts to saying that *occurrent* images, the only ones which we are indubitably aware of, still have to be recognized, even if in fact they are just short phases in the history of long-lived image continuants. And again we have to ask how this recognition is done.

One must conclude, I think, that an Imagist analysis of recognition is not at all a promising enterprise. The usual objection to it, that the image itself would have to be recognized, seems to be decisive. But it is often supposed that this objection refutes Imagist theories of conceptual cognition altogether. This is a mistake. A man might hold an Imagist theory of thinking without holding an Imagist theory of recognition; there is no inconsistency in accepting the one and rejecting the other. In actual fact, it is thinking, not recognition, which Imagist philosophers almost always discuss. I have suggested already that if the term 'abstract idea' is interpreted in a dispositional manner, the Imagists do not deny the existence of abstract ideas; it is only *occurrent* abstract ideas which they reject, abstract ideas regarded in the way that Locke usually regarded them, as occurrent introspectible entities. We saw that there are two main ways in which an abstract-idea disposition manifests itself, recognition in presence and symbolic cognition in absence. Few Imagists, if any, have wished to give an Imagist analysis of the first; and if any did wish to give one, they were very unwise to try. What they *have* done is to offer an Imagist analysis of the second, symbolic cognition in absence. And they have suggested that so far as an abstract idea manifests itself in this second way, it is to be regarded as an image-producing disposition. This is, of course, an

[1]He says that the understanding 'lays them up' (*Essay*, Book II, ch. 11, section 9).

overstatement, if words and other completely non-instantiative symbols are symbols in their own right, as we have argued they are, and are not merely substitutes for images as the Imagists, in their polemical mood, supposed. But still an abstract idea, or concept, might be *inter alia* an image-producing disposition, even if it manifests itself in other ways as well; and this might throw light on one of the sorts of thinking that we do, though it might throw no light on others. It is an obvious empirical fact that many people, unless they are *too* clever, do think in images at times. The Imagist philosophers should be able to give us an analysis of what image thinking is, if anyone can. They have at any rate studied the subject, whereas other philosophers have neglected it, and some have contented themselves with telling us that it ought not to be studied.

This brings us back to the question how an image can function as a general symbol. For that is what it must do, if there is such a thing as image thinking, as there obviously is. It must be noticed again that what we think of is not the abstract idea or concept itself, but particulars which are instances of it, or 'satisfy' it, if that word be preferred. What my dog-image means, and enables me to think of, is not Doghood, but just dogs in general. Doghood, indeed, on the Imagist view at least, is just an invented metaphysical entity, erroneously postulated to explain the fact that we think about dogs.

We must now return to the difficulty about 'too much resemblance', which was mentioned but not discussed on page 275. If my dog-image is not to be an ambiguous symbol, applicable to jackals or even sausages as much as to dogs, it would seem that it must have a pretty close resemblance to some actual dog, presumably to one which I have myself seen. But the more closely it resembles this dog, the less closely it will resemble many others. By resembling a certain dachshund too much, it will resemble a Great Dane too little. By having a vividly black and tan colouring, it will be *pro tanto* disabled from resembling white dogs or grey dogs or spotted Dalmatian hounds. Yet it ought to be a symbol for any and every dog, no matter which, as the word 'dog' quite easily contrives to be. How is this to be managed, if it symbolizes by resemblance, as the Imagist says it does? For that is what the quasi-instantiative function of images comes to, as we have seen. An image, or any other replica, is a quasi-instance of a concept by resembling, or sufficiently resembling, an actual instance.

It would seem, on the face of it, that one single dog-image could never be enough. Should we not need a large number of dog-images, all dog-like but otherwise unlike each other; as many different ones as there are sub-classes within the total class of dogs? But we do not seem to find them, when we think about dogs in an imagy way. We may occasionally find that two or three different dog-images are present in our minds on such occasions, but seldom more; and often we get on quite well with only one.

Before we consider what Imagist philosophers have to say about this, we may notice that the problem of 'too much resemblance' still arises when we consider the relation between an image and an individual object. We have hitherto supposed that our dog-image, even if it is not a very good symbol for dogs in general, can at least be a faithful copy of some individual dog, say Fido. If Fido is a class of many different appearances, as Berkeley and Lord Russell hold he is (indeed, an infinite class of different appearances according to Lord Russell) it is obvious at once that no single image can resemble them all. The more it resembles a front view of him the less closely it resembles any of the back views, side views, underneath views, top views which are also constituents of the beast, to say nothing of intermediate views from intermediate directions. The more closely it resembles a particular front view of him, say from ten yards away in full daylight, the less closely it resembles other front views of him, from fifty yards away, from six inches away, seen in lamplight or in a fog or during an eclipse. Moreover, the class of appearances contains tactual, auditory and olfactory members as well as visual ones. And if my image is visual, as we have hitherto been assuming, how is it to resemble these non-visual members of the class? Even the degree to which it can resemble the tactual ones is problematical; and as a matter of fact the Imagist Berkeley, in his *Theory of Vision*, is committed to maintaining that it is zero.

It will be objected perhaps, that Fido is not just a class of appearances, or that it makes no sense to say he is. But the difficulty is still there, no matter what our theory of perception and the external world may be. The very best a visual image can achieve is to be exactly like Fido as he looks from one particular place at one particular moment; and the more it succeeds in this task, the more it fails in resembling him as he looks from other points of view or at other moments. And if what he *is* cannot in any way be reduced to or analysed in terms of the way he *appears*, not even in terms of how he appears from many different points of view taken together; if he is a 'transcendent entity', as he is in Descartes' theory of perception, or Locke's, or any of their modern variants; then the position is still worse. For then there is nothing in him which any image can exactly resemble, and still less can it exactly resemble the whole of what he is.

The problem still arises even if the image purports to resemble just a very brief physical event, such as an explosion. For even this looks different from different points of view, and sounds different from different distances. But with persistent objects such as Fido the difficulty is even greater. Fido has quite a long history. No doubt we may fairly ignore his future (if he is to have one, and is not destroyed today by order of the magistrates). But even when we confine ourselves to his history up to now, or up to yesterday afternoon when we last saw him, it still contains a very large variety of different states and occurrences. At one time he was small and playful, but later he became large and fierce. Sometimes he is eating, sometimes sleeping, sometimes snarling, sometimes biting the postman. The more closely my image resembles him as he was at one particular time, say when he had just got his front teeth into the postman's left leg, the less closely it resembles him as he is at many other times.

It seems as if an image must have some at least of the properties of a general symbol if it is to represent even an individual object adequately. And here again it would appear that some 'bad' images— those which are schematic, sketchy, poor in detail—may actually be better than 'good' ones.

But it is time to return to images which are supposed to be general symbols in the ordinary sense, symbols used for thinking of classes. If some satisfactory account of these can be given, it can no doubt be applied *mutatis mutandis* to solve the problem just raised about images of individual objects.

To meet the difficulty about too much resemblance, Imagists have suggested several expedients. First, Hume points out that when only one image is present to the mind in fact, others may be 'present in power',[1] ready to come into consciousness when and if they are needed; that is, the thinker is ready to produce them for himself when and if they are needed. Suppose my present dog-image closely resemble a certain dachshund I have seen. It is black and tan in colour and rather sausage-like in shape. It does not, however, mislead me into thinking that all dogs are black and tan and sausage-like. If I began to be thus misled, other images of white dogs, black dogs, St. Bernard dogs not at all resembling sausages, would at once arise. Hume is partly concerned here with the word-cashing function of images. One single dog image would not, of course, suffice to cash the word 'dog' in absence, if that were the only dog-image I could produce. But it *will* suffice if I am ready at need to supplement it by other images, which are in various ways unlike itself, though also dog-like. This is an important improvement in the Imagist theory. What we now have is not just a disposition to produce quasi-instantiative images. Or at least we now see that this way of putting it is not sufficiently explicit, since it might suggest that all would be well if these quasi-instantiative particulars were exactly like each other. Instead, we now emphasize that the disposition is a disposition to produce different, alternative quasi-instantiative images, even though on a particular occasion only one of them is actually produced. This, after all, is what we might have expected. For what makes something a member of a class (an actual instance of a concept) is the fact that it resembles several *different* exemplars as closely as they resemble one another. The exemplars are 'alike in the midst of unlikeness', as I put it before.

Another and more recent suggestion for solving the difficulty is the theory of *generic images*. The term is not perhaps a very happily chosen one, and it may be interpreted in two different ways, as we shall see. Francis Galton, who first introduced it, compares a generic image to a composite photograph.[2] If you photograph all the members of a family on the same plate, all full-face, for example, the differences between their faces will be cancelled out or at least greatly weakened in the resulting picture, and the resemblances will be

[1] *Treatise of Human Nature*, Book I, Part I, section vii 'Of Abstract Ideas' (Everyman Edition, p. 28, Selby-Bigge's edition, p. 20).
[2] *Inquiries into Human Faculty*. Appendix on Composite Portraitive, section ii.

emphasized. The picture is not exactly like John Smith, or Mary Smith, or little Tommy Smith, or Aunt Jane or Great-aunt Tabitha. But it has what may be called a typical resemblance to them all. It represents the typical family face of the Smith family. Probably no one of them has exactly that face, but it is as it were the mean to which all the different Smith faces approximate, some more closely and some less. Similarly it is claimed that if a number of convicts are photographed full face on the same plate, the picture which comes out is a picture of the typical criminal face. There is probably no one member of this class of human faces which the picture exactly resembles, but it has a typical resemblance to them all.

Now some mental images, it is said, are rather like composite photographs. The early Imagists, Berkeley and Hume, assumed that a dog-image must be an exact copy of some particular dog which one has perceived, or rather of some particular dog-appearance which one has sensed. It is not denied that such exact-copy images do occur, though they may well be a good deal less common than Berkeley and Hume thought. But the images used in thinking, it is claimed, are generic ones. The dog image which one used for thinking of the class of dogs is not exactly like any dog which one has actually seen, and is not even exactly like any dog which actually exists. But it has a resemblance, and a sufficient resemblance, to any and every dog, because the features in which all dogs are alike have been strengthened, and those in which they differ have been weakened or obliterated. It has a typical resemblance to all the members of the class, but an exact resemblance to none. For that reason it is just what is needed to serve as a symbol for a class. According to this version of the Imagist theory, then, it is generic images, not exact-copy images, which are used in image thinking; and it is by generic images that words are cashed in absence.

This is not incompatible with Hume's suggestion in which 'presence in power' is brought in to supplement 'presence in fact'. Presumably a generic image could at need revive some of the non-generic images which have been, so to speak, averaged out in the making of it; just as, if I looked very carefully, I could see the faint outlines of Aunt Jane's very long nose in the composite photograph. Nevertheless, Hume did not, of course, consider the possibility that there might be generic images. If he had, he would have seen that an image which is 'present in fact' is all that is absolutely indispensable for thinking of a class, provided it is a generic image. Nor would he have needed to add an infusion of Nominalism to his Imagist theory, as he actually does, when he accounts for the 'presence in power' of additional images by supposing that a number of different images (or image-producing dispositions) are all alike associated with a single word, e.g. the word 'dog'.

It seems clear that there *are* generic images, in this sense of the term 'generic', though the adjective, as I have said, is not a very happy one. It might be better to call them 'typical images'. If we take Galton's analogy of the composite photograph for our guide, there is, of course, nothing generic about the image itself. It is a full-blooded and fully specified particular, just as the composite photograph is. What is generic about it, or rather general, is not any intrinsic characteristic which it has, but the way in which it resembles other particulars. It has a general resemblance to many different dogs, although—or rather, partly because—it does not have an exact resemblance to any one of them. As Hume says, 'some ideas (i.e. images) are particular in their existence but general in their representation'.[1] This is true of Galtonian generic images too, though Hume was not thinking of them when he said it.

But though we may agree that these generic or typical images (as opposed to exact-copy ones) are often used in image thinking, will they give us all we want? With some classes they seem to, but not with others. It depends on the nature and the degree of the unlikeness which there is between the members of the class, or between the sub-classes included in it. Galtonian generic images may suffice for thinking of crocodiles, which do not differ from each other so very much, and perhaps they will just suffice for thinking about dogs, which differ from each other a good deal more. But will they suffice for triangles, the class which gave Locke and Berkeley so much trouble? Here the analogy of a composite photograph does not seem to help. Suppose there are fifteen triangles drawn on paper, five equilateral, five isosceles, and five scalene. They all have different areas; the isosceles ones differ from each other in the sizes of their angles, and so do the scalene ones. What will happen if you photograph them all on the same plate? The result will not be any kind of picture, but just a mess—a mere blur. We cannot

[1] *Ibid.* Everyman Edition, p. 30, Selby-Bigge's edition, p. 22.

say that the feature they have in common, three sides, three angles, the equality of the angles of each to two right angles, will be emphasized, and the features on which they differ will be weakened or cancelled out. For what could a picture be like in which three-sidedness was emphasized but no sides were visible? Again, could there be a Galtonian generic image for the class of colours? If the differences between red, green, blue and yellow were cancelled out what would be left? A white image, perhaps? Or a perfect and absolute blank? But neither of these would be a very good symbol for colours in general.

For similar reasons, the Galtonian generic image does not seem to help with the other problem I mentioned in passing, about the relation between an image and an *individual* object. If I took two dozen photographs of a certain elephant on the same plate from different places, some from the front, others from the back, some from underneath, etc., what sort of a picture should I get? Again, just a mess or blur, like the composite picture of the triangles. We certainly should not get one relatively clear composite picture, as we did with the Smith family or the convicts; and whatever we did get, it could not be said to have a typical resemblance to all these different elephant appearances.

Hitherto I have followed Galton's analogy of the composite photograph, but I am not sure whether this does full justice to the theory of generic images. For sometimes the generic image is described in a way which suggests that it is a much more mysterious and even metaphysical entity than any composite photograph could be. It is spoken of as if it were a particular whose characteristics are not fully determinate.

This is a dark and tantalizing notion. In the world of everyday perceptible particulars, nothing has a determinable characteristic without having one or other of the determinate characteristics falling under it. At least that is our ordinary assumption. For instance, nothing is just triangular. It can only be triangular by being equilateral, or by being isosceles, or by being scalene. Again, nothing is just coloured. Either it must be red, or it must be green, or it must be blue, etc.; and if it is red, it must have some determinate shade of red. But this principle, it is now suggested, does not hold for mental images; or rather, with mental images it is permissive but not mandatory, and an image *can* have a determinable characteristic without having any of the determinate characteristics falling under it.

Can we make any sense of this suggestion? It will not do to dismiss it off-hand as absurd. There is no compelling *a priori* reason why the terminological rules which we use for describing the perceptible world must apply in all respects to images, though certainly they must apply in some respects, because there are certainly resemblances between images and perceptible objects. We must consider the question further, and must not allow ourselves to be prevented, or excused, from doing so by remarks about 'absurdity'. If we do sometimes have images which can only be described in this paradoxical way (given our existing terminological resources), we must put up with it as best we may.

It will be remembered that Locke describes his abstract idea of a triangle in these words: 'in effect, it is something *imperfect*, which cannot exist'. This is because it is 'neither oblique nor rectangle (i.e. right-angled), neither equilateral, equicrural nor scalenon, but all and none of these at once'.[1] When he says it cannot exist, he means that it cannot exist *in rerum naturâ*, in the physical world; for he holds that it can and does exist 'in the mind', and moreover that it exists there as an occurrent mental content. I have italicized Locke's word 'imperfect'. Is he suggesting, perhaps, that there are intra-mental occurrents which are so to speak inchoate or incomplete entities, incapable of existing in the physical world because their characteristics are not fully determinate? They can hardly be the same as the 'precise, naked appearances' which he speaks of in the other passage I have already discussed.[2] 'Precise' is just what they are not. But perhaps they *are* the same as the indeterminate generic images which we are now considering. Perhaps his abstract idea of a triangle was just a generic image in this second and more mysterious interpretation of the phrase. In that case, of course, he should not have called it an abstract idea. But then he did not have the advantage of living in the twentieth century.

Do we have images which are as it were inchoate entities, incompletely determinate particulars? I confess that I cannot confidently answer 'No', as Berkeley and Hume did. Is it possible that these great Empiricists sometimes preferred to be clear rather than

[1] *Essay*, Book IV, ch. 7, section 9.   [2] Cf. pp. 277-80, above.

empirical? If we ever are aware of such entities, we cannot, of course, expect that we shall be able to describe them in a non-paradoxical way. In describing them we shall have to use analogies drawn from the everyday perceptible world (indeed even the term 'image' itself originated in this way); and in that world such incompletely determinate entities *ex hypothesi* do not exist.

Let us now appeal to another authority, who is supposed to be much nearer to infallibility than John Locke: the Ordinary Man. Ordinary people, who are neither philosophers nor psychologists, sometimes describe their images as 'vague'. Indeed, anyone who has images at all is strongly tempted to describe some of them in this way. Yet a philosophical purist might object that it makes no sense to call an actual particular vague. When a word is called vague, for example the word 'bald', the vagueness belongs not to the sound or mark itself (there is nothing vague about that) but rather to the symbolic function it performs. We cannot draw a sharp line between the things to which it applies and the things to which it does not. But when an image is called vague, it is not vagueness of meaning that is referred to, but something in the nature of the image itself, an intrinsic or internal vagueness. If someone is asked to report what was in his mind when he heard the word 'dog' understandingly, he may quite well answer that he had a 'vague' dog-image. He is not saying that there is anything vague about the meaning which it has for him. This may, of course, also be true, but it need not be. To put it another way, he is not saying that he only vaguely understands what a dog is, or only vaguely knows what a dog is like. He is trying to describe the internal features of the particular by which, or through whose occurrence, this (dispositional) understanding of his is occurrently manifested. I would suggest that the word 'vague', in this usage, is just an untechnical and perhaps misleading equivalent for the terms 'inchoate', 'incompletely determinate', which were used in the last paragraph, and likewise for Locke's term 'imperfect'.

Lord Russell, one of the few philosophers who have discussed generic images at all, warns us in *The Analysis of Mind*[1] against identifying generic images with vague ones. Certainly we must not identify them if 'vagueness' is equivalent to 'vagueness of meaning'—the same kind of vagueness which is found, *mutatis mutandis*,

[1] *Analysis of Mind*, pp. 220-1.

T

in many verbal symbols, and perhaps in some degree in all. But we might still be right in identifying them, if the vagueness referred to is an internal characteristic of the image itself, as I believe it often is when ordinary people describe their images as vague.

This so-called vagueness, this not fully determinate or inchoate character which some images are alleged to have, might be connected with another which many images certainly do have, their evanescent or fleeting character. There are two ways of treating an image. We may dwell upon it, examine it carefully, contemplate it. This is what we do if we are asked to make an introspective report about it, for instance. An image so treated may be 'vague' in this queer sense of the word, but it need not be. It may quite well be clear, detailed and vivid. But there is another and more important way of treating images, the one which chiefly concerns us in this discussion. We may *use* them for thinking with. Then we do not dwell upon them, and it would obstruct the process of thought if we did, or even arrest it altogether. Each image, as it comes, vanishes almost at once and makes way for another. We might be inclined to say that it 'does not stay to be looked at', that is, to be attended to and inspected. This suggests that it is in itself a fully determinate entity, but we do not have time to notice what its determinate characteristics are; like a gate momentarily glimpsed out of the tail of the eye, when we did not have time to count the bars, though we are sure that there was some determinate number of bars. But another and perhaps more empirical way of describing the facts would be to say that the image does not have time to develop itself fully; it exists for so short a period that it is only half-formed, so to speak, by the time it vanishes.

I would suggest that the coming-into-being of an image is a rather mysterious process, which deserves more attention than it has received. The full-blooded, clear, detailed images which we sometimes have, the kind of images so graphically described by some of Galton's correspondents, do not necessarily spring into existence ready made and complete. Sometimes they may. But often they *grow* more detailed and more clear 'before our mental eye'. (And even when they do come into consciousness ready made and complete, are we sure that there was not a similar process of growth beneath the threshold?) This process of self-completion may take an appreciable time; and in the early stages of it, the image may perhaps be described, without too greatly straining language, as an inchoate or incompletely determinate particular, a 'half-baked' one if the reader prefers. At any rate, such phrases, however queer, do not seem to be utterly inappropriate.

With some images, however, this process of growth, or self-development, or progressive increase in determinacy, may never be completed at all. Before they have passed the inchoate and 'half-baked' stage, they cease to exist. This may be simply because the subject's imaging powers are defective, or because they are greater in some directions than in others (he might be a poor visualier, for instance, though good at producing auditory images). Again, there might be unconscious or subconscious emotional factors which prevent a given image from developing itself fully, even though the subject's imaging powers are very good. This image might distress him too much, if it was allowed time to complete itself. So it is not allowed the time, but is suppressed before it is too late. Here it is interesting to notice that in some sense we seem to know the general tendency or direction which the process of self-development has, even though nothing beyond the initial stage of it has as yet actually occurred; and that is why we prevent the later stages from occurring. We have, as it were, a fore-feeling of what will come, if we do not take steps to prevent it; at any rate, we have it when the adverse emotional factors are subconscious ('marginal') rather than unconscious.

But what is more important for our purposes is the consideration mentioned before. An image which is used for *thinking* may have so short a life-span that it simply has not time to develop itself fully. While still inchoate and incompletely determinate it vanishes, and another comes. As has been suggested already, this premature decease may even be necessary, if the process of thought is not to be obstructed. The image is banished, or murdered, on the compelling ground of *raison d'état*. For a short time, its presence at court is very useful, because its services are needed or even perhaps indispensable. But if it were allowed to stay longer, it would become a fatal embarrassment; so it must go.

Image thinkers (as opposed to image contemplators) might even form a habit of getting rid of their images very rapidly before they had time to develop themselves fully. And then they might find that such incompletely determinate images were just the ones which were most useful for image thinking. A highly determinate image of an oak tree might not be a very good symbol with which to think of trees in general, for the reasons mentioned already; by resembling oaks too much, it would resemble beeches, elms, alders, ashes too little. But something which was on the way to becoming an image of an oak, without having got there, might be much better. It would be better still if it had the potentiality of determining itself in several alternative ways, of becoming *either* oak-like *or* beech-like *or* elm-like, etc., but was not allowed time enough to determine itself actually in any of these ways. And it would be best of all if these alternatives, potentially contained in the incompletely determinate image, were felt by the subject to be there, as tendencies ready to be actualized, though in fact no one of them *is* actualized. I have suggested already that some such 'feeling of tendency' may be present when an image which is as yet not fully developed is repressed because of emotional resistances. In that case the tendency was a tendency of development in just one direction, whereas here there are alternative tendencies of development in different directions; nevertheless, I believe that these too may be 'felt' (I cannot find a better word) when none of them is as yet actualized.

In still another sense which Hume himself did not quite intend, these alternative determinations would be 'present in power' when only an incompletely determinate image is 'present in fact'. Perhaps this is also the sense in which Locke's triangle which was 'neither oblique nor rectangle, neither equilateral, equicrural, nor scalenon' could contrive to be 'all and none of these at once'. It could be all of them potentially (and felt by the subject to be so) though none of them actually. In the same way, perhaps, we may try to make sense of Kant's distinction between 'the schema' and 'the image', though I must confess I do not fully understand it. 'The image' might be what I have called a completely determinate image, while 'the schema' is an incompletely determinate image with unactualized tendencies to complete itself in several alternative ways. If this is right, both Locke and Kant were talking about generic images, though they did not know it; and Hume was on the verge of talking about them, though he did not, of course, know it either.

This is the best defence I can offer for the doctrine of generic images if they are conceived as not fully determinate particulars. It would appear that such incompletely determinate particulars do occur in image thinking, however we choose to describe them. And if indeed they do, they seem well fitted to serve as general symbols, much better fitted for the purpose than the fully determinate image-particulars which the earlier versions of the Imagist theory were concerned with. They are also better fitted for the purpose than the Galtonian generic images, analogous to composite photographs, which symbolize by typical resemblance, as I have called it; though images of this Galtonian sort do occur, and can be used for thinking of classes whose members differ from each other, provided these differences are not too great.

Finally, it should be noticed that if there are incompletely determinate images, the analogy between images and physical replicas— models, pictures, diagrams, dumb show, etc.—to that extent breaks down. It will only hold good for the images which are completely determinate particulars. We can still say of those that they are just one sort of replicas among others; and the fact that they are private and mental, instead of public and physical, makes no essential difference to the way we use them in our thinking. It may be, however, that such images are less frequent than philosophers have supposed. It may even be that, with some people at least, most or even all of their images have something 'generic' about them and fall short of being completely determinate particulars, though some come closer to complete determinateness than others. Whatever may be thought of this suggestion, it does seem that a particular which is not fully determinate is to that extent radically different from anything which exists in the public and physical world, and therefore from any physical replica. Or, if after all, there are some incompletely determinate particulars in the public physical world (as some of the queer phenomena studied by psychical researchers might possibly suggest) our ordinary conceptions of the public and physical world, and of the way in which minds are related to it, will have to be pretty drastically altered. According to our ordinary assumptions at any rate, an incompletely determinate particular can only exist 'in the mind'. We may still call it quasi-instantiative. All the same, it differs in a very important way from determinate quasi-instantiative particulars, whether physical or mental.

So much for generic images in the second and non-Galtonian interpretation of the term. As I have said, these are dark and mysterious regions, in which an analytic philosopher may well fear to tread. If we venture into them, we are coming close to what is called the 'creative' activity of mind; we are even on the fringe of dangerous topics like poetic inspiration. Anyone who thinks it is a philosopher's first duty to be clear and talk sense will do well to refrain from discussing generic images. Or are there some subjects so important or at least so intriguing, that it is better to talk nonsense about them than not talk about them at all?

There are two other topics which must be mentioned, very briefly, before I bring this long and complex discussion of image-thinking to an end. I do not know of any established terminology for referring to them. The terms which I shall use are *diagrammatic images* for the first, and *metaphorical images* for the second.

Diagrammatic images appear to play a considerable part in some people's thinking, and possibly they play some part in the thinking of everyone who uses images at all. They may be described as non-verbal ways of representing schemes of relationship. In Galton's book *Inquiries into Human Faculty* there is a very curious essay on what he calls 'number forms'. These are various sorts of diagrammatic visual images, or image diagrams, which people use for thinking of the series of cardinal numbers. The numbers are arranged in various forms of spatial order, some quite complicated. Some people use similar diagrammatic images for representing the temporal order of the days of the week, and sometimes the different days of the week have different colours as well. A genealogical table, representing the blood-relationships of the Kings and Queens of England since William the Conqueror, with their respective dates, is sometimes put up on the walls of the schoolroom. But it could equally well exist in the mind of the schoolboy (or the adult) in the form of a diagrammatic image, and would serve the same purpose in his thinking. I believe that diagrammatic images of this kind can also be used for representing the skeleton, as it were, of any scheme of classification (e.g. in zoology), or even for representing the relations between the different parts of an argument, or of a scientific or philosophical theory. I should not be surprised if many examination candidates use diagrammatic images to think about the history of British Empiricism, and answer questions about the relationships between the philosophies of Locke, Berkeley and Hume with the aid of such image-diagrams. The other way of answering them is to school oneself to repeat long verbal rigmaroles on demand; but I am not sure that it is a better one.

An example of a *metaphorical* image would be an image of a lion which is used, not for thinking about lions, but for thinking about courage. It is possible that some of our verbal metaphors, even some of those which are now mere *clichés* like 'the ship of state', may have originated in this way, by translating an image-metaphor into words. We may notice that the converse process of translating verbal metaphors into images sometimes occurs in dreams, and even in day-dreams too. What would be recognized as a mere metaphor in the verbal thinking of our waking life is presented in the dream in the form of images, as if we were picturing to ourselves an actual occurrence. A psycho-therapist, however, in interpreting such dream-images would suspect that they had a metaphorical character, and would try to discover what kind of situation, emotionally relevant to the dreamer, these images were metaphors for. Indeed, this seems to be one of the best clues we have for uncovering the 'latent content' of a dream, as opposed to its 'manifest content'. We sometimes have to use the same procedure in interpreting images, whether dream-images or waking ones, which have a tele-pathic or precognitive character. When writers on psychopathology or psychical research say that the images they are concerned with (dream-images or others, and hallucinations also) are to be regarded 'as symbols' they mean, I think, that these images are to be regarded as metaphorical ones. Furthermore, to the extent that images are used in this way, as they sometimes are even in waking life and by normal people who are neither mentally diseased nor 'psychic', I shall have to take back what was said before, that there is nothing in image-thinking which is analogous to talking nonsense in words. It is curious that the Imagist philosophers have never, so far as I know, discussed this metaphorical use of mental images, though literary critics have sometimes discussed it in connection with poetry.

Our discussion of the Imagist theory of thinking has led us into great perplexities. What conclusions, if any, may we draw from it? On its polemical side, the theory must be altogether rejected. It is not true that verbal thinking is an inferior or derivative form of thinking. Words are not merely substitutes for images. If anything, it is images which are substitutes, substitutes for percepts. And though we do sometimes cash our words with images when we are using words in absence, it is not true that this is the only way of cashing them, nor the most fundamental way. The fundamental way of cashing them is by actually perceiving the objects or situations which satisfy the ostensive definitions of the words in question. Image-cashing is only a second best, which we resort to on the principle that half a loaf is better than no bread.

On its constructive side, however, the Imagist theory has valuable lessons to teach us. As against the modern denigrators of images, we must admit that there is such a thing as image thinking. We must admit that the production of quasi-instantiative images (and other quasi-instantiative particulars) is one of the ways in which our possession of a concept is manifested, and an important way too. We must admit, moreover, that images can be used as general symbols, for thinking of classes. Certainly the Imagists do get into great difficulties in explaining how symbols which symbolize by resemblance can nevertheless be general. But it would seem that in one way or another, or by a combination of several, these difficulties can be overcome. There is Hume's suggestion that when only one image is present to the mind in fact, others are present in power. In effect this amounts to saying that a concept, in so far as it is an image-producing capacity, is a capacity to produce a range or series of *alternative* quasi-instantiative images; and that it is a range of images, not just a single image, which is needed for cashing a word in absence. Secondly, there are the two versions of the doctrine of Generic Images. For thinking of some classes, at any rate where the differences between the members of the class are not too great, we can use generic images of the Galtonian variety, which have a typical resemblance to any and every member of the class without exactly resembling any one member. But over and above these typical images, there appear also to be generic images in another and more paradoxical sense of the phrase, images which are incomplete or not fully determinate particulars. I have suggested that Locke's much-criticized passage about the abstract idea of a triangle, 'neither oblique nor rectangle, neither equilateral, equicrural nor scalenon, but all and none of these at once', may be an attempt to describe a generic image of this sort, though he was quite wrong to call it an abstract idea; and that Kant in his doctrine of the

Schema may also have been thinking of such incompletely determinate images. If there are such incompletely determinate images, they too could be used as general symbols; and they could be used when the differences between the various sub-classes within the given class are so great that a generic image of the Galtonian sort (analogous to a composite photograph) would be useless. We are inclined, perhaps, to assume that there ought to be only one way in which an image can function as a general symbol. But are there any good grounds for this assumption? As far as I can see, there might be several alternative ways.

I have already said that the Imagist theory is quite inadequate on its polemical or anti-verbal side. But even on its constructive side, despite the important lessons it has to teach us, it suffers from one very serious defect. In the Imagist theory, the *logical* aspects of thinking are almost entirely neglected; and so it does not even succeed in giving us a complete account of image-thinking itself. Berkeley's proposal that philosophical inquiries (of all things) should be conducted entirely in images is one of the most extraordinary suggestions ever made by a great thinker. How could even one paragraph of Berkeley's own *Principles* be translated into a symbolism of images, without any equivalents for the words 'not', 'if', 'any'? It is true, of course, that logical *words* need not be used. A shrug of the shoulders, or a kinaesthetic sensation of an incipient one, might be used instead of the word 'not'. But if we are to think at all, there must be something, verbal or non-verbal, to perform the functions assigned in verbal thinking to such words as 'not', 'if', 'or', 'some', 'all', 'possible', 'actual', etc. We have seen reason to think that such equivalents exist in a rudimentary form even in the tied thinking which occurs in sign-cognition. There is, for example, such a thing as a disjunctive state of preparedness, where we are ready not just for A to occur, but for *either* A *or* B *or* C to occur. *A fortiori* such equivalents for logical words must exist in the free thinking which the Imagist is trying to analyse. Perhaps they could themselves be images. Instead of using an actual shrug of the shoulders, or the kinaesthetic 'feel' of it, as our equivalent for 'not', we might perhaps use a kinaesthetic image. But if we did, it would be an image-symbol of an entirely different sort from those which the Imagist philosophers themselves have discussed.

CHAPTER X

THE CLASSICAL THEORY OF THINKING

THROUGHOUT the last four chapters we have been concerned with what may be called the Symbolistic conception of thinking. First, we had to consider in some detail the relation between symbols and signs. We found reason to reject the theory that symbols are just a special sort of signs, namely those produced by human beings. Sign-cognition and symbolic cognition are different. Since sign-cognition is undeniably thinking, it follows at once that not *all* thinking is symbolic cognition. The Symbolistic Theory of thinking, in its unrestricted form, must be mistaken. Sign-cognition, however, is a primitive kind of thinking. Certainly it is capable of great subtlety and delicacy, and there is even something which may be called a 'logic' of it, as I tried to show in Chapter V. But sign-cognition does have the defect of being tied, more closely or less, to environmental stimuli. Fully developed thinking, on the other hand, is not thus tied. It is free or autonomous. It might, therefore, be maintained that fully developed or autonomous thinking *is* nothing but symbolic cognition, in the wide sense of the term 'symbol' which I tried to explain (cf. Chapter VI, pp. 145-7). In this restricted form the Symbolistic conception of thinking might still be perfectly correct. In other words, it might be true that there is no such thing as 'bare' or 'naked' thinking, in human beings at least; that there must always be some medium in or with which we think; that in thought (as opposed to primary recognition) concepts can only be had in mind by experiencing particulars which are *not* instances of them; and that to rise above the level of sign-cognition, where such particulars are environmentally provided, we have to be able to produce suitable non-instantiative particulars for ourselves. Such autonomously produced non-instantiative particulars are just what this theory calls symbols. The most important of them are mental images on the one hand, and words on the other.

It is, therefore, not surprising that the Symbolistic conception of thinking has presented itself historically in two different forms,

Imagism and Nominalism. The one equates 'free' thinking with the using of image-symbols, the other with the using of verbal symbols (verbal images being counted for this purpose as a special sort of token-words[1]). Both are extreme theories, and it could be said roughly that the strong points of the one are the weak points of the other. I have discussed the Imagist theory in some detail, because it is nowadays the less familiar of the two. Moreover, image-thinking is worth discussing for its own sake, quite apart from any general theory of conceptual cognition which may be built upon it, especially as it has been greatly neglected by philosophers in recent years, and even declared not to exist. I have not so far said much about Nominalism. But in showing that there *is* such a thing as image-thinking and how it works, I have in effect been bringing out the weaknesses of the Nominalistic Theory, which tries to maintain that thinking is nothing but the using of words (publicly or privately) and that image-thinking is not 'really' thinking at all. On the other hand, in drawing attention to the weaknesses of the Imagist theory when *it* maintains that verbal thinking is not 'really' thinking at all, but only an operation with substitutes, I have in effect been bringing out the strong point of the Nominalist theory: the fact that words are symbols in their own right, because our basic words are linked directly to the world by ostensive definitions, without the aid of images. In this way the Imagist's very proper demand that our verbal symbols must be cashable, or that conceptual cognition must be shown to be *cum fundamento in re*, is perfectly adequately met.

The conclusion we reach is a very tame and obvious one. Both words and images are used as symbols. They symbolize in quite different ways, and neither sort of symbolization is reducible to or dependent on the other. Images symbolize by resemblance. Basic words symbolize by ostensive definition;[2] or, from the psychological point of view, by word-object associative linkages. But both words and images are perfectly good symbols, in that both are non-instantiative particulars in which or with which we think, though images (and physical replicas likewise) come closer to being instantiative particulars than words do. As we should expect of two

[1]On verbal imagery, see pp. 243-4, above.
[2]This is true even of onomatopoeic words like 'cuckoo'. It is only ostensive definition which settles that this word means a certain sort of bird, and not just the noise which that bird makes in spring and early summer.

extremist theories, both Nominalism and Imagism are right in what they affirm and wrong in what they deny.

Then should we combine them, and say that thinking in its fully developed form consists in using *either* words *or* images understandingly? Or rather, is this the way in which the Symbolistic conception of thinking (right or wrong) ought to be formulated? Not quite. Words and images are not the only non-instantiative particulars which we use for thinking with, though in human beings they happen to be the most important ones. For example, we also think sometimes by means of physical replicas, such as diagrams, models and dumb show; sometimes by non-imitative gestures, as in using the deaf and dumb alphabet; and sometimes by means of the muscular sensations which accompany incipient actions, gestures or others, when these actions are not overtly performed. Granting that conceptual cognition (above the sign-cognitive level) is rightly equated with the using of symbols in public or in private, it would be very rash to suggest that words and images are the only symbols there are. And it would be plainly wrong to suggest that they are the only ones there could conceivably be. In principle, *any* sort of non-instantiative particular might be used for thinking with, provided the thinker can learn to produce it for himself and to recognize it when produced by himself or by others.

But is the Symbolistic conception of thinking right at all? We may try to state it in a carefully guarded way, restricting it to autonomous or fully developed thinking on the one hand and excluding sign-cognition from its scope, and freeing it on the other hand from the restrictions which Imagists and Nominalists, each in their different way, have tried to impose upon it. We may insist that thinking is not just the mere occurrence of non-instantiative particulars, that we have to *produce* these particulars for ourselves, or if they are produced by others, they must at any rate be such as we are capable of producing for ourselves. We may insist too that they have to be produced in an understanding manner, or observed in an understanding manner when produced by others. Neither parrot-like production nor merely aesthetic contemplation will suffice. If they are quasi-instantiative particulars (images or physical replicas) we must recognize them to be so; if they are completely non-instantiative ones, they must not only be recognized as being the words, gestures, etc., which they are, but also they must be associatively linked to extra-mental objects, and these associative linkages must be sub-activated.

But when all this has been said and all these qualifications made, is it even then true that thinking of the free and autonomous kind is nothing but the using of symbols? In old days, few philosophers would have said so. Historically the Symbolistic theory of thinking was a heretical and left-wing view. Both Nominalism and Imagism began as movements of revolt. It is only in our own time that Nominalism has become orthodox and respectable; while Imagism has never been respectable at all, and indeed is even further from respectability now than it was when Berkeley first propounded it. And even if we try to devise a version of the Symbolist Theory less narrow than either of these, it is still radically opposed to what may be called the 'classical' conception of thinking.

By 'classical' I do not just mean Greek or Graeco-Roman. It is true that this conception of thinking did originate in Greek times, and Plato, or perhaps Socrates, was the first exponent of it. But it continued to be accepted in one form or another by the majority of philosophers until the second decade of the twentieth century. Its essential tenet is that thinking is differentiated from other forms of cognition not only by being a special sort of activity, but also by having a special sort of *objects*, which are variously called universals, concepts or abstract ideas. Thinking is conceived to be the inspection of such 'intelligible objects' and of the relationships between them. Those who hold this view would not of course deny that symbols, e.g. words or images, are very often used in thinking. But it would be said that we *can* think without them, and sometimes do. Moreover, it is held that their function, when we do use them, is a merely auxiliary or ancillary one. When used in private thinking, they direct our attention upon this intelligible object rather than that. (A similar theory is held about the function of memory-images in recollection; they are supposed to direct our retrospective powers upon this past experience rather than that.) When symbols are used in communication, it is held that they direct the hearer's or reader's attention upon the same intelligible objects to which the producer of the symbols is attending, or was attending at the time when he produced them. At least, that is what symbols are supposed to do when the attempt to communicate succeeds. When it fails, the attention of the hearer or reader is either not directed to any intelligible object, or else to intelligible objects other than those which the producer of the symbols had before his mind. Thus thinking, on this view, is sometimes not symbolic cognition at all. There is supposed to be such a thing as bare or naked thinking, in which symbols (and *a fortiori* signs) are dispensed with altogether; and even when it *is* symbolic cognition, that is not all that it is, nor the most important thing about it. The essential characteristic of thinking, on this view, is that it is the awareness or inspection of intelligible objects—universals, or concepts, or abstract ideas, or (in some versions of the theory) subsistent propositions.

It is important to understand that this Classical conception of thinking has by no means been confined to Rationalists. A man might hold that all concepts are either abstracted from experienced particulars, or else are analysable without remainder into subordinate concepts which are thus abstracted. He would then be an Empiricist. Indeed, this is the obvious way of defining 'Empiricism'. He might also hold that thought is distinguished from other forms of cognition by having concepts (as opposed to perceived or introspected particulars) for its objects. There is no inconsistency between these two tenets; and as a matter of historical fact, Locke maintained both, though later Empiricists, influenced by Berkeley and Hume, have usually rejected the Classical theory of thinking.

It should also be pointed out that this Classical conception of thinking is not by any means confined to philosophers of the Realistic school. One might deny that there are subsistent and extramental universals, whether of the *Ante rem* or *In re* variety. One might reject what I called the Philosophy of Universals altogether, and accept the Philosophy of Resemblances instead. And yet one might still hold that thinking is distinguished from other forms of cognition by having a distinctive sort of objects. One might hold that these objects of thought are intra-mental entities, concepts or abstract ideas, and that they are neither *ante rem* nor *in re* but *in intellectu*. 'General and universal,' says Locke, 'are creatures of the understanding'; they 'belong not to the real existence of things' though they 'have their foundation in the similitude of things.'[1] Probably the majority of modern western philosophers, from the

[1]*Essay*, Book III, ch. 3, sections 11 and 13.

late Renaissance to the early twentieth century, have been Conceptualists; but this has not prevented most of them from adopting what I have called the Classical conception of thinking, nor was there any logical reason why it should.

The terms 'concept' and 'abstract idea', of course, have been used by some of the Symbolist philosophers too, as well as by adherents of the Classical view. Unlike 'universal' (used as a substantive) these terms have passed into the ordinary vocabulary of educated men. They have ceased to be party labels, and may be used in a neutral sense, without committing us to any particular philosophical theory. I have myself used them in this neutral way, for example in discussing sign-cognition. In this sense, it can be said that the Symbolist philosophers are not denying the existence of concepts or abstract ideas, but are offering an analysis of what a concept or abstract idea is, or of what it is to possess one. (I have already suggested that this is what Berkeley and Hume were doing.)

Is there then no difference at all, or no substantial difference, between the Symbolists and the Conceptualists, since both of them are willing to use the terminology of concepts or abstract ideas, and both of them reject the terminology of subsistent universals, whether *in re* or *ante rem*? The Linguistic philosophers of the present day sometimes allege that the traditional Conceptualism is just an obscure and clumsy way of stating their own Symbolistic theory. Again, historians of philosophy usually tell us that there are three theories of universals, *Ante rem, In re* and *Post rem*; and according to this classification Conceptualists, Imagists and Nominalists all agree in accepting the *Post rem* theory. Of course this terminology is rather odd. It might be objected that the *Post rem* theory is not a theory of universals at all; instead of saying that someone holds 'a *Post rem* theory of universals' it would be better to say that he rejects the ontology of Universals altogether and accepts the ontology of Resemblances. But so far as the epistemology of thinking is concerned, the question still arises whether we have not been drawing the line of division in the wrong place. Perhaps it really falls between those who accept the Philosophy of Universals and those who reject it? Then the Realists, whether of the *Ante rem* or the *In re* variety, stand on one side of the line; the Conceptualists, as well as the Symbolist philosophers, stand on the other.

Of course there is this line of division too. But it is not the one which concerns us at present. The one which does concern us is the line between those who maintain that thinking is the inspection of a distinctive sort of objects, and the Symbolists who deny it. The Symbolist philosophers, when *they* talk of concepts or abstract ideas, treat them not as inspectable entities ('objects of thought') but as dispositions or capacities. To possess a concept, they tell us, is just to have the acquired capacity for using one or another sort of general symbol. From this point of view the traditional Conceptualists—Descartes, Locke, Kant—certainly fall on the 'classical' side of the line. They maintain, what the Symbolists deny, that thinking is the inspection of a distinctive type of entities, 'intelligibles' as opposed to 'sensibles'. It is true that they regard these thinkingly inspected entities as intra-mental ones, and not as extra-mental subsistents, whether *in re* or *ante rem*. But this dispute between the Conceptualists and the Realists, important as it is in its own place, is only a domestic quarrel within the Classical tradition. What matters to us is the rightness or wrongness of the 'inspective' conception of thinking. This is the conception of it which the Classical philosophers accept, whether they are Rationalists or Empiricists, Realists or Conceptualists; and this is the conception of it which the Symbolist philosophers reject, whatever minor differences there may be between them. If the reader, despite these explanations, still finds it difficult to grasp the difference between the Conceptualists and the Symbolist philosophers, perhaps an adjective may help him. The Conceptualism which falls within the Classical tradition may be called *Inspective* Conceptualism, if he pleases.

We have now to consider whether there is anything to be said for the Classical conception of thinking. We cannot just ignore it altogether, as some contemporary philosophers are inclined to do. Of course no philosopher nowadays, in English-speaking countries at least, would willingly admit that he is 'traditionally minded'. Indeed, this is one of the two accusations he fears most. (The other is that he mixes up philosophy with psychology.) But we should not be too frightened of epithets, great as their power is. There is such a thing as parochialism in time as well as in space, and perhaps the philosophers of our own age may be victims of it. In philosophy, as elsewhere, it is perfectly possible that our ancestors were wiser than we are; and if they were, we shall do well to be traditionally minded. Of course it is also possible, especially in philosophy, that men of the very highest intelligence may have fallen into fundamental mistakes. They may have failed to notice alternatives which we, who stand on their shoulders, can see quite easily. Again, they may have expressed themselves in ways which are misleading to us, with our different terminological habits and our different climate of opinion, though these modes of expression were not misleading to their original authors. It may be that the Classical conception of thinking is more wrong than right, or at least that it has come to be more misleading than illuminating. But even then, we may still have something to learn from it. Its very errors, if they are such, might be more instructive than other people's solemn platitudes.

The most plausible argument in favour of the Classical conception of thinking is an indirect one. Let us suppose that we always do use *some* symbols when we think, whether words or images or others. Even so, it may be said, our thought very frequently 'overflows' our symbols; indeed, it always overflows our symbols in some degree, though the degree varies in different cases. To put it less metaphorically: the contention is that even though *part* of what we are thinking at any give time is always symbolized in some way or other, the whole of it is not; the other parts (it would be said) are thought of asymbolically. Lord Russell remarks somewhere that 'we see more than we say'. Is it not true likewise that we *think* more than we say? Some symbols may be there, but surely they do not 'cover' the whole of what is before our minds? When symbols are used publicly for communication, it is obvious that we seldom or never communicate the whole of what we think. Perhaps we could not, even if we would. And is not the same true of the private use of symbols too? Surely one never formulates, even to oneself, the whole of what one is thinking, nor does one image the whole of it, even though some words or images or other symbols are always present to one's mind.

This contention that 'thought overflows symbols' is obviously important if true. It may be illustrated in several different ways. The first is this. It would seem that Nominalistic philosophers fix their attention too much on what may be called *full dress* thinking, where we talk to ourselves or to others in complete and fully formulated sentences, such as would satisfy a grammarian or a

U

governess. But though a few very clever people may 'talk like a book' in this full dress and fully formulated manner, it is quite certain that the vast majority of human beings do not. Even in their public talking and writing they often fall short of this ideal (if ideal it be), and still more when they use words in their private thinking. Likewise, if one thinks pictorially, in the way described by the Imagist theory, one very seldom thinks 'like a picture book' or a cinematograph film, where there is a complete and coherent series of pictures, one for each episode in the story. Full dress image thinking is as rare as full dress verbal thinking.

To put the point positively: in the thinking of most people at most times both verbal symbols and image symbols have a decidedly 'scrappy' character. Instead of a full dress sentence there may only be a single word in our minds, and even that may not be completely formed; and there may be only three or four words instead of a whole paragraph. Moreover, logical words like 'all' and 'therefore' are often left out in private verbal thinking, horrifying though this may be to a Formal Logician; yet we manage to make quite rational inferences without them. It is much the same with image thinking, especially if it is rapid. The images are often extremely sketchy and evanescent, mere wisps and shreds, rather than the complete and fully fledged mental pictures which Berkeley and Hume had in mind when they propounded the Imagist version of the Symbolist theory of thinking.

It is true, no doubt, that this scrappiness of our symbols is sometimes due to habit. The subject about which we are thinking may be very familiar to us. It may be something which we have perceived very frequently or thought about very often before. Accordingly, one key-word may come to be, for us, a substitute for a long series of words, or even for the whole of a quite complicated story or argument; and it could recall the whole series of words at need, if we wanted to write down what we are thinking of, or tell it to someone else. Also the emotion appropriate to the story (the 'feel' of it) gets attached to this one key-word. Even an argument, when familiar enough, can acquire a quasi-emotional 'feel' or 'flavour', and through habit this attaches itself to one or two key-words; and then, when they are reproduced sub-vocally or in verbal imagery, it is *as if* the whole series of words were before our minds. To make use of Hume's distinction again, it is as if the whole series of words were 'present in fact', though actually only a very few of them are present in fact and the rest are merely 'present in power'. And as there are key-words, there are also key-images, able to reinstate a whole series of other images at need. Indeed, the same thing may happen with physical replicas, such as diagrams or dumb show. If the subject thought of is very familiar, a single very sketchy diagram may be a substitute for a whole series of diagrams; and a complicated piece of dumb show or ritual may be 'condensed' into a gesture or two, or even into the muscular sensations which accompany one or two incipient gestures not overtly performed.

But can the 'scrappiness' of our symbols be explained entirely in terms of habit and familiarity? On the face of it, it cannot. Such an explanation would imply that we *first* think of a given subject in full dress symbols, and then, later, these symbols get abbreviated through habit. On the contrary, when we do a new piece of thinking, as we all do on occasion, we certainly do not use full dress symbols, completely formulated sentences and paragraphs. We use them then least of all. The full dress stage, of complete verbal formulation (or complete and full-blooded imaging) comes later, if it ever does come. When one is doing the real *work* of thinking, thinking out an argument for the first time or actually composing a complicated narrative, one is then farthest of all from full dress symbolization. It is at this stage, most of all, that the symbols are mere shreds and scraps, and their failure to 'cover' the whole of what is before one's mind is then most obvious. So even if we do sometimes talk to ourselves 'like a book' about some subjects, we certainly did not do so the first time we thought about those subjects; and that was the time when the real work of thinking was being done, when new insight was acquired or new complex ideas were formed.

To put it another way, we must distinguish between rehearsed and unrehearsed thinking. It is only rehearsed thinking which ever has a full dress and fully formulated character. But it is unrehearsed thinking which is important, because that is the stage at which something is being 'thought out' for the first time—be it an argument, or a hypothesis, or a narrative, or the solution of some practical problem. And in unrehearsed thinking our symbols are particularly scrappy and sketchy. Some symbols, no doubt, are present even then. But could it not be said that when we think most, we symbolize least?

If this is right, there are three distinct stages to consider. In the first or unrehearsed stage, when we are thinking something out for the first time, our symbolism is particularly sketchy or scrappy. Then, secondly, when the thought has become fairly familiar to us, we formulate it in more or less full dress symbols, whether privately or publicly. And then, thirdly, when the thought has become *very* familiar to us, we relapse into scrappy symbolism again, using a few key-words (or key-images) as a substitute for the complete, full dress formulation.

It would seem, then, that our use of symbols in thinking is a far less neat and tidy thing than it should be if either Nominalism or Imagism were right. Full dress symbolization, either in words or images, is the exception rather than the rule. It is the exception rather than the rule even in the public use of symbols, at least when they are used by ordinary people who are not talkers or writers by profession; and *a fortiori* it is exceptional in private thinking. Part of what we think is always symbolized, but not the whole of it, or only very seldom; and often only a small part. And it would be argued that if thinking were *nothing but* operating with symbols, whether words or images or any others, this ought not to happen.

There are two other considerations which point in the same direction; two other ways of supporting and illustrating the contention that our thought 'overflows' our symbols. The first is this. We are all familiar with the experience of looking for the right symbol and failing to find it. This happens not only with words but also with images, and indeed with physical replicas too. I know what I mean, but I cannot find the right way to say it—not even to myself. No doubt this is a puzzling statement, but surely it is often true? Sometimes we do succeed in finding the right word or image in the end. Sometimes we do not. Occasionally, especially in difficult forms of thinking such as philosophy, we can only find it by inventing it for ourselves, because no word in our existing vocabulary is quite adequate; or we have to 'stretch' the meaning of an old one, as Leibniz did with the word *monad*; or we have to resort to metaphors, for example when we are trying to describe very elusive introspectible phenomena.

But even when we do succeed in finding the right symbol in the end, or one which will serve *faute de mieux*, there may be a long period of searching and groping first, when various 'inadequate' symbols suggest themselves one after another and have to be rejected. Now what guides our search? How is it that we know what to look for? What enables us to *reject* the various inadequate symbols which suggest themselves? And equally, what enables us to *accept* the right one when (or if) it comes into our minds? It would seem that during the period of search we must have something before our minds which is not as yet symbolized at all; a *symbolizandum* which is not yet a *symbolizatum*, something which is present to the mind, for the time being, asymbolically. What could this something be, which is before our minds, and yet is neither itself a symbol nor thought of by means of a symbol? We shall be told that it is just a bare or naked thinkable, an 'intelligible object' *per se*, something of which neither Nominalism nor Imagism can give any account at all.

It may be noticed that a parallel argument is used in favour of a Realistic theory of memory. Memory-images are often inadequate and known to be so.[1] If we can detect their inadequacy and correct it, surely we must have some 'direct acquaintance' with past events themselves? Similarly with verbal memory; if I am trying to recall someone's name, various names suggest themselves which I recognize to be the wrong ones. I can also recognize that some of them are nearer the right one than others. ('Robinson' is not quite right, but it was something rather like that; 'Williams' is quite wrong.) How can I do this unless I have some 'direct access' to the past, in this case to the past experience of hearing the man addressed by someone else, or seeing his signature on a letter, or some other past experience in which his name was seen or heard?

The third and last argument in favour of the proposition that 'thought overflows symbols' is this. The Symbolist theory of thinking appears to ignore what is called the narrowness of consciousness. The number of token-symbols which can be before the mind at any one time is strictly limited. Of course we must not suppose that the present is a durationless instant. It has a finite time span. It is a specious present. Nevertheless, its duration, in normal human

[1] There is an excellent discussion of this 'negative memory-situation' in Professor E. J. Furlong's recent book *A Study in Memory*, pp. 32-7.

beings at least, is very brief. And even if we bring in the recollection of other token-words or images which were before our minds earlier, still the number of particulars which can be recollected in any one act of recollection is also very limited.

Now let us consider some long and complicated piece of verbal thinking (not necessarily an argument; it might be just a long and complicated description of some series of events, real or fictitious, or again an elaborate plan for some future course of action). Let us suppose that this piece of thinking requires a whole paragraph, say three hundred words, to formulate it. Suppose further that we do actually say to ourselves the whole three hundred words; on this occasion we are thinking in a 'full dress' manner. Clearly the whole three hundred words are not before our minds at the same time. In any one specious present five or six of them might be there, subvocally spoken or in the form of verbal imagery. But what about the others? By the time we get to the middle of the paragraph, we may indeed be recollecting *some* of the earlier ones, and possibly anticipating *some* of the later ones. But even if we bring in recollection, and anticipation too, it is quite clear that the whole three hundred are never before our minds all at once. Our consciousness would be crowded out if they were. How then do we manage to keep our heads throughout the whole process? How do we know which word to say next, and how do we fit the later ones on to the earlier ones (which have dropped out of consciousness by then) so that the whole series of words makes one coherent discourse? The obvious answer is that the 'general sense' or 'general drift' of the whole paragraph is before our minds throughout, and that it is this awareness of the 'general sense' of the whole which enables us to produce the right words one after the other in the appropriate order. Well and good; but what is this awareness? Surely *it* is not awareness of symbols? On the contrary, it dictates what symbols we are to produce and the order in which we are to produce them. Here again, it would seem that we are just directly inspecting a 'thinkable' or 'intelligible object', a highly complex one too. And here again we seem to encounter something which neither Nominalism nor Imagism can make room for, a kind of awareness which ought not to be possible if any purely Symbolistic theory of thinking were right.

It is true that the thinkable is not *wholly* naked this time, as it was in the case last considered (looking for the right word). This time it is clothed with symbols, bit by bit, as the discourse goes on. Nevertheless, the whole of this complex object of thought is never clothed with symbols simultaneously. As new symbols come into our mind, the earlier ones drop out again, and there are others still to come which are not yet before our mind at all. It is as if you first put a hat on my head, then took it off and put a collar and tie round my neck; then took *them* off and put a shirt on me; and after removing this provided me with a pair of trousers. You might clothe the whole of me in that way, but I should never be fully clothed. I never should be fully dressed, even though all the constituents of full dress were put on me one by one. Thus even 'full dress' thinking, rare though it is, turns out to be less full dress than we might suppose. It is true that in this case our thought is completely formulated, that all of it is symbolized. But the words 'all' and 'completely' are liable to mislead us. They conceal the fact that the whole series of symbols is never, as a whole, before our minds. Of course one may write them all down on paper or inscribe them on stone; and then all of them, considered as physical objects or physical marks, do exist simultaneously. But this does not help. They only function as symbols when someone reads them; and though he does not read them one by one, but rather in small blocks, it is obvious that he cannot read the whole three hundred simultaneously.

Here then we have another example of the way in which thought overflows symbols. It *still* overflows them, even when we are thinking in a full dress manner. To put it paradoxically: we do, occasionally, say all that we think, but even then there is a sense in which we still think more than we say, because the saying is bound to be successive. We may say all that we think, but we can only say it bit by bit, or image it bit by bit if the thinking is done in images. Of course there would be no problem if the thought itself were as successive as the (token) symbols are. But it is not, or not wholly. The general outline of it at least, the plot or plan of it, is somehow in our mind throughout; it dictates and controls the successive symbols as they come, so that the whole series of them makes sense.

These considerations do show that there is something wrong with the Symbolist theory of thinking, at least in the form in which we have stated it so far. But do they show that the Classical theory is right? Do they show that there is after all such a thing as 'pure' or 'naked' thinking, the direct inspection of intelligible objects? Not necessarily. What they do suggest is this: when the Symbolist philosophers tell us that thinking consists in using symbols *understandingly*, the word 'understandingly' needs further analysis. But the right analysis need not necessarily be the one which the Classical philosophers would offer. They would say that when we use symbols understandingly, there is an activity or process of understanding along with and different from the process of producing the symbols; that understanding is something which we *do* (in the sense in which mental acts are 'done') or at any rate is an occurrence which goes on in us. This activity or process, they would add, is a kind of inspection; it has objects, *inspicienda*, of a special sort, called universals by some, concepts or abstract ideas by others, and subsistent propositions by still others. Now it may well be that the Symbolist account of understanding leaves something out, but it does not follow that this is the right way to remedy the omission. In this chapter we have been considering some of the reasons which make us *want* to say that thinking is, or contains, the inspection of intelligible objects. But perhaps we ought not to say it all the same. The need which is satisfied in that way might perhaps be satisfied equally well, or better, in some different way.

CHAPTER XI

CONCEPTS AND THEIR MANIFESTATIONS

WE can all agree that thinking is rightly described as *conceptual* cognition. To use a studiously vague phrase, we can all agree that concepts somehow 'enter into' it. The question is, how or in what guise they enter into it. Do they enter into it as objects of intellectual inspection, as the Classical theory of thinking maintains? Are they 'before the mind' when we think, 'presented to it'? Or would it be better to say that they are at work in it, had in mind rather than presented to it?

Of course these expressions 'before', 'presented to', 'at work in', are all being used in an analogical sense. That cannot be helped. If we are not to use analogies, we may as well give up the inquiry altogether. We shall only be able to say 'thinking is thinking', or more grandiloquently 'thinking is a unique process which can only be understood in terms of itself'. Let us take the risk of being a little less Puritanical than this. Naturally, we must expect to find that no analogy is altogether satisfactory. 'Everything is what it is, and not another thing.' Thinking is not *quite* like any other process, and the relation between thinking and what is thought of is not *quite* like any other relation. The question is, which of several analogies is the most illuminating and the least misleading. And here we must remember that analogies which did not mislead our predecessors may nevertheless mislead ourselves. It was all very well to say that the intellect is 'the eye of the soul' at a time when very little was known about the physics and physiology of vision. Again, the ancient analogy between the Supreme Being and the sun is a hindrance rather than a help in an age when it has been discovered that there are many suns and that all of them are slowly wasting away.

We can see that it must be wrong just to equate a concept with the acquired capacity to use a general symbol, as the Symbolist philosophers wish to do. Indeed, we have seen this already, quite apart from the considerations mentioned in the last chapter about the various ways in which thought 'overflows' symbols. It was already obvious from our examination of sign-cognition in Chapters IV and V. Sign-cognition is clearly a form of thinking, though a primitive one. Concepts or abstract ideas certainly enter into it. And sign-cognition is pre-symbolic, pre-verbal and pre-imaginal. On the other hand, we cannot say that anything at all like 'intellectual inspection' occurs in it. When I have just seen a very bright flash of lightning and am expecting an almost immediate clap of thunder, we certainly cannot say that I am inspecting the concept of Thunder, still less that I am inspecting the implication-proposition 'if lightning occurs, thunder usually follows'. It looks as if the way concepts enter into sign-cognition was *neither* the way described in the Classical theory of thinking *nor* the way described in the Symbolist theory (Nominalism or Imagism or any combination of the two).

We may go further. Sign-cognition, we have seen, is connected very closely with action. Indeed, sign-cognition, as it occurs in animals and often in ourselves, could almost equally well be described as sign-responsive behaviour. The experiencing of the sign-event releases a preparedness for the significate-event; and this preparedness consists largely, and often almost wholly, in a preparedness to *act* with regard to the significate—to 'do something about it'. On the other hand, we must remember that this preparedness to act is not just a bodily posture; nor is it just a bodily movement, not even an incipient one; nor is it just the kinaesthetic sensations accompanying any of these. However practical it is, it has a cognitive aspect too, what is sometimes called a referential character. This is brought out by the phrase 'with regard to', or by the word 'about' when we say that the sign-event makes us prepared to do something *about* the thing signified. And when we are thus ready to act with regard to X, or to do something about X, this X is something absent, signified but not now experienced, or even (in disjunctive signification) a set of alternative possibilities. Thus not only does sign-responsive behaviour have a cognitive aspect as well as a practical one; in its cognitive aspect it is a form of *thinking*, and this is shewn also by the fact that sign-responsive behaviour is capable of being erroneous, which neither bodily movement nor organic sensation can be. There is such a thing as thinking *in* actions or in preparednesses to act. To put it another way, it is not true that intelligent action can always be split into two parts, a purely cognitive process of planning and a purely physical process by which the plan is executed.[1] In sign-guided action, where neither words nor images are used, our knowledge or belief as to what the sign signifies is manifested directly in the action itself.

But of course intelligent action occurs not only at the level of sign-cognition, but at higher levels of mental development too. It occurs in beings who have learned to use symbols, and consequently engage in the 'free' or 'autonomous' thinking which the use of symbols makes possible. In them too, intelligent action need not be preceded by conscious planning, though sometimes it is. Very complex concepts, which can only be *acquired* with the aid of symbols, may show themselves in action without any present *use* of symbols. When you see someone about to step on to the live rail on the Underground Railway, you pull him aside at once, without 'stopping to think', that is, without stopping to use words or images. Your action is intelligent. Your knowledge of the properties of electric currents is manifested in what you do. The action is a concept-guided one. Indeed, it could be said that quite an elaborate system of concepts 'enters into' it. These concepts, no doubt, could never have been acquired without the use of symbols, and almost certainly they could not have been acquired without the use of words. They are quite beyond the reach of any animal. Though they are linked in the end to the perceptible world, the linkage is complex and indirect; an elaborate process of symbolically conducted thinking was needed before you could grasp them at all. In spite of this, they operate on the present occasion in a non-symbolic manner. You had to act at once, if at all. There was 'no time to think', that is, to say words to yourself or produce a series of images. Yet in another sense you did think. The action itself was 'thoughtful' or intelligent. At any rate, no one would say that you acted thoughtlessly, even though there is also a sense in which you acted 'without thinking'.

Of course the current may have been turned off. The man may have been an employee of the railway company, who was stepping down from the platform to make some repair. Then you acted in error. The danger 'with reference to which' you acted did not in

[1] Cf. Professor G. Ryle, *The Concept of Mind*, ch. 2 and elsewhere.

fact exist. But this only makes the intelligent or concept-guided character of your action more evident. Only an intelligent being can err, as has been remarked before,[1] and only when his intelligence is actually being exercised. And this applies to intelligent action, no less than to other manifestations of intelligence.

On the other hand, if it is clear that concepts operate in such a case asymbolically, it is even more clear that they are not being 'inspected' or 'apprehended', in the way the Classical theory requires. Nothing which could be called a process of conceiving occurs; unless indeed we choose to say that the intelligent action *is* the conceiving in this case, and then the whole point of the Classical theory is lost. It would seem that unplanned intelligent action, whether at the sign-cognitive level of mental development or above it, is something which fits neither the Symbolistic nor the Classical account of thinking. And yet concepts somehow 'enter into' such action, to use the same studiously vague phrase as before.

We may now reconsider the examples given in the last chapter to illustrate the contention that thought overflows symbols. They do show that concepts can enter into our thinking (even our theoretical thinking) in a non-symbolic manner. As I have remarked already, these examples may properly be used *against* a purely Symbolistic analysis of conceptual cognition. They show that a concept can be 'had in mind'—to use another deliberately non-committal phrase—when the corresponding symbol is not present. A concept, then, cannot simply consist in the capacity to use a general symbol. Having the concept Cat cannot just consist in having the capacity to use the word 'cat' (or cat-like images) both in presence and in absence. But if these examples are used to *support* the Classical conception of thinking, and not merely to weaken the Symbolistic one, we can see that the support they give it is indecisive. They do not show that when our thinking 'overflows' our symbols, what is unsymbolically thought of is the object of an act of intellectual inspection, though they are, of course, compatible with such a theory. They do not show that if a concept is something more than a symbol-using capacity, it must therefore be an intelligible object somehow 'presented to' the mind of the thinker. For these are not the only two alternatives. There is another way of analysing these

[1]Cf. pp. 87, 94-5, above.

examples. It is more complicated than the analysis which the Classical theory offers, but it is also more empirical.

When our thought overflows our symbols in the various ways illustrated in the last chapter, it must be admitted that concepts enter into our thinking, are somehow had in mind, in the absence of the corresponding symbols. All the same, is such thinking completely 'naked'? Is there nothing in which or with which we think? We must agree that in private thinking, at any rate, complete and full dress symbolization is excessively rare. Yet we can still maintain that in all thinking above the purely sign-cognitive level *some* symbols are present, scrappy and fragmentary as they may be. Now if concepts are regarded as dispositions or capacities (not as inspectable entities), that does not, of course, prevent them from having all sorts of mental linkages between them. The mental linkage which a concept has to the symbol—or symbol-producing disposition—associated with it by ostensive definition need not be the only mental linkage which it has. I possess the concept of Cat; suppose that this consists in having a memory of what cats are like, in the dispositional sense of the word 'memory'. I possess the concept of Mouse; suppose that this consists likewise in having a memory of what mice are like. It is likely that these (dispositional) memories will be associated pretty closely. And if the concept of Cat is brought to mind by the occurrence of the word 'cat' or by a cat-like image, this by itself may suffice to bring the concept of Mouse to mind too, although no symbol for it has presented itself. Of course the word 'cat' is not a *symbol* for both concepts at once. Nevertheless, the occurrence of it may suffice to bring both of them to mind, and possibly other concepts too (e.g. Milk, Tiger).

Moreover, as we have seen, the 'activating' of any mental disposition is a matter of degree. Between the two extremes—complete latency and complete actualization—there are many intermediate degrees of *sub*-activation. When the word 'cat' occurs, or a cat-like image, a whole series of concepts linked in one way or another with the concept Cat may be in *some* degree brought to mind. It is true of me at all times that I am capable of recognizing mice, bowls of milk, fur, tigers, mammals, hearth-rugs, at any rate so long as I retain a moderate standard of health and sanity. At all times I have memories of what all these diverse entities are like (in the dispositional sense of the word 'memory'). But if the word

'cat' occurs to my mind—or a cat-image or a physical cat-replica—
then something comes to be true of me which is not true at all
times. All these diverse memory-dispositions are in some degree
excited or sub-activated. I am put into a state of *readiness* to recognize mice, bowls of milk, tigers, etc., if I should happen to perceive
them; and also in a state of readiness to talk of such entities or produce images of them. I am ready to do these things, even though I
do not actually do any of them.

This readiness too is a matter of degree. For some of the dispositions thus indirectly sub-activated it may be greater, for others
less. When the word 'cat' comes into my mind, I am very ready
to recognize a cat if I should see one, and much less ready to recognize a mouse, but still not entirely unready (as I am when the
concept Mouse is not being activated in any degree at all, e.g.
when I am doing a multiplication sum). But if we are willing to
regard concepts as dispositions, it is still true that the sub-activation
of one concept by means of a word or other symbol may bring
about the sub-activation of a large number of others, though for
some of these others the degree of sub-activation may be greater
and for some of them less. The mental linkages I speak of may
have various degrees of 'closeness' or 'tightness'.

If the reader finds it helpful, we may introduce two pieces of
Herbartian terminology at this point: 'the threshold' and 'the
apperception-mass'. (The first has been referred to already, in
Chapter IV,[1] but not the second.) First, we may say that our concepts come to be linked together in a number of more or less
systematic groups or apperception-masses. This could still be true
if concepts are dispositions rather than entities. And secondly, we
may say that when a concept A is above the threshold, other concepts belonging to the same apperception-mass are on the threshold,
and still others just below it. This is another way of saying that
what I have called 'being brought to mind' is a matter of degree.
A concept may be brought to mind fully, or partially, or just a
little, or not at all. And when a whole set of concepts is brought
to mind by the occurrence of the symbol for one of them, some of
these concepts may be *more* brought to mind than others are. For
example, the words for some of them may be 'on the tip of our

---

[1] pp. 114-5, above. Perhaps Herbart himself, and his disciples, did sometimes
regard 'ideas' as entities or *things*.

tongue' (though not actually produced) whereas the words for others would come if wanted, but not quite so readily or so easily.

Whatever terminology we use, it is pretty clear that the symbol for a given concept, such as Cat, may 'carry' a large number of other concepts as well. In this way, we can explain how it is possible to think without full dress symbolization, and how we can manage to keep the thread throughout a long discourse, although only a very few symbols can be in consciousness at the same time. We can explain these things without needing to suppose that when a concept is in mind without the aid of the symbol appropriated to it, it must be present *to* the mind as an object of direct intellectual inspection. Moreover, we can suggest a similar analysis for the experience of thinking of something without having a word for it, looking for the right word, etc., which seems at first sight such strong evidence in favour of the Inspection Theory of thinking. The concept for which we have at the moment no symbol is brought to mind and kept in mind because it is linked with others for which we do have present symbols. Consider the following piece of inner speech. I have dressed it up a little to make it intelligible to the reader. In actual fact it would probably be more 'scrappy' that I have made it. 'Saw . . . when out walking yesterday. Greenfinch? No. Bullfinch? No. Hawfinch? No. Brambling? Yes.' (A brambling is a species of finch.) The as yet unsymbolized concept is indicated by the. . . . In public speech, this might be replaced by the phrase 'a what-do-you-call-it'. But this unsymbolized concept need not be present to the mind *per se* or nakedly, as an object of intellectual inspection. It is carried—brought to mind and kept there—by the other words, 'saw when out walking yesterday', because it is mentally linked with what *they* bring to mind. And odd as it may sound, the concept of Brambling is likewise carried by the words 'greenfinch', 'bullfinch', 'hawfinch'—by these wrong or inappropriate words which do *not* fit it. For the concepts which they do fit have a strong linkage in my mind with the one whose symbol I am seeking for. By being in mind themselves, they hold it in mind as well, while I am waiting for the right word to come up.

These considerations do not, of course, show that the Inspective theory of conceptual cognition is false. It may be that concepts are objects of inspection after all, not only in these examples where thought 'overflows' symbols, but in all thinking whatever. It might still be true that even when we are thinking in full dress symbols, the symbols are 'transparent', that we as it were look through them or beyond them to intelligible entities to which they somehow direct our attention. What has been shown so far is only this, that a non-inspective analysis can be offered, even for those examples which seem at first sight most favourable to the Classical Inspection theory.

Let us now consider the Classical conception of thinking more closely. What exactly is the issue we have to discuss? Some people would put it thus: are concepts entities or are they dispositions? They would add that the Symbolistic theory of thinking is one form which a dispositional analysis of concepts may take, but not the only one; thus, if the Symbolistic theory is shown to be inadequate (e.g. by arguments about 'thought overflowing symbols' or about sign-cognition) it does not follow that the Classical theory is right. A concept might still be a disposition or capacity of some kind, even though it was not, or not merely, a capacity to use a general symbol, whether a word or an image or both. Or again, a concept might be a set of inter-related dispositions. In some cases a capacity to use a certain general symbol might be included in the set, in others not. When it was not, we might agree that the concept was possessed incompletely or imperfectly, but it would still be wrong to say that it was not possessed at all.

But this way of putting the issue is not altogether right. For the Classical analysis of concepts is partly dispositional too. The Classical philosophers would agree that the word 'concept' is *often* used in a dispositional sense; for instance, when we say that Jones 'possesses' or 'has acquired' such and such a concept, or again that he did possess it at one time but has since lost it. The real question is, about the *occurrences* by which such a disposition is manifested, or actualized. Perhaps both parties would agree that it is manifested in many different ways. Thus if someone possesses the concept of Dog, he recognizes a dog when he sees one, he talks understandingly about dogs in absence both publicly and privately, he understands or 'follows' the dog-mentioning talk of other people, he produces dog-like images and recognizes them to be dog-like, he takes a barking sound to be a sign of the presence of a dog. But according to the

Classical theory, all these ways in which one's possession of the concept Dog are actualized are derivative. The fundamental actualization of it, on which all the others depend, is a unique sort of cognitive act, an act of inspection or intuitive apprehension, which may be called *conceiving*. And this act has an object. Its object, in the present example, is *Doghood*. The concept of Dog, in the dispositional sense of the word 'concept', is accordingly defined as a persistent capacity for re-apprehending or re-inspecting Doghood. Without this (it would be said) we could not recognize dogs when we see them; we could not use the word 'dog' with understanding nor understand its use by others; and if by any chance we did happen to produce a dog-like image, we could not recognize that it *was* dog-like, and so could not use it as a symbol or instrument for thinking of dogs.

Some holders of the Classical theory might add that this capacity for re-apprehending Doghood is itself dependent on something else. We are *capable* of re-apprehending Doghood, they might say, because we are *actually*, all the time, in a persistent state of 'being familiar with' Doghood.[1] In making this suggestion, they are perhaps being unduly influenced by physical or physico-chemical analogies. The dispositions which material objects have (traditionally called 'powers' or 'causal properties'), for example the elasticity of a steel rod or the combustibility of a piece of coal, do depend upon the actual molecular structure of these objects. If the steel rod is stretched, it will return to approximately its original length when released; if it is bent, it will return to approximately its original shape. But these hypothetical truths about the steel rod have a categorical backing or basis, a set of categorical propositions concerning its actual molecular structure, which metallurgists have established. A metallurgist could tell us what 'makes' the steel rod elastic, and likewise what 'makes' a similar rod of lead or copper inelastic.

Such empirical discoveries, in which the *dispositional* properties of large-scale objects are shown to depend upon the *actual* structure of their minute constituents (molecular, atomic or sub-atomic as the case may be) are perhaps the most important achievements of

[1] Cf. the present writer's *Thinking and Representation* (Proceedings of the British Academy, 1946) where an attempt is made to re-state the Classical theory on these lines; and Professor A. J. Ayer's criticisms in his Inaugural Lecture *Thinking and Meaning*.

V

the physical sciences. It might be said that the whole of our modern Western European way of life depends on them. But after all, they *are* empirical discoveries. There is no *a priori* necessity for supposing that *all* dispositional properties must have a 'categorical basis'. In particular, there may be some mental dispositions which are ultimate, and the ones of which the Classical philosophers are thinking might be among them, for example the capacity for re-apprehending Doghood. Of course, such capacities might have to be acquired or learned. In that sense there would be something which 'makes' me able to re-apprehend Doghood, or Redness, or Betweenness (supposing I am capable of doing it at all). Such capacities would presumably be acquired by a process of comparison and abstraction. But this sense of the word 'make' is irrelevant. It is not the sense in which the molecular structure of the steel rod 'makes' it elastic or is the 'categorical basis' for its elasticity; for there the disposition and the actual molecular structure on which it depends are co-existent. It is true that both the disposition and the structure may have been acquired at some previous time, e.g. when the rod was being forged, and may be lost at some later time, e.g. when it is heated to a very high temperature and slowly cooled. But they are acquired or lost *together*, and so long as they exist, they exist together. With the ability to re-apprehend Doghood (assuming that there is such an ability) it might be quite different. This ability, once I have acquired it, need not be derivable, even theoretically, from some more ultimate fact about my mind, in the way that the causal properties of large-scale objects *have* turned out to be derivable from facts about their actual molecular or atomic or sub-atomic structure. Indeed, even in the physical world, it would seem that there must be some dispositional properties which are 'ultimate' in this sense, as Professor Broad has pointed out.[1] At least some of the dispositional properties of sub-atomic entities (or whatever the most minute constituents of matter may turn out to be) must be in this position.

For our purposes, then, it makes little difference whether these acquired capacities for re-apprehending Doghood, Redness, Betweenness, etc., are or are not supposed to have a 'categorical basis', in the way that elasticity or combustibility or solubility have.

[1] Cf. C. D. Broad *Examination of McTaggart's Philosophy*, Vol. I, pp. 269-72.

Such mental dispositions as these may be taken, for our purposes, as something ultimate. What does matter is that among the many different ways in which a concept (in the dispositional sense of the term) may be actualized or occurrently manifested, these re-apprehendings of 'intelligible objects' or 'abstract objects' are held in the Classical theory to be fundamental; and all the other occurrent manifestations of a concept-disposition—recognition of instances, understanding of words, production of appropriate images, etc.— are held to be derivative. If you are able to *conceive* of Doghood, that is, to apprehend or inspect that abstract entity, all these other things will be added to you; otherwise, they will not. The crucial point to consider is, whether there are apprehendings of this sort, and apprehensibles of this sort—'objects of thought', for which such words as 'doghood', 'redness', 'betweenness' would be appropriate names. It is already plain that in sign-cognition, and in at least some intelligent actions which are well above the purely sign-cognitional level, no such apprehendings are found to occur, and no such 'intelligible objects' are present to the mind. But perhaps they *are* present to it in other forms of conceptual cognition?

To answer this question, we must distinguish between the two main forms of the Classical theory, Realism and Conceptualism. Let us begin with Realism, and let us confine ourselves to the *In re* version of that doctrine. Such objects of thought as Doghood are called by the Realist 'universals'; and in the *In re* version of Realism Doghood is held to have being *in* particular dogs, and is the common factor in them all. To use the terminology of Chapter I, Doghood is supposed to be a recurrent feature of the world, found over and over again in an indefinitely large number of objects. 'In' every perceived object or event or situation, there is supposed to be a cluster of such recurrent features. By comparison and abstraction, the mind is able to single out and fix attention upon any such recurrent and apprehend it *in abstracto* apart from the particular objects in which it recurs. By so doing, we acquire the capacity of *re*-apprehending this abstracted universal whenever we are suitably reminded, e.g. by the occurrence of a new instance, or of a quasi-instance (an image or physical replica), or again by the occurrence of a word or other non-instantiative particular which has been associatively linked with our awareness of the *abstractum* in question. When we say of someone that he possesses the concept or the idea of Red or of Dog, we mean, in this theory, that he has the acquired capacity of re-apprehending Redness or Doghood; and that these apprehendings are actually occurring, these abstract objects are actually being presented to his mind, whenever he thinks about red things or dogs.

Or if not, if these abstract objects are not actually present to his mind, then he is not really *thinking* about red things or about dogs. He may, of course, appear to be thinking about them, because he is producing appropriate words in a fluent and well-trained manner. But in fact he is talking, or writing, *without* thinking, without 'having his eye on the object' as we say. The *abstracta*, the universals, which are brought before our own minds by hearing or seeing his words are not before *his* mind at all; at any rate not at that time, though at other times they may be. On the other hand, someone else who speaks or writes very clumsily, not at all fluently, with very little linguistic skill, may very well have the relevant abstract objects before his mind. Indeed, his very clumsiness may sometimes be evidence of this. It may be that the abstract objects he is talking of are very complex or not very familiar to him, or related in very complex ways which he is now noticing for the first time; and the very fact that he attends to them carefully may make him hesitant and scrupulous about the words he utters or writes. The more you have your eye on the object, the less easily, sometimes, you can talk about it or write about it. There was once a celebrated teacher of philosophy in Oxford who held this Realistic theory of thinking. It was said of him that the thing he most disliked in his pupils was mere cleverness; that is, skill and facility in word-concatenation. What is the good of being clever if you do not trouble to have and keep before your mind the abstract objects with which the discussion is supposed to be concerned? It is better to be clumsy but honest.

Now, of course, we all want to say that there is a difference between talking without thinking and talking thinkingly, though perhaps 'thinkingly' is an adverb which admits of degrees, and *completely* thoughtless talk may be a limiting case which is not very frequent in practice. The question is whether this is the right way of drawing the distinction. Does it just depend on the degree to which one attends to certain *abstracta* which are 'present to the mind' as objects of intellectual inspection? There is something suspiciously clear cut about this suggestion. One suspects that it does less than justice to the subtlety of Nature. Can things be quite as simple as all that?

The most remarkable function which concepts have is that they make cognition in absence possible. If we possess concepts, or to the extent that we possess them, we are able somehow to think of objects, events or situations which we do not at the moment see or feel. Let us suppose that we are doing so by means of symbols, not in a merely sign-cognitive manner. (We have seen already that the Classical theory of thinking does not seem to apply to sign-cognition at all.[1]) We will assume that we are thinking privately, and that the symbols in this case are sub-vocal words or verbal images. Now according to the Realist philosophers, the symbols are as it were transparent. They come into our minds, but they are not what we attend to. Their function is to draw our attention to something else; to enable us to apprehend, or be (occurrently) aware of, certain universals and the relationships between these. Well and good, but what exactly *is* this apprehending? *Ex hypothesi* it is not the recognizing of instances. If it were, one could quite plausibly say that we were apprehending universals, at any rate if one accepts the Ontology of Universals. But when I attend to Doghood in this 'absent' manner, I am not of course recognizing something to be a dog; that would be cognition in presence. What is it like to apprehend a universal such as Doghood in the *absence* of instances?

At this point, if we press him for an answer, the Realist has recourse to a very dangerous metaphor, the quasi-visual metaphor of 'inspecting' or 'intuiting'. Indeed, this metaphor is already implicit in the contention that the symbols are 'transparent'. We are supposed to look through or beyond the symbols to universals which somehow stand behind them. And it is held that we do this, even though no *instances* of these universals are being at the moment perceived or recollected. We are supposed to intuit or inspect these universals *in se*.

But does anything like this really happen when we use words in absence understandingly? When one talks to oneself about dogs in absence, understandingly, does any mental event occur which could be at all plausibly described as an act of inspection whose object is Doghood? If this is the right account of the phenomenology

[1] Cf. pp. 314-16, above.

of symbolic thinking, it would seem that very few people ever think; or if it be preferred, very few people ever 'really' think. (The rest of mankind just string symbols together and hope for the best.) And indeed how could such an act of inspection occur, if Doghood only has being 'in' the particulars which are its instances? No instances of it, *ex hypothesi*, are before one's mind at the moment. If universals are inspectable in the absence of their instances, must they not after all be *entities* or quasi-*things*? Shall we not after all be committed to the *Ante rem* theory, from which this version of Realism is so anxious to escape? And then our universals will transform themselves into supersensible particulars, and Doghood will be an eternal and archetypal Dog-in-itself.

The point may be clearer if we use the terminology of characteristics. Instead of speaking of 'Doghood', let us speak of the characteristic—the complex characteristic—of 'being a dog'. We can all recognize the characteristic of 'being a dog' when we observe some object which is characterized by it. But how *very* odd it is to suggest that 'being a dog' is something which can be inspected or intuitively apprehended by itself, in the absence of the objects which are characterized by it.

Indeed, the metaphorical phrase 'inspecting a universal' is so far from being clear, that it has itself to be elucidated by referring back to the situation which it is supposed to explain. If we are pressed to say what this inspection amounts to, we can only answer, 'Oh well, you see, it is what happens when a general symbol is used in absence with understanding'. In other words, this phraseology about inspecting universals (being directly aware of them, having them before the mind, etc.) is appropriate enough if we take it as a tentative and non-literal way of *stating* the problem which has to be solved, the problem of what thinking in absence is, or how adverbs like 'thinkingly', 'understandingly', are to be analysed. But such language does not solve the problem, as the Realists claim it does. The historical service of the Realist epistemology has in fact been to keep the problem alive by using this provocative and metaphorical language, in which thinking is spoken of as if it were somehow similar to seeing. But the task of cashing this metaphor is still on our hands.

If the Realist theory fails us at this crucial point, can the Conceptualists do any better? Perhaps there are several different versions of the Conceptualist theory. But we are only concerned at the moment with the traditional or classical version of Conceptualism, as we find it, for example, in Locke's doctrine of Abstract Ideas. The traditional Conceptualist epistemology starts from the ontological theory which I called the Philosophy of Resemblances.[1] It is supposed that we notice a number of objects which resemble the objects A, B and C as closely as these resemble one another. Then, as a result of this, we form for ourselves (or there grows up in us) an intra-mental something which is called a concept or abstract idea. Having noticed a number of creatures which resemble Fido, Tray and Spot as closely as these creatures resemble one another, we form the abstract idea of Dog. Let me quote Locke's words again. 'General and universal', he says, 'are creatures of the understanding.' 'They belong not to things themselves' (*Essay*, Book III, Chapter 3, section 11). Thus there are no general *entities*. It is only ideas which are general, and derivatively the words or other symbols which are 'signs', as Locke puts it, of such ideas. He is careful to insist, however, that these abstract ideas 'have their foundation in the similitude of things' (*Ibid.* section 13). We must not, of course, forget this part of the traditional Conceptualist epistemology. Without it, we could not explain how thought applies to reality. We might be led to suppose, as indeed some philosophers have, that thinking is just a private game we play in our own minds, constructing internally coherent structures out of bits of private mental furniture, with no reference to the real world at all. Abstract ideas, though intra-mental, the creatures of the understanding, are still *cum fundamento in re*. Because our abstract idea of Dog is 'founded on the similitude of things', it applies to or is satisfied by any object which resembles Fido, Spot and Tray as closely as they resemble one another. Nevertheless, it is the other or subjective half of the theory which concerns us at present. What *kind* of intra-mental existence is a concept or abstract idea supposed to have? This is the point at which the weakness of the traditional Conceptualism comes out; and it is a weakness very similar to the one we found in the Realistic theory.

When the traditional Conceptualists say that concepts are intra-mental, they do not seem to be using the word 'concept' in a purely dispositional sense, as when one is said to possess the concept of

[1] Cf. ch. I, pp. 13-26, above.

Dog continuously for many years, not only at times when one is actually thinking of dogs but at other times as well. Or rather, if and so far as they intend the words 'concept' or 'abstract idea' to have this dispositional sense, what they are saying is just a commonplace which everyone can accept, no matter what theory of conceptual cognition he holds. Concepts or abstract ideas, in this dispositional sense, are certainly 'in the mind' and nowhere else. 'Mind' is the word we habitually use for that part of our personality to which such dispositions belong. When the traditional Conceptualists tell us that concepts or abstract ideas are intra-mental, they are clearly speaking of some sort of *occurrent* mental contents. A concept or abstract idea, as they use these terms, seems to be something which actually occurs in consciousness from time to time. It is held that there are mental acts of a special sort, acts of conceiving or ideating, which are awarenesses of these occurrent concepts. It is not made clear whether these occurrent concepts are to be regarded as the objects of such acts of conceiving, or rather as 'internal accusatives' (cf. the theory that colour expanses and sounds are the 'internal accusatives' of visual or auditory sensation). In the latter case, these occurrent concepts would be intra-mental in the sense that their *esse* is *concipi*; as the being of colour-expanses or sounds, according to Berkeley, consists in their being 'perceived' (i.e. sensed). In the former case, they would be intra-mental in a different way; they would be psychological occurrences, items in our mental history, and conceiving would be a kind of introspection, the noticing of mental occurrences of that special sort. It makes no great difference, for our present purposes, which of these two interpretations we accept. If the being of (occurrent) concepts or abstract ideas is supposed to consist just in their being conceived, it will still have to be true that concepts, in this occurrent sense of the word, are introspectibles, even though they could not then be introspected apart from the processes of conceiving whose 'internal accusatives' they are.

In either case, these occurrent abstract ideas must of course be private, unlike the objective universals of the Realist theory. If you and I are both thinking of dogs at a particular time, you have your occurrent idea of Dog at that time, and I have mine. They might be very similar, but they would still be numerically different. Moreover, even within a given mind, an abstract idea will be private to the particular act of conceiving whose object, or internal accusative, it is. The occurrent abstract idea of Dog which I conceive at twelve o'clock must be at least numerically different from the one I conceived half an hour before. It will be impossible to conceive the same occurrent abstract idea twice. What is the same can only be the disposition of which these successive occurrent ideas are manifestations, or perhaps the class of occurrent ideas of which these two successive ones are members.

These consequences of the theory are rather disconcerting. We all want to say that many different people can 'think of the same thing' and that one person can 'think of the same thing' on many different occasions. But perhaps a tolerable interpretation could still be given to these statements. The occurrent idea of Dog which I have today may be different from the one I had yesterday; but the same object, Fido, would 'satisfy' both of them. Or rather, *any* member of the same class of mutually resembling objects would 'satisfy' both, and would 'satisfy' your occurrent idea of Dog as well as mine. In this respect, occurrent abstract ideas are no worse off than sub-vocal or imaged words, which are private in an analogous way, but may be cashed by publicly observable objects. We notice too that similar difficulties might equally be raised about the non-verbal or quasi-instantiative images used in image thinking, which are likewise private to each image-thinker and even to each act of imaging within one thinker's mental history. Here again we can say that this private image and that one, though numerically different, both represent the same publicly perceptible object, or any publicly perceptible object belonging to a certain class. If the difficulty about the privacy of images is soluble in this way, the same solution is available, *mutatis mutandis*, for the difficulty about the privacy of occurrent abstract ideas.

Thus *if* there are occurrent abstract ideas at all, we need not be greatly worried about their privacy. But are there? Or is the phrase 'occurrent abstract idea' (or 'occurrent concept') just a *vox nihili*, to which nothing that we are ever aware of corresponds? Some people will say that it is even worse, a self-contradictory phrase which not only does not, but could not, describe anything. The terms 'concept' and 'abstract idea', they will say, *can* only be used in a dispositional sense; and it is self-contradictory to suggest that something which is by definition a disposition could also be an occurrent mental event. But in saying this, they beg the question against the traditional Conceptualist theory. Even though we may grant that the terms 'concept' and 'abstract idea' are as a matter of fact used (generally or even perhaps always) in a dispositional sense, this is in itself only a generalization about the speech customs of English-speaking persons, and about the parallel speech customs of those who speak other languages. The real question is, whether it is expedient or excusable to stretch these customary usages. They *are* only usages; they are not rigid prescriptions, like those which govern the use of technical symbols in a mathematical calculus. Well then, does anything occur in our minds when we think which could be described—paradoxically, if you like—as an occurrent abstract idea? The traditional Conceptualists say it does; and if they are right in saying so, we must put up with this paradoxical phrase until we can find a better one. They cannot be refuted by merely terminological arguments. When people began to talk of black swans, we may be sure there were linguistically minded thinkers who said that such creatures were logically impossible. Did not everyone know that swans are white by definition? But if they were, at any rate it was found expedient to alter the definition. It has even been found expedient to speak of white blackbirds. Creatures for which this paradoxical-seeming description is the most natural one are occasionally observed in our gardens and hedgerows. It might be that the phrase 'occurrent abstract idea' is no worse than 'white blackbird'. Or at any rate it might be no worse than 'unconscious wish', against which the same objection of self-contradictoriness has been made by people who are more interested in the way we talk than in the way things are.

The question we have to discuss is not terminological, but phenomenological. Can we or can we not *find* entities which could be described, however surprisingly, as occurrent abstract ideas? The traditional Conceptualist, to do him justice, does tell us where to look for them. He says they are introspectibles; we are to look into our own mind when we think, and then we shall find them.

Let us try to follow his directions. I am walking by night in a dark forest in Transylvania, and my companion suddenly says 'wolf' or the equivalent word in another language which I understand. I experience a certain tenseness in my leg-muscles. I find myself beginning to hurry, or perhaps to run. I feel a sinking feeling in the stomach, and a chilly feeling in the spine and the scalp. Perhaps I also find the imaged or muttered words 'A wolf! Oh dear!' together with a visual image of a horrible beast rather like an Alsatian dog, only worse. But I do not detect any entity which could be called an occurrent abstract idea of Wolf. You may tell me that it is within my own mind, not something existing or subsisting extra-mentally *in rebus*. I look into my own mind as carefully as I can, but still I do not find it. At the most I find only a generic image, an incomplete or not-fully determinate image-particular, such as was discussed in Chapter IX. Traditional Conceptualism, when subjected to phenomenological methods, does have a tendency to turn itself into the 'Generic Image' version of the Imagist theory. Generic images *are* occurrent mental contents, and very odd ones too. They are neither words, nor organic sensations, nor are they representations of percepts, not even of possible percepts (as a determinate image of a green cat would be). Having discovered them, and lacking any better way of describing them, we might easily be tempted to say that they are at once *occurrent* and *abstract*. We have already seen reason to think that when Locke spoke of abstract ideas, generic images were what he had in mind, at least sometimes.[1] But still, whatever we call them, generic images are certainly not occurrent *concepts*. They are not ideas in the Concept sense of the word 'idea', but in the Image sense of it. Nor are they abstract in the sense in which a concept is abstract. For example, we could not say of them that they have instances. Moreover, generic images are not always present to the mind when we think, but only sometimes; whereas according to the traditional Conceptualist theory, there are always abstract ideas present to the mind whenever we think at all.

Yet I certainly understood the word 'wolf' when I heard it. I understood it in absence too; I did not see any wolf or hear one, even if my companion did. Indeed, I understood the word only too well. It was not just a noise to me, nor even a sign like the cracking of a twig or the hoot of an owl, but a symbol. A process of thinking did occur to me, an act of conceiving if you like to put it so. But I was not aware of any mental content for which 'occurrent abstract idea' would be a suitable description—not if the word 'idea' is used in the *Concept* sense, even though a generic image (supposing I had

---

[1] Cf. above, p. 288 on Locke's abstract idea of a triangle. (*Essay*, Book IV, ch. 7, section 9.)

one) might just possibly be described as 'abstract' if one had no better way of describing it.

Of course, if the terms 'concept' or 'abstract idea' are understood in their *dispositional* sense, then certainly my concept or abstract idea of Wolf was sub-activated by my hearing of what my companion said. It manifested itself occurrently by means of sub-vocal words, by the production of a wolf-like image, whether a generic image or not, and by putting me into a state of readiness for the presence of an actual wolf. This readiness, we may notice, was not merely psychical but also psycho-physical, as the accompanying organic sensations showed. I was also made ready for further wolf-mentioning discourse on my companion's part, and ready to initiate such discourse myself, either aloud or privately in the form of further sub-vocal words or verbal imagery. In all these ways, my concept of Wolf did show itself or manifest itself, both in private mental occurrences and in overt behaviour. But it did not show itself *in propriâ personâ*, if one may say so, by presenting itself to my mind in the form of an occurrent 'thinkable' or 'thought-content'. Or if someone maintains, despite the phenomenological facts, that it did, or that it must have, how are we to interpret his contention? He is maintaining on purely *a priori* grounds that thinking is a kind of inspection. He has already convinced himself that it is not the inspection of objective universals, and that 'general and universal', in Locke's words, 'belong not to the real existence of things'. He concludes accordingly that it must be the inspection of something intra-mental.

In fact, the traditional Conceptualist epistemology has more in common with the Realist epistemology than is generally supposed. That is why I said earlier that the controversy between them is only a domestic difference within the Classical tradition. Both parties agree in accepting an *inspective* conception of thinking. They both hold that thinking may be appropriately described in terms of the visual analogy of 'looking at'. The difference between them is only this:—In the Realist theory the thinker is supposed to look without, extrospectively, upon extra-mental intelligible objects (universals). In the Conceptualist theory, he is supposed to look within, introspectively, into his own mind, where he finds a special sort of mental contents (occurrent abstract ideas). Again, both parties agree that the symbols we use in thinking are 'transparent'. Here is the same visual analogy: we look through the symbols to something else beyond or behind them, and this something else is what we attend to when we think. As I have remarked already, this visual model or analogy is harmless enough if we take it as a way of posing the problem which the epistemology of thinking has to solve. But it is not a solution. If it were, there must be something, other than symbols, which is *presented to the mind* when one thinks, something which is intuitively apprehended, whether extrospectively or introspectively. And there are no such intuitively presented thinkables; unless, by saying that there are, one is merely emphasizing in a picturesque way the undoubted fact that the symbols are understood, and are not merely seen or heard or imaged.

In discussing the polemical side of the Imagist theory, its doctrine that verbal thinking, uncashed by images, is not 'really' thinking. I remarked that the Imagists do not trust their memories enough.[1] They have an uneasy feeling that cognition in absence is something which ought not to occur, and if it does, it ought to come as close to recognition in presence as possible. When one thinks of dogs in absence, it is not enough for them that one has a memory of what dogs are like. In addition, the Imagist demands that there should be some entity, actually present to the mind, which is at any rate a quasi-instance of the concept Dog. A dog-like image satisfies this demand, whereas the word 'dog' or a dog-mentioning sentence does not.

A similar distrust in memory is noticeable in the Realists and the traditional Conceptualists. It is not enough for them either that we have a perfectly good memory of what dogs are like when we use dog-referring symbols in absence. If that were all, they could not feel sure that our thought is in touch with reality. And so they demand that over and above the mere symbols there must be something actually apprehended, something actually present to the mind of the thinker which will save him from using his symbols like a parrot or a gramophone—a thinkable or intelligible, or set of related thinkables, which he inspects and attends to, whether extrospectively or introspectively. And then symbolic cognition in absence will not be 'in absence' after all. No particular dog is present to the mind, certainly. And very often no dog-like image is present to it either. But Doghood is present to it, and all is well.

[1] Cf. ch. VIII, p. 263, above.

These demands should never have been made; and if they are made they can only be satisfied in an illusory manner, with fairy gold. By ceasing to make them, we lose nothing, because we have all that we need already. So long as I really do have a (dispositional) memory of what dogs are like, this memory by itself will be enough to keep my symbol-usings 'on the rails'. This by itself is enough to ensure that my thought is 'in touch with reality', and to prevent me from talking nonsense about dogs to myself or to others. The needed link between symbol-using and reality is supplied by memory and ostensive definition. It may be pointed out that the Realist's inspectable universals were abstracted from *past* instances, and the Conceptualist's introspectible abstract ideas are the results of *past* observations of resemblance. If there are indeed such events as apprehending a universal or introspecting an occurrent abstract idea, they must themselves be *mnemic* events. Unless these alleged inspectables were connected in some way with past experiences, they would not serve the purpose for which they were introduced, which was to ensure that our thought is 'in touch with reality'. Both Realists and Conceptualists do have to trust their memories, whether they like it or not. Why are they not content to trust them, and why do they insist on fabricating pseudo-inspectables to bolster up an edifice which is already sufficiently supported by memory itself? Perhaps because they have mistakenly supposed that the recalling or recollecting of past events is the only function memory has, the only way in which a memory-disposition shows itself. Or perhaps they have supposed that when I am said to have a memory of something, what I have a memory of can only be an individual past object or event. But this is a mistake too. I can and do have a memory of what dogs are like, what red things are like, what it is like for one thing to be inside, or above, or longer than another thing. There are abstract or general memories, if one pleases to call them so, as well as memories of individual objects and events. It could even be argued that all memories have something abstract about them, though the degree of abstractness varies greatly in different cases. Once we agree that conceptual cognition is in the end a function of memory, we have no need to postulate any intuition or inspection of mysterious entities, be they extrospectible or introspectible. We can take the phenomenological facts of symbolic cognition as we find them.

If, however, we are resolved not to trust our memories, if the 'mnemic' character of conceptual cognition is ignored, it is very natural to fall back upon a visual analogy. 'Inspection' and 'intuition' are visual words. Intelligence is easily thought of as 'the eye of the soul'. Visual perception is the most important source of knowledge of the world, in human beings at least. We are naturally inclined to take it as a model of what all cognition ought to be, and to assimilate all other forms of cognition to it as far as we can. If no 'objects' of conceptual cognition can be found, in the sense in which visual perception has an object, we tend to suppose that these thought-objects must, nevertheless, be there; and so we are tempted to postulate mysterious abstract entities, whether extra-mental or intra-mental, to provide what is needed. In this way we are led to offer analyses of conceptual cognition which are more metaphysical than phenomenological. Perhaps we should never have asked 'what are the objects of thought' at all. At any rate, we should not have asked the question with this visual analogy in mind. For then we are obliged to seek for the objects of thought among entities which 'present themselves to consciousness' or 'stand over against it' in the way that visual percepts do. If that is the principle which guides our search, we shall find only images, generic images at the most. But these are not what we wanted, and they are not always present when we think. Very often we can find nothing but words or other non-instantiative particulars.

If the traditional visual analogy leads us into so much trouble, it may be useful to try quite a different one. Suppose we said that possessing a concept is something like having a disease. Acquiring the concept Cat or the concept Red, let us say, is something like catching influenza, though when once acquired it usually lasts longer than influenza does, and may last all the rest of one's life. Now we may imagine a medical sceptic, who refuses to believe in the existence of these mysterious entities called 'diseases'. All I can find, he says, are *symptoms*, high temperature, shivery feelings, aches in the back, feelings of lassitude; this mysterious something called 'a disease', which is supposed to be behind and beyond the symptoms, does not exist at all—neither inside the patient nor anywhere else. (This is like what Berkeley, the Imagist, said about Locke's abstract ideas.) Now there is clearly something wrong with this medical sceptic. He is assuming that a disease *ought* to be something which is seen or felt, either by the patient himself or by others, like a flushed countenance or an ache in one's back. If this assumption were true, his sceptical conclusion would be the right one. All you can see or feel, even if you are the patient yourself, are the symptoms. Must we suppose, then, that diseases are supersensible entities, detectable by an act of 'medical intuition'? Is that the way to answer this medical sceptic? By no means. Diseases cannot be seen or felt, but they can be detected by examining what *is* seen or felt. We may notice too that it is not enough to examine the symptoms one by one. We also have to notice the relations between them, the order in which they occur, whether simultaneously or successively.

If this analogy shocks us, let us try another; a physical one this time, though just because it is physical and not biological, it may lead us to over-simplify the facts. A concept, let us say, is more like a *force* than an entity. A sceptical student of physics may complain that he has no notion of what magnetism is. Certainly he has seen magnets with little bits of steel sticking to them. He has seen compass needles too. He has noticed how they maintain a constant orientation when the compass-case is shifted or rotated, and also how they lose it when a steel pocket-knife or machine-gun is in their near neighbourhood, and how the original orientation can be restored by sticking little magnets into the compass-case. But, he asks, what is this mysterious 'magnetic force' which is supposed somehow to inhabit these observable objects? What reason is there to think it exists at all? To convince him, we exhibit other magnetic phenomena to him. We put a piece of paper over the magnet; on the paper we scatter little iron filings, which then arrange themselves in curvilinear patterns around the magnet's poles. We take him to Northern Labrador, and ask him to notice how the compass needle behaves there. We introduce him to what aerial navigators call the Northerly Turning Error. We heat the magnet red hot, and when it has cooled again we show him that the little bits of steel no longer stick to it, and the iron-filings no longer arrange themselves around the poles in the way they did. If he is still unconvinced, what shall we do? We shall say he has a mistaken assumption about what he is looking for, and that is why he fails to find it. He is looking for some sort of perceptible thing or stuff, over and above the various perceptible occurrences which we have exhibited to him. But if he has attended to these occurrences and to the relations between them, then he *already* has some grasp, at any rate, of 'what magnetism is'.

These two analogies are not very good ones. I offer them to the reader because they are entirely different from the traditional visual analogy, which treats concepts as inspectable entities and conceptual cognition as the inspection of them. Whatever defects these new analogies may have, they do at least have the merit of suggesting a new question, and it may be a more fruitful one. In what ways, by what occurrences, does a concept manifest itself when we possess it? And how are its different occurrent manifestations related to one another? To find out what a concept is, let us ask what it does; or rather what its possessor does, what happens in him both mentally and psychophysically, which would not happen if he lacked it. In answering this question, I shall in effect be drawing together a number of scattered hints which have been given piecemeal in earlier chapters. When this has been done, with any amplification which may be needed, we may hope that a constructive theory of concepts may emerge; or at any rate a constructive theory of what an *empirical* concept is, and of what it is to possess one.

It is agreed on all hands that a concept manifests itself occurrently by the recognition of instances. A man who has the concept Cat will recognize this perceived object to be as like Pussy, Tabitha and Tiger Tim as they are to one another. When this happens, his concept is 'satisfied' by the perceived object. If someone lacks the concept of Cat, either because he has never acquired it or because he has lost it ('forgotten what a cat is like'), such recognition will not occur in him. We shall return to recognition later. But for the moment we are more concerned with other concept-manifestations, with the ways in which a concept occurrently manifests itself 'in absence', i.e. when we are *not* perceiving any object which satisfies it.

The first is sign-cognition and sign-guided behaviour. My concept of Rain is manifesting itself when I take a black cloud as a sign of a coming rain-storm which I do not as yet see or feel. Here the concept shows itself by putting me into a state of psycho-physical preparedness for an instance. This preparedness may take the form of appropriate action, such as running indoors, or taking out a mackintosh from my haversack. But sign-cognition, and the con-

W

ceptual character which it has, was discussed so fully in Chapters IV and V that no more need be said about it now. We have merely to notice that it *is* one of the ways, and a very important way, in which our concepts operate or manifest themselves, both mentally and psycho-physically; and that this operation of them, like recognition, is pre-symbolic. Perhaps it should also be said that when a concept is sub-activated by a sign, its whole power of self-manifestation may be exhausted in the production of appropriate behaviour; as when I see a bull issuing from a gate, and run away at top speed to a place of safety.

Let us next consider the way our concepts manifest themselves in image-thinking. First, they manifest themselves by the occurrence of quasi-instantiative images, and by the recognition of these (in the sense of 'recognize' which is appropriate to quasi-instances). My concept of Cat manifests itself occurrently when a cat-like image presents itself to my mind and is recognized to be cat-like. But this is not all. Sometimes I feel dissatisfied with my image; something is wrong with the ears, or the whiskers are missing. My (dispositional) knowledge or memory of what cats are like—in other words, my concept of Cat—is again occurrently manifested by this feeling of inadequacy; and sometimes by the production of a better image which has fewer defects than the first. Again, perhaps my first image represented a side view of a cat. Other images may then come up to supplement it, images of top views or back views, or tactual images of the feel of a cat's fur, or auditory images of purrings or mewings. In any case, I am in a state of readiness to produce them. Moreover (as Hume pointed out) if my original image represented a thin, short-haired tabby, I am ready to supplement it by other images representing Persian cats, or Siamese cats, or black ones or fat ones. Thus the concept manifests itself not merely by the production of a single image, but by our readiness to produce a whole series of different images, related in such a way that one supplements another and corrects its deficiencies; and if several members of such a series are actually produced, we are ready to produce still others.

Another way in which a concept manifests itself is by the occurrence of a *generic* image; either of the Galtonian sort (better called a typical image) or of the more mysterious sort described in Chapter IX as an incomplete or imperfect particular, which is sometimes mistakenly supposed to be itself a concept or abstract idea. It would seem that the readiness to produce supplementary quasi-instantiative images, in the way referred to by Hume, is connected with the actual production of a generic one.

Sometimes, again, our concept shows itself by the production of quasi-instantiative particulars which are not mental but material. We produce a physical replica of a cat, a drawing or painting or clay model, or a piece of cat-like behaviour in a charade or other form of dumb show. Here our concept of Cat, our (dispositional) knowledge or memory of what cats are like, is manifested in a psycho-physical way, by a piece of intelligent action. It is well to repeat that the two sorts of replica-production, the production of mental images on the one hand and physical replicas on the other, are parallel and mutually independent. Each of them is a direct manifestation of the concept, and neither is subordinate to the other. In particular, the production of a physical replica does not depend on the prior production of an image, an intra-mental blueprint, which is then copied as it were on paper or in clay, or reproduced in dumb show. If I tell you to draw a cat on the blackboard at once, without giving you 'time to think' (i.e. to form images) you will be able to do it straight off. Your drawing may not be a very good one, but it will have some considerable likeness to a cat; and having done it, you will be able to correct it more or less satisfactorily, by trial and error methods perhaps, without any need of consulting an image blueprint. By this time, it is true, an image may have presented itself. By now you have had 'time to think'. But you can make your drawing, and correct it too in some measure, even if you are so deficient in imagery that you cannot form a cat-like image at all. Similarly, if I tell you to behave in a cat-like manner, you will at once go down on all fours and produce mewing or purring sounds without any need of images to guide you. Of course an image *is* sometimes present when a physical replica is produced, and it may even be used as a kind of blueprint. It appears that some painters paint 'from' images, and even occasionally from eidetic images projected on to the canvas. But the point is that this need not happen. A physical replica, a public and perceptible quasi-instantiative particular, is often produced 'straight off', just as the image itself is produced 'straight off' and does not have to be copied from a pre-image which is there beforehand. My (dispositional) knowledge of what cats are like, when once it has been sub-activated by a suitable stimulus, can overflow as it were into bodily move-ments—say, those of drawing or dumb show—just as it can also overflow into an act of mental imaging.

We now come to another sort of concept-manifesting occur-rence which has not been mentioned in earlier chapters, and in some ways it is the most remarkable of all. Sometimes a concept manifests itself not just by the production of replicas, mental or physical, but by the production of an actual real-life instance. Of course this only happens with some concepts, not with all. My concept of Cat or Earthquake, however complete my possession of it may be, does not enable me to produce an actual cat or an actual earthquake. But suppose one asks a golfer what a mashie-shot is. He may answer in words. But he need not. Instead, he might take a walking-stick and a stone and produce an imitation of a mashie-shot. This would be a kind of physical replica, analogous to a drawing or a piece of dumb show. It would be only a quasi-instance of the concept, not an actual one. But he may do more than this. Without a word, he goes into his bedroom, fetches a mashie and a golf ball, places the ball on the lawn, and lofts it gracefully over the roof of the College Chapel. His concept of Mashie-shot manifests itself occurrently by the production of a real-life instance, and thereby provides me with an ostensive definition of the phrase which I used in asking my question. Similarly, if you are in an aeroplane for the first time and ask the pilot what 'a stall' is, he may answer by actually doing one. Again, the Ancients were much interested in what they called 'the form in the soul of the craftsman', e.g. the concept of Pot in the soul of the potter, which likewise manifests itself by the production of real-life instances; though unfortunately they supposed that he had to inspect this form in his soul, as if it were a sort of intelligible blueprint, in order to make his pot.

It may be objected, perhaps, that what the golfer or the aeroplane pilot or the craftsman possesses is a skill rather than a concept. But in fact he possesses both. He can *recognize* the mashie shots or stalls or pots produced by others, he can detect the deficiencies there may be in them, and can grade the instances, as better or worse, or suggest ways of improving them. And likewise, when he produces the instance himself he recognizes it to be one, and grades it too, as a good instance or middling or not very good one. What the golfer cannot do, perhaps, is to give a description in words of the complicated series of events, partly in his own body and partly outside it, which constitute a mashie-shot. All he can do, perhaps, is to reproduce the 'feel' of the performance in kinaesthetic imagery, and the 'look' of it in visual imagery. Possibly he cannot do even that. But it is sufficient if he can *recognize* this feel or look when they recur, and distinguish between the cases where the performance 'feels right' (if done by himself) or 'looks right' (if done by another) from those in which it feels or looks wrong, or not quite right. One may possess a concept, and it may manifest itself occurrently in one's cognitions as well as in one's actions, even though one possesses it pre-analytically.

The performances I have mentioned are beyond the reach of most of us. But we all possess some concepts which show themselves on occasion by the production of real-life instances. Everyone knows what it is to walk or to sit. He can recognize the walkings and sittings of himself and other people. He can probably produce images of them, visual or kinaesthetic or both. He can draw at least a rough sketch of a man walking or sitting, which is a public quasi-instantiative particular. And he can also produce real-life instances by walking and sitting himself, unless he is paralysed or crippled. Again nearly everyone can *make* something, even if it is only a walking-stick crudely fashioned out of the branch of a bush. When he does, a concept of his is occurrently manifested by the production of an actual real-life instance.

When we review the different sorts of concept-manifestations mentioned in the last few pages, two remarks naturally suggest themselves. In the first place, these manifestations seem to form a graded series. It is as if a concept were striving, so to speak, for material embodiment, and progressed towards this end in a series of stages. First there is the generic image, which is not even a completely determinate image-particular. Then there is the complete and detailed image, which resembles, but is not, a physical and public instance of the concept. Then there is the physical replica; and now the concept has manifested itself by the occurrence of something physical and public, though only in a quasi-instantiative way.

Finally, there is the real-life instance. This is physical and public, as the replica already was; but in addition, it not only resembles an instance of the concept but actually *is* an instance. Perhaps if we reflected on this ordered series of concept-manifestations, it might throw some light on the relations of mind and body, and on the relations between mind and the material world in general.

The second remark which suggests itself is this. The images, replicas and real-life instances are not, of course, the concept itself, any more than a disease is the symptoms. We ought rather to say that the occurrence of such particulars, and the recognition of them as quasi-instances or actual instances, are ways in which a concept manifests itself or shows itself, both mentally and psycho-physically. And perhaps it is most clearly manifested in the way in which different particulars succeed each other, so that later ones correct the deficiencies of earlier ones. Moreover, this correction and supplementation do not come about in at all the way the traditional visual analogy would lead us to expect. One does not *compare* the defective images or replica with the concept, as one might compare rough sketches of a machine with a perfect blueprint, or refer back from an imperfectly drawn graph to the algebraical formula which determines what sort of curve it ought to be. The concept is not *before* the mind as an object of inspection. It is at work *in* the mind, but not as one inspectable content among others, as the traditional Conceptualists supposed. It shows itself not as a detectable item of mental furniture, but rather as a guiding force, determining the direction which the series of presented particulars takes, whether they are images, or physical replicas, or real-life instances. In one of my examples, the concept at work was the concept of Cat. If it had been the concept of Mammal instead, the series of images might have started in the same way, with a cat-image, but it would have gone on quite differently. Instead of other cat-images, there would have been perhaps a dog-image, an elephant-image, a whale-image, a man-image. And so too if the series had consisted of physical replicas, such as drawings or clay models, instead of images.

In this connection, we may observe that the inadequacy of our images and the detection and correction of it, is noticeable in recollection also. We often do have images when we recall past events. And so it has been thought that remembering (in the sense of recalling) just consists in having images of some sort. Against this, Realist philosophers have protested that we can often detect the inaccuracy of our memory-images. And how could we do this, unless we *compared* the defective image with the past event itself? They have concluded that remembering is a direct apprehension of past events. Their protest is justified, but not the conclusion they draw from it. If we look into our minds when we recall something, no such act of direct retro-apprehension can be found. There is no presented past object, with which the defective memory-image is compared and found wanting. Here again, our knowledge of the past event does not manifest itself by an act of direct inspection or intuition. It manifests itself, rather, as a guiding force, which substitutes a better image for the original inadequate one; in the discontent we feel about the earlier image, and the satisfaction or smaller dissatisfaction which we feel about the later one. Indeed, the notion of 'comparing' a present image with a past event is so obscure and metaphorical that we can only make sense of it by referring back to the phenomenon it is intended to elucidate. The so-called comparing of an image just *consists* in the detection of the first image's inadequacy and the substitution of a better one. Much the same could be said where the recalling is done by means of words instead of images, by describing a past event verbally to oneself or to others. Here again we often detect some inaccuracy in our first description, and often we can substitute a better one; but not by 'comparing' the description with the past event itself, unless this 'comparing' is just another name for the process which it purports to explain.

It is clear that this Realistic theory of remembering has much in common with the Realistic theory of conception which has already been discussed. In both cases there is the obscure analogy of 'looking through' or 'beyond' the actually presented contents of the mind, and 'inspecting' something else which lies behind them. In both cases, the analogy will serve well enough as a way of drawing attention to the epistemological problem which has to be solved; in neither, as a solution.

Similarly if the inspective account of recalling is combined with the theory that remembered events are always intra-mental (either because all of them are in the end past experiences of our own, or because they have to be 'retained in the mind' in order to be recollected), we then have a parallel with the traditional Conceptualism, which regards concepts as introspectible mental contents.

If I was right in suggesting that conceptual cognition is in the last resort a function of memory, these parallels are not, of course, surprising. If conceiving, which is one function of memory, is analysed in an inspective manner, it is to be expected that recalling, which is another function of memory, would also be analysed in an inspective manner. Philosophers who hold an inspective theory of the one might be expected to hold an inspective theory of the other.

We now come to the most obvious of all the ways in which our concepts manifest themselves. They manifest themselves by the production and understanding of words, both in public and in private, by the understanding of words produced by others, and by the production and understanding of other 'non-resemblant' symbols, for example signalling with a flag, blowing blasts on a whistle, pointing or beckoning with the hand. Here the particulars produced are not even quasi-instantiative ones, like images and physical replicas; still less are they real-life instances of the concepts which are manifested by their means. On the other hand, the understanding of such non-instantiative symbols is something different from the understanding of signs, as we have explained earlier.

It is often supposed that such symbolic operations, those in which the symbols are completely non-instantiative particulars, are the only ones in which our concepts are occurrently manifested; or even that concepts are only manifested in *word*-using operations, whether public or private. To possess the concept of ϕ, it is thought, consists simply in the capacity to use the *word* 'ϕ' with understanding, both publicly and privately, both in the presence of instances of ϕ and in their absence. Throughout this book I have been protesting against such narrow views of conceptual cognition. The production and understanding of non-instantiative symbols, and *a fortiori* the production and understanding of verbal symbols, is only one of the many different ways in which our concepts are occurrently manifested. They are manifested also by the recognition of instances; by the production of quasi-instantiative particulars, whether images or physical replicas; by the production (sometimes) of real-life instances; by sign-cognition in its various forms, including secondary recognition; by intelligent action of all kinds, both at the sign-cognitive level and above it. If we must have paradoxes, it would be better to say that a concept-possessing being is one who can make mistakes; or that he is one who has learned from experience and can use what he has learned.

Nevertheless, it is true that the higher levels of intelligence, so far as human frailty can attain to them, are only to be reached by the use of words. Sign-cognition is restricted within very narrow bounds, despite the subtlety and delicacy of which it is capable. It is founded upon the observation of easily noticeable constant or near-constant conjunctions. It is tied to sensible cues, and we must wait till environmental causes produce them. Image-thinking, though relatively autonomous and independent of environmental happenings, is unsuitable for very abstract and very complex subjects. To go farther, we must learn to use words, or other non-instantiative particulars which symbolize in the same non-resemblant way as words do (e.g. the manual symbols of the deaf and dumb). I am only protesting against the doctrine that a concept is *nothing but* a word-using capacity, and that intelligence consists wholly in the power of using words understandingly.

The concept in the mind of the craftsman or other practical expert manifests itself in what he does, without being present *to* his mind as an object of inspection. Similarly, the concepts in the mind of the word-user manifest themselves in what *he* does, in his production of (token) words, public or private, spoken or written or whispered or imaged in one form or another of verbal imagery; for all of these are forms of doing, even where the particulars produced are private and inaccessible to outside observers. In these doings of his, as in the craftsman's, concepts are at work in his mind without being present *to* his mind as 'thought-objects' or 'objects of intellectual inspection'. In both cases, the requisite productive dexterity must have been acquired already, perhaps by a long and laborious process of learning. But once the dexterity is there, the man's concepts manifest themselves occurrently by means of it. Once I have learned to draw, my concept of Cat can manifest itself thenceforward by the production of cat-like pictures and sketches. It manifested itself from the first by the production of cat-like mental images (the capacity of producing mental images seems to be an unlearned one, even though it can be improved by practice).

But now it can also manifest itself in a new way, by means of this new productive capacity which I have acquired. And so far as mere introspection can tell, this new manifestation is often as direct and spontaneous as the old. The concept, when it has been sub-activated by some suitable stimulus, overflows of itself into the production of drawings (or models, or dumb show as the case may be) as it overflows of itself into the production of mental images. If one may say so, my concept of Cat has as it were assimilated or absorbed this newly acquired muscular dexterity, and thereby has come to be, or has grown into, a more complex disposition than it was before.

In the same sort of way, our concepts enrich themselves by absorbing or assimilating our acquired dexterity in producing articulate sounds (private or public) and written marks. This comes about through the process of ostensive definition. The 'bare bones' of my concept of ϕ consist in a (dispositional) memory of what ϕ things are like. This memory, which can also be called a recognitional capacity, is the concept of ϕ in its minimal form, the indispensable basis for any further developments it may undergo. By means of ostensive definitions, associative linkages are gradually set up between recognitional capacities and word-producing skills. Henceforth my memory of what ϕ things are like is able to manifest itself in a new way, through the production of words. And in time this new kind of concept-manifestation comes to be, introspectibly, as direct and effortless as the old. To all appearance, the concept now manifests itself immediately by means of words. When once sub-activated, it just 'overflows' into the production of words, spontaneously and smoothly. This is the excuse for the erroneous theory that a concept *is* nothing but a word-producing capacity. In any normal person brought up in an English-speaking community, the capacity for using the sound 'cat' or the written mark 'c-a-t' may fairly be called a part, and an important part, of the concept of Cat which he possesses. If he did not possess this word-using capacity, one could properly say that he did not possess the concept of Cat completely (we have already seen reason for thinking that the possession of a concept is a matter of degree). But one would not be justified in concluding that he did not possess it at all. He already possesses it in some degree if he can recognize cats when he sees them. And although this capacity of recognizing instances is the minimal degree of concept-possession, it is also the indispensable basis for any advance towards higher degrees of possession.

If a concept in its fully developed form is—among other things—a word-using capacity (even though that is not the whole of what it is) we need not be surprised to discover that in verbal thinking nothing is present to the mind except the token-words themselves, be they public or private, overtly uttered or sub-vocally produced or imaged in some form of verbal imagery (auditory, or visual, or kinaesthetic). It is true that this discovery is, at first sight, very disconcerting. It seems to suggest, at first sight, that when we think in words we are not really *thinking*; it suggests that concepts enter in no way into the process. But that is only because we have an erroneous preconception about the way they must enter into it, if they enter into it at all: either they play no part whatever in our word-using operations, or if they do, they must be before the mind as inspectable 'objects of thought'. We must give up this preconception, and make up our minds to accept the phenomenological facts. We must take verbal thinking as it is, instead of distorting it into something else which we suppose it ought to be.

It is just a phenomenological truth that there is a form of thinking in which nothing else is present to the mind except a succession of (token) words. Yet this truth is so stated as to conceal the essential point. Why just these words, rather than quite different ones? And why in just this order, rather than a different one? 'Cupboard in cat' is as good a concatenation of sounds as 'cat in cupboard'. That is where our concepts manifest themselves—in determining just what words shall occur in a given occasion, and what order they shall occur in. It will be remembered that concepts operate in a rather similar manner in image-thinking. Nothing is present to the mind except the images themselves. But concepts enter into the process by determining the direction which the flow of images takes. In verbal thinking too they manifest themselves by determining the direction which the flow of words takes. They operate as guiding forces, preventing us from saying *this* and permitting us to say *that*. If we are to use perceptual metaphors, a tactual metaphor would be less misleading than the traditional visual one. Imagine that a mouse is running about under a thin carpet on which our hands are laid. The creature is not seen at all. It never presents itself to our gaze as an object of inspection. But it makes itself felt by means of the upward pressures we feel, first in one part of the carpet and then in another. We can say, if we must have a perceptual metaphor, that in verbal thinking our concepts 'make themselves felt' through the way in which first one word comes up and then another and then another. Of course a concept is not an *entity*, as the mouse is, but a disposition or capacity. And the mouse could be inspected on other occasions, even though it is not inspected now; or at any rate other mice could be. This tactual metaphor, then, is not to be taken very seriously. I only recommend it as being a little less misleading than the traditional visual one.

However this may be, the important point is not the occurrence of a single word in isolation, but the transition from one word to another. If I just produced the isolated word 'red', you could not tell—neither could I—whether I possessed the concept of Red or not. A blind man, or a colour-blind man, or even a parrot, could produce this sound as well as I. If the production of a word is to be a manifestation of a concept of mine, there must be at least a preparedness to pass from this word to others, e.g. to say 'red is the colour of ripe tomatoes' or 'red sky at sunset, so fine day tomorrow'. Sometimes, of course, our talk (especially our private talk or verbal imagery) is discontinuous and fragmentary, in the way I tried to describe in the last chapter.[1] It may appear that then we really do think in isolated words. But even so, there is still a *series* of words, although the series is a gappy one; and there is a felt preparedness to fill in the gaps if need be, for example when someone challenges us by saying 'a penny for your thoughts'.

Again, I say 'a dodecahedron', and I go on from this to 'is a solid figure', instead of going on 'is an extinct reptile', as I might have if I had been using the word *dodecahedron* without understanding. My concept of Dodecahedron shows itself in the way I join this word to others. Even then, of course, it does not show itself unambiguously. I might have learned the whole sentence 'a dodecahedron is a solid figure' like a parrot. When I produce it now, privately or publicly, this performance might just be manifesting an acquired dexterity in word-concatenation. If others doubt whether I uttered these words with understanding, or if I myself doubt it, how is the question to be settled? Shall I not have to look

[1]See pp. 306-8, above.

into my own mind and find whether there is or not an object of thought there of which the 'dodecahedron' is the name? Or perhaps I should look for a more complex object of thought which the whole sentence 'a dodecahedron is a solid figure' corresponds to, whereas 'a dodecahedron is an extinct reptile' discords with it? I look, but I find no such entities. Must I conclude, then, that I *was* talking like a parrot? Not at all. If the concept of Dodecahedron was indeed manifested in what I said, I shall be able to produce other utterances, I shall be able to 'put it another way'. Instead of saying a dodecahedron is a solid figure, I can say 'it is a three-dimensional shape' and add 'it has twelve corners', or I can translate my original remark into French or Latin; or again, I can draw a rough sketch of a dodecahedron on a piece of paper.

This brings out an important point which may perhaps be overlooked when we say that our concepts manifest themselves by 'determining' the flow of words. Our concepts manifest themselves in a readiness to produce *alternative* verbal formulations. It is not like what happens when the mechanism of a clock determines the movement of the clock hands. The determination of the series of words is not rigid, but flexible. This flexibility is the production of words or other symbols is one of the characteristic features of intelligence, and is shown equally in intelligent action. Nevertheless, the flexibility does, of course, have limits. My hearer perhaps is very obstinate or very stupid. He keeps begging me 'to put it another way', and I go on doing so as long as I can. Yet I shall not say, 'Oh, a dodecahedron is an extinct reptile'. Or if by any chance I do say this, I say it in jest, just to be naughty, with an acute feeling of absurdity or incongruity; and this feeling of absurdity which I have in joining the word 'dodecahedron' to these others is itself a manifestation of my concept of Dodecahedron—still another way in which this concept works in my mind or makes its presence felt.

In all this process there is nothing which could reasonably be called 'inspecting the concepts (or sets of interrelated concepts), which the words stand for'. If that were the only way in which concepts enter into intelligent speech or other forms of verbal thinking, we should have to conclude that they do not enter into it at all. In verbal thinking our concepts do not present themselves to the mind *in propriâ personâ*, as one sort of mental contents among others; nor by means of particulars which are recognized to be instances of them; nor by means of quasi-instantiative or 'illustrative' particulars, as they do in image thinking. They are not 'before the mind' at all. Or rather, the suggestion that they are, if it is intended as any more than a provisional way of labelling the problem which has to be solved, misleads us fatally, by putting our inquiry on a wrong track which can only lead to a blind alley. We shall end in the monstrous paradox that verbal thinking is not thinking at all, and thus deny the existence of the very thing we are supposed to be analysing. Let us be content to say that in verbal thinking our concepts manifest themselves as guiding forces, directing the flow of words both public and private; as in image thinking they manifest themselves by directing the flow of images, and in intelligent action, by directing the flow of muscular movements which are the successive stages of execution. If the reader is inclined to complain that on such a view verbal thinking is 'not in touch with reality', we remind him that concepts can be regarded as *memory*-dispositions, and that possessing the concept ϕ is equivalent to having a memory of what ϕ things are like. At any rate, that is what our basic concepts are; and all other concepts (with the word using capacities which have been absorbed into them) are dependent in one way or another on these. It is memory, or retentiveness if that term be preferred, which supplies the link between word-using and extra-verbal reality.

The furthest we can go towards agreeing with the traditional Inspective theory of thinking is this: we may admit that the directing or guidance of which I spoke just now is sometimes actually *felt* as the successive words present themselves, at any rate when it meets with resistance, either from our own wishes, or our mental habits, or from some other person who objects to the words we utter. In such cases we often hesitate what to say, whether publicly or privately. The words which at first suggest themselves have a *felt* inappropriateness about them; and then, perhaps, after a period of mental blankness, others come into our minds, or our mouths, which have a felt appropriateness or at least a felt permissibility. (Sometimes we actually make comments to ourselves about our own discourse, even our private discourse. 'No, one cannot quite say that. . . . Perhaps one might say this.') Here there is some excuse for maintaining that something else does present itself to the mind over and above the words themselves. Yet even so, it is not exactly 'something else', presented alongside the words as an additional and non-verbal mental content. It is rather that there is a certain felt flavour or quality *in* the words themselves, a feel of inappropriateness or appropriateness or permissibility as the case may be. Sometimes it is there as soon as the words present themselves, and sometimes it develops itself later when they have been reflected on for a while. But in any case these 'feels' are not detectable in ordinary unstudied discourse. There the words 'just come', as we say, without any special felt quality attached to them. This added quality, which the Classical theory inflates into an apprehension of intelligible entities, is only present when we do *not* fully understand what we are saying, and is absent when we do.

So far, I have been considering what happens when the thinker produces words himself, public or private, and does so understandingly. I have been trying to say what 'understandingly' might mean in this case. I have suggested that this adverb does not have to be interpreted as the Classical theory would interpret it, and that concepts may still be manifesting themselves in our verbal thinking (or 'are operative' in it, if the reader prefers) even though they are not present to the mind as objects of intellectual inspection.

But, of course, our concepts manifest themselves also by our understanding of the words spoken or written by others. Here again, it is not single words taken separately which are important, but rather the way they succeed one another, the way they are ordered. As we sometimes put it, understanding someone consists in 'following' what he says. Here my own concepts do not determine or direct the flow of words. It is the speaker's concepts which do that (if *he* is speaking understandingly). But still my own concepts are at work. They are associatively linked to *any* recognizable token of those particular type-words, no matter how produced, and are sub-activated when these token-words are heard. And they manifest themselves by *permitting* that particular succession of words, though not by determining it. Or if at any point they do not permit it, I have a feeling of bafflement. I no longer 'follow' what is being said; and by this very feeling my own concepts are manifesting themselves in another way. Moreover, if I have indeed understood him, I shall be able to repeat what he has said, not necessarily in the very same words he used, but very likely in different ones; or perhaps I shall be able to repeat it in images or dumb show or pictures.

Thus when I follow what someone else says, or what he has written, I am myself thinking in words, though the words in which I think are not produced by me but by him. The understanding of other people's words is derived from and dependent on the understanding of one's own. If I can think in or with the words I myself utter, then I can also think in or with the words other people utter, provided they are tokens of the same type-words which I know how to use myself. Other people may of course combine them in combinations which are entirely new to me; and so I can acquire information from others which I did not have before, including false information. But still the words combined must be tokens of the same type-words which I already use in my own discourse, public or private. Moreover, the combinations must be such as my own concepts *permit*, however incapable I might have been of actually producing these combinations myself. It would never have occurred to me to say, 'there is an elephant in the garden'. But my own concepts of Elephant, Garden, and Being In, do permit this combination; and so I follow or understand this utterance, even though I may not believe it.

Perhaps it sounds paradoxical to say that the understanding of other people's words is dependent on the understanding of one's own. Surely ostensive definition is something which must be done for me by other people, and I must understand *their* words first, if I am ever going to understand my own? True enough, the process of ostensive definition has to be initiated by someone else, but he cannot complete it. His services are indispensable, but they are not sufficient. The process of ostensive definition is only complete when I have learned to use this mark or noise for myself. Until then it is not a *word* for me, but only a noise or mark, though doubtless it is already a word for him. At that stage, I am only noticing constant conjunctions (between this sort of noise and that sort of situation) and do not yet understand. The noise or mark, so long as I merely observe other people producing it, is not yet a symbol for me, but only at most a sign. It only becomes a symbol for me when I have learned to use it for myself.

After all, every man must understand for himself what others say or write. The others cannot understand for him. It is *his* concepts, not theirs, which are operative when he 'follows' what his neighbours say. His concepts, and not only theirs, must be associatively linked with the sounds or marks which he hears or sees. And that is only another way of saying that he must already be able to use these words understandingly in his own thinking. Each of us must understand for himself, and no one else can understand for him. Even in a Collectivistic age, this last shred of Liberal Individualism cannot be surrendered.

We have now surveyed a number of different ways in which our concepts occurrently manifest themselves both in consciousness and in behaviour. I would like to emphasize the word 'different'. There is not just one single way in which a concept *must* manifest itself if it is to manifest itself at all, as philosophers have tended to assume. There are many alternative ways. Our concepts manifest themselves through the recognition of instances; in sign-cognition, and in the actions and incipient actions which are characteristic of sign-guided behaviour; by the production and recognition of quasi-instantiative particulars, whether images or physical replicas (including dumb show and other forms of mimetic behaviour); by the detection of the inadequacies of these, and the substitution of others more adequate; by the production of generic images, both of the Galtonian and the 'incomplete particular' variety; by the production of real-life instances, and the detection and correction of *their* inadequacies; by the production and understanding of words and other non-instantiative symbolic particulars (e.g. gesture symbols) through the associative linkages established by ostensive definition.

In discussing these many different ways in which our concepts are occurrently manifested, by occurrences of many different sorts, both mental and psycho-physical, I have been trying to show how concepts may 'enter into' our thinking and our action without ever being objects of intellectual inspection. I have been explaining how concepts or abstract ideas may operate *in* our minds (and in our behaviour too) without ever being present *to* our minds, as the Classical theory of conceptual cognition supposes they are.

In effect, I have been recommending a *dispositional* version of Conceptualism, instead of the traditional *inspective* or introspective Conceptualism, which holds that concepts or abstract ideas present themselves to the mind as one sort of occurrent mental contents

x

among others. It is true that we may still speak, if we please, of 'having an abstract idea occurrently' as distinct from 'having it dispositionally'.[1] But having it occurrently does not consist in directing a kind of mental gaze at it. It is not any sort of intuitive apprehension or direct awareness. The nearest we get to anything of the kind is the inspection of generic images. (We have seen reason to think that Locke did sometimes confuse abstract ideas with generic images.[2]) Moreover, if we do speak of having an abstract idea occurrently, we must insist that there is not just *one* way of having it occurrently, or of 'conceiving' it if that word be preferred. There are many different ways, all the different ways which have been mentioned in our survey of concept-manifestations; and doubtless there are others which have not been mentioned. The occurrent manifestation of concepts is as multiform as the exercise of intelligence is. In fact it is just another name for the exercise of intelligence.

Here we must remember that intelligence shows itself not only in cognitive activities, but in all sorts of practical activities as well, from the level of sign-guided behaviour upwards. For example, it does not show itself only in the high-grade practical activities to which Moral Philosophers confine their attentions, but also in the skill of the craftsman or the golfer; and likewise in the skill of the hunter, even if he is only a bird or beast of prey, and equally in the skill of his intended victim in evading him. Anyone, beast or man or any other creature, who uses past experience for adapting himself to new situations is showing intelligence, even if he does no more than respond to inductive signs. What he does is a manifestation of some concept or concepts which he possesses, though a concept may be possessed in different degrees, more fully or less. Indeed, we should not be far wrong if we said that the operation of concepts is co-terminous with conscious life itself. At any rate we may say so if we are willing to admit that the possession of a concept is a matter of degree. For if conscious life consisted just in sensation, with no recognition of recurrences, not even the dimmest, and no learning from experience of past conjunctions, not even when they are of the highest biological importance, a conscious creature might

[1]This terminology is a slight modification of the one suggested by Professor C. D. Broad, *Examination of McTaggart's Philosophy*, Vol. I, p. 38. He distinguishes there between 'occurrent ideas' and 'dispositional ideas'.

[2]Cf. pp. 288-9, above.

as well lack consciousness altogether. A mere mechanism of conditioned reflexes would do as well, and indeed better.

One task remains if this dispositional analysis of concepts is to be made intelligible to the reader. We have seen that a concept may manifest itself occurrently in many different ways, both mental and psycho-physical. How are these different manifestations related to each other? Or if a concept be regarded as a complex of many capacities (more of them in some cases and fewer in others, according to the degree in which the concept is possessed) what relations are there between these capacities? If we could answer these questions completely, we should have solved almost all the problems of the Philosophy of Mind. We must be content with the beginnings of an answer. Perhaps we can say this much: the recognition of instances is the primary and fundamental way in which a concept is manifested, and all the other manifestations it has, or may come to have as it develops towards completeness, are dependent upon this one. Fundamentally a concept is a recognitional capacity, whatever else it may be besides.

It has been remarked before that conceptual cognition is a function of memory in the widest sense of that term. To have the concept of Cat is to have a (dispositional) memory of what cats are like. The basic way in which this memory shows itself is in the recognition of cats when I perceive them, and in the distinguishing between cats and non-cats according as they do or do not resemble the past particulars which are my Cat-examplars as closely as these examplars resembled one another. Such recognition is, of course, only the minimal manifestation of a concept. If that is all I can do, my concept of Cat is a very incomplete one. But though minimal, this capacity to recognize instances is also indispensable. If I have it, I may come in time to possess the concept more fully. If I lack it, I do not possess the concept at all; and I still do not possess it whatever skill I may acquire in using the *word* 'cat', because I shall be using this word without understanding.

On the other hand, once the capacity to recognize instances is there, the way is open for all the other varieties of concept-manifestation which have been mentioned: the understanding of signs, when the requisite inductive learning has been done; the production and recognition of images and other quasi-instantiative particulars, and the correction and supplementation of these; the production of real-life instances (of some concepts, though not all); and finally, when our recognitional capacities have been associatively linked with sound-producing skills by means of ostensive definitions, the most remarkable of all concept-manifestations begins to be possible, namely verbal thinking, the production of words with understanding, both in public and in private, and the understanding or 'following' of words produced by others.

These developments, from the bare capacity to recognize instances to the full-blown complex of interlinked capacities which is a complete concept, would, however, be quite unintelligible if we thought that a mental capacity must either be fully actualized or else not actualized at all. For then it would appear that my capacity for recognizing cats or red objects is only actualized when I do happen to see a red object or a cat. The way in which concepts manifest themselves 'in absence' (and all their other manifestations *are* in absence) would then become utterly mysterious. And in the unbearable perplexity which this mystery would engender, we should be driven to postulate an equally mysterious act of intuitive apprehension or intellectual inspection, to ensure that conceptual cognition in absence was not altogether in absence after all. We have seen that this motive operates not only in the Classical Inspective theory of thinking, but also in the Imagist theory, which holds that thinking is not 'really' thinking unless quasi-instantiative particulars, at least, are being intuitively apprehended.

To solve the mystery, or prevent it from arising, we must introduce the notion of degrees of actualization. My capacity for recognizing cats or red objects may be *sub-activated*, even when it is not fully actualized. It then manifests itself in my state of readiness or preparedness for fresh instances, even though no fresh instance is actually there. My memory of what cats or red objects are like is aroused from its normal condition of complete latency; yet not so fully aroused as it would be if a cat or a red object were actually being perceived.

We all know that when someone describes an absent object in appropriate words, and we follow attentively what he says or writes, it is sometimes almost as if we saw such an object before our eyes. To the feeling, there may be very little difference. A vivid narrative can arouse our passions of pity or terror almost as the actual events themselves would. My hair stands on end as I read, almost as if I actually saw the ghost. So too if the object is vividly imaged or vividly depicted on paper. This is one source of the temptation to suppose that thinking is itself a sort of seeing, seeing with the intellect, 'the eye of the soul'.

Why is it that symbols have this extraordinary power of making us feel as if the absent were present; and especially, why do words have it, which are not even quasi-instances of the concepts they arouse? Because recognitional capacities can be sub-activated by suitable stimuli even when they are not being fully actualized; and words come to be such stimuli, once they have been associatively linked with our recognitional capacities by the process of ostensive definition. And when this sub-activation occurs, the state we are put into approximates in some degree to the recognition of an actually present instance, and has similar emotional and conative repercussions to those which actual recognition would have.

The error of the traditional Inspective theory is after all excusable. It arises partly from assimilating the derivative manifestations of a concept to the fundamental one, recognition; and partly from the quite natural assumption that if a capacity is actualized at all, it must be fully actualized. The important truth that in every conceptual operation (cognitive or practical) a recognitional capacity is in *some* degree actualized is exaggerated into the error of supposing that it is always *fully* actualized. Something which could not unreasonably be called 'awareness of a universal' really does occur whenever we recognize an instance; at any rate we are aware of a recurrence, to use the language of Chapter I, however the term 'recurrence' is analysed. And so it is supposed that awareness of a universal must be happening whenever a recognitional capacity is actualized at all, because it has not been noticed that there are degrees of actualization.

Finally, it is the fact that concepts are recognitional capacities which keeps our thought in touch with reality. When we think in absence, by means of symbols, we are not cut off from the experienceable world, as if we were just playing an elaborate game with words or images, either in a social way or in the privacy of our own minds. By being recognitional capacities, our concepts are *cum fundamento in re*. They are founded in the similitude of things, as Locke says; that is, in the remembered similitudes of remembered things. What keeps thought in touch with reality is not any mysterious sort of intellectual intuition. It is the fact that conceptual cognition is a function of memory or retentiveness. There are general memories as well as particular ones. It could even be argued that all memory has something general or abstract about it. And that is the sense in which our symbols may be said to stand for realities other than themselves. They do so because in one way or another they sub-activate our memories of what such realities are like.

The basic empirical concepts are memory-dispositions. All other concepts, however complex, however remote from the experience-able world they may appear, must in the end be cashable in terms of these basic ones, as they in turn are cashable in terms of experienceable objects and situations. (It does not, of course, follow that sense-experience is the only sort of experience there is, as some Empiricists have rashly assumed.) If the concept ϕ is a basic one, having the concept ϕ consists in having a memory of what ϕ things are like. Whatever other manifestations this concept may have, or may come to have in the course of our intellectual development, the recognition of instances is the fundamental one, upon which all the others depend. That is how complex concepts, not themselves acquired by direct experience of instances, are also recognitional capacities, and a man who has the complex concept of Dragon or Jet-propelled Helicopter would be able to recognize a dragon or a jet-propelled helicopter if he should ever happen to perceive one. Because he has a memory of what lizards are like, and of what winged things are like, and of what fire and breathing are like, he could recognize a fire-breathing winged lizard if he saw one; even though he has never yet observed any object by which all these recognitional capacities were conjointly actualized, and probably never will. Without recognitional capacities there would be no thinking and no intelligent action.

INDEX

359